American College of Physicians

MKSAP® 15

Medical Knowledge Self-Assessment Program®

Endocrinology and Metabolism

Endocrinology and Metabolism

Contributors

Henry B. Burch, MD, Book Editor[1]
Chief, Endocrinology
Walter Reed Army Medical Center
Professor of Medicine and Chair, Endocrinology Division
Uniformed Services University of the Health Sciences
Bethesda, Maryland

Howard H. Weitz, MD, FACP, Associate Editor[2]
Professor of Medicine
Director, Division of Cardiology
Vice-Chairman, Department of Medicine
Jefferson Medical College, Thomas Jefferson University
Philadelphia, Pennsylvania

Baha M. Arafah, MD[2]
Professor of Medicine
Director, Clinical Program & Fellowship Training Program
Division of Endocrinology
Case Western Reserve University and University Hospitals
    Case Medical Center
Cleveland, Ohio

Richard J. Auchus, MD, PhD[2]
The Charles A. and Elizabeth Ann Sanders Chair in
    Translational Research
Professor of Internal Medicine
Division of Endocrinology and Metabolism
University of Texas Southwestern Medical Center at Dallas
Dallas, Texas

Victor J. Bernet, MD, FACP[1]
Director, National Capital Consortium Endocrinology
    Fellowship Program
Walter Reed Army Medical Center—Bethesda Naval
    Medical Center
Associate Professor
Uniformed Services University of the Health Sciences
Bethesda, Maryland

Silvio E. Inzucchi, MD[2]
Professor of Medicine
Clinical Director, Section of Endocrinology
Director, Yale Diabetes Center
Yale University School of Medicine
New Haven, Connecticut

Mark E. Molitch, MD, FACP[2]
Professor of Medicine
Division of Endocrinology, Metabolism and Molecular
    Medicine
Northwestern University Feinberg School of Medicine
Chicago, Illinois

Meeta Sharma, MD[2]
Assistant Chief
Division of Endocrinology
Director, Diabetes Team
Washington Hospital Center
Washington, DC

Editor-in-Chief

Patrick C. Alguire, MD, FACP[1]
Director, Education and Career Development
American College of Physicians
Philadelphia, Pennsylvania

Endocrinology and Metabolism Reviewers

Amindra S. Arora, MD[1]
Arnold A. Asp, MD, FACP[1]
Dawn E. DeWitt, MD, MSc, FACP[2]
Cheryl A. Fassler, MD, FACP[2]
Jason L. Gaglia, MD[1]
William James Howard, MD, MACP[2]
Steven Ricanati, MD[1]
Ingram Roberts, MD, FACP[2]
Cynthia M. Tracy, MD[2]

Endocrinology and Metabolism ACP Editorial Staff

Ellen McDonald, PhD, Senior Staff Editor
Sean McKinney, Director, Self-Assessment Programs
Margaret Wells, Managing Editor
Charles Rossi, Senior Associate of Clinical Content
    Development
Shannon O'Sullivan, Editorial Coordinator

ACP Principal Staff

Steven E. Weinberger, MD, FACP[2]
Deputy Executive Vice President
Senior Vice President, Medical Education and Publishing

D. Theresa Kanya, MBA[1]
Vice President, Medical Education and Publishing

Sean McKinney[1]
Director, Self-Assessment Programs

Margaret Wells[1]
Managing Editor

Charles Rossi[1]
Senior Associate of Clinical Content Development

Becky Krumm[1]
Senior Staff Editor

Ellen McDonald, PhD[1]
Senior Staff Editor

Amanda Neiley[1]
Staff Editor

Katie Idell[1]
Production Administrator/Editor

Valerie Dangovetsky[1]
Program Administrator

John Murray[1]
Editorial Coordinator

Shannon O'Sullivan[1]
Editorial Coordinator

Developed by the American College of Physicians

---

1. Has no relationships with any entity producing, marketing, re-selling, or distributing health care goods or services consumed by, or used on, patients.

2. Has disclosed relationships with entities producing, marketing, re-selling, or distributing health care goods or services consumed by, or used on, patients. See below.

Conflicts of Interest

The following contributors and ACP staff members have disclosed relationships with commercial companies:

Baha M. Arafah, MD
Consultantship
Novartis

Richard J. Auchus, MD, PhD
Consultantship
Cougar Biotechnology, Takeda
Stock Options/Holdings
Merck, Bristol-Myers Squibb

Research Grants/Contracts
Novartis

Dawn E. DeWitt, MD, MSc, FACP
Honoraria
Sanofi-Aventis
Consultantship
Sanofi-Aventis
Other
Sanofi-Aventis

Cheryl A. Fassler, MD, FACP
Stock Options/Holdings
Amgen
Research Grants/Contracts
Eli Lilly
Speakers Bureau
Tercica, Sanofi-Aventis

William James Howard, MD, MACP
Research Grants/Contracts
Pfizer, AstraZeneca
Honoraria
Pfizer, AstraZeneca, Merck, Schering-Plough, Abbott, Sankyo
Consultantship
Merck, Schering-Plough
Speakers Bureau
Pfizer, AstraZeneca, Merck, Schering-Plough, Abbott, Sankyo

Silvio E. Inzucchi, MD
Research Grants/Contracts
Eli Lilly
Honoraria
Pfizer, Takeda, Novartis, Merck, NovoNordisk
Consultantship
Takeda, Novartis, Merck, Daiichi-Sankyo, Amylin
Speakers Bureau
Takeda, Merck

Mark E. Molitch, MD, FACP
Research Grants/Contracts
Amgen, Tercica, Ardana, Lilly
Consultantship
Sanofi-Aventis, Abbott, Tercica, Novartis
Speakers Bureau
Sanofi-Aventis, Abbott, Merck
Stock Options/Holdings
Amgen, Abbott, Pfizer

Ingram Roberts, MD, FACP
Royalties
UpToDate

Meeta Sharma, MD
Honoraria
Procter & Gamble, Takeda, Merck, Sanofi-Aventis
Speakers Bureau
Procter & Gamble, Takeda, Merck, Sanofi-Aventis

Cynthia M. Tracy, MD
Honoraria
Medtronic

Steven E. Weinberger, MD, FACP
Stock Options/Holdings
Abbott, GlaxoSmithKline

Howard H. Weitz, MD, FACP
Other
GlaxoSmithKline (member of adverse events review committee of a clinical research trial)

Acknowledgments

The American College of Physicians (ACP) gratefully acknowledges the special contributions to the development and production of the 15th edition of the Medical Knowledge Self-Assessment Program® (MKSAP 15) of Scott Thomas Hurd (Senior Systems Analyst/Developer), Ricki Jo Kauffman (Manager, Systems Development), Michael Ripca (Technical Administrator/Graphics Designer), and Lisa Torrieri (Graphic Designer). The Digital version (CD-ROM and Online components) was developed within the ACP's Interactive Product Development Department by Steven Spadt (Director), Christopher Forrest (Senior Software Developer), Ryan Hinkel (Senior Software Developer), John McKnight (Software Developer), Sean O'Donnell (Senior Software Developer), and Brian Sweigard (Senior Software Developer). Computer scoring and reporting are being performed by ACT, Inc., Iowa City, Iowa. The College also wishes to acknowledge that many other persons, too numerous to mention, have contributed to the production of this program. Without their dedicated efforts, this program would not have been possible.

Continuing Medical Education

The American College of Physicians is accredited by the Accreditation Council for Continuing Medical Education (ACCME) to provide continuing medical education for physicians.

The American College of Physicians designates this educational activity for a maximum of 166 *AMA PRA Category 1 Credits*™. Physicians should only claim credit commensurate with the extent of their participation in the activity.

AMA PRA Category 1 Credit™ is available from July 31, 2009, to July 31, 2012.

Learning Objectives

The learning objectives of MKSAP 15 are to:
- Close gaps between actual care in your practice and preferred standards of care, based on best evidence
- Diagnose disease states that are less common and sometimes overlooked and confusing
- Improve management of comorbidities that can complicate patient care
- Determine when to refer patients for surgery or care by subspecialists
- Pass the ABIM certification examination
- Pass the ABIM maintenance of certification examination

Target Audience

- General internists and primary care physicians
- Subspecialists who need to remain up-to-date in internal medicine
- Residents preparing for the certifying examination in internal medicine
- Physicians preparing for maintenance of certification in internal medicine (recertification)

How to Submit for CME Credits

To earn CME credits, complete a MKSAP 15 answer sheet. Use the enclosed, self-addressed envelope to mail your completed answer sheet(s) to the MKSAP Processing Center for scoring. Remember to provide your MKSAP 15 order and ACP ID numbers in the appropriate spaces on the answer sheet. The order and ACP ID numbers are printed on your mailing label. If you have <u>not</u> received these numbers with your MKSAP 15 purchase, you will need to acquire them to earn CME credits. E-mail ACP's customer service center at custserv@acponline.org. In the subject line, write "MKSAP 15 order/ACP ID numbers." In the body of the e-mail, make sure you include your e-mail address as well as your full name, address, city, state, ZIP code, country, and telephone number. Also identify where you have made your MKSAP 15 purchase. You will receive your MKSAP 15 order and ACP ID numbers by e-mail within 72 business hours.

Disclosure Policy

It is the policy of the American College of Physicians (ACP) to ensure balance, independence, objectivity, and scientific rigor in all its educational activities. To this end, and consistent with the policies of the ACP and the Accreditation Council for Continuing Medical Education (ACCME), contributors to all ACP continuing medical education activities are required to disclose all relevant financial relationships with any entity producing, marketing, re-selling, or distributing health care goods or services consumed by, or used on, patients. Contributors are required to use generic names in the discussion of therapeutic options and are required to identify any unapproved, off-label, or investigative use of commercial products or devices. Where a trade name is used, all available trade names for the same product type are also included. If trade-name products manufactured by companies with whom contributors have relationships are discussed, contributors are asked to provide evidence-based citations in support of the discussion. The information is reviewed by the committee responsible for producing this text. If necessary, adjustments to topics or contributors' roles in content development are made to balance the discussion. Further, all readers of this text are asked to evaluate the content for evidence of commercial bias so that future decisions about content and contributors can be made in light of this information.

Resolution of Conflicts

To resolve all conflicts of interest and influences of vested interests, the ACP precluded members of the content-creation committee from deciding on any content issues that involved generic or trade-name products associated with proprietary entities with which these committee members had relationships. In addition, content was based on best evidence and updated clinical care guidelines, when such evidence and guidelines were available. Contributors' disclosure information can be found with the list of contributors' names and those of ACP principal staff listed in the beginning of this book.

Educational Disclaimer

The editors and publisher of MKSAP 15 recognize that the development of new material offers many opportunities for error. Despite our best efforts, some errors may persist in print. Drug dosage schedules are, we believe, accurate and in accordance with current standards. Readers are advised, however, to ensure that the recommended dosages in MKSAP 15 concur with the information provided in the product information material. This is especially important in cases of new, infrequently used, or highly toxic drugs. Application of the information in MKSAP 15 remains the professional responsibility of the practitioner.

The primary purpose of MKSAP 15 is educational. Information presented, as well as publications, technologies, products, and/or services discussed, is intended to inform subscribers about the knowledge, techniques, and experiences of the contributors. A diversity of professional opinion exists, and the views of the contributors are their own and not those of the ACP. Inclusion of any material in the program does not constitute endorsement or recommendation by the ACP. The ACP does not warrant the safety, reliability, accuracy, completeness, or usefulness of and disclaims

any and all liability for damages and claims that may result from the use of information, publications, technologies, products, and/or services discussed in this program.

Publisher's Information

Unauthorized Use of This Book Is Against the Law

MKSAP 15 ISBN: 978-1-934465-25-7
Endocrinology and Metabolism ISBN: 978-1-934465-37-0

Printed in the United States of America.

For order information in the U.S. or Canada call 800-523-1546, extension 2600. All other countries call 215-351-2600. Fax inquiries to 215-351-2799 or e-mail to custserv@acponline.org.

Errata and Norm Tables

Errata for MKSAP 15 will be posted at http://mksap.acponline.org/errata as new information becomes known to the editors.

MKSAP 15 Performance Interpretation Guidelines with Norm Tables, available December 31, 2010, will reflect the knowledge of physicians who have completed the self-assessment tests before the program was published. These physicians took the tests without being able to refer to the syllabus, answers, and critiques. For your convenience, the tables are available in a printable PDF file at http://mksap.acponline.org/normtables.

Table of Contents

Calcium and Bone Disorders

Endocrinology and Metabolism

Diabetes Mellitus

Diagnosis and Classification of Diabetes Mellitus

Diabetes mellitus, a chronic metabolic disease characterized by increased circulating blood glucose levels, results from the inadequate supply or action of insulin. Insulin is the main hormonal regulator of intermediary metabolism. Its most prominent effects are the stimulation of glucose uptake by peripheral tissues (mainly skeletal muscle) and the suppression of endogenous glucose production (mostly by the liver). This anabolic hormone also suppresses lipolysis in adipocytes and proteolysis in muscle.

Patients with diabetes mellitus exhibit variable degrees of hyperglycemia in both fasting and postprandial states that is related to specific defects in insulin secretion, the response to insulin, or both. Hyperglycemia is associated with an increased risk of chronic micro- and macrovascular complications.

The two major forms of diabetes are type 1 and type 2 (**Table 1**). Type 1 diabetes is usually diagnosed early in life and results from autoimmune destruction of insulin-producing pancreatic beta cells. The more common type 2 diabetes typically results from both insulin resistance and relative insulin deficiency. The prediabetic states of impaired fasting glucose and impaired glucose tolerance are transitional phases; patients with these conditions are at increased risk for type 2 diabetes. The diagnostic criteria for diabetes and prediabetes are shown in **Table 2**.

Diabetes mellitus is diagnosed in most patients on the basis of their fasting plasma glucose level. The more sensitive oral glucose tolerance test is less frequently performed, although it remains a standard way to diagnose diabetes during gestation. A diagnosis of diabetes also can be made if a random plasma glucose level equals or exceeds 200 mg/dL (11.1 mmol/L) in the setting of symptomatic hyperglycemia, such as polyuria, polydipsia, or blurred vision. The hemoglobin A_{1c} value is a long-term (2-3 month) marker of glycemic control. A recent expert committee statement recommended that the hemoglobin A_{1c} test be used to diagnose diabetes, but major professional organizations have not yet endorsed this recommendation.

Although a recent literature review for the U.S. Preventive Services Task Force (USPSTF) found no direct evidence of health benefits with mass screening for diabetes, the USPSTF does recommend screening for type 2 diabetes in asymptomatic adults with a sustained blood pressure greater than 135/80 mm Hg (either treated or untreated). The more comprehensive American Diabetes Association (ADA) guidelines for diabetes screening are listed in **Table 3**.

TABLE 1 Classification of Diabetes Mellitus

Type 1 Diabetes Mellitus
Beta cell destruction, usually leading to absolute insulin deficiency 　Autoimmune 　Idiopathic ("seronegative")
Type 2 Diabetes Mellitus
Ranging from predominant insulin resistance with relative insulin deficiency to a predominant secretory defect with insulin resistance
Gestational Diabetes Mellitus
Similar pathogenesis to that of type 2 diabetes
Other Specific Types
Genetic defects in beta cell function (including MODY syndromes)
Genetic defects in insulin action
Diseases of the exocrine pancreas (pancreatitis, pancreatic cancer, cystic fibrosis, hemochromatosis)
Endocrinopathies (Cushing syndrome, acromegaly, glucagonoma, pheochromocytoma)
Drug- or chemically induced (corticosteroids, niacin, diazoxide)
Infections (CMV, congenital rubella)
Rare forms of immune-mediated diabetes
Other genetic syndromes associated with diabetes (Down, Turner, Klinefelter, Prader-Willi, Laurence-Moon-Biedl syndromes; myotonic dystrophy; Huntington chorea)

CMV = cytomegalovirus; MODY = maturity-onset diabetes of the young.

Adapted with permission from American Diabetes Association. Diagnosis and classification of diabetes mellitus. Diabetes Care. 2008;31 Suppl 1:S58. [PMID: 18165338]

Type 1 Diabetes Mellitus

Type 1 diabetes mellitus mainly affects lean children, teenagers, and young adults. The disorder is characterized by absolute insulin deficiency from selective autoimmune destruction of insulin-secreting pancreatic beta cells. After diagnosis, residual insulin secretion can persist for several months or even years. When there is enough insulin to control blood glucose, a "honeymoon" phase occurs during which the patient may transiently be able to markedly reduce or even eliminate insulin therapy. In type 1A diabetes, one or more autoantibodies directed against the beta cells or their products (such as anti–glutamic acid decarboxylase, anti–islet cell autoantigen 512, and anti-insulin antibodies) can usually be detected. Strong HLA associations exist, with linkage to the *DQA* and *DQB* genes. Type 1B diabetes is idiopathic, has

TABLE 2 Diagnostic Criteria for Diabetes Mellitus and Prediabetic States

Diagnosis	Fasting Plasma Glucose	Random Plasma Glucose[a]	2-Hour Plasma Glucose[b]
Normal glucose homeostasis	<100 mg/dL (5.6 mmol/L)	—	<140 mg/dL (7.8 mmol/L)
Impaired glucose metabolism ("prediabetes")	100-125 mg/dL (5.6-6.9 mmol/L) (impaired fasting glucose)	—	140-199 mg/dL (7.8-11.0 mmol/L) (impaired glucose tolerance)
Diabetes	≥126 mg/dL (7.0 mmol/L)	≥200 mg/dL (11.1 mmol/L) (with symptoms of diabetes)	≥200 mg/dL (11.1 mmol/L)

[a]Without regard to previous meal.

[b]During 75-g oral glucose tolerance test.

Data from American Diabetes Association. Diagnosis and classification of diabetes mellitus. Diabetes Care. 2008;31 Suppl 1:S55-S60. [PMID: 18165338]

TABLE 3 American Diabetes Association Screening Guidelines for Diabetes Mellitus

Consider screening every 3 years in all persons beginning at age 45 years

Consider screening more frequently and at an earlier age in overweight persons (BMI >25) with any of the following additional risk factors:

Physical inactivity

First-degree relative with diabetes

Membership in a high-risk ethnic group (Hispanic, American Indian, African American, Asian American, and Pacific Islander)

History of gestational diabetes or previous delivery of an infant ≥4.1 kg (9 lb)

Hypertension (≥140/90 mm Hg)

Low HDL-cholesterol level (≤35 mg/dL [0.91 mmol/L])

High triglyceride level (≥250 mg/dL [2.83 mmol/L])

Polycystic ovary syndrome

Acanthosis nigricans

Impaired fasting glucose or impaired glucose tolerance on prior testing

History of vascular disease

Adapted with permission from American Diabetes Association. Standards of medical care—2008. Diabetes Care. 2008;31 Suppl 1:S14. [PMID: 18165335]

no autoimmune markers, and occurs more commonly in persons of Asian or African descent.

At presentation, patients with type 1 diabetes mellitus often have severe hyperglycemia with associated fatigue, polyuria, polydipsia, visual blurring, weight loss, and dehydration. The main acute complication of this type of diabetes is diabetic ketoacidosis. Type 1 diabetes is usually treated solely with insulin. Some older patients in whom type 2 diabetes was previously diagnosed develop gradual autoimmune beta cell destruction and are said to have late-onset autoimmune diabetes of adulthood. These patients are usually lean, have evidence of lower insulin secretory capacity and positive autoimmune markers, and manifest more labile glycemic control. Over time, they develop absolute insulin deficiency.

Type 2 Diabetes Mellitus

Type 2 diabetes mellitus accounts for 90% to 95% of diabetes worldwide and has a more insidious onset than type 1. Patients with type 2 diabetes are usually older than 40 years and typically overweight or obese. Because of increasing obesity rates in the young, type 2 diabetes is becoming more common in teenagers and older children.

The pathogenesis of type 2 diabetes involves the dual defects of insulin resistance and relative insulin deficiency. Patients at risk for type 2 diabetes initially develop insulin resistance alone, accompanied by augmented pancreatic insulin secretion. Because of the resulting hyperinsulinemia, plasma glucose levels are maintained in the normal range. In most patients, however, pancreatic beta cell function ultimately falters, with deterioration of endogenous insulin secretory capacity over time. The beta cell defect heralding the transition from normal to impaired glucose tolerance and then to frank diabetes is not well understood.

Because insulin secretion persists in almost all patients with type 2 diabetes mellitus, ketoacidosis is rare. Most patients with type 2 diabetes have other coexisting clinical and biochemical features, including central adiposity, hypertension, and dyslipidemia. This collection of findings is often referred to as the metabolic syndrome (**Table 4**). Hyperuricemia, polycystic ovary syndrome, obstructive sleep apnea, and nonalcoholic steatohepatitis are other manifestations of the metabolic syndrome in patients with type 2 diabetes.

Treatment for type 2 diabetes should include lifestyle changes, but patients usually will eventually require treatment with one or more oral antihyperglycemic agents. Additionally, as insulin secretory capacity further falters, most patients will ultimately need insulin. The need for insulin to control hyperglycemia in a patient with type 2 diabetes does not, however, indicate a transformation to type 1. This stage is instead often referred to as insulin-requiring type 2 diabetes.

Other Types of Diabetes Mellitus

The pathogenesis of gestational diabetes is similar to that of type 2 diabetes, with the acute insulin resistance of pregnancy

TABLE 4 Diagnostic Criteria for the Metabolic Syndrome[a]

Risk Factor	Defining Level
Abdominal obesity (waist circumference)	
Men	>102 cm (>40 in)
Women	>88 cm (>35 in)
Triglycerides	≥150 mg/dL (1.70 mmol/L)
HDL-cholesterol	
Men	<40 mg/dL (1.04 mmol/L)
Women	<50 mg/dL (1.30 mmol/L)
Blood pressure	
Systolic	≥130 mm Hg
Diastolic	≥85 mm Hg
Fasting glucose	≥100 mg/dL (5.6 mmol/L)

[a]According to National Cholesterol Education Program Guidelines; diagnosis is established when at least three of these risk factors are present.

Adapted with permission from Grundy SM, Cleeman JI, Daniel SR, et al. Diagnosis and management of the metabolic syndrome: an American Heart Association/National Heart, Lung, and Blood Institute Scientific Statement. Circulation. 2005;112(17):2739. [PMID: 16157765] Copyright 2005, The American Heart Association.

posing too great a stress to the pancreatic beta cells, which are not able to increase their insulin production to maintain euglycemia. Gestational diabetes currently affects approximately 7% of pregnancies in the United States. The American Diabetes Association recommends that high-risk patients (those from high-risk ethnic groups or with obesity, glycosuria, a history of gestational diabetes, or a family history of diabetes) should undergo screening as soon as pregnancy is recognized and that, if gestational diabetes is not found, these patients be retested at 24 to 28 weeks of gestation, when average-risk patients should be screened. Notably, the USPSTF recently has concluded that current evidence is insufficient to assess the balance of benefits and harms of universal screening for gestational diabetes and recommends that until there is better evidence, clinicians should discuss screening for gestational diabetes with their patients and make case-by-case decisions. Low-risk patients (those <25 years of age, not a member of high-risk ethnic group, and with normal prepregnancy weight, no family history of diabetes, and no history of abnormal glucose testing or poor obstetric outcomes) do not require testing. Diagnostic criteria for gestational diabetes are shown in **Table 5**.

Gestational diabetes mellitus is associated with an increased risk of fetal macrosomia, neonatal hypoglycemia, jaundice, polycythemia, and hypocalcemia. Maternal hypertension and cesarean delivery risks also are increased. Gestational diabetes typically resolves after delivery but frequently recurs during future pregnancies. Women with a history of gestational diabetes are at very high risk (~50%) of developing type 2 diabetes within a decade. A repeat oral glucose tolerance test is recommended 6 weeks after delivery, as is ongoing periodic surveillance.

Secondary diabetes mellitus is diabetes resulting from a drug, such as a corticosteroid, or another disease, such as pancreatic disorders, other endocrinopathies, and several genetic syndromes. Other hyperglycemic diseases that are collectively known as maturity-onset diabetes of the young (MODY) develop early in life (teens to early 20s); the pattern of inheritance is autosomal dominant. Several described subtypes of MODY are associated with specific genetic defects in enzymes or transcription factors affecting beta cell function. The identification of MODY will not necessarily alter management, but insulin-sensitizing drugs may be less effective therapies.

KEY POINTS

- Patients with impaired fasting glucose levels and impaired glucose tolerance are at increased risk for developing type 2 diabetes mellitus.
- Women with a history of gestational diabetes mellitus are at very high risk (~50%) of developing type 2 diabetes within a decade.

Treatment of Diabetes Mellitus

The Diabetes Control and Complications Trial (DCCT) showed that improved control of blood glucose levels mitigates the incidence of microvascular complications, such as

TABLE 5 Diagnosis of Gestational Diabetes Mellitus

Test	Measurement Time	Plasma Glucose Level
Step 1: 50-g oral glucose challenge test	1 hour	If >140 mg/dL (7.8 mmol/L), proceed to step 2
Step 2: 100-g oral glucose tolerance test[a,b]	Baseline (fasting)	95 mg/dL (5.3 mmol/L)
	1 hour	180 mg/dL (10.0 mmol/L)
	2 hours	155 mg/dL (8.6 mmol/L)
	3 hours	140 mg/dL (7.8 mmol/L)

[a]Diagnosis is made if two or more of the values listed are reached or exceeded.

[b]Should be performed in the morning after an overnight fast (8-14 h) and 3 days of unrestricted diet (≥150 g carbohydrates/d).

retinopathy and nephropathy, in patients with type 1 diabetes mellitus. The United Kingdom Prospective Diabetes Study (UKPDS) made similar observations in patients with type 2 diabetes. Given these results, the ADA currently advises stringent glycemic control in most patients with diabetes, allowing for individualized treatment goals under certain circumstances (**Table 6**). There is conflicting evidence about whether improving glucose levels similarly benefits macrovascular (cardiovascular) complications, although a UKPDS substudy showed that initial therapy with metformin in overweight patients reduced myocardial infarction rates.

Achieving glycemic control is a challenge in managing diabetes, as is achieving control of other cardiovascular risk factors. The most reliable assessment of overall glycemic status is a periodic measurement of the hemoglobin A_{1c} value. This test allows practitioners to determine the average degree of glycemia over the previous 2 to 3 months. Ideally, the hemoglobin A_{1c} value should be below 7.0% (normal range, 4.0%-6.0%). Home capillary glucose monitoring can be helpful as an adjunct to hemoglobin A_{1c} measurement, especially in patients on insulin. The exact frequency of this testing should be individualized.

Plasma glucose levels should be between 70 and 130 mg/dL (3.9 and 7.2 mmol/L) before meals and below 180 mg/dL (10.0 mmol/L) 2 hours after meals. Caution is advised, however, in patients with preexisting severe cardiovascular or cerebrovascular disease because hypoglycemia can predispose to cardiac arrhythmia or cerebral dysfunction. In addition, any patient with either type 1 or type 2 diabetes who has hypoglycemia unawareness (see later discussion of hypoglycemia) should have less stringent treatment goals, as should patients with significant comorbidities or with limited

life expectancy. In contrast, patients with diabetes during pregnancy should be kept to even stricter targets, including a normal hemoglobin A_{1c} value.

Education and Self-Management in Diabetes Mellitus

Patient education and self-management are critical in the management of diabetes mellitus. Training is optimally provided outside of routine physician office visits by health care professionals who devise individual programs for patients' specific needs. Such education should provide information about the disease process itself, its complications, its relationship to metabolic control, and the key role of diet and exercise in its management. Glucose-monitoring techniques, the proper administration of oral agents and insulin, the treatment of hypoglycemia, and the situations in which medical care should be sought must also be carefully reviewed. Diabetes self-management training is optimally provided by an interdisciplinary team composed, at minimum, of a diabetes educator and a nutritionist, who work in conjunction with the patient's primary care physician.

The widespread use of periodic capillary glucose monitoring has facilitated better glycemic control. For patients on intensive insulin regimens, information from premeal glucose testing assists in insulin dosing.

Continuous subcutaneous glucose monitoring devices are now available, but their role in diabetes management is unclear. Such devices are mainly used by patients on insulin pumps, who can adjust their insulin doses on the basis of the frequent feedback from the monitor. Issues involving precision, reproducibility, convenience, and cost remain, however. Some companies are developing monitoring units that communicate with insulin infusion pumps to create a virtual artificial pancreas.

Noninsulin Agents for Diabetes Mellitus

Type 2 diabetes mellitus is conventionally treated first with diet, weight loss, and exercise. Such lifestyle modifications reduce insulin resistance and blood glucose levels and also improve cardiovascular risk factors. However, these steps are usually insufficient to attain glucose targets. The pharmacologic approach to type 2 diabetes has changed markedly over the past decade, with nine drug classes now available, each with unique mechanisms of action to address the various pathophysiologic defects of this disease (**Table 7**). It should be noted, however, that a recent meta-analysis suggested that older, less expensive agents were just as effective as newer ones.

Most physicians use metformin as first-line therapy in patients whose diabetes is not controlled by diet and exercise alone. This approach was endorsed in an ADA–European Association for the Study of Diabetes (EASD) consensus statement advising initiation of metformin monotherapy, in conjunction with diet and exercise, once the diagnosis of diabetes is made. Because type 2 diabetes mellitus is a progressive

TABLE 6 Metabolic Targets for Nonpregnant Patients with Diabetes Mellitus	
Variable Measured	**Target Value**
Hemoglobin A_{1c}[a]	<7.0%
Preprandial plasma glucose	70-130 mg/dL (3.9-7.2 mmol/L)
Postprandial plasma glucose[b]	<180 mg/dL (10.0 mmol/L)
Blood pressure	<130/80 mm Hg
LDL-cholesterol	<100 mg/dL (2.59 mmol/L)[c]
HDL-cholesterol	
Men	>40 mg/dL (1.04 mmol/L)
Women	>50 mg/dL (1.30 mmol/L)
Triglycerides	<150 mg/dL (1.70 mmol/L)

[a]Normal range, 4.0% to 6.0%.

[b]1 to 2 hours after a meal.

[c]In patients with overt cardiovascular disease, a lower goal of <70 mg/dL (1.81 mmol/L) may be preferred.

Data from American Diabetes Association. Standards of medical care in diabetes—2008. Diabetes Care. 2008;31 Suppl 1:S12-S54. [PMID: 18165335]

TABLE 7 Noninsulin Antihyperglycemic Agents for Type 2 Diabetes Mellitus

Class	Mechanism of Action	Benefits	Risks/Concerns
Sulfonylureas Glyburide Glipizide Glimepiride	Bind to sulfonylurea receptor on beta cells, stimulating insulin release; long duration of action	Extensive clinical experience; improved microvascular outcomes in UKPDS; low cost; once-daily dosing possible	Hypoglycemia; weight gain; potential impairment of cardiac ischemic preconditioning
Glinides (meglitinides) Repaglinide Nateglinide	Bind to sulfonylurea receptor on beta cells, stimulating insulin release; short duration of action	Target postprandial glucose; mimics physiologic insulin secretion	Hypoglycemia; weight gain; no long-term studies; expensive; frequent dosing (compliance an issue)
Biguanides Metformin	Decrease hepatic glucose production	Extensive clinical experience; no hypoglycemia; weight loss or weight neutral; lipid and other nonglycemic vascular benefits; improved macrovascular outcomes; low cost; once-daily dosing available (sustained-release product)	Diarrhea, abdominal discomfort; many contraindications to consider, including serum creatinine >1.4 mg/dL (123.76 µmol/L) and lactic acidosis risk (rare); lowers vitamin B_{12} levels (without apparent effects on hematologic indices or neurologic function)
α-Glucosidase inhibitors Acarbose Miglitol	Retard gut carbohydrate absorption	Target postprandial glucose; weight-neutral; nonsystemic	Flatulence, abdominal discomfort; frequent dosing (compliance); expensive
Thiazolidinediones Rosiglitazone Pioglitazone	Activate the nuclear receptor PPARγ, increasing peripheral insulin sensitivity. May also reduce hepatic glucose production	Address primary defect of T2DM; no hypoglycemia; lipid and other nonglycemic vascular benefits; probable decreased macrovascular outcomes with pioglitazone; greater durability of effectiveness; once-daily dosing	Edema and heart failure risk; weight gain; possible increased fracture risk in women; possible increased myocardial infarction risk with rosiglitazone; slow onset of action; expensive
Amylinomimetics Pramlintide	Activate amylin receptors, decreasing glucagon secretion, delaying gastric emptying, and enhancing satiety	Weight loss	Nausea, vomiting; hypoglycemia risk when used with insulin; no long-term studies; injectable; expensive; frequent dosing (compliance)
Incretin modulators GLP-1 mimetics Exenatide	Activate GLP-1 receptors, increasing glucose-dependent insulin secretion, decreasing glucagon secretion, delaying gastric emptying, and enhancing satiety	No hypoglycemia; weight loss	Nausea, vomiting; possible pancreatitis (rare); no long-term studies; injectable; expensive
DPP-IV inhibitors Sitagliptin	Inhibit degradation of endogenous GLP-1 and GIP, thereby enhancing the effect of these incretins on insulin and glucagon secretion	No hypoglycemia; weight neutral; once-daily dosing	Possible urticaria/angioedema (rare); no long-term studies; expensive
Bile acid sequestrants Colesevelam	Bind cholesterol within bile acid; unknown mechanisms of antihyperglycemic effect	No hypoglycemia; weight neutral; lowers LDL-cholesterol	Constipation; may increase triglycerides; no long-term studies; expensive

DPP-IV = dipeptidyl peptidase-IV; GIP = gastric inhibitory peptide; GLP-1 = glucagon-like peptide-1; PPARγ = peroxisome proliferator–activated receptor-γ; T2DM = type 2 diabetes mellitus; UKPDS = United Kingdom Prospective Diabetes Study.

disease, drugs with different mechanisms of action are typically added to metformin when therapy beyond lifestyle changes is required. The exact sequence of agents remains somewhat controversial. An individualized approach that incorporates efficacy, side effect profiles, and cost is encouraged. Single agents consisting of two drugs in fixed combinations (metformin plus a sulfonylurea and/or a thiazolidinedione) are now also available and may improve compliance. As described in the ADA-EASD consensus statement, early initiation of insulin therapy may be appropriate in many patients, especially if glycemic targets are not being achieved after a trial of two to three oral agents at a time (**Figure 1**).

Insulin Therapy for Diabetes Mellitus

As beta cell function declines in type 2 diabetes mellitus, the attainment of adequate glycemic control with multiple oral

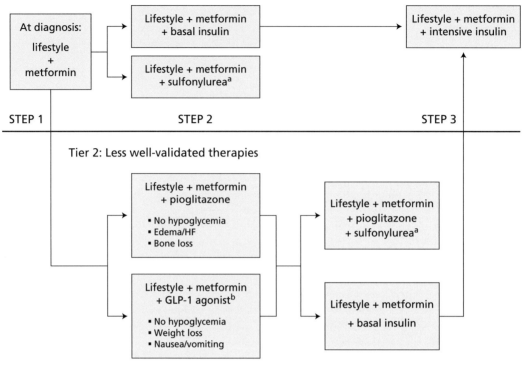

Tier 1: Well-validated core therapies

STEP 1   STEP 2   STEP 3

Tier 2: Less well-validated therapies

FIGURE 1.

Metabolic management of type 2 diabetes mellitus.

Algorithm for the metabolic management of type 2 diabetes from the American Diabetes Association and the European Association for the Study of Diabetes.

GLP-1 = glucagon-like peptide 1; HF = heart failure.

[a]Sulfonylureas other than glyburide or chlorpropamide.

[b]Insufficient clinical use to be confident regarding safety.

Adapted with permission from Nathan DM, Buse JB, Davidson MB, et al. Medical management of hyperglycemia in type 2 diabetes: a consensus algorithm for the initiation and adjustment of therapy: a consensus statement from the American Diabetes Association and the European Association for the Study of Diabetes. Diabetes Care. 2009;32(1):200. [PMID: 18945920]

agents becomes elusive, and insulin is ultimately required in most patients. Several strategies exist to transition patients from oral agents to insulin, and several insulin types are available (**Table 8**). The most popular method is to begin with a single, typically nighttime injection of a basal insulin, such as insulin glargine or insulin detemir, because this simple approach minimizes the risk of hypoglycemia. Starting doses in the 0.2 to 0.3 U/kg range are well tolerated in most patients, with future titration based on the results of home glucose monitoring. Dose changes are typically made in increments of 10% to 15% every few days or weekly. A more cost-effective approach involves the use of neutral protamine Hagedorn (NPH) insulin once at night or twice daily, although this may result in hypoglycemia because of an unpredictable peak between 4 and 8 hours of injection. Because of this peak, NPH insulin given at bedtime may be preferred for patients who manifest the "dawn phenomenon," defined as an increase in blood glucose levels during the early morning hours (4 AM-8 AM) that is thought to be related to increased levels of cortisol and growth hormone at this time. Basal insulin, although effective in many patients, does not address postprandial glucose excursions. Another method involves the use

premixed products that contain both intermediate and short- or rapid-acting insulins in fixed ratios, administered twice daily. More intensive regimens are described below.

Oral agents are usually continued when basal insulin is initiated, although secretagogues can be stopped once prandial insulin is added to the treatment regimen. There may be some advantage to continuing insulin sensitizers to improve control and minimize the insulin dose required. With thiazolidinediones, however, the side effects of weight gain and edema are accentuated when used in combination with insulin, so a dose reduction should be considered. Although better control of hemoglobin A_{1c} was recently shown with a rapid-acting insulin analogue at mealtime and a premixed insulin analogue twice daily than with a once-daily basal insulin (detemir), this improved control was at the expense of more weight gain and hypoglycemia.

In patients with type 1 diabetes mellitus, an intensive insulin regimen involving at least three to four daily injections or a continuous subcutaneous insulin infusion with a programmable insulin pump is preferable and is often managed by an endocrinologist. Regimens involving one to two injections

TABLE 8 Pharmacokinetic Properties of Insulin Products[a]

Human Insulins and Insulin Analogues	Onset	Peak	Duration
Rapid-acting (lispro, aspart, glulisine)	10-15 min	1-2 h	3-5 h
Short-acting (regular)	0.5-1 h	2-4 h	4-8 h
Intermediate-acting (NPH)	1-3 h	4-10 h	10-18 h
Long-acting			
Glargine	2-3 h	none	24+ h
Detemir	1 h	none	12-24 h
Premixed insulins			
70% NPH/30% regular	0.5-1 h	2-10 h	10-18 h
50% NPH/50% regular	0.5-1 h	2-10 h	10-18 h
75% NPL/25% lispro	10-15 min	1-3 h	10-16 h
50% NPL/50% lispro	10-15 min	1-3 h	10-16 h
70% NPA/30% aspart	10-20 min	1-4 h	10-16 h

NPA = neutral protamine aspart; NPH = neutral protamine Hagedorn; NPL = neutral protamine lispro.

[a]The time course of each insulin may vary among persons or at different times in the same person. Because of this variation, the time periods here should be considered general guidelines only.

per day will likely prevent ketosis only and should not be considered standard therapy. Most patient with type 1 diabetes require between 0.6 and 0.8 U/kg/day of insulin. Variables, including diet, exercise, stress, and illness, can alter these requirements, sometimes significantly.

The optimal insulin replacement regimen mimics the two components of insulin secretion: a basal component, mainly to suppress hepatic glucose production, and a prandial (or bolus) component, to metabolize ingested calories. Insulin pumps deliver rapid-acting insulin analogues at a continuous basal rate, with additional premeal doses calculated based on the anticipated carbohydrate intake of the patient; this allows for more refined control. The basal-bolus method of insulin replacement is an alternative to the insulin pump and has many of the same benefits. This method uses long-acting basal insulin products, such as insulin glargine or detemir, and premeal adjusted doses of a rapid-acting analogue, such as insulin aspart, insulin lispro, or insulin glulisine. Because basal insulins cannot be mixed with other types of insulin, four daily injections are required.

Optimally, the total daily insulin requirements are equally divided into basal and bolus components, with approximately one third of the bolus component taken prior to each meal. More precisely, the premeal bolus is based on the anticipated carbohydrate intake for each meal (carbohydrate counting), which typically uses an insulin unit to carbohydrate gram ratio of 1:15. Adjustments can also be made for premeal hyperglycemia by using correction doses, typically 1 to 2 units of rapid-acting insulin for every 40 to 50 mg/dL (2.2 to 2.8 mmol/L) of glucose above the premeal target. The older NPH insulin can serve as the basal insulin but requires dosing twice daily. Premixed insulins incorporate both intermediate and short- or rapid-acting components and are given two to three times per day.

Prevention of Type 2 Diabetes Mellitus

Interest in preventing type 2 diabetes in patients with prediabetes is high, with most efforts focused on improving insulin sensitivity through either lifestyle modifications or drug therapy. The Finnish Diabetes Prevention Study and the U.S. Diabetes Prevention Program (USDPP) both demonstrated a 58% relative risk reduction in the progression to diabetes with these methods in (generally) obese, middle-aged individuals with impaired glucose tolerance. However, the active therapy required significant clinical support (nutritionists, exercise physiologists, behavior modification experts), which is not readily available in clinical practice.

The USDPP reported a 31% risk reduction in the development of diabetes in those treated with metformin. Acarbose reduced the risk of diabetes by 25% in the Study to Prevent Non–Insulin-Dependent Diabetes Mellitus (STOP-NIDDM) trial but had a high drop-out rate due to gastrointestinal side effects. Other studies have shown a 62% reduction in progression to diabetes with rosiglitazone in patients with impaired glucose tolerance or impaired fasting glucose and an 82% reduction in the progression to diabetes with pioglitazone. The precise role of each of these interventions is evolving, and no drug is currently approved for diabetes prevention. In their consensus statement, the ADA-EASD advise that lifestyle modifications continue to be the standard approach, with the goal being to increase regular physical activity by approximately 30 minutes on most days of the week and to reduce calories (to reduce weight) by 7%; they also recommend that metformin therapy be considered in very high-risk patients. Other cardiovascular risk factors should be aggressively addressed in any of these patients predisposed to macrovascular disease.

Diabetes Mellitus During Pregnancy

Once identified, gestational diabetes mellitus is typically managed with diet, but some women require pharmacologic support. Studies have demonstrated the safety and efficacy of both metformin and sulfonylureas in pregnancy, but insulin remains the mainstay of therapy. Tight glycemic control minimizes maternal, fetal, and neonatal complications, including defective embryogenesis during the first trimester and macrosomia.

To avoid birth defects, women with type 1 diabetes should attain excellent glycemic control prior to conception. Glycemic control needs to be maintained compulsively throughout gestation, with current glucose targets of 60 to 90 mg/dL (3.3 to 5.0 mmol/L) premeal and less than 120 mg/dL (6.7 mmol/L) 1 hour postmeal.

Inpatient Management of Hyperglycemia and Diabetes Mellitus

Many retrospective investigations have linked hyperglycemia in the hospital with adverse clinical outcomes; this association appears to be greater in patients without a history of diabetes. Intensive intravenous infusion of insulin to normalize blood glucose levels was shown to reduce mortality in one study, but this benefit has not been confirmed by others. Current recommendations from a consensus statement from the ADA and the American Association of Clinical Endocrinologists are to use insulin infusions to reduce blood glucose levels in critically ill patients to the more modest range of 140 to 180 mg/dL (7.8 to 10.0 mmol/L). In noncritically ill patients, a premeal target of less than 140 mg/dL (7.8 mmol/L) and a target of less than 180 mg/dL (10.0 mmol/L) for random glucose were endorsed by the statement. The guidelines also emphasize the need to reconsider the widespread use of regular insulin sliding scales as the sole antihyperglycemic therapy in hospitalized patients with diabetes. Instead, more proactive, physiologic insulin regimens, such as a basal-bolus approach, are advisable (**Figure 2**). Also, patients identified as being hyperglycemic during the stress of illness should have their glycemic status reassessed after recovery because many of them will ultimately be shown to have diabetes.

KEY POINTS

- Metformin is widely considered the best first-line antihyperglycemic agent for type 2 diabetes mellitus and may help prevent progression from prediabetes to diabetes; sulfonylureas are typically used as second-line therapy.

- In type 1 diabetes mellitus, an intensive insulin regimen involving at least three to four daily insulin injections or a continuous subcutaneous insulin infusion with a programmable insulin pump is preferable.

- Glycemic control needs to be maintained compulsively throughout gestation, with current glucose targets of 60 to 90 mg/dL (3.3 to 5.0 mmol/L) premeal and less than 120 mg/dL (6.7 mmol/L) 1 hour postmeal.

Complications of Diabetes Mellitus

Acute Complications of Diabetes Mellitus

Hyperglycemic and hypoglycemic emergencies are the major acute complications of diabetes mellitus. Hyperglycemic emergencies include diabetic ketoacidosis and hyperglycemic hyperosmolar syndrome.

Diabetic Ketoacidosis

The most life-threatening acute complication of diabetes is diabetic ketoacidosis, which mostly affects patients with type 1 disease and is sometimes its presenting manifestation. This complication can occur in those with superimposed acute infections, such as influenza, pneumonia, or gastroenteritis; those on insulin pumps, when there is a technical interruption of insulin infusion; and those who are nonadherent to their medication regimen. In almost all instances, diabetic ketoacidosis is entirely preventable if patients practice regular glucose monitoring and understand the need for increased insulin doses during stress. Although less common in patients with type 2 diabetes mellitus, diabetic ketoacidosis can occur in that setting during severe medical stress.

The syndrome of diabetic ketoacidosis indicates profound insulin deficiency combined with excess circulating levels of counterregulatory hormones, particularly glucagon. Hyperglycemia, ketosis, and dehydration are directly or indirectly related to insulin deficiency. A lack of insulin prevents glucose uptake by muscle and allows unrestrained hepatic glucose production. Lack of suppression of lipolysis also leads to excess circulating free fatty acids, which are converted into the ketoacids β-hydroxybutyrate and acetoacetate by the liver, and ultimately results in acidemia, which may impair vascular tone and cardiac function. Marked hyperglycemia and ketonemia result in an osmotic diuresis with loss of water and electrolytes.

At presentation, patients with diabetic ketoacidosis usually report a several-day history of polyuria, polydipsia, and blurred vision, culminating in nausea, vomiting, abdominal pain, dyspnea, and altered mental status. Physical examination typically reveals deep, labored breathing (Kussmaul respirations), a fruity odor to the breath (from acetone), poor skin turgor, tachycardia, and hypotension. Bowel sounds are commonly absent, and the abdomen may be diffusely tender. Laboratory findings will include marked hyperglycemia (plasma glucose 400 to 900 mg/dL [22.2 to 50.0 mmol/L]), an anion gap metabolic acidosis, increased urine and plasma ketones, and elevated blood urea nitrogen and serum creatinine levels. Arterial blood gas findings usually show acidemia with respiratory compensation. The serum sodium level will often be low, a response to the osmotic shifts that result from hyperglycemia. The serum potassium level is often high because of the acidosis, although total body potassium stores are usually low.

Diabetic ketoacidosis should generally be managed in the intensive care unit. In patients with uncomplicated findings,

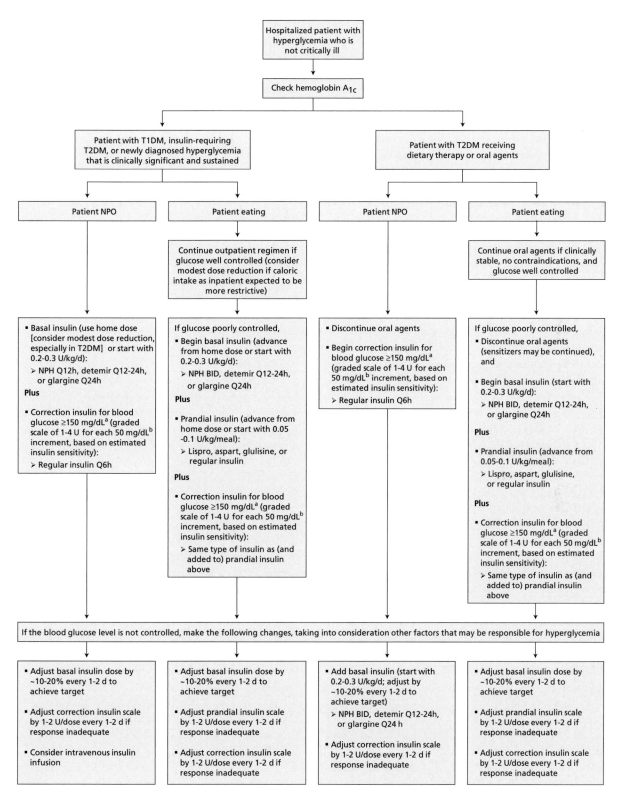

FIGURE 2.

Algorithm for glucose control in noncritically ill hospitalized patients (not in the intensive care unit) with diabetes mellitus.

BID = twice daily; NPH = neutral protamine Hagedorn insulin; NPO = receiving nothing by mouth; Q6h = every 6 hours; Q12h = every 12 hours; Q12-24h = every 12-24 hours; Q24h = every 24 hours; T1DM = type 1 diabetes mellitus; T2DM = type 2 diabetes mellitus.

[a]SI value, 8.3 mmol/L.

[b]SI value, 2.8 mmol/L.

Adapted from Inzucchi SE. Clinical practice. Management of hyperglycemia in the hospital setting. N Engl J Med. 2006;355(18):1907. [PMID: 17079764] Copyright 2006, Massachusetts Medical Society.

diabetic ketoacidosis should resolve within 12 hours of hospital presentation, with transition to subcutaneous administration of insulin and transfer to a general medical ward accomplished by 24 hours. The major management goals are to correct the acidosis, volume deficits, and hyperglycemia; to ensure the stability of electrolytes; and to correct any precipitating cause. Rapid normalization of the plasma glucose levels is not necessary and actually may be harmful because of the effects of rapid osmotic shifts, especially as they relate to cerebral edema. Instead, glucose levels should be lowered gradually.

The mainstays of therapy include intravenous insulin to reduce glucose and suppress lipolysis and ketogenesis and intravenous fluids to replenish volume, improve hemodynamics, and reduce counterregulatory factors. Given the severe volume deficits typically associated with diabetic ketoacidosis, intravenous normal saline should be administered initially as quickly as possible until clinical signs of intravascular volume contraction improve. Once plasma volume deficits are largely corrected, as assessed by clinical and laboratory findings, a more hypotonic solution, such as 0.45% sodium chloride, is advisable so that free water losses, predominantly from the intracellular space, can be replenished.

If possible, insulin should be administered intravenously to ensure adequate systemic delivery and to enable the dose to be altered from hour to hour. An initial bolus of 0.15 U/kg is recommended, followed immediately by infusion at a rate of 0.1 U/kg/h. The goal should be to reduce the plasma glucose level by 50 to 100 mg/dL/h (2.8 to 5.6 mmol/L/h). Once the glucose is in the 200 mg/dL (11.1 mmol/L) range, continued insulin is required until ketones are cleared and the anion gap has closed. Because this may take several more hours, glucose levels may fall into the hypoglycemic range; intravenous fluids should be changed at this point to dextrose-containing solutions. The insulin infusion rate can be decreased to that required to suppress lipolysis (in most adults, 1 to 2 U/h). An adequate amount of dextrose (5-10 g/h) will maintain circulating glucose levels between 150 and 200 mg/dL (8.3 and 11.1 mmol/L). Once the anion gap has closed and the patient is ready to eat, the transition to subcutaneous injections of insulin should occur. A mixture of long- and short-acting insulin, overlapped with an insulin drip, is provided at this time for at least 1 hour to ensure adequate insulin levels.

Because cardiac dysfunction can occur if the arterial pH falls below 7.0, intravenous bicarbonate can be considered, although randomized trials have generally not shown any benefit on outcomes. Theoretically, too much bicarbonate can lead to cerebral alkalosis, which can impair the respiratory compensation for systemic acidosis. Additionally, as ketone body production is halted, a correction alkalosis may occur. Of greater concern, large infusions of bicarbonate may potentially lead to severe hypokalemia.

Although potassium deficits may be greater than 100 meq/L (100 mmol/L), the serum potassium level on admission is typically elevated because of the systemic acidosis, with resultant movement of the cation from the intracellular to the extracellular space. Frequent monitoring of the potassium level is therefore mandatory, and aggressive repletion is critical. As the glucose level falls and the pH normalizes, the potassium level will decrease rapidly and must be corrected to avoid cardiac arrhythmias. All intravenous fluids should contain at least 20 meq/L (20 mmol/L) of potassium, unless the serum potassium level is already in excess of 5.0 meq/L (5.0 mmol/L). Additional potassium should be administered either orally or intravenously once the level falls below 4.0 meq/L (4.0 mmol/L). Phosphate levels may also be labile during the management of diabetic ketoacidosis. Initially elevated, particularly in those with renal insufficiency, these levels also drop substantially once metabolic correction has been established. Although maintaining a normal phosphate level is recommended, complications related to hypophosphatemia are rare, and no clear benefit of routine phosphate repletion has been shown. Concurrent replacement of both potassium and phosphate with intravenous potassium phosphate is a convenient way to maintain the serum phosphorus level above 1.0 mg/dL (0.323 mmol/L).

Cerebral edema is a rare but life-threatening complication of diabetic ketoacidosis, primarily in children and adolescents. Its manifestations include headache, an altered level of consciousness, and subsequent neurologic deterioration several hours after the initiation of therapy.

Hyperglycemic Hyperosmolar Syndrome

A complication of type 2 diabetes mellitus, hyperglycemic hyperosmolar syndrome is defined as a plasma osmolality greater than 320 mosm/kg, a plasma glucose level greater than 600 mg/dL (33.3 mmol/L), either no or low serum levels of ketones, and a relatively normal arterial pH and bicarbonate level. The diagnosis is considered in any elderly patient with altered mental status and dehydration, particularly if a diagnosis of diabetes is already established. Rarely, the syndrome is the presenting feature in a patient with a recent diagnosis of diabetes. Some patients have an "overlap" hyperglycemic syndrome with features of both hyperglycemic hyperosmolar syndrome and diabetic ketoacidosis, such as severe hyperosmolarity and mild acidosis.

The profound volume depletion associated with hyperglycemic hyperosmolar syndrome and the older age of patients predispose to more serious complications. Patients with this disorder usually have a precipitating factor, such as severe infection, myocardial infarction, or new renal insufficiency, which can complicate therapy. The syndrome is sometimes encountered in debilitated patients who, after an initial illness, develop worsening hyperosmolality and volume contraction because of insensible fluid losses and possibly abnormal thirst mechanisms. In response, counterregulatory factors lead to hyperglycemia, which, in turn, results in more fluid losses. Eventually, glucose clearance by the kidney declines, which results in extreme hyperglycemia and hyperosmolality; coma may ensue.

Management of hyperglycemic hyperosmolar syndrome mainly involves identifying the underlying precipitating illness and restoring a markedly contracted plasma volume. Both the type of intravenous solution and the rate depend on the degree of hyperosmolality and the extent of intravascular volume depletion, as determined by clinical examination and laboratory measurements. Normal saline, which is already comparatively hypotonic in such patients, is usually chosen first to replenish the extracellular space. If the patient has hypotension, fluids should be administered as rapidly as tolerated to restore plasma volume. Once blood pressure is restored and urine output established, rates should be slowed and hypotonic solutions should be administered. The total body water deficit can be calculated by using standard formulas, with the goal of replacing one half the deficit during the first 24 hours and the remainder over the course of the next 2 to 3 days. Ongoing, insensible fluid losses must be incorporated into these calculations. Because patients are usually older and prone to cardiovascular impairments, close monitoring of their pulmonary status and oxygenation is necessary.

Insulin reduces glucose levels but should be administered only after expansion of the intravascular space has begun. If given earlier, movement of glucose into cells theoretically can reduce circulating volume further, which threatens cerebral and coronary perfusion. Intravenous administration of insulin is preferred, with an initial bolus of 0.1 U/kg and a rate of 0.1 U/kg/h. Electrolytes should be monitored, especially potassium because the potassium level may fall as urine output is restored and renal function improves. The serum potassium level should be maintained at 4 meq/L (4 mmol/L) or higher. Mild metabolic acidosis does not require bicarbonate therapy because normalization of circulating volume will quickly correct this defect. Once the plasma glucose level decreases to less than 200 mg/dL (11.1 mmol/L) and the patient is eating, subcutaneous insulin injections should begin.

Hypoglycemia

Hypoglycemia (plasma glucose level <70 mg/dL [3.9 mmol/L]) in patients with diabetes occurs because of excess insulin supply at a particular time. Hypoglycemia usually occurs in patients taking insulin but can also occur in those on insulin secretagogues. Hyperadrenergic signs, such as diaphoresis, tachycardia, anxiety, and tremor, initially develop. When the plasma glucose level falls below 50 mg/dL (2.8 mmol/L), neuroglycopenic signs and symptoms (such as slurred speech, cognitive impairment, change in personality, loss of consciousness, focal neurologic deficits, and seizures) emerge. In severe and prolonged hypoglycemia, coma and irreversible brain injury can occur. Hypoglycemia usually occurs in the setting of missed meals, excess exercise, alcohol use (which suppresses hepatic glucose production), or excessive insulin

dosing. If the patient maintains consciousness, the symptoms can quickly be reversed with the ingestion of rapidly absorbed carbohydrates, such as glucose- or sucrose-containing foods. If the patient is unconscious or otherwise unable to swallow, intravenous infusion of dextrose or intramuscular injection of glucagon should be initiated. Identification of the precipitating factors is vital so that future events can be prevented. The antihyperglycemic regimen should also be adjusted, depending on the causes of the event.

Hypoglycemia remains the primary impediment to achieving tight glycemic control in insulin-treated patients. An increase in severe hypoglycemic episodes requiring the assistance of another was observed in the intensive therapy group in the DCCT. Careful longitudinal assessment of these patients has not identified any decrease in cognitive function. Hypoglycemia unawareness is often encountered in patients with tightly controlled glucose levels. This complicates management significantly because the normal adrenergic symptoms of mild hypoglycemia are absent, and the first manifestation may be loss of consciousness. Hypoglycemia unawareness appears to be due to an abnormality within centers of the hypothalamus involved in glucose sensing; awareness may be improved by several weeks of compulsively avoiding hypoglycemia. Given the sometimes life-threatening nature of severe hypoglycemia, maintaining glucose levels in a higher, safer range must be stressed for patients prone to frequent episodes of hypoglycemia.

Chronic Complications of Diabetes Mellitus

Besides ischemic insults, microvascular disease in diabetes mellitus involves the kidneys (diabetic nephropathy), the retinae (diabetic retinopathy), and the peripheral nerves (diabetic neuropathy), although the pathogenesis of diabetic neuropathy is probably related to intracellular metabolic abnormalities. The origin of microvascular disease remains poorly understood. Such disease does not occur to a significant degree in conditions other than diabetes and largely correlates with the degree of hyperglycemia. Causes include the interrelated processes of oxidative stress, protein kinase C activation, polyol flux, and the development of advanced glycosylation end products and endothelial dysfunction. The result is tissue ischemia and, eventually, cell death. Microvascular complications occur infrequently in patients with prediabetes and rarely in those with insulin resistance or the metabolic syndrome. Accordingly, their onset usually correlates with the onset of hyperglycemia.

Macrovascular complications of diabetes mellitus involve the coronary, carotid, cerebral, and peripheral arteries (myocardial infarction); the aorta (stroke); and the arterial supply to the lower extremities (gangrene). This atherosclerosis is similar to that seen in patients without diabetes who share other cardiac risk factors. Generally, however, macrovascular disease in those with diabetes appears at an earlier age and to a greater degree and extent than in those without diabetes. In addition, macrovasculopathy also exists, with more distal small vessel involvement, which compounds the resultant tissue ischemia.

All patients with diabetes may develop microvascular and macrovascular complications. Patients with type 2 diabetes more commonly have macrovascular complications because of their generally older age and the frequent coexistence of cardiovascular risk factors. The development of microvascular complications is determined in part by the duration of disease, the quality of blood glucose control, and the coexistence of hypertension.

Diabetic Retinopathy

The highly vascular retina is often affected in patients with long-standing diabetes mellitus, with most cases of legal blindness in adults in the United States being attributable to the disease. Hard exudates, microaneurysms, and minor hemorrhages on funduscopic examination—collectively known as background diabetic retinopathy—are among the early changes. Although these changes are not typically associated with any decline in visual acuity, they are a marker for the future development of more significant abnormalities that can lead to visual loss. Preproliferative retinopathy is manifested by the presence of "cotton-wool spots," which are indicative of retinal infarcts. This ischemia provides a stimulus for the growth of new blood vessels (neovascularization) that are abnormal in both appearance and structure and are prone to hemorrhage (**Figure 3**). Blood vessel fragility in proliferative retinopathy predisposes affected patients to significant retinal and vitreous hemorrhage. Edema of the retina can also occur; when this edema affects the macula, loss of central vision results.

Studies have shown a beneficial effect on sight preservation with laser photocoagulation if either macular edema or proliferative retinopathy is present. In addition, control of blood glucose levels decreases the occurrence and progression of eye disease. Protein kinase C inhibitors (such as ruboxistaurin) have shown a modest benefit in stabilizing vision in subsets of patients with proliferative retinopathy. Blood pressure reduction appears to exert as great a beneficial effect on retinopathy as glycemic control does. The control of plasma lipids may also affect the progression of eye disease.

Diabetic Nephropathy

One of the most common causes of chronic kidney disease worldwide, diabetic nephropathy begins with a period of glomerular hyperfiltration and intraglomerular hypertension. Glomerular injury subsequently develops, with the eventual loss of filtration capacity and consequent renal insufficiency. This process is accelerated by coexisting systemic hypertension. Abnormal albumin excretion is an early sign of glomerular disease and may progress slowly from microalbuminuria (30-300 mg/24 h) to macroalbuminuria (>300 mg/24 h) to frank nephrotic syndrome (>3.5 g/24 h). Aggressive blood pressure control, particularly with angiotensin-converting enzyme (ACE) inhibitors or angiotensin-II receptor blockers (ARBs) slows this progression. Tight glycemic control is also known to prevent the development and slow the progression of chronic kidney disease in both type 1 and type 2 diabetes.

Early screening for diabetic kidney disease, with annual measurement of the serum creatinine level and the albumin-creatinine ratio in spot urine samples, is recommended. The use of either an ACE inhibitor or an ARB in patients with albuminuria but normal blood pressure is recommended to slow deterioration of renal function. Because these agents reduce the glomerular filtration rate, a small increase in the serum creatinine level is expected. However, the presence of advanced renal insufficiency and hyperkalemia limits their use. Serum electrolyte, blood urea nitrogen, and serum creatinine levels should be checked 1 to 2 weeks after initiation of therapy. Once chronic kidney disease develops, attention must be paid to any related anemia or hyperparathyroidism, and referral to a nephrologist should be considered.

Diabetic Neuropathy

Diabetic neuropathy involves injury to sensory, motor, and autonomic nerves. Loss of sensation in a "stocking-glove" distribution that is associated with paresthesia or painful dysesthesias is its most common presentation. Loss of sensation in the lower extremities also plays a major part in the development of foot ulcerations, which can lead to limb loss. Acute mononeuropathies are less common and can involve the cranial or peripheral nerves and sometimes even entire spinal nerve roots (radiculopathy). Radiculopathy may involve pain that mimics the pain associated with acute myocardial infarction, acute cholelithiasis, or nephrolithiasis. Autonomic neuropathy presents as erectile dysfunction in men and as orthostatic hypotension, gastroparesis, diabetic diarrhea, and

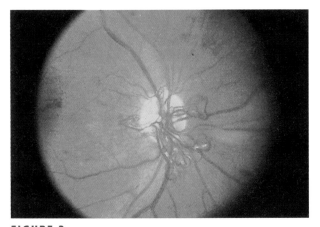

FIGURE 3.
Proliferative retinopathy.
Neovascularization and microaneurysms of the eye are evident.

atonic bladder in both sexes. The presence of cardiac auto-nomic dysfunction, which is established by the loss of the dynamic responses of the cardiac rate to physiologic stimuli (such as deep breathing, standing, the Valsalva maneuver), identifies a high-risk cohort of patients with an increased risk of coronary artery disease, silent ischemia, and cardiovascular morbidity. Therefore, patients with diabetes who are identified as having autonomic neuropathy may benefit from a comprehensive cardiac evaluation to exclude ischemic heart disease.

No direct treatment for diabetic neuropathy exists, other than improving glycemic control. Pharmacologic therapy may, however, help symptoms. Partial serotonin and norepinephrine reuptake inhibitors (duloxetine), tricyclic antidepressants (amitriptyline), and various antiseizure medications (gabapentin, phenytoin, carbamazepine) are frequently used to treat the pain associated with this condition; occasionally, opiate analgesics may be required. Autonomic failure is a considerable problem that is best dealt with on a patient-by-patient and symptom-by-symptom level.

The Diabetic Foot

Because patients with diabetes mellitus often have peripheral vascular disease and peripheral neuropathy, careful examination of the feet must be part of the diabetic assessment. These conditions, especially when they coexist, place the diabetic foot at extreme risk for ulceration, infection, and ultimate amputation. Clinical evaluation should include an assessment of the vascular status of the leg and an evaluation of foot sensation with a standard 10-g monofilament.

The early detection of foot sensory deficits involves the patient making a meticulous visual inspection of the feet. Daily self-care, including bathing, rehydration with emollient creams, and the use of comfortable, protective, and well-fitting shoes and plain cotton socks, is recommended. Patients should also avoid walking barefoot. When examining their feet, patients with diabetes should look for callus formation, new growths, and evidence of newly developing points of friction from new footwear or of irritation from improperly fitting shoes. Ongoing foot care by a qualified podiatrist is central to the multidisciplinary management of diabetes, particularly in patients with "high-risk feet," such as those with vascular insufficiency, sensory deficits, and bony deformities. The coexistence of two or more of these abnormalities mandates earlier and more frequent attention. Once ulceration or infection is established, treatment is extraordinarily difficult because of abnormal host defenses and vascular insufficiency. Therefore, preventive foot care is critical.

Treatment of a foot ulcer or infection must be aggressive. Ulcerations, which can involve gram-negative organisms, should be treated with broad-spectrum antibiotics, often for long periods of time. Adequate débridement of nonviable tissues necessitates referral to a surgical specialist, as does vascular insufficiency. Glycemic control remains key to optimizing healing and promoting immune mechanisms.

Cardiovascular Disease

Diabetes mellitus carries a two- to fourfold increased risk of major cardiovascular events, including myocardial infarction, stroke, and heart failure. The relative risk is enhanced in women. Diabetes is considered a coronary heart disease risk equivalent on the basis of data showing that patients with diabetes but no history of coronary artery disease have a similar risk of myocardial infarction as do patients without diabetes who have survived a previous infarction. The detrimental long-term vascular effects of hyperglycemia in patients with type 2 diabetes may be compounded by the presence of insulin resistance. These detrimental effects include not only hypertension and dyslipidemia, but also endothelial dysfunction, hypercoagulability, and vascular inflammation. With the exception of the metformin arm of the UKPDS, no study has conclusively shown a reduction in cardiovascular events after treatment of hyperglycemia.

In a long-term follow-up of the DCCT cohort, the original intensively treated group experienced 42% fewer cardiovascular events after a mean of 13 years posttreatment than patients initially treated conventionally; this difference was impressive because the two randomized groups experienced coalescence of their hemoglobin A_{1c} values (to ~8.0%) over most of the follow-up period. Although these findings suggest a long-lasting effect of periods of tight glycemic control, this observation has not been made consistently in all studies of type 2 diabetes. For example, whereas the addition of pioglitazone to the drug regimen of patients with type 2 diabetes and macrovascular disease in the Prospective Pioglitazone Clinical Trial in Macrovascular Events (PROactive) seemed to reduce secondary end points of death, myocardial infarction, and stroke, this benefit may have actually resulted from the improvement in the glucose level, blood pressure, and lipid levels of the active-therapy patients. More recently, the glucose-lowering substudy of the Action to Control Cardiovascular Risk in Diabetes (ACCORD) trial was prematurely terminated because of excess deaths in the intensive therapy group in whom the target hemoglobin A_{1c} value was less than 6%. Two other studies, the Action in Diabetes and Vascular Disease: Preterax and Diamicron MR Controlled Evaluation (ADVANCE) trial (hemoglobin A_{1c} target <6.5%) and the Veterans Affairs Diabetes Trial (VADT) (hemoglobin A_{1c} target <6.0%), found no cardiovascular benefit with more stringent glucose control but did not identify a significant risk. The reason for the increased mortality risk in the ACCORD trial is unknown but may relate to an increased risk of hypoglycemia or weight gain or simply to the complexity of care required to achieve such stringent targets in this older group of patients, many of whom had preexisting cardiovascular complications. At this time, the cardinal goal of tight glycemic control should be the prevention of microvascular disease; blood pressure control and lipid lowering appear to have much more profound effects on cardiovascular disease risk. Whether stricter glucose control might lead to a cardiovascular benefit in younger patients over a longer period of time than is realistically possible to study in the context of a clinical trial is not known.

Barring contraindications, all adult patients with diabetes mellitus who are older than 40 years are now advised to take daily aspirin (81-325 mg). Blood pressure control is also critical. In the UKPDS, more intensive blood pressure management (mean, 144/82 mm Hg) reduced rates of myocardial infarction by 21% and stroke by 44%. The ADA's current stricter treatment target (<130/80 mm Hg; see Table 6) is based on the results of randomized clinical trials in which control of diastolic blood pressure to less than 80 mm Hg significantly reduced cardiovascular events and mortality. Studies have also shown a reduction in cardiovascular events with a variety of antihypertensive drug classes, including ACE inhibitors, ARBs, β-blockers, calcium channel blockers, and diuretics. Most authorities recommend starting with an ACE inhibitor or ARB because of these agents' documented benefit on albuminuria. Currently, the ADA endorses the use of ACE inhibitors in patients with type 1 diabetes and proteinuria; for type 2 diabetes, an ACE inhibitor or ARB is recommended if microalbuminuria is present and an ARB if macroalbuminuria is present.

Lipid-lowering guidelines are equally aggressive (see Table 6) after several large clinical trials in patients with and without diabetes confirmed a reduction in the relative risk of cardiovascular events in patients receiving statin therapy. Several major studies have conclusively shown a benefit of lowering LDL-cholesterol levels below 100 mg/dL (2.59 mmol/L) in patients with diabetes, both with and without known coronary disease.

Lifestyle modifications with increased physical activity, weight loss, and a focus on reducing saturated fat, *trans* fat, and total cholesterol intake are recommended to improve lipid profiles. Statin therapy is recommended by the ADA for patients with diabetes who have overt cardiovascular disease, regardless of their baseline LDL-cholesterol level. This therapy is also recommended for those without known cardiovascular disease who are older than 40 years and have one or more additional risk factors. For lower-risk patients (those with no overt cardiovascular disease and age <40 years), statin therapy should be considered if the LDL-cholesterol level is greater than 100 mg/dL (2.59 mmol/L) or if multiple cardiovascular disease risk factors are present. The LDL-cholesterol goal in persons without overt cardiovascular disease is less than 100 mg/dL (2.59 mmol/L); in those with overt disease, a lower goal of less than 70 mg/dL (1.81 mmol/L) is an option. If statin-treated patients do not achieve these targets, then an LDL-cholesterol reduction of at least 40% from the baseline level should be considered as an alternative goal. Although a triglyceride level below 150 mg/dL (1.7 mmol/L) in both sexes and an HDL-cholesterol level greater than 40 mg/dL (1.04 mmol/L) in men and greater than 50 mg/dL (1.3 mmol/L) in women are also desirable, LDL-cholesterol–targeted therapy is the primary strategy. Combination therapy with other lipid-lowering agents can be considered to either reduce the LDL-cholesterol level (ezetimibe, binding resins, niacin) or address the triglyceride and/or HDL-cholesterol level (fibrates, niacin), but outcomes data are sparse.

Other Comorbidities in Diabetes Mellitus

Because chronic hyperglycemia alters immune function and impairs wound healing, patients with diabetes mellitus are at increased risk for various infections and other complications of surgical and nonsurgical wounds. Other evidence suggests that patients with diabetes also are predisposed to nonalcoholic steatosis and steatohepatitis, obstructive sleep apnea, venous thrombosis, bone fracture, dementia, depression, and several cancers, including colorectal carcinoma and endometrial carcinoma (in women).

KEY POINTS

- The mainstays of therapy for diabetic ketoacidosis are intravenous insulin and intravenous fluids.

- Microvascular complications in diabetes mellitus involve the kidneys (diabetic nephropathy), retinae (diabetic retinopathy), and peripheral nerves (diabetic neuropathy); macrovascular complications involve the coronary, carotid, and cerebral arteries (myocardial infarction); the aorta (stroke); and the arterial supply to the lower extremities (gangrene).

- Aggressive blood pressure control, particularly with angiotensin-converting enzyme inhibitors or angiotensin-II receptor blockers, slows the progression of diabetic nephropathy.

- Clinical evaluation of the diabetic foot includes assessment of the vascular status of the leg and an evaluation of foot sensation with a standard 10-g monofilament.

- Barring contraindications, all adult patients with diabetes mellitus who are older than 40 years are now advised to take daily aspirin.

Hypoglycemia in Patients Without Diabetes Mellitus

In persons without diabetes mellitus, hypoglycemia results from failure of the normal homeostatic mechanisms to maintain the balance between glucose production and use. As glucose levels fall below the physiologic range, counterregulatory factors (epinephrine, glucagon, cortisol, and growth hormone) are released. The clinical response to hypoglycemia has adrenergic and neuroglycopenic manifestations.

Hypoglycemic disorders can occur in either the postprandial or the fasting state. Because symptoms of hypoglycemia are nonspecific, the presence of an abnormally low blood glucose level must be documented. The diagnostic criteria for hypoglycemia are summarized in the Whipple triad: hypoglycemic symptoms, a simultaneous low blood glucose level, and the resolution of symptoms as hypoglycemia is corrected. Glucose measurement should involve whole blood or plasma samples collected in specialized tubes that inhibit glycolysis; home glucose meters may be inaccurate in the hypoglycemic range, so their results should be interpreted cautiously.

Reactive (Postprandial) Hypoglycemia

Postprandial alimentary hypoglycemia, which typically occurs after gastric surgery, is manifested by hypoglycemia occurring approximately 30 to 60 minutes after meals. It may be related to the loss of the stomach's normal reservoir, with glucose being rapidly absorbed and insulin released in excess. In contrast, reactive (idiopathic) hypoglycemia in patients with no history of gastric surgery is more controversial and is likely diagnosed too frequently. Although the term previously encompassed various postprandial somatic symptoms, true reactive hypoglycemia is a rare entity. Because many patients with this diagnosis have normal blood glucose levels during symptoms, the oral glucose tolerance test adds little to the diagnostic evaluation and is not recommended. The pathogenesis is likely a temporal mismatch between insulin levels and glucose supply after a large carbohydrate challenge. Reactive hypoglycemia is best treated by nutritional interventions, such as high-complex carbohydrate foods and smaller, more frequent meals.

Fasting Hypoglycemia

If evaluation confirms the presence of hypoglycemia during fasting periods, the differential diagnosis includes several clinical entities.

Exogenous Hypoglycemia

In patients without diabetes who develop hypoglycemia, inadvertent or surreptitious use of oral antihyperglycemic agents or insulin must be excluded. Exogenous insulin administration is best confirmed by measuring serum insulin and plasma glucose levels and simultaneously measuring the serum C-peptide level to confirm endogenous insulin production. In a patient whose hypoglycemia results from insulin injections, insulin levels will be elevated but the C-peptide level will be suppressed; if hypoglycemia results from the use of insulin secretagogues (such as sulfonylureas or glinides), both insulin and C-peptide levels will be inappropriately elevated. Measurement of blood or urine levels of the suspected pharmacologic agent is then required to confirm its inappropriate use.

Endogenous Hypoglycemia

Endogenous hypoglycemia is classified as that related to increased peripheral glucose utilization, usually resulting from excess insulin or insulin-like compounds, or that related to decreased glucose supply or production.

Hypoglycemia Due to Increased Glucose Utilization

An insulin-secreting islet cell tumor, or insulinoma, is the most serious diagnosis in a patient with fasting hypoglycemia. The biochemical diagnosis of insulinoma is made when the fasting plasma glucose level falls below 45 mg/dL (2.5 mmol/L) and there are accompanying hypoglycemic symptoms and inappropriate hyperinsulinemia (insulin level >5-6 μU/mL [36-43 pmol/L) after exogenous factors have been eliminated. Nesidioblastosis and islet cell hyperplasia are rare causes of hyperinsulinemic hypoglycemia in adults. Several genetic diseases have been implicated in these syndromes, including constitutive activation of the sulfonylurea receptor on pancreatic beta cells and abnormalities of the glucokinase gene. Recently, islet cell hyperplasia has also been reported in patients with hypoglycemia after gastric bypass surgery.

Evaluation of patients for insulinoma usually requires a prolonged fast (up to 72 hours) under strict medical observation. The fast is discontinued once the glucose level falls below 45 mg/dL (2.5 mmol/L), there are associated symptoms of hypoglycemia, and appropriate laboratory tests (measurement of plasma glucose, insulin, and C-peptide levels) are performed. Once the diagnosis of insulinoma is confirmed biochemically, imaging studies of the pancreas are required, beginning with a CT of the abdomen. Although these typically benign lesions are usually too small to be seen on CT scans, this modality is essential to exclude larger lesions or those already metastatic to the liver. If there are no significant findings, further evaluation may include MRI or endoscopic ultrasonography of the pancreas, hepatic venous sampling with arterial calcium stimulation, or pancreatic arteriography. Octreotide scans are usually not helpful in detecting these small, localized tumors. Once the lesion is identified, surgical resection should follow. When preoperative localization has been unsuccessful, operative exploration by an experienced pancreatic surgeon should proceed, with the lesion detected by palpation or on an intraoperative ultrasound. In patients who are not surgical candidates, medical therapy with diazoxide, octreotide, or corticosteroids (or some combination) can be attempted.

Other rare causes of hypoglycemia include tumors that secrete insulin-like growth factor 2 (which has insulin-like properties), other malignancies (typically, massive, rapidly growing tumors that lower glucose levels simply by gross consumption), and insulin antibody syndromes.

Hypoglycemia Due to Decreased Glucose Supply

Fasting hypoglycemia can also occur as a result of gluconeogenic substrate deficiency, as in severe starvation, even if insulin secretion is appropriately suppressed. Alcohol ingestion, which suppresses hepatic glucose production, can accentuate hypoglycemia. Various systemic illnesses, such as sepsis, profound hepatic dysfunction, and severe and prolonged nutritional deficiency, are also associated with hypoglycemia. Hypoglycemia may also be seen in certain endocrine disorders, such as Addison disease (because of the lack of cortisol) and hypopituitarism (because of the lack of adrenocorticotropic hormone [and, as a result, cortisol] and growth hormone).

Bibliography

American Diabetes Association. Standards of medical care in diabetes—2008. Diabetes Care. 2008;31 Suppl 1:S12-54. [PMID: 18165335]

Baggio LL, Drucker DJ. Biology of incretins: GLP-1 and GIP. Gastroenterology. 2007;132(6):2131-2157. [PMID: 17498508]

Bolen S, Feldman L, Vassy, J, et al. Systematic review: comparative effectiveness and safety of oral medications for type 2 diabetes [erratum in Ann Intern Med. 2007;147(12):887]. Ann Intern Med. 2007;147:386-399. [PMID: 17638715]

Buse JB, Ginsberg HN, Bakris GL, et al. Primary prevention of cardiovascular diseases in people with diabetes mellitus: a scientific statement from the American Heart Association and the American Diabetes Association. Circulation. 2007;115(1):114-126. [PMID: 17192512]

Costa J, Borges M, David C, Vaz Carneiro A. Efficacy of lipid lowering drug treatment for diabetic and non-diabetic patients: meta-analysis of randomised controlled trials. BMJ. 2006;332(7550): 1115-1124. [PMID: 16585050]

Diabetes Control and Complications Trial/Epidemiology of Diabetes Interventions and Complications Study Research Group; Jacobson AM, Musen G, Ryan CM, et al. Long-term effect of diabetes and its treatment on cognitive function. N Engl J Med. 2007;356(18):1842-1852. [PMID: 17476010]

Gaede P, Lund-Andersen H, Parving HH, Pedersen O. Effect of a multifactorial intervention on mortality in type 2 diabetes. N Engl J Med. 2008;358(6):580-591. [PMID: 18256393]

Grundy SM. Metabolic syndrome: a multiplex cardiovascular risk factor. J Clin Endocrinol Metab. 2007;92(2):399-404. [PMID: 17284640]

Inzucchi SE. Clinical Practice. Management of hyperglycemia in the hospital setting. N Engl J Med. 2006;355(18):1903-1911. [PMID: 17079764]

Inzucchi SE, McGuire DK. New drugs for the treatment of diabetes: part II: Incretin-based therapy and beyond. Circulation. 2008;117(4):574-584. [PMID: 18227398]

Kahn SE. The relative contributions of insulin resistance and beta-cell dysfunction to the pathophysiology of type 2 diabetes. Diabetologia. 2003;46(1):3-19. [PMID: 12637977]

Kitabchi AE, Umpierrez GE, Murphy MB, Kreisberg RA. Hyperglycemic crises in adult patients with diabetes: a consensus statement from the American Diabetes Association. Diabetes Care. 2006;29(12):2739-2748. [PMID: 17130218]

McGuire DK, Inzucchi SE. New drugs for the treatment of diabetes mellitus: part I: Thiazolidinediones and their evolving cardiovascular implications. Circulation. 2008;117(3):440-449. [PMID: 18212301]

Nathan DM, Cleary PA, Backlund JY, et al; Diabetes Control and Complications Trial/Epidemiology of Diabetes Interventions and Complications (DCCT/EDID) Study Research Group. Intensive diabetes treatment and cardiovascular disease in patients with type 1 diabetes. N Engl J Med. 2005;353(25):2643-2653. [PMID: 16371630]

Nathan DM, Davidson MB, DeFronzo RA, et al; American Diabetes Association. Impaired fasting glucose and impaired glucose tolerance: implications for care. Diabetes Care. 2007;30(3):753-759. [PMID: 17327355]

Disorders of the Pituitary Gland

Hypothalamic Disease

The pituitary stalk arises from the median eminence, a vascular region at the base of the hypothalamus. Hypothalamic hormones, including corticotropin-releasing hormone, gonadotropin-releasing hormone, thyrotropin-releasing hormone, and growth hormone (GH)–releasing hormone, travel to the median eminence via axonal pathways to be released into the portal plexus and then into the pituitary gland through the hypothalamic-pituitary portal vessels carried in the pituitary stalk. Disruption of these axons by certain pathologic conditions leads to substantial decreases in the secretion of pituitary hormones, with the exception of prolactin, whose secretion may actually increase because of the elimination of tonic inhibition by dopamine. Symptoms result from both the location of lesions and the rapidity of increase in lesion size.

Congenital hypothalamic structural lesions are often due to mutations in the genes for transcription factors expressed sequentially during embryogenesis and vital to the development of pituitary cells. For example, in 85% of patients with Kallmann syndrome, a disorder characterized by anosmia (lack of a sense of smell) and hypogonadotropic hypogonadism, a defect exists in the protein that facilitates the embryologic migration of both olfactory neurons and the neurons that produce gonadotropin-releasing hormone.

Acquired hypothalamic conditions include tumors, such as craniopharyngiomas and pituitary adenomas with suprasellar extension; infiltrative disease, such as sarcoidosis and Langerhans cell histiocytosis; and trauma due to head injury, neurosurgery, or cranial irradiation. When hypopituitarism is accompanied by diabetes insipidus or hyperprolactinemia, hypothalamic causes should be suspected.

KEY POINT

- Hypothalamic causes of pituitary dysfunction should be suspected when hypopituitarism is accompanied by diabetes insipidus or hyperprolactinemia.

Hypopituitarism

Causes and Treatment of Hypopituitarism

The congenital combined deficiencies of GH, prolactin, and thyroid-stimulating hormone (TSH) are a major cause of hypopituitarism and are themselves caused by mutations in the genes for transcription factors (**Table 9**). Gene mutations have also been found for releasing factor receptors, pituitary hormones, and pituitary target organ receptors. Neoplastic lesions, particularly pituitary adenomas, cause hypopituitarism by direct compression of the normal pituitary gland or by disruption of the pituitary stalk. Conventional and stereotactic

TABLE 9 Causes of Hypopituitarism
Genetic defects
Hypothalamic hormone gene defects
Hypothalamic hormone receptor gene defects
Pituitary hormone gene defects
Pituitary hormone receptor gene defects
Transcription factor gene defects (affecting multiple pituitary hormones)
Embryopathies
Anencephaly
Midline cleft defects
Pituitary aplasia
Kallmann syndrome (anosmin gene defect)
Acquired defects
Tumors (pituitary adenomas, craniopharyngiomas, dysgerminomas, meningiomas, gliomas, metastatic tumors, Rathke cleft cysts)
Irradiation
Trauma (neurosurgery, external blunt trauma)
Infiltrative disease (sarcoidosis, Langerhans cell histiocytosis, tuberculosis)
Empty sella syndrome
Vascular (apoplexy, Sheehan syndrome, subarachnoid hemorrhage)
Lymphocytic hypophysitis
Metabolic causes (hemochromatosis, critical illness, malnutrition, anorexia nervosa, psychosocial deprivation)
Idiopathic causes

gamma knife irradiation causes a progressive hypopituitarism through damage to the hypothalamus and the pituitary gland. Hypopituitarism also has been found to occur after traumatic brain injury and subarachnoid hemorrhage in 35% to 50% of patients studied.

Pituitary tumor apoplexy, which is due to hemorrhagic infarction and is characterized by the sudden onset of headache, stiff neck, fever, and (sometimes) ophthalmoplegia, can also cause hypopituitarism. Acute hormone replacement and surgical decompression are often necessary to treat this disorder. Sheehan syndrome, another cause of hypopituitarism, is due to silent pituitary infarction and is usually associated with obstetric hemorrhage and hypotension. Acutely, vascular collapse may occur, but this syndrome more commonly presents with amenorrhea, a postpartum inability to lactate, and fatigue due to central hypothyroidism or secondary adrenal insufficiency.

In lymphocytic hypophysitis, a destructive lymphocytic infiltration causes hypopituitarism and, possibly, symptoms of a mass lesion. Adrenocorticotropic hormone (ACTH) insufficiency and adrenal insufficiency are particularly common with this disorder and can be lethal if undetected. Most cases of lymphocytic hypophysitis occur during or after pregnancy. Resolution of hypopituitarism in patients with lymphocytic hypophysitis is uncommon.

Adjustment of the dosages of replacement hormones in treating hypopituitarism is based primarily on clinical findings (**Table 10**). GH and gonadotropins are generally lost before ACTH and TSH in most patients, but this finding is not consistent. Because ACTH/cortisol deficiency can be potentially life-threatening, the hypothalamic-pituitary axis should always be assessed in patients suspected of having hypopituitarism and should be assessed before other axes. An 8 AM measurement of a patient's serum cortisol level is helpful in diagnosing ACTH deficiency (see Disorders of the Adrenal Glands). Cortisol deficiency must always be addressed first in patients who have hypopituitarism because doing so can be life-saving. If thyroid hormone is replaced before cortisol, the

TABLE 10 Hormonal Replacement Therapy in Hypopituitarism	
Hormone	**Treatment**
TSH	Levothyroxine, 50-200 mg/d; adjust by measuring free T_4 levels.
ACTH	Hydrocortisone, 10-20 mg in AM and 5-10 mg in PM, *or* prednisone, 2.5-5.0 mg in AM and 2.5 mg in PM; adjust clinically. Stress dosage, hydrocortisone, 50-75 mg IV every 8 hours.
LH/FSH	
Men	Testosterone: 1% gel, 1-2 packets (5-10 g) daily; transdermal patch, 5 g daily; or testosterone enanthate or cypionate, 100-300 mg IM every 1-3 weeks. Adjust by measuring testosterone levels. May need injectable gonadotropins (LH, FSH) or GnRH (if a primary hypothalamic lesion) for spermatogenesis.
Women	Cyclic conjugated estrogens (0.3-0.625 mg) and medroxyprogesterone acetate (5-10 mg) *or* low-dose oral contraceptive pills. Estrogen patches also available. May need injectable gonadotropins (LH, FSH) for ovulation or in vitro fertilization techniques.
GH	Adults start at 200-300 µg subcutaneously daily and increment by 200 µg at monthly intervals. Adjust to maintain IGF-1 levels in the midnormal range. Women receiving oral estrogens require higher doses.
Vasopressin	Desmopressin: metered nasal spray, 10-20 µg once or twice daily; or tablets, 0.1-0.4 mg every 8-12 h; or injected, 1-2 µg SC or IV, every 6-12 h.

ACTH = adrenocorticotropic hormone; FSH = follicle-stimulating hormone; GH = growth hormone; GnRH = gonadotropin-releasing hormone; IGF-1 = insulin-like growth factor 1; IM = intramuscularly; IV = intravenously; LH = luteinizing hormone; SC = subcutaneously; T_4 = thyroxine; TSH = thyroid-stimulating hormone.

former would speed the body's metabolism so that the small amount of cortisol that could be made would be metabolized more rapidly, and the patient could potentially go into a hypoadrenal crisis. Despite conventional hormone replacement, there is a twofold excess mortality in patients with hypopituitarism.

KEY POINTS

- Hypopituitarism is commonly seen in patients after various brain injuries or insults, including traumatic brain injury, subarachnoid hemorrhage, neurosurgery, and cranial irradiation.

- Lymphocytic hypophysitis, which usually occurs during or after pregnancy, causes hypopituitarism, possible symptoms of a mass lesion, and often adrenocorticotropic hormone insufficiency.

Growth Hormone Deficiency

GH deficiency in adults can either be a continuation of a childhood condition or be newly acquired. Adults with this deficiency have decreased muscle mass, increased fat mass, and decreased bone mineral density, and many have decreased strength, endurance, and well-being. A GH stimulation test, such as insulin-induced hypoglycemia or use of a combination of arginine and GH-releasing hormone, is necessary for diagnosis. Testing may not be necessary if three or more other pituitary hormones are shown to be deficient and insulin-like growth factor 1 (IGF-1) levels are below normal. Only approximately one third of children with isolated idiopathic GH deficiency are found to be GH deficient when retested as adults; therefore, these patients should be retested before continuing GH as an adult. Given that GH-dependent bone remodeling continues into the mid-20s, stopping childhood GH replacement when final height has been achieved may be inappropriate.

GH treatment of adults with GH deficiency can increase lean body mass, decrease fat mass, and improve the sense of well-being without long-term adverse effects. The short-term adverse effects of edema, joint pain, and carpal tunnel syndrome can be avoided by using a low starting dose and gradually increasing it.

KEY POINTS

- Adults with growth hormone deficiency have decreased muscle mass, increased fat mass, and decreased bone mineral density; many also have decreased strength, endurance, and well-being.

- A growth hormone stimulation test is necessary to diagnose growth hormone deficiency.

Gonadotropin Deficiency

Clinical features of hypogonadotropic hypogonadism in women include amenorrhea, breast atrophy, vaginal dryness,

diminished libido, and loss of bone density. In men with the disorder, decreased libido, erectile dysfunction, anemia, and loss of bone density occur. Acquired hypogonadotropic hypogonadism in women commonly results from weight loss, anorexia nervosa, stress, heavy exercise, or severe illness, although it may also be idiopathic. Structural disease must be excluded by MRI or CT. Hyperprolactinemia can suppress gonadotropin-releasing hormone and lead to reduced gonadotropin levels.

Treatment of hypogonadism is addressed in Reproductive Disorders.

Adrenocorticotropic Hormone Deficiency

ACTH deficiency causes hypocortisolism, with symptoms of nausea, vomiting, weakness, fatigue, fever, and hypotension. Mineralocorticoids are not generally affected by this deficiency because they are controlled by the renin-angiotensin system, so hyperkalemia is not present. In women, reduced adrenal androgens can decrease libido and cause loss of axillary and pubic hair. However, patients with significant ACTH and cortisol deficiency may occasionally be asymptomatic.

The most common cause of ACTH deficiency is suppression of ACTH secretion with exogenous corticosteroids. If another cause is responsible, ACTH deficiency usually occurs in combination with the loss of other pituitary hormones. Acquired isolated ACTH deficiency can occur, however, particularly in women with lymphocytic hypophysitis. Finally, the use of megestrol acetate for appetite stimulation can occasionally suppress the secretion of ACTH and lead to its deficiency.

Details regarding diagnosis and therapy of primary and secondary adrenal insufficiency are provided in Disorders of the Adrenal Gland.

Thyroid-Stimulating Hormone Deficiency

Acquired central forms of hypothyroidism are usually associated with deficiencies of TSH and other pituitary hormones. A low free thyroxine (T_4) level without an elevated TSH level is consistent with central hypothyroidism. In some patients with hypothalamic disease, the TSH level is partially elevated in the presence of low levels of free T_4, but TSH bioactivity is reduced. It may be difficult to distinguish between central forms of hypothyroidism and the euthyroid sick syndrome in patients with severe illness. Generally, those with euthyroid sick syndrome have elevated levels of reverse triiodothyronine (T_3), but those with central forms of hypothyroidism do not.

Thyroid hormone dosing in patients with central hypothyroidism should be adjusted according to clinical symptoms and free T_4 levels because TSH levels cannot be used.

Pituitary Tumors

Pituitary tumors can be microadenomas (<10 mm) or macroadenomas (>10 mm). These tumors are very rarely malignant but can be locally invasive. Pathogenetic mutations have been found in only a subset (35%-40%) of somatotroph adenomas, which have an activating mutation of the gene for the $G_s\alpha$-subunit involved in transduction of the GH-releasing hormone signal.

Mass Effects of Pituitary Adenomas

The mass effects of an enlarging tumor may be the primary clinical manifestation of a pituitary adenoma. Headaches are common, and sudden worsening may indicate apoplexy. Macroadenomas abutting the optic chiasm can cause visual field defects, and those invading the cavernous sinus can cause cranial nerve palsies.

Hypopituitarism is reversible in up to 50% of patients with pituitary adenomas after surgical decompression. Slightly elevated serum prolactin levels (generally, less than 100 ng/mL [100 µg/L]) occur in patients with stalk compression. Diabetes insipidus is rarely caused by pituitary tumors and should instead raise suspicion of a craniopharyngioma.

Treatment of Pituitary Adenomas

Therapy goals for pituitary adenomas are to reduce tumor mass (and any attendant mass effects), prevent tumor recurrence, and correct any hormone oversecretion without causing damage to the normal pituitary gland. Except for prolactinomas, for which medical therapy is usually preferred, surgery is the primary mode of therapy for tumors that warrant intervention. The standard sublabial transsphenoidal approach is gradually being replaced by an endoscopic endonasal approach. In experienced hands, complications of transsphenoidal surgery occur in less than 5% of patients and include transient diabetes insipidus, cerebrospinal fluid leak, hemorrhage, optic nerve injury, and hypopituitarism. Craniotomy, which is reserved for very large tumors, is associated with greater morbidity and mortality.

Irradiation is generally used as adjunctive therapy after surgery or in combination with medical therapy. Radiation has generally been administered over 5 weeks, but recently, gamma knife or stereotactic radiotherapy administered over a single day from multiple ports has come into use. Primary radiation therapy is reserved for patients who cannot undergo surgery. Adjunctive radiotherapy is performed for any residual tumor and/or continued hormone hypersecretion. The most common complications include hypopituitarism, second tumors, and stroke; rarer complications are optic nerve damage, brain necrosis, and cognitive dysfunction.

Prolactinomas and Hyperprolactinemia

Causes

Prolactinomas are the most common type of pituitary adenoma (25%-40%), but not all patients with hyperprolactinemia have prolactinomas (**Table 11**). The serum prolactin level in patients with hyperprolactinemia caused by drugs and other nonprolactinoma causes is usually less than 150 ng/mL (150 µg/L).

TABLE 11 Causes of Hyperprolactinemia	
Pituitary disease	Prolactinomas
	Growth hormone–secreting tumors (cosecretion or pituitary stalk effects)
	Nonfunctioning pituitary tumors (pituitary stalk effects)
	Lymphocytic hypophysitis (pituitary stalk effects)
	Empty sella syndrome (pituitary stalk effects)
	Cushing disease (cosecretion or pituitary stalk effects)
Nonpituitary sellar and parasellar lesions	Craniopharyngioma
	Hypothalamic disease (sarcoidosis, Langerhans cell histiocytosis, lymphoma)
	Metastatic tumors to pituitary/hypothalamus
	Meningiomas
	Dysgerminomas
	Irradiation
Neurogenic	Chest wall or spinal cord disease
	Breast stimulation/lesions
Drugs	Psychotropic agents (butyrophenones and phenothiazines, MAO inhibitors, tricyclic antidepressants, fluoxetine, molindone, risperidone, cocaine)
	Antihypertensive agents (verapamil, α-methyldopa, reserpine)
	Metoclopramide
	(Estrogen in conventionally used doses does not cause hyperprolactinemia.)
Other	Pregnancy
	Hypothyroidism
	Chronic renal failure
	Cirrhosis
	Macroprolactinemia
	Idiopathic
	Adrenal insufficiency
	Ectopic secretion

MAO = monoamine oxidase.

Many medications block dopamine release or action, the most common being antipsychotic medications, verapamil, and metoclopramide. Various suprasellar lesions cause hyperprolactinemia because of compression of the hypothalamus or pituitary stalk, which causes decreased amounts of dopamine to reach the lactotrophs. Because high estrogen levels in pregnancy cause lactotroph hyperplasia and hyperprolactinemia, pregnancy must always be excluded when hyperprolactinemia is found in a woman of childbearing potential. Hypothyroidism and renal failure (serum creatinine level >2 mg/dL [176.8 µmol/L]) can also cause hyperprolactinemia. Unless there is very good evidence for these conditions or drug-induced hyperprolactinemia, even patients with mild hyperprolactinemia should be evaluated with CT or MRI to distinguish between idiopathic hyperprolactinemia, microprolactinomas, and large mass lesions.

A special caution is needed when some prolactin assays are used because patients with large prolactinomas (and very high prolactin levels) can appear to have prolactin levels that are normal or only modestly elevated, thus mimicking a large, nonfunctioning adenoma. This "hook effect" is due to saturation of the assay antibodies. Therefore, prolactin levels should always be remeasured at a 1:100 dilution in patients with macroadenomas and normal to modestly elevated prolactin levels.

When no pituitary lesions are present on radiographic studies and other known causes of hyperprolactinemia have been excluded, the diagnosis of idiopathic hyperprolactinemia is made. Over time, only 10% to 15% of patients with this condition develop microadenomas, and very few develop macroadenomas. Hyperprolactinemia resolves in one third of patients with idiopathic hyperprolactinemia without specific intervention.

Macroprolactinemia

Macroprolactins are high-molecular-weight prolactin variants that are either aggregates with immunoglobulins or dimers. These variants have diminished biologic potency. Evidence of macroprolactinemia can be detected in the serum by precipitating the aggregate or dimer with polyethylene glycol. If more than 50% of the prolactin can be precipitated in this fashion, the patient is said to have macroprolactinemia. Macroprolactinemia has usually been found in patients with equivocal symptoms and not those typically due to hyperprolactinemia.

Clinical Features and Therapy of Hyperprolactinemia

Hyperprolactinemia can cause galactorrhea, oligomenorrhea, and amenorrhea in premenopausal women; erectile dysfunction in men; and decreased libido, infertility, and osteopenia in both sexes. Large tumors also may cause mass effects, which are often the presenting feature in men and postmenopausal women.

For most symptomatic patients with hyperprolactinemia, a dopamine agonist is the therapy of choice (**Table 12**). However, in some women with idiopathic hyperprolactinemia or microadenomas who do not desire fertility but are estrogen deficient, simple replacement of estrogen with oral contraceptives may be preferable. Dopamine agonists normalize prolactin levels, correct amenorrhea and galactorrhea, and decrease tumor size by more than 50% in 80% to 90% of patients (**Figure 4**). Cabergoline is generally more efficacious and better tolerated, although more expensive, than bromocriptine. Thus, it is reasonable to use a dopamine agonist as first-line therapy, even in patients with visual field defects, as long as visual acuity is not threatened by rapid progression or recent tumor hemorrhage. Approximately 25% to 75% of patients whose prolactin levels normalize and tumors shrink to the point of nonvisualization can be tapered off dopamine agonists without tumor reexpansion. It is critical to ensure adherence to medical therapy, although, in some patients, prolactinomas appear to be resistant to dopamine agonists. It is equally necessary to be certain that the underlying lesion is a prolactinoma and that there is no other cause of the hyperprolactinemia. Although some patients respond to larger dosages of cabergoline, caution is needed because recent reports in patients taking cabergoline for Parkinson disease have shown that doses greater than 3 mg/d may be associated with cardiac

TABLE 12 Medical Therapies for Pituitary Adenomas	
Type of Pituitary Adenoma	**Medication**
Prolactinoma	Cabergoline
	Bromocriptine
Adenomas causing acromegaly	Somatostatin analogue (octreotide, lanreotide)
	Cabergoline
	Pegvisomant
Adenomas causing Cushing disease	Ketoconazole
	Metyrapone
	Cabergoline
	Mifepristone
	Mitotane
	Etomidate
TSH-secreting adenomas	Somatostatin analogues (octreotide, lanreotide)
Nonfunctioning adenomas	Cabergoline
	Somatostatin analogues (octreotide, lanreotide)

TSH = thyroid-stimulating hormone.

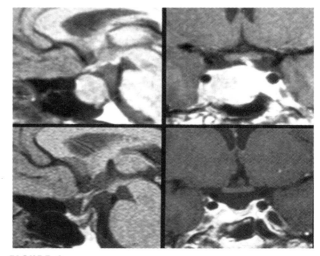

FIGURE 4.
Sagittal and coronal MRIs showing a prolactin-secreting macroadenoma.
Sagittal (*left*) and coronal (*right*) MRIs of a patient with a prolactin-secreting macroadenoma before (*top*) and during (*bottom*) bromocriptine treatment. Note the marked decrease in tumor size after treatment began.

Reprinted from Molitch ME. Prolactinoma. In: Melmed S, ed. The Pituitary. 2nd ed. Malden, MA: Blackwell Publishing; 2002:457.

valvular abnormalities. Echocardiographic monitoring may be useful; however, the dose threshold for doing so remains to be established. Alternatively, transsphenoidal surgery can be performed; studies have shown initial remission rates of 70% to 80% for microprolactinomas and 25% to 40% for macroadenomas, with long-term recurrence rates of 20%. Radiation therapy, usually gamma knife irradiation, is reserved for those patients with macroadenomas who do not respond to either medical or surgical treatment.

KEY POINTS

- In addition to prolactinomas, possible causes of hyperprolactinemia include medications, suprasellar lesions, hypothyroidism, renal failure, hypothalamic disease, and pregnancy.

- Hyperprolactinemia also may be due to decreased clearance of prolactin because of chronic renal failure and the presence of macroprolactin.

- Dopamine agonists, in particular cabergoline, are the primary treatment for patients with prolactinomas.

Acromegaly and Growth Hormone Excess

Etiology, Clinical Features, and Evaluation

Acromegaly is most often caused by a GH-secreting adenoma. If GH excess occurs before epiphyseal closure, a condition known as pituitary gigantism results; when it occurs in adulthood after epiphyseal closure, acromegaly ensues. Clinical features of acromegaly include prognathism; enlargement of the nose, lips, and tongue; frontal bossing; malocclusion; increased spacing between the teeth; sleep apnea; enlargement of the hands and feet; arthritis of the hips and knees; carpal tunnel syndrome; oily skin; and skin tags.

Prolactin is coproduced with GH in approximately 40% of patients with acromegaly. Some of these patients also may have amenorrhea and/or galactorrhea. Ectopic production of GH-releasing hormone is a rare (<1%) cause of acromegaly.

There is a two- to threefold increase in mortality rate associated with GH excess because of its association with cardiovascular and cerebrovascular diseases. Cardiac hypertrophy is common, and hypertension and diabetes mellitus occur in many patients with GH excess. Because of an increased risk of premalignant polyps and colon cancer, screening with colonoscopy is recommended for all persons with GH excess.

Random GH level measurements are not useful because of pulsatile secretion, and demonstration of nonsuppression during a glucose tolerance test is needed for making the diagnosis. IGF-1 levels provide an integrated index of GH production, correlate well with clinical activity, and serve as a better screening test for acromegaly. An MRI evaluates the extent of tumor growth; approximately 60% of patients have macroadenomas.

Treatment

Correction of GH oversecretion prevents further physical disfigurement, reverses the increased mortality rate, and can lead to substantial improvement of soft-tissue changes and metabolic derangements. Transsphenoidal surgery results in plasma GH levels below 1 ng/mL (1 µg/L) and normal IGF-1 levels in approximately 80% to 90% of patients with microadenomas and 30% to 40% of patients with macroadenomas when performed by experienced neurosurgeons.

Medical therapies are used in patients who are not cured by surgery or in whom surgery is very unlikely to result in a cure. Although cabergoline is successful in only approximately 10% to 20% of patients with GH excess, an initial trial may be warranted because it can be given orally and is relatively inexpensive compared with somatostatin analogues. Long-acting preparations of the somatostatin analogues octreotide and lanreotide can be given by injection every 4 weeks and reduce GH and IGF-1 levels to normal in approximately 60% of patients. Tumor size is reduced modestly in most instances. Adverse effects of somatostatin analogues include diarrhea and an increased risk of cholelithiasis; cholecystitis and the need for cholecystectomy occur rarely. Some patients experience additive beneficial effects from adding cabergoline to somatostatin analogues.

Pegvisomant is a biosynthetic GH analogue that prevents binding of GH to its receptor. It has been shown to normalize IGF-1 levels in more than 90% of patients with GH excess, with corresponding clinical benefits, but has no effects on tumors. Pegvisomant is given by daily injection; long-term experience with its use is limited.

Adjunctive radiation therapy may be required when elevated GH levels or mass effects persist after surgery and medical therapy.

KEY POINTS

- Acromegaly carries a two- to threefold increased risk of mortality when levels of growth hormone and insulin-like growth factor 1 are not normalized.

- Long-acting preparations of the somatostatin analogues octreotide and lanreotide have been shown to reduce growth hormone and insulin-like growth factor 1 levels to normal in approximately 60% of patients with acromegaly but result in only modest reductions in tumor size.

Cushing Disease

Cushing disease denotes Cushing syndrome caused by excess production of ACTH by a pituitary adenoma. Cushing syndrome is discussed in Disorders of the Adrenal Glands.

Gonadotropin-Producing and Clinically Nonfunctioning Adenomas

Gonadotropin-producing and clinically nonfunctioning adenomas generally manifest with symptoms and signs related to local mass effects, such as headache, visual field loss, and hypopituitarism. Although most clinically nonfunctioning adenomas produce low levels of intact gonadotropins or their uncombined α- or β-subunits, these hormones usually cause no symptoms. Treatment primarily aims to reduce the size of the tumor. Complete or partial reversal of visual field defects and hypopituitarism can be accomplished by surgery, unless these conditions are of long duration. An MRI performed 3 to 4 months postoperatively serves as a baseline for follow-up, which should include yearly MRI monitoring for tumor recurrence or growth. When follow-up studies show tumor growth, repeat surgery or radiation therapy (or both) is indicated. Cabergoline reduced the rate of regrowth of tumor remnants in one study and can be considered in patients with a visible tumor on postoperative MRI. Octreotide also has been used in some patients with clinically nonfunctioning adenomas with varying success.

Incidentalomas

Many nonfunctioning adenomas are discovered as incidental findings on CT scans or MRIs performed for other reasons (hence the term "incidentaloma"). Patients with such findings should be screened for hormone overproduction by measurement of prolactin and IGF-1 levels and, possibly, by an overnight dexamethasone suppression test or midnight salivary cortisol measurement to exclude Cushing syndrome (see Disorders of the Adrenal Glands). If a macroadenoma is present, patients should also be screened for hypopituitarism; if the tumor abuts the optic chiasm, visual field testing also should be performed. Treatment is indicated for hormone over- or underproduction and for visual field defects. Careful follow-up of asymptomatic patients with incidentalomas shows that 10% of microadenomas enlarge, 6% get smaller, and 84% remain unchanged; in contrast, 24% of macroadenomas enlarge, 13% get smaller, and 63% remain unchanged. Therefore, periodic monitoring with MRI is warranted to detect an enlarging tumor that may require surgery.

> **KEY POINT**
> - Incidentally found macroadenomas carry a 24% risk of enlargement over time and must be followed periodically.

Thyroid-Stimulating Hormone–Secreting Tumors

TSH-secreting tumors are rare. The diagnosis is usually made when the serum TSH level is found not to be suppressed during the evaluation of a patient with hyperthyroidism. Surgery and adjunctive irradiation are often needed because of the large size of most of these tumors. Somatostatin analogues control TSH levels and hyperthyroidism in approximately 80% of treated patients, but consistent effects on tumor growth have not been demonstrated. The hyperthyroidism in patients with such tumors can also be treated with antithyroid drugs or radioiodine.

> **KEY POINT**
> - Somatostatin analogues are effective as adjunctive treatment of patients with thyroid-stimulating hormone–secreting adenomas.

Posterior Pituitary Deficiency and Excess

Diabetes Insipidus

Diabetes insipidus can result from a deficiency of arginine vasopressin (AVP) secretion (central diabetes insipidus) or from a defect in the ability of AVP to act on the kidney (nephrogenic diabetes insipidus). With both disorders, the patient excretes dilute urine excessively; the resultant serum hyperosmolality stimulates thirst receptors, causing polydipsia.

Rare congenital defects in the gene for AVP and embryopathic disorders leading to diabetes insipidus have been identified in children with this disorder. Most adults develop central diabetes insipidus as a result of hypothalamic mass lesions, traumatic brain injury, or infiltrative diseases, such as Langerhans cell histiocytosis and sarcoidosis.

Patients with partial diabetes insipidus may be asymptomatic and only manifest the disease if they are deprived of water (as with a comatose patient) or become pregnant and experience an increased degradation of circulating AVP levels by placental vasopressinase.

Testing for diabetes insipidus involves a water deprivation test, as long as the baseline serum osmolality is not substantially elevated. Patient weight and urine and serum osmolalities are obtained every 2 hours until the urine and serum osmolalities have stabilized (serum osmolality >295 mosm/kg) and the patient has lost no more than 3% of body weight. The patient is then given 5 μg of desmopressin intranasally; urine osmolality continues to be measured hourly for the next 2 to 3 hours. During water deprivation and before desmopressin administration, healthy persons will increase their urine osmolality to greater than 800 mosm/kg, but those with diabetes insipidus will not increase theirs above 300 mosm/kg. In response to desmopressin, patients with central diabetes insipidus will increase their urine osmolality by at least 50%, but those with nephrogenic diabetes insipidus will not respond appreciably to desmopressin administration. Patients with partial diabetes insipidus will increase their urine osmolality to 300 to 500 mosm/kg with dehydration and by at least another 9% with desmopressin.

Treatment of central diabetes insipidus includes desmopressin administered either orally via a metered nasal spray or subcutaneously by injection. In the unconscious patient or one whose thirst mechanisms are not operative, extreme care must be exerted to avoid under- and overtreatment; accurate daily body weights, fixed dosages of fluid intake, and frequent monitoring of the serum sodium are necessary.

Pregnancy and Pituitary Diseases

Prolactinomas and Pregnancy

For women with prolactinomas, dopamine agonists are stopped once pregnancy is achieved. There are no documented risks of fetal malformations or other adverse pregnancy outcomes for these agents; the collection of available data on the safety of bromocriptine is approximately 10-fold larger than that for cabergoline. Dopamine agonists are reinstituted when breast feeding is completed. Symptomatic growth occurs in approximately 30% of macroprolactinomas and 3% of microprolactinomas in the second or third trimester, which necessitates reinstitution of the dopamine agonist, transsphenoidal surgical decompression, or delivery if the pregnancy is sufficiently advanced.

Acromegaly in Pregnancy

The diagnosis of acromegaly during pregnancy can be difficult because the placental variant of GH increases substantially in the second half of pregnancy as measured in the standard GH assays. It may be necessary to wait until the postpartum period to confirm the diagnosis. As with prolactinomas, dopamine agonists (if taken) are stopped when the pregnancy is diagnosed. Somatostatin analogues also are generally stopped when pregnancy is planned or diagnosed. Although no adverse outcomes have occurred in the 14 reported cases in which somatostatin analogues have been used by pregnant women, the facts that these drugs cross the placenta and that there are somatostatin receptors in many fetal tissues make use of such drugs during pregnancy problematic. Hypertension and gestational diabetes mellitus in pregnant women with acromegaly can generally be managed conventionally.

Cushing Disease in Pregnancy

Active Cushing syndrome, including Cushing disease, is associated with a substantially increased risk of prematurity and stillbirth. The diagnosis of Cushing syndrome during pregnancy may be difficult because signs and symptoms overlap with those of normal pregnancy; 24-hour urine free cortisol and serum cortisol levels increase in normal pregnancy, and there is impaired suppression of cortisol levels by dexamethasone. Outcome analyses suggest that pregnant patients with newly diagnosed Cushing syndrome of all causes should undergo surgery, unless they are near term.

Clinically Nonfunctioning Adenomas and Thyroid-Stimulating Hormone–Secreting Adenomas in Pregnancy

There are few reports of women with either clinically nonfunctioning adenomas or thyroid-stimulating hormone–secreting adenomas becoming pregnant. Hyperthyroidism needs to be controlled, but pituitary surgery for these tumors can usually be deferred until after delivery.

Hypopituitarism During Pregnancy

Only thyroid and adrenal hormone replacement need be performed during pregnancy in patients with hypopituitarism. Extrapolating from data of patients with primary hypothyroidism, physicians usually increase the levothyroxine dosage by 0.025 mg daily at the end of the first trimester and by another 0.025 mg daily at the end of the second trimester. Corticosteroid replacement does not have to be increased, except in women under stress or undergoing labor.

Bibliography

Casanueva FF, Molitch ME, Schlechte JA, et al. Guidelines of the Pituitary Society for the diagnosis and management of prolactinomas. Clin Endocrinol (Oxf). 2006;65(2):265-273. [PMID: 16886971]

Gillam MP, Molitch MP, Lombardi G, Colao A. Advances in the treatment of prolactinomas. Endocrine Rev. 2006;27(5):485-534. [PMID: 16705142]

Laws ER, Jane JA Jr. Neurosurgical approach to treating pituitary adenomas. Growth Horm IGF Res. 2005;15 Suppl A:S36-S41. [PMID: 16039890]

Loh JA, Verbalis JG. Disorders of water and salt metabolism associated with pituitary disease. Endocrinol Metab Clin North Am. 2008;37(1):213-234. [PMID: 18226738]

Melmed S. Medical progress: Acromegaly [erratum in N Engl J Med 2007;356(8):879]. N Engl J Med. 2006;355(24):2558-2573. [PMID: 17167139]

Molitch ME. Nonfunctioning pituitary tumors and pituitary incidentalomas. Endocrinol Metab Clin North Am. 2008;37(1):151-171. [PMID: 18226735]

Molitch ME, Clemmons DR, Malozowski S, et al. Evaluation and treatment of adult growth hormone deficiency: an Endocrine Society Clinical Practice Guideline. J Clin Endocrinol Metab. 2006;91(5):1621-1634. [PMID: 16636129]

Schneider HJ, Kreitschmann-Andermahr I, Ghigo E, Stalla GK, Agha A. Hypothalamopituitary dysfunction following traumatic brain injury and aneurysmal subarachnoid hemorrhage: a systematic review. JAMA. 2007;298(12):1429-1438. [PMID: 17895459]

Sheehan JP, Niranjan A, Sheehan JM et al. Stereotactic radiosurgery for pituitary adenomas: an intermediate review of its safety, efficacy, and role in the neurosurgical treatment armamentarium. J Neurosurg. 2005;102(4):678-691. [PMID: 15871511]

Toogood AA, Stewart PM. Hypopituitarism: clinical features, diagnosis, and management. Endocrinol Metab Clin North Am. 2008;37(1):235-261. [PMID: 18226739]

Disorders of the Thyroid Gland

Thyroid Physiology

Thyroid hormone production is under the control of the hypothalamic-pituitary axis by means of thyrotropin-releasing hormone (TRH) and thyroid-stimulating hormone (TSH) secretion through a negative feedback loop involving thyroxine (T_4) and triiodothyronine (T_3). The thyroid gland primarily produces T_4 (80-100 µg/d) and only a small amount of T_3 (4-8 µg/d). Most T_3 (8-22 µg/d) comes from peripheral conversion by 5'-deiodinase enzymes. Hypothalamic-pituitary axis disorders lead to central causes of thyroid dysfunction (such as secondary hypothyroidism) or, more rarely, thyrotoxicosis from excess TSH secretion. Most patients with thyroid dysfunction have an intact hypothalamic-pituitary axis with either low TSH levels reflective of thyrotoxicosis or elevated TSH levels indicative of hypothyroidism.

The free forms of T_4 and T_3 are biologically active, whereas moieties bound to thyroxine-binding globulin (TBG), albumin, or prealbumin remain biologically unavailable until released into the free form. Conditions affecting protein binding of thyroid hormone can significantly affect measured total thyroid hormone levels, which makes interpretation of testing more challenging.

Because iodide is an essential component of thyroid hormone, adequate dietary iodine intake is essential for adequate thyroid hormone production. Although iodine deficiency is a worldwide health problem, data from the National Health and Nutrition Examination Survey (NHANES) study indicate generally adequate iodine intake in the United States except for pregnant and lactating women, who require approximately 50% or 100%, respectively, more daily iodine than the general population.

The potential effects on thyroid function by environmental exposure to endocrine disrupters has recently become concerning. For example, perchlorate, a rocket fuel waste product, has been found in small amounts in some U.S. drinking water sources. In high enough doses, it can negatively affect thyroid function by competitively inhibiting iodide transport. Although current perchlorate levels in drinking water have not breached recommended safety thresholds, the clinical impact of low-level environmental exposure is not yet fully known.

KEY POINTS

- The thyroid gland primarily secretes thyroxine with peripheral conversion to bioactive triiodothyronine as required.
- Adequate iodine intake is imperative for thyroid hormone production; pregnant and lactating women require 50% or 100%, respectively, more iodine intake than the general population.

Evaluation of Thyroid Function

Various tests can evaluate thyroid function (**Table 13**). Serum TSH levels are generally the most sensitive indicator of thyroid dysfunction, but in patients with possible thyroid-related symptoms, a free T_4 level should be obtained concurrently to assess the degree of hyper- or hypothyroidism and to detect secondary hypothyroidism in patients with hypothyroidism and TSH levels that are low or inappropriately normal.

The functional sensitivity of the TSH assay has improved over time. Third-generation TSH assays are generally reliable and can measure TSH levels as low as 0.01 µU/mL (0.01 mU/L). Total and free T_4 levels can both be measured, with the former comprising both bound and free T_4. Because total T_4 levels are greatly affected by any variation in binding proteins, they may not accurately reflect free T_4 levels. Free T_4 represents the prohormone available for conversion to active T_3, and its precise measurement is imperative for the accurate assessment of thyroid status. Many laboratories measure free T_4 levels by means of analogue assays, but various medications, antibodies, and (counterintuitively) fluctuations in binding protein levels can interfere with these assays, thereby yielding artificially low or high results. Free T_4 measurement by equilibrium dialysis remains the gold standard. Although more expensive, this assay is also more accurate and has fewer problems with interference overall. If antibodies against T_4 are suspected, as in patients with a pattern of erratic results on thyroid function testing that are inconsistent with the clinical picture, confirmation is possible by a T_4 antibody assay.

Measurement of the T_3 level can provide essential information in some patients with thyrotoxicosis, in which T_3 production predominates over T_4 production (T_3 toxicosis). However, the routine measurement of T_3 levels is rarely indicated in patients with hypothyroidism because the levels are conserved and generally remain within the reference range, even in the presence of significant hypothyroidism.

The thyroid antibodies anti–thyroid peroxidase antibody and anti–thyroglobulin antibody can be measured in serum. Their presence indicates underlying autoimmune thyroid disease. Increased titers of thyroid antibodies, especially anti–thyroid peroxidase antibody, confer an increased risk of hypothyroidism (~4% per year), which escalates as TSH levels rise above the reference range. However, some patients with positive thyroid antibodies may remain euthyroid for many years.

TSH receptor antibodies can be measured as serum thyroid-stimulating immunoglobulins (TSIs) and thyrotropin-binding inhibitory immunoglobulins (TBIIs). Although pathognomonic for Graves disease, the TSI and TBII assays are expensive and generally not required for diagnosis of routine Graves disease. These assays can be helpful in evaluating

TABLE 13 Common Tests of Thyroid Function

Measurement	Normal Range	Indication	Comment
Serum TSH	0.5-5.0 µU/mL (0.5-5.0 mU/L)	Suspected thyroid dysfunction	Misleading results in central hypothyroidism because of inappropriately low or normal TSH level
Serum free T_4	0.9-2.4 ng/dL (11.61-31 pmol/L)	Suspected thyroid dysfunction	Variable normal ranges depending on assay
Serum free T_3	3.6-5.6 ng/L (5.6-8.6 pmol/L)	T_3 thyrotoxicosis	May substitute with total T_3 (In contrast to free thyroid hormone assays, total T_4 or T_3 measurement is affected by the serum binding protein level.)
Serum thyroglobulin	3-40 ng/mL (3-40 µg/L)	Suspected subacute thyroiditis	Variable levels with nodular thyroid disease
Serum TSI	0-125%	Graves disease in pregnancy; euthyroid ophthalmopathy	Very expensive test, not generally needed to diagnose Graves disease
Serum TBII	<10%	Same as TSI; also useful in assessing fluctuating thyroid function in Graves disease	Detection of both blocking and stimulating antibodies against the TSH receptor; not generally needed to diagnose Graves disease
Anti–thyroid peroxidase antibodies	<2 U/mL	Suspected Hashimoto thyroiditis	Predictive value for development of overt hypothyroidism
Radioactive iodine uptake	10%-30% of dose at 24 hours	Suspected thyrotoxicosis	Contraindicated in pregnancy and breastfeeding

T_3 = triiodothyronine; T_4 = thyroxine; TBII = thyrotropin-binding inhibitory immunoglobulin; TSH = thyroid-stimulating hormone; TSI = thyroid-stimulating immunoglobulin.

patients with euthyroid Graves ophthalmopathy, pregnancy complicated by Graves disease, and unusual cases of hypothyroidism alternating with hyperthyroidism because of changes in stimulating and blocking TSH receptor antibodies. In such patients, titers of TSI and TBII may help predict clinical disease course or confirm the presence of antibodies with conflicting impacts on thyroid function.

Thyroglobulin, a glycoprotein integral in follicular storage of thyroid hormone, can be detected in serum. Thyroglobulin levels can be elevated in both hyperthyroidism and destructive thyroiditis. Intake of exogenous thyroid hormone generally suppresses thyroglobulin levels, which makes its measurement useful in patients with thyrotoxicosis due to surreptitious use of thyroid hormone. Thyroglobulin is also an effective tumor marker in patients with papillary or follicular thyroid cancer after thyroidectomy and radioactive iodine ablation therapy because normal thyroid release of thyroglobulin should no longer be present. The presence of thyroglobulin antibodies interferes with accurate measurement of thyroglobulin, so such antibodies should be checked simultaneously when using thyroglobulin as a tumor marker.

The primary clinical use of calcitonin measurement is as a tumor marker for medullary thyroid cancer, and some have advocated measuring the calcitonin level to screen patients with thyroid nodules for such cancer. Given the relative infrequency of medullary thyroid cancer, however, the efficacy of generalized screening of all thyroid nodules is uncertain. Calcitonin measurement is recommended in higher-risk scenarios, such as in patients with a positive family history of known medullary thyroid cancer (or a thyroid cancer of unknown type) that has features of multiple endocrine neoplasia type 2 (such as concurrent pheochromocytoma or hyperparathyroidism) or with thyroid biopsy results suggestive of medullary thyroid cancer.

The radioactive iodine uptake (RAIU) test measures thyroid gland iodine uptake over a timed period, usually 24 hours. Patients with thyrotoxicosis typically have an above-normal or high-normal RAIU, which is inappropriate in the context of a suppressed TSH level. In patients with thyroiditis or exposure to exogenous thyroid hormone, the RAIU will be below normal (<5% at 24 hours). A thyroid scan shows where in the thyroid gland the uptake is occurring (diffusely in Graves disease or focally within autonomous nodules). Radionuclide studies should not be performed during pregnancy or in women who are breast feeding.

Functional Thyroid Gland Disorders

Thyrotoxicosis

The term thyrotoxicosis encompasses all forms of thyroid hormone excess, whether primary or secondary, endogenous or exogenous, related to excess hormone production by the thyroid gland, or a result of damage-related thyroid hormone release (**Figure 5**). Hyperthyroidism specifically refers to thyroid gland overactivity, which most commonly occurs in Graves disease, toxic multinodular goiter, and toxic adenoma. The wide array of thyrotoxic symptoms reflects the effects of thyroid hormone on various body systems. The severity of symptoms is variable between patients and does not always correlate with the extent of thyroid hormone elevation. For example, elderly patients with apathetic hyperthyroidism may have minimal hyperadrenergic symptoms and instead have atrial fibrillation and/or heart failure at presentation. Symptoms of thyrotoxicosis include fatigue, anxiety, insomnia, weight loss (despite increased appetite), tremulousness, heat intolerance, irregular menses, hyperdefecation, palpitations, shortness of breath or dyspnea on exertion, and muscle weakness. Patients with Graves ophthalmopathy may note proptosis, dry eyes, tearing, double or blurred vision, and photophobia.

The evaluation of thyrotoxicosis involves the correlation of history and physical examination findings with laboratory and anatomic study findings (**Table 14**). In addition to TSH and free T_4 measurements, laboratory studies should include a basic electrolyte panel, liver chemistry tests, and a complete blood count because each may be affected by either the

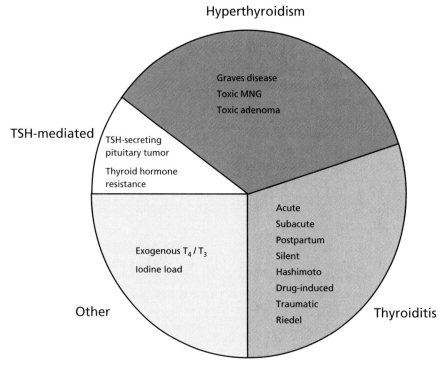

FIGURE 5.
Types of thyrotoxicosis.

MNG = multinodular goiter; T_3 = triiodothyronine; T_4 = thyroxine; TSH = thyroid-stimulating hormone.

TABLE 14 Classic Test Result Patterns in Thyrotoxicosis

	Graves Disease	Toxic Adenoma/ MNG	SAT Thyrotoxic Phase	Postpartum Thyroiditis	Exogenous T$_4$	Exogenous T$_3$	TSH-Secreting Pituitary Tumor	Reference Range
TSH	↓	↓	↓	↓	↓	↑	Normal/↑	0.5-5.0 µU/mL (0.5-5.0 mU/L)
FT$_4$	Normal/↑	Normal/↑	Normal/↑	Normal/↑	Normal/↑	Normal/↓	Normal/↑	0.9-2.4 ng/dL (11.61-31 pmol/L)
FT$_3$	Normal/↑	Normal/↑	Normal/↑	Normal/↑	Normal/↑	↑	Normal/↑	3.6-5.6 ng/L (5.6-8.6 pmol/L)
TPO Ab	+/−	+/−	+/−	+/−	−	−	−	<35 U/mL
TG Ab	+/−	+/−	+/−	+/−	−	−	−	<20 U/mL
TSI	+	−	−	−	−	−	−	<125%
TBII	+	−	−	−	−	−	−	<16%
TG	↑	↑	↑	↑	↓	↓	↑	3-40 ng/mL (3-40 µg/L)
RAIU	Normal/↑	Normal/↑	<5%	<5%	<5%	<5%	Normal/↑	10-30% at 24 h

Ab = antibody; FT$_3$ = free triiodothyronine; FT$_4$ = free thyroxine; MNG = multinodular goiter; RAIU = radioactive iodine uptake; SAT = subacute thyroiditis; TBII = thyrotropin-binding inhibitory immunoglobulin; TG = thyroglobulin; TPO = anti–thyroid peroxidase; TSH = thyroid-stimulating hormone; TSI = thyroid-stimulating immunoglobulin; ↓ = decreased; ↑ = increased; + = present; − = absent.

underlying disorder or its therapy. A T$_3$ level (total or free) should be obtained in patients with a suppressed TSH level but a normal free T$_4$ level because some patients have T$_3$ toxicosis. Usual laboratory findings of thyrotoxicosis include a suppressed TSH level and high-normal to frankly elevated T$_4$ or T$_3$ levels. Anti–thyroid peroxidase and anti–thyroglobulin antibody levels are elevated at times, but the TSH receptor antibodies TSI and TBII are more classically associated with Graves disease.

A thyroid scan and radioactive iodine uptake test (with ^{123}I or technetium Tc 99m and ^{131}I) are useful in the differential diagnosis of thyrotoxicosis. A thyroid scan typically reveals diffuse radionuclide uptake in Graves disease; an autonomously functioning thyroid nodule exhibits a prominent solitary focus, and multiple foci of uptake are seen with a toxic multinodular goiter. Radioactive iodine uptake is inappropriately elevated in hyperthyroidism and inappropriately low in destructive thyroiditis and exogenous thyroid hormone exposure.

Thyroid ultrasonography is usually reserved for patients with clinically suspected thyroid nodules. Thyroid gland vascular flow can be assessed with color-flow Doppler ultrasonography, which can help distinguish the high-flow pattern seen with hyperthyroidism from the low-flow pattern seen in thyroiditis or exogenous thyroid exposure. This is particularly helpful in diagnosing amiodarone-induced thyrotoxicosis or in differentiating postpartum thyroiditis from postpartum Graves disease in a woman who is breastfeeding and cannot be exposed to radioactive iodine.

KEY POINTS

- Thyrotoxicosis encompasses all forms of thyroid hormone excess, whereas hyperthyroidism relates specifically to excess hormone production by the thyroid gland.

- Radioactive iodine uptake is elevated in hyperthyroidism and low in destructive thyroiditis and exogenous thyroid hormone exposure.

- Color-flow Doppler ultrasonography is used to distinguish hyperthyroidism (high flow) from thyroiditis (low flow).

Graves Disease

Graves disease is an autoimmune process characterized by the production of antibodies against the TSH receptor. On TSH receptor binding, these antibodies stimulate autonomous thyroid gland function and lead to excess serum T$_4$ or T$_3$ levels. Graves disease can present with either subclinical or overt thyrotoxicosis. Factors associated with its occurrence include a positive family history, the presence of other autoimmune conditions, recent severe stressors, tobacco use, and possible viral exposures. Physical examination may reveal tachycardia; an elevated systolic blood pressure with a widened pulse pressure; a palpable goiter, which is classically smooth; a thyrotoxic stare due to lid retraction; proptosis; and, infrequently, an infiltrative dermopathy.

Adrenergic symptoms from thyrotoxicosis can be effectively treated with prompt β-blocker therapy. Antithyroidal drugs, radioactive iodine (^{131}I), and thyroid surgery are the three main treatments available for Graves disease. Thyroid surgery is typically reserved for patients with concurrent suspicious nodules, extremely large goiters, or ophthalmopathy in whom radioactive iodine has aggravated their eye condition. There is geographic variation in the choice of a first-line therapy for Graves disease, with radioactive iodine being most commonly used in the United States and antithyroidal drugs in other parts of the world.

Antithryoidal drugs can be used either short term, to control hyperthyroidism in preparation for thyroidectomy, or for longer periods (6-18 months), in an attempt to achieve disease remission. Propylthiouracil and methimazole are the two antithyroidal drugs available in the United States. Because of a presumed immunomodulatory effect, antithyroidal drugs result in drug-free remission rates of between 30% and 50% in patients with Graves disease who are treated for 1 year. Higher remission rates have been described in patients who also have mild hyperthyroidism, small goiters, and lower initial antithyroidal drug requirements. Although antithyroidal drugs are generally well tolerated, they have some notable adverse effects. Drug rashes occur in approximately 2% of patients taking antithyroidal drugs. Propylthiouracil has been associated with elevated aminotransferase levels and a higher rate of serious adverse effects on the liver than methimazole. Rarely, severe hepatic necrosis has been reported, predominantly with propylthiouracil. Therefore, a recent advisory suggested that propylthiouracil should not be used as a first-line antithyroidal medication, with the possible exception of the first trimester of pregnancy, during which methimazole has been associated with possible teratogenicity. A mild and usually reversible cholestatic pattern on liver chemistry tests can be seen with methimazole. Both drugs are associated with agranulocytosis, at a rate of one occurrence per 250 to 500 patients.

Radioactive iodine can effectively ablate an overactive thyroid in greater than 90% of patients, characteristically after a single dose. Adverse effects are uncommon. Patients may (rarely) develop neck pain or tenderness from radiation thyroiditis, which may also be associated with an exacerbation in the thyrotoxic state for several weeks because of the release of preformed hormone. If thyrotoxicosis still persists 6 months after the initial treatment, repeat dosing should be considered. Although an occasional patient becomes euthyroid after radioactive iodine administration, the expected outcome is hypothyroidism, which typically occurs within 2 to 3 months of therapy, at which time thyroid hormone replacement therapy is begun. TSH receptor antibodies can persist for decades after successful treatment with radioactive iodine and can have future clinical effects, even in patients who are euthyroid on stable levothyroxine replacement therapy. For example, Graves ophthalmopathy can present years after the initial treatment, and TSH receptor antibodies can cross the placenta in pregnant patients during their third trimester and have a potentially negative effect on fetal thyroid function.

Clinically significant Graves ophthalmopathy occurs in approximately 5% to 10 % of patients with Graves disease and is more common in smokers and those with a family history of Graves ophthalmopathy. Ophthalmopathy severity varies from mild to severe and may involve lid changes, proptosis or exophthalmos, and inflammatory eye changes, such as chemosis, conjunctival injection, periorbital edema, or iritis. Extraocular muscle involvement can result in double vision, whereas optic nerve compression can result in reduced visual acuity and even blindness. A primary management focus in Graves ophthalmopathy is to establish a euthyroid state because persistent hypo- and hyperthyroidism exacerbate disease activity. Radioactive iodine treatment has been associated with worsening of Graves ophthalmopathy, at least transiently. Therefore, its use for treatment of hyperthyroidism in patients with severe Graves ophthalmopathy is not recommended. In patients with mild to moderate eye disease, prophylactic administration of prednisone should be considered if radioactive iodine treatment is selected. Treatment choices for Graves ophthalmopathy include local measures (such as artificial tears) to treat conjunctival dryness and corticosteroid regimens to treat moderate inflammation. Orbital irradiation may also be considered in patients with advanced ophthalmopathy not responsive to corticosteroids, although long-term benefit is controversial. Orbital decompression is done emergently in patients with optic nerve compression. Successful management of Graves ophthalmopathy requires a team approach, with involvement of experienced endocrinologists and ophthalmologists.

KEY POINTS

- The drug-free remission rate in patients with Graves disease who are treated with antithyroidal drugs is between 30% and 50% after 1 year of therapy.
- Therapy with radioactive iodine (^{131}I) should be avoided in patients with significant Graves ophthalmopathy.

Toxic Multinodular Goiter and Toxic Adenoma

Toxic multinodular goiter and toxic adenoma frequently result from a somatic mutation in the $G_s\alpha$-subunit or TSH receptor causing constitutive activation in one or more nodule(s), which leads to autonomy of function and secondary thyrotoxicosis. Recent exposure to iodine should be determined because acute iodine loads, either in the diet or intravenously from medical testing, can lead to iodine-induced thyrotoxicosis in patients with preexisting thyroid autonomy (Jod-Basedow phenomenon). Physical examination may reveal one or more palpable nodule(s) and overall gland enlargement. Patients can be asymptomatic or exhibit classic signs of thyrotoxicosis. Obstructive symptoms can occur if the gland is large, especially if there is any significant substernal extension. With toxic adenoma, a thyroid scan will reveal a solitary overactive ("hot") nodule with suppression of the nonautonomous extranodular tissue. In contrast, with toxic multinodular goiter, a thyroid scan will reveal patchy uptake of radioactive iodine with increased uptake in autonomous regions and reduced uptake outside those areas; in areas of decreased uptake, determining if the reduced uptake correlates with normal-appearing tissue or a distinct thyroid ("cold") nodule is essential because the latter requires specific evaluation, including aspiration biopsy. Ultrasonography is useful is assessing toxic multinodular goiters because scan findings can be correlated with normal thyroid architecture and functional nodules can be delineated from nonfunctional ones. Iodinated contrast should be avoided in patients with toxic thyroid nodules, if possible, and close monitoring by thyroid function tests is indicated.

Antithyroidal drugs can achieve drug-free remission in Graves disease but only modulate thyroid hormone production in toxic multinodular goiter and toxic adenoma and thus would be required continuously to control hyperthyroidism. In contrast, radioactive iodine can be definitive treatment of toxic multinodular goiter and toxic adenoma because hyperactive nodules take up the iodine, with suppressed normal tissue (ideally) receiving minimal radiation exposure. As the hyperthyroid tissue is destroyed over the subsequent few months, the residual normal tissue resumes function, which allows a return to euthyroidism without a need for thyroid hormone replacement therapy. Surgical options include removal of the involved lobe in toxic adenoma and total thyroidectomy in toxic multinodular goiter. Patients who undergo total thyroidectomy will require lifelong levothyroxine therapy, but those who have only the involved lobe resection may have enough residual tissue to remain euthyroid.

KEY POINT

- Radioactive iodine (^{131}I) or surgery can be definitive treatment of hyperthyroidism in patients with toxic multinodular goiter and toxic adenoma.

Destructive Thyroiditis

Thyroiditis entails transient destruction of thyroid tissue, leading to disruption of follicles and release of preformed thyroid hormone into the circulation. Forms of destructive thyroiditis include subacute (de Quervain), postpartum, and silent (painless) thyroiditis. Subacute thyroiditis is thought to occur after a viral infection, whereas silent thyroiditis is generally considered to be autoimmune. The former usually involves thyroid tenderness, whereas the later is generally painless. Postpartum thyroiditis is a painless autoimmune thyroiditis that affects approximately 5% of pregnant women in the United States and typically occurs within a few months of delivery. This disorder can recur with each pregnancy, and the risk for permanent hypothyroidism increases with each episode. There also have been reports of an HLA haplotype associated with an increased familial risk for thyroiditis.

The classic course of destructive thyroiditis consists of a thyrotoxic release phase followed by a hypothyroid recovery stage, which is in turn followed by a return to euthyroidism. The TSH level responds in a converse fashion in that it is suppressed during the toxic phase and then increases to above-normal levels in the hypothyroid phase. Although TSH and free T$_4$ levels often normalize after these events, some patients will remain permanently hypothyroid or become hypothyroid again in the future. Patients often are not diagnosed until after the thyrotoxic phase has passed. The severity and duration of a course of destructive thyroiditis vary between patients. In some patients, the hypothyroid phase will be mild, whereas in others, it will be so severe that replacement with levothyroxine should be considered. In such patients, levothyroxine is typically prescribed for approximately 6 months (to allow time for gland recovery) and then tapered and stopped, with ongoing monitoring for recurrent hypothyroidism. Recurrence of subacute thyroiditis can occur in approximately 4% of these treated patients.

Findings on physical examination and laboratory study will depend on the phase of destructive thyroiditis the patient is experiencing at the time of evaluation. Typical results of thyroid function and radioactive iodine uptake tests are shown in **Figure 6**. The course of destructive thyroiditis can be lengthy and, at times, associated with a moderate thyrotoxic phase. Although many patients can be treated expectantly with only β-adrenergic blocker therapy, prednisone is indicated in patients with significant hormone elevation or pain. NSAIDs have also been used to treat the discomfort associated with subacute thyroiditis but are not as effective as corticosteroids.

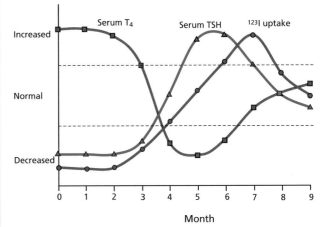

FIGURE 6.

Triphasic changes in thyroid hormone levels associated with destructive thyroiditis.

Measurement of TSH and radioactive iodine (^{123}I) uptake shows thyrotoxicosis during the first 3 months, followed by hypothyroidism for 3 months, and then by euthyroidism.

^{123}I = radioactive iodine; T$_4$ = thyroxine; TSH = thyroid-stimulating hormone.

Adapted with permission from Pearce EN, Farwell AP, Braverman LE. Thyroiditis [erratum in N Engl J Med. 2003;349(6):620]. N Engl J Med. 2003;348(26):2650. [PMID: 12826640] Copyright 2003, Massachusetts Medical Society.

- The classic course of destructive thyroiditis consists of a thyrotoxic release phase followed by a hypothyroid recovery stage, which in turn is followed by a return to euthyroidism.
- Radioactive iodine uptake will be very low during the thyrotoxic phase of destructive thyroiditis but can then rise to above-normal levels during the hypothyroid phase.

Drug-Induced Thyrotoxicosis

Several drugs can cause thyrotoxicosis, including lithium carbonate, interferon alfa, interleukin 2, and (especially) amiodarone. Iodine loads from drugs, iodinated contrast, and, in rare cases, significant betadine exposure can trigger hyperthyroidism in predisposed persons. Lithium is more commonly associated with hypothyroidism than hyperthyroidism. The average American diet contains approximately 150 µg/d of iodine, but amiodarone contains 75 mg of iodine per tablet and has a half-life of months; persistent effects on thyroid function can be seen for up to 1 year after discontinuation.

Amiodarone-induced thyrotoxicosis has two forms: iodine-induced hyperthyroidism (type 1) and destructive thyroiditis (type 2). Type 1 thyrotoxicosis is more commonly seen in iodine-deficient areas, and type 2 generally occurs in iodine-sufficient regions, such as the United States. In practice, the distinction can be difficult to make. The types cannot be distinguished by changes on thyroid function testing alone; for example, the high iodine load associated with type 1 iodine-induced hyperthyroidism may result in low radioactive iodine uptake, as is seen in type 2 thyroiditis. Ultrasonography of the thyroid gland with color-flow Doppler imaging has shown promise in that it can distinguish the high vascular flow pattern of type 1 amiodarone-induced thyrotoxicosis from the low vascular flow pattern of type 2.

The management of amiodarone-induced thyrotoxicosis can be very complex and should be handled by an endocrinologist. When possible, discontinuation of amiodarone should be considered, although this is often not possible from a cardiac perspective. Because amiodarone reduces T_4 to T_3 conversion, T_3 levels may appear lower than expected; levels typically increase after discontinuing the drug. First-line therapy for amiodarone-induced thyrotoxicosis is antithyroidal drugs for type 1 and prednisone for type 2. In practice, both drug types may be needed to effectively control amiodarone-induced thyrotoxicosis for patients in whom a clear distinction between subtypes is not possible.

- Amiodarone can induce two forms of thyrotoxicosis: iodine-induced hyperthyroidism (type 1) and destructive thyroiditis (type 2).

Subclinical Hyperthyroidism

Subclinical hyperthyroidism is defined as the presence of a suppressed serum TSH level with concomitant T_4 and T_3 levels within the reference range. Symptoms of hyperthyroidism are usually mild, and many patients are asymptomatic. Radioactive iodine uptake typically is within the reference range in patients with subclinical hyperthyroidism, and thyroid scan findings are consistent with the underlying cause (Graves disease, autonomously functioning thyroid nodule, multinodular goiter). There has been substantial debate about the appropriate therapy for subclinical hyperthyroidism, especially because of the paucity of symptoms and spontaneous normalization of TSH levels seen with serial follow-up. However, recent data have increasingly raised concern about the potential negative effects of persistent mild thyrotoxicosis on the heart, bones, and central nervous system. Consensus exists for intervention when the TSH level is less than 0.1 µU/mL (0.1 mU/L) or when patients are convincingly symptomatic. Debate still surrounds the management of less suppressed TSH levels, although recent data indicate an increased risk of atrial fibrillation when the TSH level is below 0.3 µU/mL (0.3 mU/L). In patients with unclear findings, the use of antithyroidal drugs is a reasonable first step to gauge the response to normalization of the TSH level. More definitive therapy can be pursued later if a positive response is observed.

Hypothyroidism

Hypothyroidism is a common disorder with a higher prevalence in women than men (2% versus 0.2%) and in persons with other underlying autoimmune diseases. Hashimoto thyroiditis is the most frequent cause, followed distantly by iatrogenic hypothyroidism, which can occur after radioactive iodine ablation for Graves disease, external-beam radiation to the thyroid bed, or surgical removal of the thyroid gland. Certain medications, such as lithium carbonate, interferon alfa, interleukin 2, and amiodarone, also can cause hypothyroidism. Pituitary tumors and/or pituitary surgery can cause central hypothyroidism. Congenital forms of hypothyroidism, such as thyroid agenesis or dyshormonogenesis (a genetic defect in the synthesis of thyroid hormone), constitute rarer causes of hypothyroidism. Celiac disease also can be associated with inadequate levothyroxine absorption and resultant increased levothyroxine dosing requirements in patients with established hypothyroidism. Clinical manifestations of hypothyroidism include fatigue, reduced endurance, weight gain, cold intolerance, constipation, impaired concentration and short-term memory, dry skin, edema, mood changes, depression, psychomotor retardation, muscle cramps, myalgia, and menstrual changes, such as menorrhagia. Physical examination findings include a reduced basal temperature, diastolic hypertension, a possibly enlarged thyroid gland, bradycardia, pallor, dry and cold skin, brittle hair, hoarseness, and a delayed recovery phase of deep tendon reflexes. Results of laboratory studies can confirm hypothyroidism (**Table 15**). Although serum T_4 levels are helpful, T_3 levels are generally not needed. The presence of anti–thyroid peroxidase antibodies suggests Hashimoto thyroiditis as the cause of hypothyroidism and is associated with an increased risk of overt hypothyroidism of 4% per year. Thyroid imaging is not required unless concurrent thyroid nodules are suspected on physical examination.

The mainstay of thyroid hormone replacement is levothyroxine therapy, which should always be taken on an empty stomach 1 hour before or 2 to 3 hours after intake of food or other medications. Although much attention has recently been focused on therapy with liothyronine or combination T_3/T_4 therapy using either thyroid hormone extract or synthetic T_3/T_4 combinations, most evidence to date shows no clinical advantage of combined T_3/T_4 therapy over traditional levothyroxine treatment. Available T_3 preparations have a short half-life and can be associated with acute spikes in serum T_3 levels, which are of particular concern in elderly patients or patients with cardiac abnormalities.

Data from recent studies, including NHANES III, are challenging the validity of the traditional TSH reference range of 0.5 to 5.0 µU/mL (0.5 to 5.0 mU/L). When patients with a family history of thyroid disease or the presence of thyroid antibodies are excluded from the reference population, the TSH normal range appears to be more narrow (0.5-2.5 µU/mL [0.5-2.5 mu/L]). Therefore, a target range of approximately 1.0 to 2.5 µU/mL (1.0 to 2.5 mU/L) seems appropriate for patients with defined thyroid disease receiving replacement levothyroxine. Whether patients without known thyroid disease or risk factors whose serum TSH levels are between 2.5 and 5.0 µU/mL (2.5 and 5.0 mU/L) should be treated remains less clear, especially older patients. At least one study indicated that patients age 80 years and older with subclinical or overt hypothyroidism are more likely to survive to age 89 than their contemporaries with normal or low serum TSH values.

KEY POINTS

- The presence of anti–thyroid peroxidase antibodies suggests Hashimoto thyroiditis as the cause of hypothyroidism.
- Levothyroxine remains the mainstay of thyroid hormone replacement therapy in patients with hypothyroidism.
- The suggested goal for serum thyroid-stimulating hormone levels in patients on levothyroxine therapy is 1.0 to 2.5 µU/mL (1.0 to 2.5 mU/L).

Subclinical Hypothyroidism

Subclinical hypothyroidism is defined by the presence of an elevated serum TSH level with concomitant T_4 and T_3 levels in the reference range. Patients typically have mild or no symptoms of hypothyroidism. The potential causes of subclinical hypothyroidism are the same as for overt hypothyroidism. Evidence suggests that patients with subclinical hypothyroidism also have mild elevations in total cholesterol, LDL-cholesterol, and even C-reactive protein levels, and some recent meta-analyses have shown an increased risk for atherosclerosis and cardiac events. However, no data support treatment with levothyroxine to reverse or improve outcomes for these risks. Consensus does exist for treatment of patients with serum TSH levels greater than 10 µU/mL (10 mU/L). Additionally, many advocate a lower threshold for institution of levothyroxine therapy in patients with anti–thyroid peroxidase antibodies, a strong family history of thyroid disease, a goiter (or signs of thyroid failure), or pregnancy.

TABLE 15 Classic Test Result Patterns in Hypothyroidism

	Hashimoto Thyroiditis	Subclinical Hypothyroidism	SAT Recovery Phase	Postpartum Thyroiditis Hypothyroid Phase	Central Hypothyroidism	Reference Range
TSH	↑	↑	↑	↑	↓/Normal	0.5-5.0 µU/mL (0.5-5.0 mU/L)
FT_4	Normal/↓	Normal	Normal/↓	Normal/↓	↓/Normal	0.9-2.4 ng/dL (11.61-31 pmol/L)
FT_3	Normal/↓	Normal	Normal/↓	Normal/↓	Normal/↓	3.6-5.6 ng/L (5.6-8.6 pmol/L)
TPO Ab	+	+/−	−	+	−	<35 U/mL
TG Ab	+/−	+/−	+/−	+/−	−	<20 U/mL

Ab = antibody; FT_3 = free triiodothyronine; FT_4 = free thyroxine; SAT = subacute thyroiditis; TG = thyroglobulin; TPO = anti–thyroid peroxidase antibody; TSH = thyroid-stimulating hormone; ↓ = decreased; ↑ = increased; + = present; − = absent.

- Subclinical hypothyroidism may be associated with an increased risk of atherosclerosis and cardiac events, but reversal of these effects with levothyroxine therapy has not been systematically studied.
- Levothyroxine therapy is reasonable in patients with subclinical hypothyroidism who have increased risk factors for development of overt hypothyroidism.

Structural Disorders of the Thyroid Gland

The primary structural disorders of the thyroid gland are nodules, goiters, and cancers. Rarer aberrant or ectopic structural disorders include agenesis, hemiagenesis, substernal and lingual abnormalities, and struma ovarii.

Thyroid Nodules

The prevalence of palpable thyroid nodules is 4% to 7% and of thyroid nodules detected on ultrasounds is 20% to 65%. An increasing number of thyroid nodules are detected incidentally on imaging tests performed for unassociated reasons. Nodules are more common with aging and occur more frequently in women. The differential diagnosis of thyroid nodules is varied (**Table 16**). The cancer risk for a thyroid nodule is 5% to 10%. Because most thyroid nodules are benign, the clinician's focus is to accurately identify malignant lesions in the most efficient and cost-effective manner possible (**Figure 7**). Factors associated with increased cancer risk include extremes of age (<20 or >60 years), male sex, a history of head or neck irradiation, a family history of thyroid cancer (especially medullary thyroid cancer), rapid nodule growth, and hoarseness. Nodule pain is uncommon and is more often associated with benign than malignant processes. Findings of a hard nodule (or nodules), local cervical lymphadenopathy, fixation to adjacent tissue, and vocal cord paralysis increase the risk of cancer.

Limited laboratory testing is typically required in the workup of a thyroid nodule. Beyond a routine complete blood count and serum chemistry panel, the serum TSH level should be measured because the result will help guide the workup. Concomitant measurement of the serum free T_4 level is also reasonable if patients have thyroid-related symptoms. Measurement of thyroid antibodies is unnecessary unless there is a clinical suspicion of autoimmune thyroid disease. Presently in the United States, routine calcitonin measurement is not recommended but should be considered in patients with hypercalcemia or a family history of thyroid cancer or multiple endocrine neoplasia type 2. Although measurement

TABLE 16 Differential Diagnosis of Thyroid Nodules

Diagnosis	Notes
Benign	
Thyroid nodule	Adenomatoid hyperplasia, colloid nodule, adenomatoid nodule, follicular or Hürthle cell adenoma, and hylanizing trabecular adenoma
Thyroglossal duct cyst	Midline cystic mass at level of hyoid bone; moves upward with protrusion of the tongue; may become infected; rarely malignant
Pyramidal lobe of thyroid	Cephalad projection of thyroid tissue from isthmus; may be palpable in autoimmune thyroid disease
Lipoma	Benign focal subcutaneous accumulation of fat
Dermoid cyst	Soft mass in the suprasternal notch
Teratoma	Type of germ cell tumor possibly containing several different types of tissue (such as hair, muscle, and bone); mediastinal location at times
Branchial cyst	Soft, lateral neck mass anterior to upper third of sternocleidomastoid muscle; usually seen in adults; cholesterol crystals in cyst fluid
Cervical lymphadenopathy	Possibly benign or may be associated with malignancy, including thyroid cancer
Malignant	

Thyroid cancer	Primary thyroid cancer
	    Papillary (variants: follicular, diffuse sclerosing, columnar, tall cell)
	    Follicular (variants: Hürthle cell [oncocytic])
	    Medullary
	    Anaplastic

Thyroid lymphoma	Enlarging, firm neck mass; often bilateral; classically seen in older women with a history of Hashimoto thyroiditis
Metastatic carcinoma	Metastases of other primary carcinoma to thyroid (breast, melanoma, kidney)
Sarcoma	Tumors usually arising from connective tissue, with most being malignant

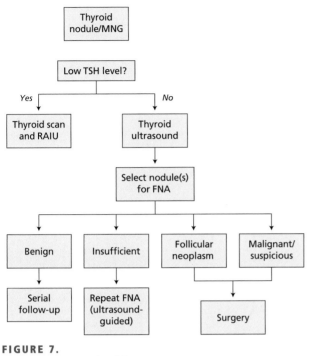

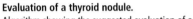

FIGURE 7.
Evaluation of a thyroid nodule.
Algorithm showing the suggested evaluation of a thyroid nodule.

FNA = fine-needle aspiration; MNG = multinodular goiter; RAIU = radioactive iodine uptake; TSH = thyroid-stimulating hormone.

TABLE 17 Ultrasound Characteristics of Thyroid Nodules	
Cancerous Nodules	**Benign Nodules**
Microcalcifications	Comet tail
Increased central nodule vascularity	Increased peripheral nodule vascularity
Hypoechogenicity	Hyperechogenicity
Irregular border	Halo present
Taller than wide (sagittal view)	Pure cyst

of the thyroglobulin level is an excellent thyroid cancer marker in patients who have undergone thyroidectomy or radioactive iodine ablation, it is not useful in patients with an intact thyroid gland.

Thyroid ultrasonography is most useful in the evaluation of thyroid nodules. Not only does it allow for accurate detection and sizing of all nodules on the thyroid gland, but ultrasound characteristics can be used to further delineate cancer risk (**Table 17**). Additional characteristics worrisome for malignancy include a size greater than 3 cm, speckled calcification within the nodule, and high intravascular flow in the nodule's center. Nodules with a surrounding hypolucency (halo) or peripheral vascular flow are less concerning. Ultrasound findings have a reasonable specificity for thyroid cancer but a poor sensitivity, so they cannot by themselves be used to determine the presence or absence of cancer. CT and MRI are not routinely used but may sometimes be appropriate, as in the presence of a substernal goiter, cervical lymphadenopathy, or tracheal deviation. A thyroid scan and radioactive iodine uptake test are appropriate in the context of a suppressed serum TSH level because a toxic nodule or multinodular goiter may be present. Because such hyperfunctional nodules rarely harbor cancer (<1%), their previously discussed workup and management are far different.

Fine-needle aspiration, performed either by nodule palpation or under ultrasonographic guidance, is essential in the evaluation of thyroid nodules. In the hands of a trained physician, this procedure is a simple and relatively inexpensive method of determining the presence of malignancy. Sensitivity is approximately 90% to 95%, with a false-negative rate of 1% to 11%. Because a potential sampling error is of concern with large nodules (>3 cm), resampling of such nodules at a future time is prudent, even if the nodule remains stable in size. Papillary thyroid cancer, when present, is often diagnosed at the time of the fine-needle aspiration. However, one cannot know if a follicular neoplasm is benign or malignant without histologic examination to determine if the nodule capsule demonstrates vascular and/or capsular invasion. Therefore, surgical removal of the nodule is required, generally by lobectomy. Some management guidelines stipulate that a nodule found to be "hot" on a thyroid scan can instead be monitored if a previous cytologic study reported it as a follicular neoplasm. Benign nodules on cytologic examination can be monitored, whereas suspicious or malignant nodules require surgical removal. Surgical complications of thyroidectomy include hypoparathyroidism and recurrent laryngeal nerve paresis. The lowest complication rates are associated with thyroid surgery performed by experienced thyroid surgeons at large-volume medical centers. Levothyroxine therapy was previously used in an attempt to shrink thyroid nodules, but this practice has largely been abandoned because of inefficacy. Ethanol injection and radiofrequency treatment of nodules also have been advocated in a few reports, but their usefulness is debatable.

According to several guidelines on the management of thyroid nodules, biopsy of any nodule greater than 1 cm in diameter is reasonable, and biopsy of smaller nodules should be considered in patients with risk factors, such as a history of radiation exposure, a family history of thyroid cancer, cervical lymphadenopathy, or worrisome ultrasound characteristics. Patients require serial follow-up even when results of the initial biopsy show a benign nodule. Repeat fine-needle aspiration is appropriate when the initial sample proves insufficient or when there has been interval nodule growth (50% by volume) or development of concerning ultrasound characteristics.

- Selection of thyroid nodules for fine-needle aspiration should be guided by nodule size and the presence of worrisome ultrasound features (such as an irregular border, prominent central intranodular vascularity, microcalcifications, and hypoechogenicity).

Incidentalomas

Incidental thyroid nodules, commonly referred to as incidentalomas, are often encountered during the course of patient evaluation with carotid artery ultrasonography, CT or MRI of the neck or carotid arteries, and, most recently, ^{18}F-fluoro-2-deoxy-D-glucose positron emission tomography (^{18}FDG-PET). Overall, incidentally found thyroid nodules have a cancer risk similar to that of nodules presenting clinically, except for ^{18}FDG-positive nodules, which harbor a 14% to 50% cancer risk. Because many patients undergo ^{18}FDG-PET scanning for cancer surveillance, focal thyroid uptake may indicate a metastasis from an already diagnosed cancer. Diffuse ^{18}FDG uptake suggests benign thyroid conditions and is generally not concerning for cancer. The workup and management of incidentally found thyroid nodules are guided by the same principles used for palpable nodules.

Goiters

Multinodular Goiter

Multinodular goiters occur more frequently with advancing age, low iodine intake, and Hashimoto disease. In recent series, the cancer risk was similar for a thyroid gland with a solitary nodule or with multiple nodules (approximately 5%-9%). Multinodular goiters are associated with hypothyroidism, hyperthyroidism, and, most commonly, a euthyroid state. Multiple nodules are generally assessed similarly to solitary nodules, with nodule size and ultrasound characteristics used to select the nodules to be biopsied. As with solitary thyroid nodules, multinodular goiters require serial follow-up to check for significant nodule growth (50% by volume) or new worrisome ultrasound findings; repeat biopsy may be necessary. Large multinodular goiters, especially those with a substernal extension, may present with local symptoms, such as dysphagia, hoarseness, or even dyspnea. Barium swallow, direct vocal cord visualization and/or spirometry with flow volume loops, and chest CT may be used to quantify the severity of any mass effect. As with solitary nodules, the use of levothyroxine to suppress TSH secretion and thereby reduce goiter size is generally not helpful and not routinely recommended. Radioactive iodine can be used in select circumstances to shrink a multinodular goiter but is generally not a first-line option except in patients with thyrotoxicosis due to autonomous function. Thyroid surgery is indicated when local symptoms are prominent, malignancy is suspected, or cosmetic intervention is desired by the patient.

Simple Goiter

Simple goiter is defined as the presence of an enlarged thyroid gland without nodules. Simple goiters can be homogeneous or heterogeneous. Dyshormonogenesis is an occasional cause of simple goiter. Patients with asymptomatic, stable simple goiters can be serially monitored. Goiters exhibiting serial growth may stabilize or even be reduced in size with levothyroxine given at dosages that keep the TSH level in the low-normal range. In patients with concomitant autoimmune thyroid disease, thyroid antibodies may be measurable. Although rare, primary thyroid lymphoma, which is more likely to occur in patients with Hashimoto thyroiditis, can present as a rapidly enlarging goiter, usually with a very firm texture.

- The thyroid cancer risk is approximately the same for multinodular goiters and solitary nodules, whether found clinically or incidentally.

Thyroid Cancer

Recent data from the Surveillance, Epidemiology, and End Results (SEER) program indicate an increase in the incidence of thyroid cancer in the United States, although it is unclear whether this has resulted from increased detection or increased disease occurrence. See MKSAP 15 Hematology and Oncology for a discussion of thyroid cancer.

Medications That Alter Thyroid Function

Many medications can affect thyroid hormone status (**Table 18**) and alter thyroid hormone levels in various ways, including inhibition and reduction of TSH synthesis and release, alteration in the thyroxine-binding globulin level (either increase or decrease), displacement of thyroid hormone from binding globulins, decrease in T_4 to T_3 conversion, enhanced clearance of thyroid hormone, interference with gastrointestinal absorption and/or enterohepatic circulation, and induction of thyroiditis. Some alterations affect thyroid status to the point of causing hypothyroidism or thyrotoxicosis, as previously discussed. At other times, patients may remain euthyroid, but the alterations complicate the interpretation of thyroid function test results. As Table 18 suggests, several drugs can affect thyroid function by more than one mechanism. When one of these drugs is discontinued, the response in thyroid function has to be monitored as the drug's effect diminishes. Additionally, conditions such as celiac disease and malabsorption from various causes (including certain bariatric procedures) also can be associated with inadequate levothyroxine absorption and resultant hypothyroidism.

TABLE 18 Medications with Effects on Thyroid Function

Inhibition of thyroid-stimulating hormone synthesis or release
Bexarotene	Dopamine
Corticosteroids[a]	Octreotide

Decreased thyroid hormone synthesis or release
Iodine	Potassium perchlorate
Lithium[a]	Propylthiouracil[a]
Methimazole	

Decreased conversion of total thyroxine to total triiodothyronine
Amiodarone[a]	Propranolol (high doses)
Corticosteroids[a]	Propylthiouracil[a]
Ipodate/iopanoic acid	

Decreased thyroxine-binding globulin
Androgen therapy	Corticosteroids[a]
L-Asparaginase	Niacin

Increased thyroxine-binding globulin
Estrogen	Raloxifene
5-Fluorouracil	Tamoxifen
Heroin, methadone	

Enhanced metabolic clearance rate of thyroid hormone
Carbamazepine[a]	Rifampin
Phenobarbital	Sertraline[b]
Phenytoin[a]	

Displacement of thyroid hormone from binding proteins
Aspirin	Heparin
Carbamazepine[a]	Phenytoin[a]
Furosemide	Salsalate

Drugs inhibiting absorption or enterohepatic circulation
Aluminum hydroxide	Psyllium
Calcium	Raloxifene
Cholestyramine/colestipol	Soybean oil
Iron	Sucralfate
Proton pump inhibitors	

Drugs causing thyroiditis
Amiodarone[a]	Interleukin 2
Interferon alfa	Lithium[a]

[a]Drugs with more than one mechanism of interaction.

[b]Data to date are very suggestive but limited in number.

Effects of Nonthyroidal Illness on Thyroid Function Tests

Severe nonthyroidal illness can alter the results of thyroid function tests, an effect referred to as the euthyroid sick syndrome. Most commonly, T_3 levels decline sharply, whereas reverse T_3 levels increase. T_4 levels typically remain relatively unchanged, but low levels have been reported in some patients with prolonged severe illness. The TSH response is less consistent, with low, normal, and elevated levels reported. These changes appear related to cytokines and various other mediators of inflammation. The thyroid hormone patterns associated with nonthyroidal illness appear to be an adaptive response to mitigate catabolism associated with severe stress. As such,

intervention with thyroid hormone therapy has not proved beneficial and is not indicated. Thyroid hormone levels typically normalize 4 to 8 weeks after recovery from the illness.

KEY POINT

- Nonthyroidal illness is commonly associated with changes in thyroid function tests; levothyroxine therapy is not indicated.

Thyroid Function and Disease in Pregnancy

Abnormalities in thyroid function during pregnancy can profoundly affect the health of both mother and fetus. The increase in estrogen causes an increase in thyroxine-binding globulin. To keep the free T_4 level stable, extra T_4 is required, either by increased production or—in patients on thyroid hormone replacement therapy—an increase in the levothyroxine dosage (as much as 35% to 50% during the first or second trimester). In areas of iodine sufficiency, such as the United States, thyroid size tends to remain stable during pregnancy. In contrast, an increase in thyroid size of approximately 30% can occur during pregnancy in iodine-deficient regions. Additionally, the β-subunit of human chorionic gonadotropin can stimulate thyroid hormone production via cross-reactivity with the TSH receptor. Serum TSH levels may drop to low-normal or even below-normal ranges in the first trimester and then slowly rise back to normal by 16 weeks' gestation. Total T_4 levels increase to approximately 1.5 times the normal range, whereas the normal range for free T_4 tends to be lower as pregnancy progresses. If using free T_4 levels to monitor thyroid function during pregnancy, an assay with trimester-specific normal ranges should be used. A direct-dialysis free T_4 assay is preferred in this setting.

During the first 12 weeks of gestation, the fetus is very dependent on transplacental transfer of maternal thyroid hormone. Fetal thyroid tissue is not functional until 10 to 12 weeks of gestation. Several studies have indicated that maternal and/or fetal thyroid hormone deficiency can negatively affect fetal neurocognitive development. Therefore, women on thyroid replacement therapy should have their thyroid hormone status monitored frequently during pregnancy, and adjustments in dosage should be made promptly with timely repeat thyroid function testing to assess effect. Presently, debate exists on the value of general prenatal maternal screening of thyroid function. At a minimum, thyroid function tests should be obtained in patients with strong risk factors for thyroid disease, and close monitoring is required in those with a known history of a thyroid disorder.

Because some symptoms of thyrotoxicosis overlap with symptoms of normal pregnancy (tachycardia, heat intolerance, fatigue), changes in thyroid function test results that are associated with pregnancy may be difficult to distinguish from underlying hyperthyroidism. This problem is compounded because some traditional diagnostic techniques, such as thyroid scans and radioiodine uptakes tests, are contraindicated during pregnancy to avoid radiation exposure of the fetus. The presence of a moderate goiter, ophthalmopathy, or TSH receptor antibodies can help indicate the presence of Graves disease. Whereas human chorionic gonadotropin–mediated TSH receptor stimulation tends to resolve by 12 to 16 weeks' gestation, primary thyroid disease changes persist longer, albeit with some improvement. Although both antithyroidal medications (propylthiouracil and methimazole) can be used safely in pregnancy, propylthiouracil is generally preferred during the first trimester because of the potential negative effects of methimazole on embryogenesis. Propylthiouracil dosages should be maintained at less than 300 to 450 mg/d. The goal of antithyroidal drug therapy during pregnancy is to keep the serum TSH level slightly suppressed and the free T_4 level in the high-normal range to avoid the deleterious effects of overtreatment, such as fetal hypothyroidism and goiter. Selective β-blockers can be used sparingly when required but are best avoided because of the risk of fetal bradycardia. Thyroid surgery can be performed in the second trimester when absolutely necessary. However, it is rarely indicated and is reserved for special circumstances, such as a patient who is unable to tolerate antithyroidal drugs or who achieves inadequate control on medical therapy. Radioactive iodine is not an option during pregnancy or during subsequent lactation; iodine (^{131}I) concentrates in breast milk and has half-life of 8 days.

KEY POINTS

- The fetus is dependent on maternal thyroid hormone until its own thyroid becomes functional at 10 to 12 weeks of gestation.
- Maternal thyroxine demand increases substantially during pregnancy, and pregnant patients on levothyroxine therapy may require a 35% to 50% increase in levothyroxine dosage during the first or second trimester.
- Thyroid scans and radioactive iodine uptake testing are contraindicated in pregnant patients.

Thyroid Emergencies

Although most thyroid conditions are nonurgent, thyroid storm and myxedema coma are life-threatening conditions that require prompt diagnosis and intervention.

Thyroid Storm

Thyroid storm is a severe manifestation of thyrotoxicosis associated with amplified signs and symptoms coupled with secondary systemic decompensation. Although reported to occur with many causes of thyrotoxicosis, thyroid storm most commonly occurs in Graves disease and, therefore,

has a higher frequency in younger women. An underlying precipitating condition is commonly present, such as surgery, infection or sepsis, trauma, myocardial infarction, pulmonary embolism, diabetic ketoacidosis parturition, acute iodine exposure, radioactive iodine (^{131}I) therapy, or ingestion of medications, including salicylates and pseudoephedrine. Potential symptoms include the full spectrum of those seen in thyrotoxicosis. These can be quantified using well known scoring systems for gauging the severity of thyrotoxicosis and for diagnosing thyroid storm (**Table 19**).

Treatment of thyroid storm should reduce thyroid hormone production/secretion by the thyroid gland, decrease peripheral conversion of T_4 to bioactive T_3, address associated adrenergic and thermoregulatory changes, treat all precipitating factors, and aggressively reverse any systemic decompensation. Once the patient is stable, definitive therapy of the causative thyroid disorder should begin. Therapeutic interventions include a combination of antithyroidal drugs (propylthiouracil or methimazole), iodine-containing products, corticosteroids, β-blockers, and, less frequently, lithium and resin binders (**Table 20**). Propranolol and propylthiouracil have the added benefit over atenolol and methimazole of reducing T_4 to T_3 conversion. Additionally, cooling blankets and acetaminophen can be used to reduce increased core body temperature. Even with aggressive appropriate therapy, however, mortality rates can still be as high as 15% to 20%.

KEY POINTS

- Targeted therapy for thyroid storm should reduce thyroid hormone production/secretion by the thyroid gland, decrease peripheral conversion of T_4 to bioactive T_3, address associated adrenergic and thermoregulatory changes, treat all precipitating factors, and aggressively reverse any systemic decompensation.
- Thyroid storm is associated with a mortality rate of 15% to 20%.

Myxedema Coma

Myxedema coma is an extreme manifestation of hypothyroidism, to the point of systemic decompensation. This thyroid emergency can be life-threatening, especially without prompt diagnosis and treatment. Myxedema coma tends to occur more often in women than men and in elderly patients and tends to occur during periods of cold weather. Occurrence in patients with a history of antecedent thyroid disease predisposing to hypothyroidism is common. Primary hypothyroidism accounts for greater than 95% of all occurrences, but episodes in patients with central hypothyroidism also have been reported. Common precipitating factors include hypothermia, stroke, heart failure, infection, metabolic disturbances, trauma, gastrointestinal bleeding, acidosis, hypoglycemia, and hypercalcemia. Patients taking certain

TABLE 19 Point Scale for the Diagnosis of Thyroid Storm

Thermoregulatory Dysfunction

Temperature	Points
37.2-37.7 °C (99.0-99.9 °F)	5
37.8-38.3 °C (100.0-100.9 °F)	10
38.4-38.8 °C (101.0-101.9 °F)	15
38.9-39.3 °C (102.0-102.9 °F)	20
39.4-39.9 °C (103.0-103.9 °F)	25
≥40 °C (≥104.0 °F)	30

Cardiovascular

Tachycardia (beats/min)	Points
100-109	5
110-119	10
120-129	15
130-139	20
≥140	25

Atrial Fibrillation	Points
Absent	0
Present	10

Heart Failure	Points
Absent	0
Mild	5
Moderate	10
Severe	20

Gastrointestinal-Hepatic Dysfunction

Manifestation	Points
Absent	0
Moderate (diarrhea, abdominal pain, nausea/vomiting)	10
Severe (jaundice)	20

Central Nervous System Disturbance

Manifestation	Points
Absent	0
Mild (agitation)	10
Moderate (delirium, psychosis, extreme lethargy)	20
Severe (seizure, coma)	30

Precipitant History

Status	Points
Positive	0
Negative	10

Scores Totaled

Diagnosis	Points
Thyroid storm	>45
Impending storm	25-44
Storm unlikely	<25

Adapted with permission from Burch HB, Wartofsky L. Life-threatening thyrotoxicosis. Thyroid storm. Endocrinol Metabol Clin North Am. 1993;22(2):263. [PMID: 8325286] Copyright 1993, with permission from Elsevier.

TABLE 20 Treatment of Thyroid Storm

Medication	Comments
Inhibition of hormone production	
Propylthiouracil	Inhibits T_4 to T_3 conversion
Methimazole	Does not block T_4 to T_3 conversion; typically an alternative to propylthiouracil
Inhibition of hormone release	
Iodine-potassium solutions (SSKI, Lugol)	Begun ≥1 h after first antithyroidal drug
β-Adrenergic blockers	
Propranolol	Inhibits T_4 to T_3 conversion at higher doses (>240 mg)
Atenolol	Cardioselective
Esmolol	Can be considered in patients with heart failure; allows active dose titration
Supportive therapies	
Hydrocortisone	Inhibits T_4 to T_3 conversion; used with possible adrenal insufficiency or hypotension
Acetaminophen	Decreases hyperthermia

SSKI = saturated solution of potassium iodide; T_3 = triiodothyronine; T_4 = thyroxine.

medications, including anesthetics, sedatives, tranquilizers, narcotics, amiodarone, and lithium, are likewise more at risk for myxedema coma.

Mental status changes and hypothermia (temperature less than 34.4 °C [94.0 °F]) are hallmark findings of myxedema coma, with hypothermia occurring in 88% of patients. Additional common findings are hypoxemia (80% of patients) and hypercapnia (54% of patients). The combination of mental status changes, hypothermia, hypoventilation, and hyponatremia in a patient whose clinical picture is consistent with hypothyroidism strongly suggests the diagnosis of myxedema coma. The mortality rate from myxedema coma has decreased over the past 20 years from approximately 50% to 20%. Elderly patients tend to do worse, as do those with evidence of severe illness (high Acute Physiology and Chronic Health Evaluation [APACHE] Scale score, low Glasgow Coma Scale score).

Controversy exists regarding the most efficacious thyroid hormone replacement regimen to use for myxedema coma. Traditionally, intravenous levothyroxine has been administered, with an initial bolus of 200 to 500 μg followed by daily doses between 50 and 100 μg until transition to oral administration is feasible. Supplementation with liothyronine (oral or intravenous, if available) at doses between 2 and 10 μg twice daily has been advocated, but definitive benefit is still unproved. If liothyronine is used, it should be administered in lower doses and in combination with levothyroxine (**Table 21**). As with thyroid storm, all underlying precipitating conditions must be addressed.

TABLE 21 Treatment of Myxedema Coma

Levothyroxine, 100 mg and 500 mg vials

   Initial 100-600 μg IV bolus (4 μg/kg lean body weight)

   Follow-up with 50-100 μg IV until conversion to PO replacement

Liothyronine, 5 and 25 μg PO or 10 μg/mL IV

   Consider 10 μg/mL IV or 10 μg PO every 8-12 h

   Use with extreme caution (best avoided in elderly patients and those with cardiac disorders)

   If used, give in conjunction with levothyroxine therapy

Admit to monitored ward, such as a medical intensive care unit

Treat underlying precipitants and complications

Consider CVP line for volume repletion monitoring

Consider empiric antibiotic therapy after panculture

Carefully adjust dosing for all medications

Hydrocortisone, 50-100 mg IV every 6-8 h, until patient is stable

CVP = central venous pressure; IV = intravenously; PO = oral(ly).

KEY POINTS

- Mental status changes and hypothermia are hallmark findings for myxedema coma.
- The primary pharmacologic therapy for myxedema coma is levothyroxine; use of liothyronine is more controversial.
- Underlying precipitants are common in myxedema coma and must be addressed along with the patient's thyroid abnormalities.

Bibliography

Cooper DS. Approach to the patient with subclinical hyperthyroidism. J Clin Endocrinol Metab. 2007;92(1):3-9. [PMID: 17209221]

Devdhar M, Ousman YH, Burman KD. Hypothyroidism. Endocrinol Metab Clin North Am. 2007;36(3):595-615. [PMID: 17673121]

Franklyn JA. Subclinical thyroid disorders—consequences and implications for treatment. Ann Endocrinol (Paris). 2007;68(4):229-230. [PMID: 17651685]

Hegedüs L. Clinical practice. The thyroid nodule. N Engl J Med. 2004;351(17):1764-1771. [PMID: 15496625]

Nayak B, Burman K. Thyrotoxicosis and thyroid storm. Endocrinol Metab Clin North Am. 2006;35(4):663-686. [PMID: 17127140]

Nayak B, Hodak SP. Hyperthyroidism. Endocrinol Metab Clin North Am. 2007;36(3):617-656. [PMID: 17673122]

Pearce EN, Farwell AP, Braverman LE. Thyroiditis [erratum in N Engl J Med. 2003;349(6):620]. N Engl J Med. 2003 Jun 26;348(26):2646-2655. [PMID: 12826640]

Poppe K, Velkeniers B, Glinoer D. Thyroid disease and female reproduction. Clin Endocrinol (Oxf). 2007;66(3):309-321. [PMID: 17302862]

Surks MI, Ortiz E, Daniels GH, et al. Subclinical thyroid disease: scientific review and guidelines for diagnosis and management. JAMA. 2004;291(2):228-238. [PMID: 14722150]

Wartofsky L. Myxedema coma. Endocrinol Metab Clin North Am. 2006;35(4):687-698. [PMID: 17127141]

Disorders of the Adrenal Glands

Adrenal Insufficiency

Adrenal insufficiency refers to the many clinical features associated with partial or complete loss of secretion of adrenal corticosteroids. Diseases of the adrenal glands themselves, such as autoimmune adrenalitis, lead to primary adrenal insufficiency, in which secretion of all adrenal corticosteroids (aldosterone, cortisol, dehydroepiandrosterone [DHEA], and DHEA sulfate) is impaired. In contrast, central or secondary adrenal insufficiency is caused by loss of adrenocorticotropic hormone (ACTH) secretion, which leads to decreased production of ACTH-dependent corticosteroids (cortisol, DHEA, and DHEA sulfate). The clinical manifestations of adrenal insufficiency are subtle (**Table 22**) but become more apparent at times of increased stress, which is associated with a higher need for corticosteroids.

Common causes of primary and central adrenal insufficiency are shown in **Table 23**. Exogenous corticosteroid administration at supraphysiologic dosages for the treatment of various illnesses suppresses ACTH secretion, which leads to central or secondary adrenal insufficiency when such therapy is discontinued. This is the most common cause of central adrenal insufficiency. The suppressive effects of exogenous corticosteroids on ACTH secretion are influenced by the structure of the corticosteroid used, its dose, and the duration of therapy. Corticosteroids with a long biologic half-life (such as dexamethasone) suppress ACTH secretion more than others with a shorter half-life (such as hydrocortisone).

The time of administration of exogenous corticosteroids has a greater role than does the delivered dose in causing suppression of the hypothalamic-pituitary-adrenal (HPA) axis. For example, even a small amount of prednisone, the most commonly used agent, given at night can cause suppression of the HPA axis because it will prevent the physiologic early morning increase in the ACTH level. In contrast, higher doses given once daily between 9 and 10 AM are less likely to suppress the HPA axis, even after prolonged administration. Although individual patients' responses to exogenous corticosteroids vary, a morning measurement of the serum cortisol level obtained before scheduled dosing will generally confirm this lack of suppression. On the other hand, patients given multiple daily doses of corticosteroids are likely to have a suppressed HPA axis for 8 to 12 months. To minimize suppression of the HPA axis, physicians should (whenever possible) administer the smallest amount of corticosteroid possible as a single dose in the morning.

The diagnosis of adrenal insufficiency should be suspected in patients with suggestive symptoms, especially those at increased risk (see Table 23). The diagnosis relies on demonstrating a low basal serum cortisol level that does not increase appropriately after stimulation with the ACTH

TABLE 22 Characteristics of Adrenal Insufficiency

Characteristic	Primary Adrenal Insufficiency	Central Adrenal Insufficiency
Symptoms	Fatigue, nausea, anorexia, weight loss, abdominal pain, arthralgia, low-grade fever; salt craving, postural dizziness; decreased libido	Same symptoms as primary insufficiency but no salt craving and postural dizziness
Signs	Hyperpigmentation[a] Dehydration Hypotension Decreased pubic/axillary hair in women	Normal pigmentation Normal volume Slight decrease in blood pressure Decreased pubic/axillary hair in women
Major laboratory findings	Low basal serum cortisol level (<5.0 µg/dL [138 nmol/L]) with a suboptimal response (<18.5 µg/dL [510.6 nmol/L]) to cosyntropin; low serum DHEA and DHEA-S levels but high plasma renin activity and ACTH level	Same cortisol findings as primary insufficiency except low or inappropriately normal ACTH level; normal aldosterone and plasma renin activity
Other laboratory findings	Hyponatremia, high potassium level, azotemia, anemia, hypoglycemia, and leukopenia (with a high % of eosinophils and lymphocytes)	Same findings as primary insufficiency but also normal potassium level

ACTH = adrenocorticotropic hormone; DHEA = dehydroepiandrosterone; DHEA-S = DHEA sulfate.

[a]Occurs only in patients with primary adrenal insufficiency as a result of increased secretion of adrenocorticotropic hormone and its precursor, pro-opiomelanocortin. An increase in the latter leads to increased secretion of one of its products, melanocortin-stimulating hormone, which causes the hyperpigmentation.

analogue cosyntropin. Random serum cortisol levels vary, depending on the time of day and the degree of stress encountered at the time of measurement. Available assays for measuring the serum cortisol level determine the total (protein-bound and free) hormone level. The physiologic effects of cortisol are determined by the free (or unbound) fraction of the hormone pool. Because over 90% of the cortisol in the circulation is protein bound, an increase in binding proteins, such as occurs during pregnancy or with estrogen therapy (including oral contraceptive pills), results in increased serum cortisol levels without altering the physiologically important free hormone concentrations. This fact should always be considered in the interpretation of serum cortisol measurements. For example, the serum cortisol level may be misleadingly normal in a patient with adrenal insufficiency receiving estrogen therapy. Similarly, patients with hypoproteinemia have lower total serum cortisol levels but may have normal serum free cortisol levels. The latter situation becomes clinically relevant in critically ill patients with hypoproteinemia.

When primary adrenal insufficiency is present, plasma ACTH levels are increased and serum cortisol and aldosterone levels are low. A minimal or no increase in serum cortisol level in response to cosyntropin stimulation confirms the diagnosis. In normal persons, serum cortisol levels increase to 18.5 µg/dL (510.6 nmol/L) or greater 60 minutes after 250 µg of cosyntropin is administered intravenously (mean response, 28 µg/dL [772.8 nmol/L]). Patients with central adrenal insufficiency have low or low-normal plasma ACTH levels and normal plasma aldosterone levels. Although patients with central adrenal insufficiency usually have a subnormal response to cosyntropin, some with partial deficiency display normal responses; in such patients, using a lower dose of cosyntropin (1 µg instead of 250 µg) improves the diagnostic accuracy of the test. Serum levels of DHEA and DHEA-S are low in both primary and central adrenal insufficiency.

Patients with primary adrenal insufficiency require corticosteroid therapy and mineralocorticoid replacement, whereas those with central disease need corticosteroid therapy only. Although any of the corticosteroids can be used, the preferred drug is hydrocortisone (**Table 24**). The doses should be titrated according to symptoms and adverse events. An important part of treating adrenal insufficiency is educating the

TABLE 23 Causes of Adrenal Insufficiency

Primary Adrenal Insufficiency	Central Adrenal Insufficiency
Autoimmune adrenalitis (most common)	Exogenous corticosteroid administration (most common)

Infection
  Tuberculosis
  Mycosis
  Bacterial
  HIV associated
	Hypothalamic/pituitary disease, such as:
	  Pituitary adenoma
	  Rathke cyst or craniopharyngioma
	  Hypothalamic tumors
	  Sarcoidosis

Metastatic cancer	Cranial irradiation

Medications
  Etomidate
  Ketoconazole
  Metyrapone
	Chronic administration of drugs with corticosteroid activity
	  Megestrol acetate

Adrenal hemorrhage	

TABLE 24 Examples of Hydrocortisone Therapy in Established Adrenal Insufficiency

Condition	Hydrocortisone
Physiologic daily dosing	15-25 mg PO in three divided doses,[a] at 8:00 AM (7.5-12.5 mg), 12:00 noon (5.0-7.5 mg), and 6:00 PM (2.5-5.0 mg)
Minor stress (symptoms of a cold or mild influenza)	30-50 mg/d PO in three divided doses
Moderate stress (UTI, minor/moderate surgical procedure [such as cataract surgery])	45-75 mg/d PO or IV in three or four divided doses; can use prednisone or dexamethasone instead
Severe stress (major surgical procedure, such as cardiac surgery, hip replacement), sepsis without shock	100-150 mg/d IV in four divided doses
Septic shock	150-200 mg/d IV in four divided doses

IV = intravenously; PO = orally; UTI = urinary tract infection.

[a]For twice daily dosing, the morning dose is 10-15 mg PO, and the late afternoon dose is 5-10 mg PO.

patient about his or her own illness and the need for dosage adjustments with intercurrent illnesses or surgery (see Table 24). Patients are advised to carry medical alert identification that indicates the diagnosis and dependence on corticosteroids. The standard mineralocorticoid replacement therapy (for patients with primary adrenal insufficiency) is fludrocortisone, 0.05 to 0.1 mg/d. Patients with either primary or central adrenal insufficiency are adrenal androgen–deficient, but replacement therapy (such as with DHEA, 25 to 50 mg/d) is not essential for survival (although it may help some women who report diminished libido).

Although true adrenal insufficiency is not common in critically ill patients, it should always be considered in those at risk for the condition. Establishing the diagnosis can be difficult in that setting because of many confounding factors. The effect of hypoproteinemia on measured serum cortisol levels becomes critical when serum albumin levels are below 2.5 g/dL (25 g/L); although measured serum cortisol levels may appear low, serum free cortisol levels are appropriately elevated. Some critically ill patients, such as those with septic shock, may develop severe, protracted hypotension that is not responsive to standard therapy. Most of these patients have elevated serum total and free cortisol levels. A recent study showed that hydrocortisone therapy (300 mg/d) given to patients with septic shock did not influence mortality but resulted in a faster reversal of shock. Such therapy is not directed at treating an adrenal dysfunction, but rather at controlling the associated overwhelming inflammatory response. For more information on hydrocortisone therapy in patients with septic shock, see MKSAP 15 Pulmonary and Critical Care Medicine.

KEY POINTS

- Central or secondary adrenal insufficiency results from loss of adrenocorticotropic hormone secretion from either chronic exogenous corticosteroid use or hypothalamic/pituitary diseases.
- The diagnosis of primary adrenal insufficiency is suspected when the serum cortisol level is low and the adrenocorticotropic hormone level is high; the plasma aldosterone level is also low in primary disease but not in central (or secondary) adrenal insufficiency.
- Therapy for primary adrenal insufficiency includes corticosteroid therapy (hydrocortisone, prednisone, or dexamethasone), mineralocorticoid replacement (fludrocortisone), and (occasionally) adrenal androgen therapy (in women); therapy for central or secondary adrenal insufficiency involves corticosteroids alone at appropriate dosages.

Cushing Syndrome

The term Cushing syndrome refers to the collection of signs and symptoms that occur after prolonged exposure to supraphysiologic doses of corticosteroids. Causes of Cushing syndrome are outlined in **Table 25**, with the most common being exogenous corticosteroid use to treat various illnesses. Although many of the initial manifestations

TABLE 25 Common Causes of Cushing Syndrome

Cause	Percentage of Patients[a]
Endogenous Cushing syndrome	
ACTH-dependent	75-80
ACTH-secreting pituitary adenomas	60-65
Ectopic ACTH secretion by tumors	10-15
CRH-secreting tumors	<0.5
ACTH-independent	20-25
Adrenal adenoma	10-15
Adrenal carcinoma	5-10
Exogenous Cushing syndrome	
Administration of corticosteroids (prednisone, dexamethasone, hydrocortisone)[b]	—
Administration of drugs with corticosteroid activity (progestational agents, such as megestrol acetate)	—

ACTH = adrenocorticotropic hormone; CRH = corticotropin-releasing hormone; — = not applicable.

[a]With endogenous Cushing syndrome.

[b]Most common cause of Cushing syndrome.

of Cushing syndrome (such as weight gain) are nonspecific (**Figure 8**), others—such as muscle weakness, ecchymosis, hypokalemia, unexplained osteoporosis, new-onset hypertension, and diabetes mellitus—are more alarming and collectively should raise concern for a state of hypercortisolism.

The diagnosis of Cushing syndrome involves confirmation of persistent hypercortisolism associated with poor cortisol suppressibilty with dexamethasone. Three approaches are used to screen for hypercortisolism: (1) assessment of cortisol secretion in a 24-hour period, (2) documentation of the loss of normal diurnal variation in cortisol secretion (late-night salivary cortisol level measurement), and (3) documentation of loss of feedback inhibition of cortisol on the hypothalamic-pituitary-adrenal axis (dexamethasone suppression testing) (**Figure 9**). The serum cortisol level, measured the morning after 1 mg of dexamethasone is given, is generally less than 2 μg/dL (55 nmol/L) in healthy persons. Although a postdexamethasone cortisol level greater than 5 μg/dL (138 nmol/L) is clearly suggestive of Cushing syndrome, values of 2 to 5 μg/dL (55 to 138 nmol/L) require additional testing. As discussed earlier, an increase in binding proteins (such as corticosteroid-binding globulin in patients receiving estrogen therapy or oral contraceptives) leads to false-positive results. In this instance, the other two tests (salivary cortisol and urine free cortisol measurements) can more reliably establish the presence of hypercortisolism. When urine free cortisol excretion is clearly elevated (>200 μg/24 h [551 nmol/24 h]), the diagnosis of hypercortisolism is reasonably established. For patients in whom the overnight dexamethasone suppression test or urine free cortisol excretion is equivocal, other confirmatory studies,

such as the low-dose dexamethasone suppression test, need to be performed. With the latter test, dexamethasone administration (0.5 mg every 6 hours for 48 hours) results in suppression of serum cortisol levels to less than 2 μg/dL (55.2 nmol/L) and in a 24-hour urine free cortisol excretion of less than 20 μg (55.1 nmol/24h) in healthy persons; higher levels are diagnostic of Cushing syndrome. Once hypercortisolism is established, further studies are needed to determine the cause.

Measurements of ACTH can differentiate ACTH-dependent states of hypercortisolism, in which ACTH levels are inappropriately normal or elevated (as with a pituitary adenoma), from ACTH-independent ones, in which ACTH levels are low or undetectable (as with adrenal neoplasms). A high-dose dexamethasone suppression test (2 mg every 6 hours for 48 hours) is sometimes used to distinguish a pituitary source of ACTH-dependent hypercortisolism, which is often suppressible with such dosing, from ectopic ACTH-dependent hypercortisolism, which frequently is not. There are exceptions, however, such as pituitary tumors that do not suppress ACTH and ectopic sources that do suppress ACTH, so caution must be exercised in interpretation. In such instances, expert consultation is highly recommended. Other approaches used to determine the cause of hypercortisolism include dynamic testing with dexamethasone alone or in combination with metyrapone. However, the value of these tests is limited by the degree of overlap in responses observed among patients with different forms of hypercortisolism.

Imaging studies should be obtained only after biochemical documentation of hypercortisolism is established. Although an MRI of the sella turcica is appropriate for patients with ACTH-dependent hypercortisolism, MRI findings are normal in 40% to 50% of patients with documented ACTH-secreting pituitary adenomas because most of these adenomas are too small to be detected. This makes differentiating ACTH-secreting adenomas from ectopic ACTH secretion difficult on the basis of MRI alone. There is significant overlap between these two entities regarding their biochemical features and responsiveness to dexamethasone suppression or other dynamic testing (such as with vasopressin or corticotropin-releasing hormone). One way of confirming a central source of ACTH secretion in patients with negative results on pituitary MRIs is bilateral inferior petrosal sinus catheterization with measurements of ACTH levels from both sides simultaneously before and after stimulation with corticotropin-releasing hormone. This test, however, is technically difficult and potentially dangerous and should only be done at experienced centers.

In patients with hypercortisolism associated with suppressed ACTH secretion, a CT scan of the adrenal glands often shows a tumor (adenoma or carcinoma). Although the differentiation between adrenal adenoma

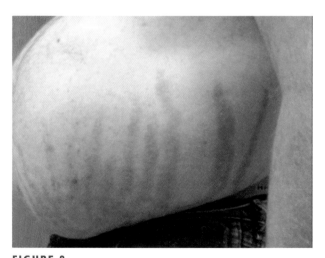

FIGURE 8.
Patient with the central obesity and purple striae characteristic of Cushing syndrome.

Photograph courtesy of Rebecca L. Adochio, MD, University of Colorado Health Science Center.

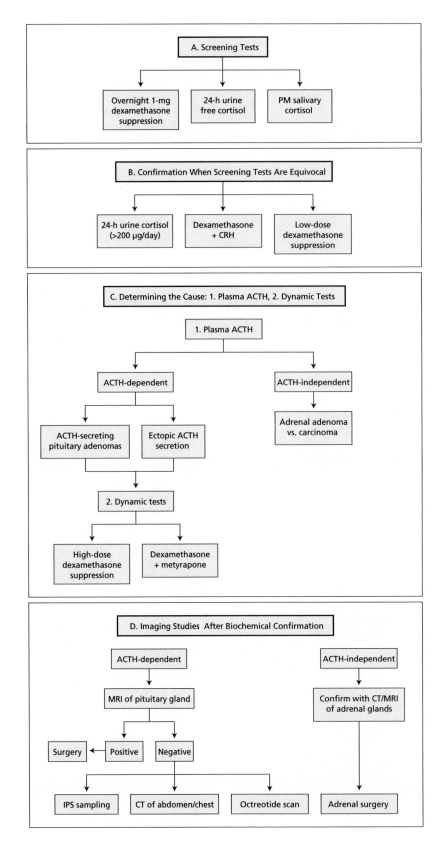

FIGURE 9.
Workup of patients with suspected Cushing syndrome.
After the diagnosis of Cushing syndrome is suspected on clinical assessment, the further workup of patients involves four distinct phases.

ACTH = adrenocorticotropic hormone; CRH = corticotropin-releasing hormone; IPS = inferior petrosal sinus.

and carcinoma can usually be made by using clinical, biochemical, and imaging features, histologic confirmation may be necessary in early disease.

The treatment of Cushing syndrome depends on the cause, the certainty of the diagnosis, and the expertise of the managing team. The treatment of choice for patients with ACTH-secreting pituitary adenomas is pituitary adenomectomy, immediately after which patients develop ACTH deficiency requiring 9 to 18 months of corticosteroid replacement therapy. Patients with residual disease after surgery may benefit from gamma knife irradiation and adjuvant medical therapy. The latter includes drugs that inhibit corticosteroid synthesis (ketoconazole, metyrapone), others that block its effects (mifepristone), and some that are cytotoxic to the adrenal cortical cells (mitotane).

The treatment of adrenal adenomas and carcinomas is surgical resection of the tumor, preferably with a laparoscopic approach in the case of an adenoma. Postoperatively, most patients develop adrenal insufficiency lasting 6 to 9 months. Whereas cortisol-secreting adrenal adenomas are generally curable with surgical resection, adrenal carcinomas may not be totally resectable and can recur; the treatment of patients with such carcinomas is discussed later. The treatment of Cushing syndrome resulting from ectopic ACTH secretion should be directed at the cause, which is often difficult to determine because many different malignant tumors are capable of secreting ACTH, including small cell carcinoma of lung, bronchial or thymic carcinoid, pancreatic carcinoid, pancreatic islet cell tumor, pheochromocytoma, neuroblastoma, ganglioma, paraganglioma, and medullary carcinoma of the thyroid gland. Most patients with ectopic ACTH secretion require medical therapy to control hypercortisolism.

KEY POINTS

- Cushing syndrome occurs after prolonged exposure to endogenous or, more commonly, exogenous corticosteroids; its diagnosis involves confirmation of persistent hypercortisolism associated with poor cortisol suppressibilty with dexamethasone.

- Adrenocorticotropic hormone–independent hypercortisolism is frequently due to a cortisol-producing adrenal tumor that is biochemically characterized by an elevated serum cortisol level associated with a suppressed adrenocorticotropic hormone level.

- The most appropriate treatment of Cushing syndrome is often surgery; for patients with adrenocorticotropic hormone–secreting pituitary adenomas, pituitary adenomectomy is appropriate therapy.

Adrenal Incidentaloma

The increasing use of imaging studies has revealed many previously unrecognized, often asymptomatic adrenal masses (adrenal incidentalomas) in 2% to 3% of the scanned population older than 50 years and in up to 7% of those older than 70 years. Adrenal masses in younger patients are more clinically important. The evaluation of adrenal masses should address the origin and nature of the mass (primary versus metastatic, benign versus malignant). For a primary tumor, whether it is functioning or not must be determined. Nearly 10% of all adrenal incidentalomas are functioning, although most do not have overt clinical manifestations. Functioning tumors can originate from any of the three layers of the adrenal cortex or from the adrenal medulla and secrete products of the respective portion of the adrenal glands.

Initial assessment should include a careful history and physical examination to find any suggestion of malignant disease or clinical evidence of hormone hypersecretion (**Figure 10**). Most patients with metastatic cancer of the adrenal glands have clinical evidence of disease elsewhere. Imaging characteristics of the mass (size, CT attenuation, vascularity) can provide important clues. The risk of primary or metastatic cancer is nearly 2% for tumors less than 4 cm in diameter but increases to 25% for tumors 6 cm or larger. Metastatic lesions to the adrenal glands tend to have a high CT attenuation (greater than 20 Hounsfield units) and are often bilateral. Primary adrenocortical carcinoma tends to be large with irregular borders and may include areas of necrosis. Pheochromocytoma, adrenal carcinoma, and metastatic disease to the adrenal glands are often vascular, whereas benign adrenal adenomas are not highly vascular. Additionally, T2-weighted MRIs of benign adrenal adenomas are usually isointense (compared with the liver), but those of adrenocortical carcinoma, pheochromocytoma, and metastatic disease are hyperintense. The possibility of adrenal hypofunction should be investigated in patients with large, bilateral adrenal masses. Up to 15% of adrenal incidentalomas are bilateral, so bilateral adrenal hyperplasia is part of their differential diagnosis, as are metastatic cancer and adrenocortical carcinoma.

Because overt clinical manifestations are typically scant, screening tests are often necessary to identify potentially functioning adrenal incidentalomas that are secreting cortisol, aldosterone, or catecholamines. Measurements of plasma catecholamines (epinephrine and norepinephrine) and their metabolites (metanephrines and normetanephrines) are reasonable screening tests to rule out pheochromocytoma (see later discussion); further testing can be done when the results are abnormal.

Although adrenal incidentalomas are unlikely to secrete aldosterone, patients should be screened for that possibility if they have hypertension and/or hypokalemia. Appropriate screening for primary hyperaldosteronism is discussed later. Similarly, excess adrenal androgen production is rare, except when the mass represents adrenal

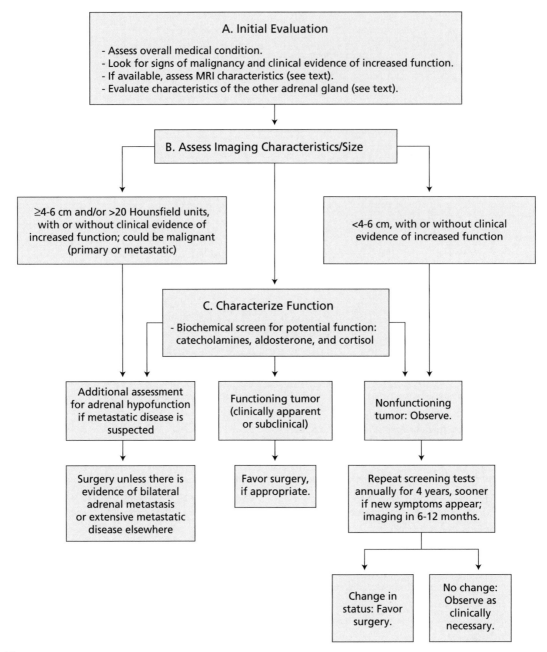

FIGURE 10.
Workup and management of an incidentally discovered adrenal mass.
The initial approach to patients with an incidentally discovered adrenal mass includes three steps: initial evaluation, assessment of imaging characteristics/size, and assessment of function. Masses larger than 6 cm are more likely to be malignant.

cancer, and screening is not routinely performed in the absence of clinical signs or symptoms of feminization in men or hyperandrogenism in women.

Management of an adrenal incidentaloma depends on its size, potential malignancy, and functional status (see Figure 10). All functioning tumors and those larger than 6 cm in diameter should be considered for surgical removal. Patients with nonfunctioning tumors smaller than 4 cm are often followed; tumors measuring 4 to 6 cm can be either surgically removed or clinically observed, depending on the presence or absence of other suspicious clinical and radiographic features. A follow-up CT scan should be obtained in 6 to 12 months for nonfunctioning masses. There is no consensus on how often the screening tests should be repeated (if at all), with some experts recommending repeat tests annually for 3 to 4 years.

Pheochromocytoma

Pheochromocytomas are relatively rare tumors composed of chromaffin cells derived from the neural crest that occur in 0.1% to 0.6% of persons with hypertension. Chromaffin cells can secrete biogenic amines (epinephrine, norepinephrine, and dopamine) and their metabolites. Most pheochromocytomas predominantly secrete norepinephrine, which results in sustained or episodic hypertension. An occasional tumor may secrete epinephrine and cause hypotension. Nearly 90% of pheochromocytomas arise in the adrenal medulla; 10% are extra-adrenal and occur along the sympathetic chain. Approximately 25% of pheochromocytomas are familial, 10% are asymptomatic, and 10% are malignant. Most familial pheochromocytomas are in multiple sites, are more likely to recur after surgery, and are associated with other benign or malignant tumors. Therefore, genetic testing should be considered in patients with a family history of pheochromocytoma, in patients with bilateral disease or an extra-adrenal location, and in younger persons with other tumors.

The clinical manifestations of pheochromocytomas are variable, with hypertension (episodic or sustained) observed in over 90% of patients. Other major symptoms include diaphoresis, pallor, palpitations, and headaches; the classic triad of sudden severe headache, diaphoresis, and palpitations is highly suggestive of pheochromocytoma. Other manifestations include hyperglycemia, weight loss, arrhythmias (atrial and ventricular fibrillation), and catecholamine-induced cardiomyopathy.

The diagnosis of pheochromocytoma relies on documenting excessive secretion of catecholamines and/or their metabolites. Resting and supine levels of combined plasma catecholamines (epinephrine and norepinephrine) obtained through an indwelling intravenous catheter are often clearly elevated (greater than 2000 ng/L [10,920

pmol/L]) in patients with pheochromocytoma. Lower levels are equivocal and require further biochemical confirmation, such as with a clonidine suppression test. The administration of clonidine (0.3 mg orally) will suppress plasma norepinephrine levels to less than 500 ng/L (2956 pmol/L) in persons whose plasma catecholamine levels are elevated for reasons other than pheochromocytoma. Milder elevations in plasma norepinephrine levels (600-1000 ng/L [3547-5911 pmol/L]) can be seen in many stressed persons and those with essential hypertension. Except for labetalol, antihypertensive drugs do not interfere with the assays used for fractionated catecholamine determination. Measurements of plasma levels of catecholamine metabolites (metanephrines and normetanephrines) are similarly sensitive and specific in screening patients for pheochromocytoma. Additional biochemical diagnostic tests include measurement of fractionated catecholamines and their metabolites (metanephrines, normetanephrines, and vanillylmandelic acid) in the urine. Although measurements of urinary excretion of vanillylmandelic acid are not highly sensitive (65%), they have a greater than 95% specificity when dietary sources of interference are eliminated. The use of β-blockers in patients suspected of having pheochromocytoma should be avoided until the patients receive adequate α-adrenergic blocker therapy because β-blockade will result in unopposed α-stimulation, which can further exacerbate the features of pheochromocytoma.

CT scans and MRIs should be obtained only after the diagnosis of pheochromocytoma is biochemically confirmed. Pheochromocytomas are often characteristically hyperintense on T2-weighted MRIs. Scintigraphic localization with iodine-131–metaiodobenzylguanidine (^{131}I-MIBG) is used when CT scans and MRIs are negative for pheochromocytoma; ^{131}I-MIBG can also help distinguish metastasis from malignant pheochromocytoma.

Laparoscopic surgical resection by an experienced surgeon is the most effective treatment for pheochromocytomas. Preoperative medical therapy should be instituted once the diagnosis is confirmed; what it should consist of is less clear, given the lack of controlled studies. In the past, most patients with pheochromocytoma were treated with a competitive α-adrenergic blocking agent (such as phenoxybenzamine) for several weeks before surgery at an initial dose of 10 mg twice daily, with upward titration of 80 mg/d every 2 to 3 days. However, phenoxybenzamine has long-lasting effects that contribute to the hypotension commonly observed during the first day after tumor removal. Recent data suggest that short-acting specific α-antagonists, such as prazosin (2-5 mg, three times daily), doxazosin (2-8 mg/d), or terazosin (2-5 mg/d), may be better preoperative choices. Besides these α-blocking drugs, blood pressure control can be achieved with the calcium channel blockers amlodipine or verapamil, as needed. Labetalol, a combined α- and β-blocking agent, can also be used, especially in patients with tachyarrhythmias. Treatment with α-blockers and calcium channel blockers should be titrated to maintain the systolic blood pressure near 150 mm Hg for more than 7 days before surgery. Normotensive patients with pheochromocytomas should also be treated with α-blockers because they often become hypertensive during surgery. A nitroprusside intravenous drip is used to control intraoperative hypertension. In the perioperative period, changes in blood pressure during tumor manipulation are possible, and volume expansion during and after tumor resection may be needed.

Additional therapy includes control of catecholamine-related symptoms with α-blockers and catecholamine synthesis inhibitors. Other therapeutic options for malignant pheochromocytomas include external irradiation or targeted radiotherapy using ^{131}I-MIBG. Systemic cytotoxic chemotherapy has also been used, although the response rates are usually low and short-lived.

The long-term prognosis after resection of a solitary, sporadic pheochromocytoma is excellent, but some patients may have persistent hypertension and up to 17% have tumor recurrence. All patients should be followed for at least 10 years for tumor recurrence, and those with extra-adrenal lesions or with familial disease should be followed indefinitely.

KEY POINTS

- Pheochromocytoma can be diagnosed by measuring the plasma level and urinary excretion of catecholamines or their metabolites.

- β-Blocker therapy should be avoided in patients suspected of having pheochromocytoma until they receive adequate α-adrenergic blocker therapy.

- Treatment of pheochromocytoma involves laparoscopic adrenalectomy after appropriate preparation with α-adrenergic blocking agents and reasonable control of blood pressure.

Primary Hyperaldosteronism

Primary hyperaldosteronism is characterized by excessive and autonomous aldosterone production by the adrenal zona glomerulosa independent of its physiologic regulator, the renin-angiotensin system. Diagnosed biochemically, primary hyperaldosteronism is associated with several pathologic entities, including solitary aldosterone-producing adrenal adenoma, bilateral adrenal hyperplasia (or idiopathic primary hyperaldosteronism), unilateral hyperplasia, and adrenal carcinoma. Most patients with primary hyperaldosteronism have either bilateral adrenal hyperplasia (50%-60%) or an aldosterone-secreting adenoma (40%-50%). Aldosterone acts on the distal convoluted tubule to reabsorb sodium, which causes excessive potassium and hydrogen ion secretion in the collecting duct. When aldosterone is secreted excessively, the expected outcome is hypertension, hypokalemia, and metabolic alkalosis. For these reasons, patients with hypertension should be screened for primary hyperaldosteronism, especially when the hypertension is difficult to control or associated with hypokalemia.

Screening of patients for primary hyperaldosteronism focuses on the physiologic changes (namely, suppressed renin activity) and thus involves the simultaneous measurements of the plasma aldosterone level and plasma renin activity. A ratio of plasma aldosterone (measured in ng/dL) to plasma renin activity (measured in ng/mL/h) of greater than 20 is highly suggestive of primary hyperaldosteronism, especially when the plasma aldosterone level is greater than 15 ng/dL (414 pmol/L). This ratio is particularly helpful in patients taking angiotensin-converting enzyme (ACE) inhibitors or angiotensin-II receptor blockers (ARBs), in whom plasma renin activity is expected to be generally high but plasma aldosterone levels are usually low. In a patient receiving an ACE inhibitor or an ARB, one would expect the plasma aldosterone level to be lower than 10 ng/dL (276 pmol/L) and the plasma renin activity to be greater than 3 ng/mL/h (3 µg/L/h) with an aldosterone-to-renin ratio of less than 5. Thus, in a patient receiving an ACE inhibitor or ARB, an aldosterone-to-renin ratio of 10 or more would be highly suggestive of hyperaldosteronism.

The screening tests can be performed on random blood samples, even in patients on antihypertensive medications (except the aldosterone receptor antagonists spironolactone and eplerenone). Confirmation of the biochemical diagnosis involves showing persistent elevation (poor suppressibility) of plasma aldosterone in response to a high salt load. Salt can be given orally (sodium chloride, 2 g three times daily for 3 days) or intravenously (with normal saline, 500 mL/h for 3 hours). During either method of salt loading, plasma aldosterone levels are suppressed to less than 5 ng/dL (138 pmol/L) in normal subjects but remain elevated (often greater than 10 ng/dL [276 pmol/L]) in patients with primary hyperaldosteronism. Because an increased salt intake promotes kaliuresis, serum potassium levels should be monitored and adequately replaced during salt loading.

After a biochemical diagnosis of primary hyperaldosteronism is confirmed, further studies are appropriate to help define the pathologic cause. The simplest is CT of the adrenal glands. A solitary adrenal adenoma, often 2 cm or less in diameter, can be visualized on a CT scan. Notably, the other adrenal gland would appear normal. In contrast, the CT scan of a patient with bilateral adrenal hyperplasia would show diffuse or focal enlargement of all limbs of the two adrenal glands. Requesting expert consultation is recommended in unusual or nonclassic cases. Distinguishing between a single adenoma and bilateral hyperplasia is essential because it will substantially affect therapy. However, imaging studies are not always accurate in defining the cause of hyperaldosteronism. A more definitive approach is to catheterize both adrenal veins and measure the plasma aldosterone levels from both sides to determine if aldosterone production is unilateral or bilateral. Given this procedure's technical difficulty and association with adverse events, such as adrenal vein dissection and hemorrhage, it should be used selectively and only at centers with appropriate expertise.

Aldosterone-producing adrenal carcinoma is very rare, tends to be larger in size and have irregular contours (in contrast to adrenal adenomas), and is often associated with increased production of other adrenal corticosteroids. Other rare causes of excessive corticosteroid secretion can mimic the metabolic and clinical manifestations of primary hyperaldosteronism. Some examples include corticosteroid-remediable hypertension and congenital adrenal hyperplasia. Patients with these conditions are often young and have a family history of similar abnormalities at presentation.

Therapeutic goals for primary hyperaldosteronism include normalization of blood pressure, resolution of hypokalemia, and attainment of normal aldosterone levels and effects. The last goal is essential because aldosterone can have adverse effects over and above its influence on blood pressure and potassium level. Although laparoscopic surgical resection of a solitary aldosterone-secreting adrenal adenoma is recommended in most patients, medical therapy can be an effective alternative approach when it includes aldosterone receptor blockers (discussed subsequently). After removal of the aldosterone-producing adrenal adenoma, potassium levels become normal in over 90% of patients, blood pressure normalizes in two thirds of patients, and blood pressure control improves in the remaining third.

The treatment of choice for primary hyperaldosteronism caused by bilateral adrenal hyperplasia is medical therapy with spironolactone or eplerenone, the two available aldosterone antagonists. These medications also are given to medically treated patients with aldosterone-secreting adenomas. Spironolactone is often effective in controlling hypertension and hypokalemia. In addition to being an aldosterone-receptor blocker, spironolactone also blocks the androgen receptor, thus causing gynecomastia, impotence, and diminished libido in men and menstrual irregularities in women. Eplerenone is a more selective aldosterone-receptor blocker and has fewer adverse effects but is more expensive than spironolactone. Most medically treated patients with adrenal adenomas and bilateral adrenal hyperplasia will also require another antihypertensive drug (or drugs), with thiazide diuretics (such as hydrochlorothiazide, 12.5-25 mg/d) being the most effective. Patients should be followed indefinitely for monitoring of blood pressure, renal function, and potassium levels.

KEY POINTS

- An aldosterone-to-renin ratio greater than 20 is highly suggestive of primary hyperaldosteronism.

- Confirmation of biochemically established hyperaldosteronism requires documentation of nonsuppressibilty of elevated aldosterone secretion after high salt (oral or intravenous) intake.

- Primary hyperaldosteronism caused by a solitary aldosterone-secreting adenoma is best treated surgically; bilateral adrenal hyperplasia is best managed medically with an aldosterone-receptor blocking agent.

Adrenocortical Carcinoma

Adrenocortical carcinoma is a rare malignancy in which up to 60% of patients have symptoms of hormone (such as cortisol) excess. Other patients may have mechanical symptoms (abdominal fullness, nausea, back pain) related to rapid tumor growth, and a few have an incidentally discovered mass on presentation. Thus, depending on the patient's clinical presentation, the diagnostic approach can vary, but definitive diagnosis requires integration of the clinical, biochemical, and imaging data discussed earlier. Most functioning adrenocortical carcinomas produce multiple corticosteroids, including biologically inactive precursors.

The treatment of adrenocortical carcinoma depends on the extent of disease at presentation. Surgical removal after appropriate endocrine and imaging assessment remains the best option, especially in patients with early disease. Even after apparently complete resection, adjuvant therapy using mitotane, a known adrenal cytotoxic drug, can be beneficial. Treatment with mitotane is recommended for patients with persistent disease and others with known metastases. This treatment is associated with objective remissions in approximately 25% of patients. The main limiting factor for mitotane use is its associated adverse effects, including nausea, vomiting, lethargy, and other neurologic symptoms. Experience with chemotherapy is limited, but this treatment is usually ineffective.

KEY POINTS

- The typical manifestations of adrenocortical carcinoma include clinical evidence of increased hormone secretion (such as cortisol) or mechanical symptoms caused by a rapidly growing mass.

- Surgical resection is the best therapeutic option for adrenocortical carcinomas and is best followed by use of mitotane.

Bibliography

Allolio B, Fassnacht M. Clinical review: Adrenocortical carcinoma: clinical update. J Clin Endocrinol Metab. 2006;91(6):2027-2037. [PMID: 16551738]

Arafah BM. Hypothalamic pituitary adrenal function during critical illness: limitations of current assessment methods. J Clin Endocrinol Metab. 2006;91(10):3725-3745. [PMID: 16882746]

Bornstein SR. Predisposing factors for adrenal insufficiency. N Engl J Med. 2009;360(22):2328-2339. [PMID: 19474430]

Findling JW, Raff H. Cushing's syndrome: important issues in diagnosis and management. J Clin Endocrinol Metab. 2006;91(10):3746-3753. [PMID: 1686805]

Grumbach MM, Biller BM, Braunstein GD, et al. Management of the clinically inapparent adrenal mass ("incidentaloma"). Ann Intern Med. 2003;138(5):424-429. [PMID: 12614096]

Lenders JW Eisenhofer G, Mannelli M, Pacak K. Phaeochromocytoma. Lancet. 2005;366(9486):665-675. [PMID: 16112304]

Oelkers W. Adrenal insufficiency. N Engl J Med. 1996;33(16):1206-1212. [PMID: 8815944]

Sprung C, Annane D, Keh D, et al; CORTICUS Study Group. Hydrocortisone therapy for patients with septic shock. N Engl J Med. 2008;358(2):111-124. [PMID: 18184957]

Young WF. Primary aldosteronism: renaissance of a syndrome. Clin Endocrinol (Oxf). 2007;66(5):607-618. [PMID: 17492946]

Young WF Jr. Clinical practice. The incidentally discovered adrenal mass. N Engl J Med. 2007;356(6):601-610. [PMID: 17287480]

Reproductive Disorders

Basic Concepts and Common Features

Despite their respective purposes of spermatogenesis and ovulation, the male and female reproductive axes share many features. The pulsatile release of gonadotropin-releasing hormone (GnRH) from the supraoptic nucleus of the hypothalamus every 90 to 120 minutes elicits the secretion of luteinizing hormone (LH) and follicle-stimulating hormone (FSH) from the pituitary gonadotropes. LH drives steroidogenesis from the androgen-producing cells of the testis and ovary, and FSH aids in the maturation and release of sperm and oocytes. Both androgens and estrogens exert feedback inhibition on GnRH and gonadotropin production, but FSH secretion is regulated primarily by inhibin B, a product of Sertoli and granulosa cells, which are the targets of FSH action.

Physiology of Male Reproduction

Introduction

The two main products of the adult testis are testosterone and mature sperm. Every LH pulse elicits a corresponding pulse of testosterone by the Leydig cells, although changes in circulating testosterone levels are dampened by testosterone binding to plasma proteins, primarily sex hormone–binding globulin (SHBG) and albumin. Testosterone is also metabolized to dihydrotestosterone in some target tissues, such as the prostate and genital skin fibroblasts, and some testosterone is converted to estradiol in the Leydig cell itself and in peripheral tissues, such as fat. Exogenous estrogens, progestins, and androgens all decrease gonadotropin

secretion by suppressing GnRH and LH pulsations, which then reduces testosterone synthesis by Leydig cells; spermatogenesis is also impaired.

The seminiferous tubules account for approximately 80% of the testicular mass, and germ cells form the bulk of the seminiferous epithelium. The much larger Sertoli cells are closely associated with the developing germ cells and are essential for sperm maturation. Although an inability to synthesize testosterone often causes oligo- or azospermia, poor spermatogenesis can occur despite normal testosterone production. FSH acts on Sertoli cells, which in turn aid in sperm maturation; Sertoli cells secrete inhibin B, which feeds back to attenuate FSH production. For this reason, an elevated serum FSH level is indicative of Sertoli cell dysfunction, primary testicular damage, and low sperm production. The male reproductive axis is depicted in **Figure 11**.

Only 1% to 3% of testosterone in the circulation is free, whereas approximately 60% is bound to SHBG and the remainder to albumin. Testosterone binds tightly to SHBG and is in slow equilibrium with the free fraction. SHBG-bound testosterone dampens the fluctuations in testosterone concentrations that may result from the pulsatile secretion of testosterone from the testis. In contrast, testosterone binds to albumin weakly and dissociates readily, forming a rapid equilibrium with free testosterone. The free and albumin-bound portions of testosterone are collectively known as bioavailable testosterone. The bioavailable testosterone and free

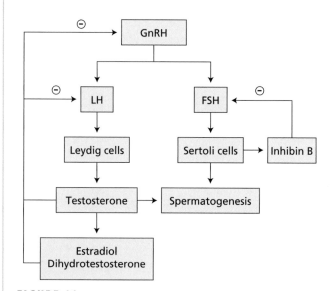

FIGURE 11.
Male reproductive axis.
Pulses of GnRH elicit pulses of LH and FSH. FSH acts on Sertoli cells, which assist sperm maturation and make inhibin B, the major negative regulator of basal FSH production. The Leydig cells make testosterone, which feeds back to inhibit GnRH and LH release. Some testosterone is irreversibly converted to dihydrotestosterone or estradiol, which are both more potent than testosterone in suppressing GnRH, LH, and FSH.

FSH = follicle-stimulating hormone; GnRH = gonadotropin-releasing hormone; LH = luteinizing hormone; ⊖ = negative feedback.

testosterone levels vary in parallel, except at the extremes of SHBG levels. Borderline-low values for total serum testosterone (200-350 ng/dL [6.94-12.15 nmol/L]) should therefore be further evaluated with measurement of the free or bioavailable testosterone level, particularly in elderly men (in whom the SHBG level is increased) and obese men (in whom the SHBG level is decreased).

Primary Hypogonadism

The etiologic categories of primary hypogonadism are chromosomal/congenital, toxic/traumatic, and infiltrative. Overt primary hypogonadism almost always causes infertility. Although unilateral or even bilateral cryptorchidism usually does not prevent pubertal development and fertility, cryptorchidism may be associated with a premature decline in testosterone production later in life. Primary hypogonadism is usually caused by congenital or genetic disorders, such as Klinefelter syndrome (46,XXY karyotype). Acquired primary hypogonadism, which is uncommon in men, most often results from toxic exposures, such as to the alkylating agents used in cancer chemotherapy.

Secondary Hypogonadism

Acquired hypogonadism is usually secondary to hypothalamic and/or pituitary dysfunction in men. However, pinpointing the site(s) of dysfunction is difficult, and the etiology is often multifactorial. Because hypogonadism may be the initial sign of a pituitary tumor or systemic disease, careful evaluation is essential, especially in younger men. Secondary hypogonadism generally prompts a broader assessment of pituitary function, particularly measurement of prolactin, which suppresses gonadotropins directly and may indicate the presence of a pituitary tumor (see Disorders of the Pituitary Gland). Causes of secondary hypogonadism include pituitary (or adjacent) tumors (the most common cause), congenital/genetic disorders, infiltrative disorders, and traumatic/iatrogenic disorders. Certain drugs (such as corticosteroids and narcotic agents), chronic illness, malnutrition, obesity, and aging also contribute to hypogonadism, primarily by acting on the central components of the male reproductive axis.

Androgen Deficiency in the Aging Male Syndrome

Testosterone production begins to decline at a rate of approximately 1% per year after age 25 years. GnRH and LH pulse frequency and amplitude decline with age, and less testosterone is produced after each pulse of LH. In addition, the free testosterone level tends to decline even further because of the increased peripheral conversion of androgens to estrogens and the higher circulating SHBG concentrations. These insults, which affect all levels of the male reproductive axis, are further exacerbated by intercurrent illnesses and medications, which can decrease circulating testosterone concentrations to abnormally low values. Collectively, these features are known as the androgen deficiency in the aging male (ADAM) syndrome. Spermatogenesis in ADAM syndrome is typically normal or slightly reduced, but the testosterone deficiency can cause symptoms and quantifiable consequences, such as osteoporosis and cognitive decline.

Classic symptoms of androgen deficiency (and male hypogonadism) at any age include fatigue, loss of muscular strength, poor libido, hot flushes, and sexual dysfunction, but none of these may be the presenting symptom. In older men who report a vague and gradual deterioration in their sense of well-being, particularly those who also have depression or cognitive disturbances, screening for hypogonadism should be considered. Although mild erectile dysfunction or, more specifically, poor libido often accompanies hypogonadism, severe erectile dysfunction typically derives from coexisting vascular, neurologic, or cavernosal conditions, and testosterone replacement therapy alone rarely restores normal sexual function when erectile dysfunction is severe.

Diagnosis and Workup of Male Hypogonadism

Because the symptoms of male hypogonadism are highly variable and often nonspecific, the diagnosis requires laboratory confirmation. The best screening test for male hypogonadism is measurement of the total serum testosterone level no later than 10:00 AM; an assay of three pooled specimens drawn at 20- to 30-minute intervals (pooled morning testosterone) is preferable. A random serum testosterone level greater than 350 ng/dL (12.15 nmol/L) excludes hypogonadism. Values consistently less than 200 ng/dL (6.94 nmol/L) almost always confirm hypogonadism, but values in the 200 to 350 ng/dL (6.94-12.15 nmol/L) range are equivocal. Unless the total testosterone level is markedly reduced and the patient has a known pituitary or gonadal pathologic abnormality, a screening testosterone value of 350 ng/dL (12.15 nmol/L) or lower requires confirmation by a second measurement that includes determination of the free and/or bioavailable testosterone level.

Immunoassays performed after testosterone extraction and chromatography and assays using liquid chromatography coupled with tandem mass spectrometry are the most reliable methods, with direct immunoassays on serum being less accurate, particularly at the low end of the normal range of male testosterone levels, where accuracy is most critical. In this situation, measuring free and bioavailable testosterone levels is necessary. The free testosterone level can be measured by equilibrium dialysis or by calculation after measuring the total serum testosterone, SHBG, and albumin levels. A direct assay kit for measuring free testosterone is available but is notoriously unreliable, and its use is strongly discouraged.

During or after confirmatory testing, serum levels of gonadotropins and prolactin should be measured before starting treatment. The FSH level, which reflects Sertoli cell function and sperm production, may be omitted if fertility is not desired or in the evaluation of ADAM syndrome. Typically, findings of a normal prolactin and inappropriately normal LH levels associated with a low testosterone level in men older than 60 years are consistent with ADAM syndrome, and further evaluation of other pituitary hormones and pituitary imaging are not necessary. Further assessment of pituitary anatomy and function should be considered in younger men and in older men with a testosterone level less than 150 ng/dL (5.21 nmol/L). A high prolactin level suggests pituitary disease and necessitates an MRI of the sella turcica with further pituitary and thyroid testing. A very low serum LH level (<0.5 mU/mL [0.5 U/L]), particularly if the serum prolactin level is high, also suggests pituitary disease. A low LH level and a normal or low prolactin level with otherwise normal anterior pituitary function is commonly seen in patients taking exogenous androgens, estrogens, progestins, or narcotics but also can be seen in hemochromatosis or congenital disorders of GnRH production (such as Kallman syndrome). Primary testicular failure is suggested by a high serum FSH level (>15 mU/mL [15 U/L]) and is confirmed by an inhibin B level of less than 100 pg/mL (normal, >150 pg/mL). Semen analysis is reserved for patients being evaluated for current or future fertility. **Figure 12** provides a diagnostic algorithm for male hypogonadism.

KEY POINTS

- A morning measurement of total serum testosterone level is the screening test of choice for male hypogonadism.
- Patients with moderately low (200-350 ng/dL [6.94-12.15 nmol/L]) total serum testosterone levels should have their free or bioavailable testosterone level determined.

Testosterone Replacement Therapy

The benefits of testosterone replacement therapy in men with hypogonadism include an increased libido, increased bone density, improved cognitive function and sense of well-being, and an increased hematocrit; such therapy is thus appropriate for men with unequivocal hypogonadism. In one study, an inverse correlation between the magnitude of benefit in elderly men and the pretreatment total serum testosterone level (in the 100-350 ng/dL [3.47-12.15 nmol/L] range) was shown, but no improvement occurred when the testosterone level was greater than 350 ng/dL (12.15 nmol/L). Infertility, on the other hand, is not treated with testosterone replacement therapy but with injectable gonadotropins because testosterone replacement suppresses LH and FSH production, reduces testosterone production by Leydig cells, and impairs spermatogenesis.

Preparations of testosterone esters (enanthate or cypionate) in oil are administered every 1 to 3 weeks by deep intramuscular injection. A regimen of 200 mg every 2 weeks is most commonly employed to balance convenience with serum testosterone fluctuations, but more stable serum testosterone levels are maintained by using 100 mg every week. The dosage is titrated to maintain the trough serum testosterone level near the low end of the normal range before the next injection.

The first transcutaneous testosterone preparations marketed were the testosterone patches; availability is now limited to 2.5- and 5-mg patches. The normal starting dose for adults is one 5-mg patch at bedtime; the 2.5-mg patch is for smaller men, young adults, and prepubertal adolescents. Therapy is best monitored by measuring the serum testosterone level in the early morning to detect the increase in testosterone level, but the peak may occur during the night. Dosage adjustments are limited to up to two patches of the available sizes. The most common adverse effect of skin irritation can be minimized by smearing a small drop of 0.1% triamcinolone cream on the drug reservoir in the center of the patch before application and by not placing the patch on pressure points, such as the shoulder blades and hips.

Hydroalcoholic testosterone gels are the most popular preparations. The starting dose is one 5-g packet or tube of 1% gel applied once daily to specified areas (either the trunk and shoulders or the abdomen). After a few weeks, a steady state is reached in which testosterone is delivered to the circulation from an intradermal storage pool with essentially zero-order kinetics, and the applied dose replaces the portion delivered to the blood. Consequently, serum levels of circulating testosterone remain fairly constant throughout the day; the dosage can be monitored at any time by sampling the serum testosterone level. Skin irritation is rare, but showering and swimming for several hours after application must be avoided to allow complete absorption of the testosterone dose. Transference to partners and children through contact can occur, necessitating handwashing and contact precautions. The

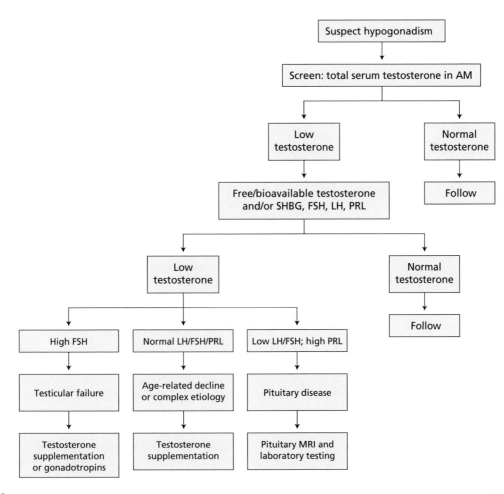

FIGURE 12.
Algorithm for evaluating male hypogonadism.
The best screening test for male hypogonadism is an early morning measurement of the total testosterone level. If the level is low or equivocal, a second measurement, which includes free and bioavailable testosterone levels and/or the SHBG level, will resolve the diagnosis. PRL, LH, and FSH levels also are measured to determine the type of hypogonadal state and to guide further evaluation and treatment.

FSH = follicle-stimulating hormone; LH = luteinizing hormone; PRL = prolactin; SHBG = sex hormone–binding globulin.

dosage may be increased by up to 10 g/d if needed on the basis of measured testosterone levels; higher dosages are costly and difficult to apply properly.

The buccal system involves a lozenge containing testosterone (30 g) in a mucoadhesive matrix that is applied between the cheek and gums of the upper teeth. The testosterone is delivered through the gingival mucosa into the superior vena cava, which bypasses first-pass hepatic metabolism. The system is applied daily in the morning and evening, with testosterone levels peaking toward the end of a 12-hour application. The dose is not titrated, but the serum testosterone level may be monitored, preferably towards the end of the 12-hour application. Some men cannot use the system comfortably because of gum irritation or bitter taste.

Testosterone replacement therapy also can be used in patients with hypogonadism caused by prolactinomas. Correction of the hyperprolactinemia often reestablishes pulsatile GnRH secretion and thus testosterone production, but

those with undetectable FSH and LH levels and very low serum testosterone levels despite dopamine agonist treatment should be considered for testosterone replacement therapy.

Recommendations for periodic monitoring of testosterone replacement therapy appear in **Table 26**. Because testosterone replacement therapy can exacerbate polycythemia, prostatic hyperplasia, dyslipidemia, and sleep apnea, patients with those disorders should be counseled and closely reassessed. Men with dyslipidemia, particularly a low HDL-cholesterol level, should have another lipid profile after several months of testosterone replacement therapy. Although no evidence suggests that testosterone replacement therapy causes prostate cancer, such therapy can enable the growth of occult prostate cancer. Active prostate cancer is an absolute contraindication to testosterone replacement therapy. The prostate-specific antigen level is often low (<1 ng/mL [1 µg/L]) in men with hypogonadism but often doubles and then stabilizes after 3 to 6 months of testosterone replacement

---

TABLE 26 Monitoring of Testosterone Replacement Therapy

For adequacy and efficacy, serum total testosterone measurement using:

Injectable esters: trough prior to fourth injection (goal is low end of normal range)

Androderm™ patch: morning testosterone level 4-6 weeks after initiating therapy

Androgel™/Testim™ gel: random testosterone level 4-6 weeks after initiating therapy

Striant™ buccal system: testosterone level 1 week after initiating therapy; obtain just before applying a new buccal lozenge

For potential untoward events:

Relative contraindications of testosterone replacement therapy include obstructive uropathy, cirrhosis, and sleep apnea; absolute contraindication is prostate cancer

Digital screening prostate examination, determination of PSA level and hemoglobin or hematocrit before treatment

Hemoglobin or hematocrit; PSA level 3, 6, and 12 months after start of therapy, then annually (expect PSA level to increase <50% to <2 ng/mL [2 µg/L] and PSA velocity <0.75/year)

Monitor serum lipid levels if initially abnormal

PSA = prostate-specific antigen.

---

therapy. If the PSA increases by more than a factor of two (to a value >4 ng/mL [4 µg/L]) or continues to increase after 6 to 12 months of treatment, testosterone therapy should be interrupted until a urologic evaluation is completed.

KEY POINT

- Currently available testosterone replacement systems include injections, patches, gels, and buccal mucosa lozenges.

Male Anabolic Steroid Abuse

Although androgen abuse is found in persons of all ages, professions, and socioeconomic levels, the use of performance-enhancing substances, especially anabolic steroids (androgens) and growth hormone, is particularly pervasive today in professional and elite sports. The self-administration of androgens is also common in recreational bodybuilders and persons who want to improve their physique. Androgens, which are inexpensive and easy to obtain, are unequivocally effective agents in promoting weight gain and strength, particularly when used in combination with enhanced nutrition and training regimens. Adolescent and young adult males have the highest prevalence of androgen abuse.

A particular psyche known as muscle dysmorphia or reverse anorexia nervosa predisposes to chronic androgen abuse and addiction. Persons with this condition perceive themselves as being small when they are muscular and hold unrealistic goals about size and strength. Because self-administered androgens advance them toward these

unachievable goals and because they lose strength, size, and vigor on androgen withdrawal, such persons are vulnerable to psychological and physical addictions to androgens. Androgen withdrawal places such persons in a functionally hypogonadal state lasting months to years, depending on prior use, which may be accompanied by depression, lassitude, emotional lability, and hot flushes.

When persons who abuse androgens seek medical attention, it is usually at the insistence of a spouse or partner because of infertility. Physical examination typically shows irritability, tangential or evasive speech, muscular hypertrophy, testicular atrophy, gynecomastia (if abusing testosterone), and acne, including the pustular type, particularly on the back. The gynecomastia is often self-managed with tamoxifen and aromatase inhibitors and the acne with tretinoin. Laboratory data show suppressed LH and FSH levels, variable testosterone levels (depending on whether testosterone or synthetic androgens only are being used), and otherwise normal pituitary function. The thyroid-stimulating hormone and free thyroxine levels are low if liothyronine (T$_3$) is being self-administered, and the insulin-like growth factor 1 level can be elevated if growth hormone is being self-administered; both are common practices in patients abusing androgens. Few of these patients are willing to abstain from androgens voluntarily or to adhere to prescribed regimens.

Male Infertility

The evaluation of an infertile couple should involve both partners because up to half of infertility cases involve a male-related problem. Fertility induction requires both Leydig cell testosterone production and gonadotropin action on Sertoli cells. The cornerstone of the male infertility examination is analysis of semen, which should be obtained after 48 to 72 hours of sexual abstinence and analyzed immediately by a qualified laboratory. The parameters monitored in the semen analysis and their significance are shown in **Table 27**.

In secondary hypogonadism, fertility may be restored with injectable gonadotropins or, in the specific case of hypothalamic hypogonadism, with pulsatile GnRH delivered by a programmable infusion pump. Human chorionic gonadotropin (HCG), 1000 to 5000 units two to three times per week, is generally used because of its lower cost and longer duration of action than LH. Recombinant FSH is added to the HCG treatment, particularly when the hypogonadism is severe or spontaneous puberty did not occur, but HCG alone often restores fertility in previously fertile men with acquired secondary hypogonadism, particularly if incomplete or of recent onset.

KEY POINT

- The cornerstone of the male infertility examination is analysis of semen, which should be obtained after 48 to 72 hours of sexual abstinence and analyzed immediately by a qualified laboratory.

TABLE 27 Semen Analysis Parameters

Parameter	Normal Range	Significance
Volume	>2 mL	Low with ductal obstruction, retrograde ejaculation, and lack of abstinence
pH	8-9	Low with ductal obstruction
Fructose	Positive	Negative with ductal obstruction
Sperm count	2-10 million/mL	Correlates with other parameters
Motility	>50%	Decreased by toxins, sperm pathology
Sperm morphology	>14% normal forms	Prognostic for fertility

Female Reproductive Physiology

In females, GnRH pulses also drive secretion of LH and FSH. LH acts on the androgen-producing theca cells to stimulate androstenedione and testosterone synthesis, and FSH acts on the granulosa cells to stimulate expression of aromatase, which converts androstenedione and testosterone to estradiol and triggers ovulation. Inhibin B from granulosa cells exerts feedback inhibition on FSH secretion (**Figure 13**). The granulosa cells undergo a process called luteinization after ovulation, forming a corpus luteum that produces progesterone. Progesterone withdrawal follows 2 weeks later and leads to menstrual bleeding unless fertilization and implantation occur. The parallels of the male and female reproductive axes include the action of LH on androgen synthesis, the action of FSH on the supporting cells for the developing gametes, the reciprocal feedback, and the dampening with stress and aging. The female axis features a more complex pattern, with both negative and positive feedback, a monthly cycle with an ovulatory gonadotropin surge yielding one or a few mature germ cells, and more abrupt and consistent age-related decline.

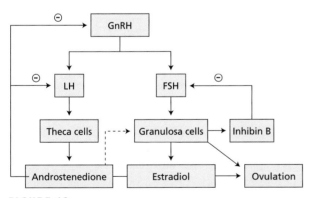

FIGURE 13.
Female reproductive axis.
As in the male reproductive axis, pulses of GnRH drive LH and FSH production. LH acts on theca cells to stimulate androgen (principally androstenedione) production. Androstenedione is metabolized to estradiol in granulosa cells. FSH also acts on granulosa cells to enhance follicle maturation. Granulosa cells produce inhibin B as a feedback regulator of FSH production.

FSH = follicle-stimulating hormone; GnRH = gonadotropin-releasing hormone; LH = luteinizing hormone; ⊖ = negative feedback.

Primary Amenorrhea

By definition, primary amenorrhea is the absence of spontaneous menses by age 16 or age 14 in the absence of secondary sexual characteristics. After pregnancy is excluded, possible causes fall into four categories: (1) anatomic defects, (2) ovarian failure, (3) chronic anovulation with a normal estrogen level, and (4) chronic anovulation with a low estrogen level. The most common causes of primary amenorrhea include ovarian failure due to Turner syndrome, müllerian duct agenesis, congenital hypopituitarism, anorexia nervosa (or other causes of a low BMI), and systemic illnesses. Primary amenorrhea always requires a thorough evaluation by a gynecologist and/or endocrinologist.

Secondary and Hypothalamic Amenorrhea

By definition, secondary amenorrhea is the absence of menses for 3 or more consecutive months in a woman who previously has menstruated. Oligomenorrhea (irregular and infrequent menses) is much more common than complete amenorrhea, but the diagnostic considerations are similar, and the same four diagnostic categories of primary amenorrhea apply. The incidence of an underlying pathologic process in women with amenorrhea after the use of cyclic oral contraceptive regimens is the same as in women with spontaneous amenorrhea. Therefore, women who do not resume their menstrual cycle after discontinuing an oral contraceptive should be evaluated just as women with spontaneous amenorrhea.

Excluding pregnancy, polycystic ovary syndrome (PCOS), a form of chronic anovulation with normal estrogen levels, is the most common cause of secondary amenorrhea. Asherman syndrome due to endometrial scarring should be considered as the cause in any woman who previously had dilation and curettage or a uterine infection. Hyperprolactinemia causes chronic anovulation with normal or low estrogen levels. Premature ovarian failure may be caused by mosaic Turner syndrome or autoimmune oophoritis. Hypothalamic amenorrhea may be caused by a tumor or infiltrative lesion (such as lymphoma or sarcoidosis). More commonly, hypothalamic amenorrhea is functional and due to stress, excessive loss of body weight, excessive exercise, or some combination thereof and is a diagnosis of exclusion. The effects of prior chemotherapy or radiation therapy should be considered in cancer survivors.

- After pregnancy is excluded, polycystic ovary syndrome is the most common cause of secondary amenorrhea.

Diagnosis and Workup of Amenorrhea

The female reproductive axis is particularly vulnerable to disruption by systemic illnesses and weight loss. Therefore, obtaining a good general history and performing a thorough physical examination are essential for diagnosis. In primary amenorrhea, the absence of secondary sexual characteristics and the finding of masculinization are both features that can guide further evaluation. A pregnancy test is customary, although women with primary amenorrhea and no secondary sexual characteristics are unlikely to be pregnant.

To screen for ovarian failure and other common endocrinologic causes of amenorrhea, initial laboratory studies should include measurement of FSH, prolactin, thyroid-stimulating hormone, and free thyroxine levels. Serum FSH values greater than 35 mU/mL (35 U/L) are consistent with ovarian failure, and values of 20 to 35 mU/mL (20-35 U/L) suggest low ovarian reserve. In women younger than 30 years with primary amenorrhea, a karyotype (using blood or skin fibroblasts) should be obtained to exclude Turner variants, even in the absence of classic stigmata. Hyperprolactinemia requires further pituitary testing and imaging; referral to an endocrinologist is recommended.

If the screening laboratory studies do not reveal a diagnosis, the cornerstone of further evaluation is a progestin withdrawal challenge with medroxyprogesterone acetate, 10 mg/d orally for 10 days, or micronized progesterone, 200 mg/d orally for 12 days. Menstruation with progestin withdrawal indicates normal estrogen production and a patent outflow tract, which categorizes the amenorrhea as chronic anovulation with a normal estrogen level. The absence of menses with progestin withdrawal indicates a low estrogen level and/or an anatomic defect. The pelvic anatomy, therefore, should be assessed with ultrasonography, MRI, or hysterosalpingography.

PCOS is by far the most common cause of secondary amenorrhea or oligomenorrhea. Other causes of chronic anovulation in patients with normal estrogen levels include hyperprolactinemia, Cushing syndrome, and mild (nonclassic) 21-hydroxylase deficiency, all of which are states of androgen excess. Because an ovarian ultrasound shows polycystic ovarian morphology in at least 25% of normal cycling women and does not distinguish primary from secondary PCOS, ultrasonography is not routinely recommended. A total serum testosterone level greater than 150 ng/dL (5.21 nmol/L) suggests an androgen-producing ovarian or adrenal tumor or other significant disorder and requires further evaluation and imaging.

- A high follicle-stimulating hormone level indicates ovarian failure in a patient with amenorrhea.
- Withdrawal bleeding after progestin challenge indicates normal estrogen production and a normal outflow tract, whereas the absence of bleeding indicates a low estrogen level and/or an anatomic defect.

Hirsutism and Polycystic Ovary Syndrome

Hirsutism is a common problem in young women and should be evaluated in the context of the patient's history and ethnic extraction. The history of a woman with hirsutism should ascertain the age of onset, rate of progression, presence of virilization (voice deepening, clitoral enlargement), and presence of other symptoms, such as galactorrhea, bruising, or myopathy. PCOS, the most common cause of hirsutism, normally starts during pubertal development, progresses slowly, and does not cause virilization or cushingoid features. A measurement of the total serum testosterone level is recommended to exclude androgen-producing tumors, Cushing syndrome, and occult 21-hydroxylase deficiency, particularly when the hirsutism involves sudden onset and rapid progression. Exogenous androgen use, including use of nutraceuticals (such as dehydroepiandrosterone), should be considered in the differential diagnosis of hirsutism.

The diagnosis of PCOS, according to the current Rotterdam criteria, requires two of the three following findings: ovulatory dysfunction, laboratory or clinical evidence of hyperandrogenism, and ultrasonographic evidence of polycystic ovaries. Additional diagnostic testing for Cushing syndrome, 21-hydroxylase deficiency, hyperprolactinemia, and other disorders is based on the history and physical examination findings. Because PCOS is associated with progression to diabetes mellitus and the metabolic syndrome, the measurement of fasting glucose and lipid levels also is appropriate in women with PCOS.

The management of hirsutism and PCOS varies according to the patient's symptoms and needs. If fertility is not desired, spironolactone plus an oral contraceptive pill containing a progestin with low androgenicity (desogestrel, norgestimate, gestodene, or drospirenone) is a good first-line combination therapy. Other androgen antagonists, such as flutamide, bicalutamide, and 5α-reductase inhibitors (finasteride, dutasteride), offer little advantage and are more costly. Metformin decreases the serum testosterone level and improves ovulation rates in women with PCOS, even in those with normal insulin sensitivity. Although metformin is effective and does not appear to be teratogenic, patients should be counseled that the treatment of PCOS with metformin is an off-label indication and that ovulation and pregnancy may occur. Given the favorable effect of metformin on lipid profiles and progression to diabetes in selected populations, chronic metformin therapy offers many advantages and should be considered, either alone or in combination with other agents, a first-line therapy when metabolic abnormalities are significant. All women require endometrial protection and withdrawal bleeding every 1 to 3 months at a minimum.

Clomiphene is superior to metformin for producing live births with oral therapy alone in women with PCOS who desire children, but infertility treatments such as clomiphene should be prescribed only by a reproductive endocrinologist, who may also recommend in vitro fertilization.

The transition to a coarse terminal hair is irreversible, and the effects of oral therapy on hirsutism will not be evident for at least 3 months. Antiandrogen therapy renders the hair shafts thinner and maintains follicles in the resting (telogen) state longer, which yields fewer and less conspicuous terminal hairs at any given time. Topical eflornithine cream can be useful for treating small problem areas of hirsutism. Mechanical methods, including plucking, shaving, waxing, electrolysis, and laser therapy, provide more rapid and, in some cases, permanent cosmetic effects without systemic exposure to drugs. Risks, benefits, and costs of various monotherapies and combination therapies for hirsutism must be weighed for each patient.

KEY POINTS

- The most common cause of hirsutism is polycystic ovary syndrome, which normally starts during puberty, progresses slowly, and does not cause virilization or cushingoid features.

- Measurement of the total serum testosterone level is recommended in patients with suspected polycystic ovary syndrome to exclude Cushing syndrome, androgen-producing tumors, and 21-hydroxylase deficiency.

Female Anabolic Steroid Abuse

Some women also abuse androgens for reasons similar to those of men but usually at lower doses for physique enhancement. In addition to breast atrophy, anovulation, hirsutism, and acne, the virilizing side effects of androgen abuse (voice deepening and enlargement of the clitoris) are particularly specific and often irreversible. Unlike men, women do not experience a physiologic hypogonadism on androgen withdrawal, but the psychological changes of withdrawal can be severe.

Bibliography

Bhasin S, Cunningham GR, Hayes FJ, et al. Testosterone therapy in adult men with androgen deficiency syndromes: an Endocrine Society clinical practice guideline [erratum in J Clin Endocrinol Metab. 2006;91(7):2688]. J Clin Endocrinol Metab. 2006;91(6):1995-2010. [PMID: 16720669]

Legro RS, Barnhart HX, Schlaff WD, et al; Cooperative Multicenter Reproductive Medicine Network. Clomiphene, metformin, or both for infertility in the polycystic ovary syndrome. N Engl J Med. 2007;356(6):551-566. [PMID: 17287476]

Nestler JE. Metformin for the treatment of the polycystic ovary syndrome. N Engl J Med. 2008;358(1):47-54. [PMID: 18172174]

Rosner W, Auchus RJ, Azziz R, Sluss PM, Raff H. Position statement: Utility, limitations, and pitfalls in measuring testosterone: an Endocrine Society position statement. J Clin Endocrinol Metab. 2007;92(2):405-413. [PMID: 17090633]

Calcium and Bone Disorders

Regulation of Calcium Metabolism

Maintenance of the body calcium stores depends on dietary calcium intake, absorption of calcium from the gastrointestinal tract, and regulation of renal calcium excretion. In a balanced diet, roughly 1000 mg/d of calcium is ingested. Depending on the concentration of circulating vitamin D, 200 to 400 mg of calcium is absorbed from the intestine each day, with the remainder appearing in the stool. Calcium balance is maintained through renal calcium excretion, which averages 200 mg/24 h (5 mmol/24h).

Normal total serum calcium levels range from 9.0 to 10.5 mg/dL (2.3 to 2.6 mmol/L). Despite its important intracellular roles, roughly 99% of body calcium exists in bone, mainly as hydroxyapatite crystals, and approximately 1% of bone calcium is freely exchangeable with the extracellular fluid, which makes it available for buffering changes in calcium balance. Approximately 40% of the total blood calcium is bound to plasma proteins, primarily albumin; the remaining 60% includes ionized calcium and calcium complexed with phosphate and citrate. The total calcium level is usually determined by clinical laboratory measurement. Ideally, the ionized or free calcium level also should be determined because it is the physiologically active form of calcium in serum. Given the technical difficulty involved, however, this measurement is usually restricted to patients in whom significant alteration of the protein binding of serum calcium is suspected (such as those with hypoalbuminemia). The ionized calcium level is generally assumed to be roughly 50% of the total serum calcium level.

Calcium metabolism and phosphorus metabolism are intimately related. The regulation of calcium and phosphorus balance within a narrow physiologic range occurs through the interactions of circulating parathyroid hormone (PTH), vitamin D, and, to a lesser extent, calcitonin. Calcium and inorganic phosphate concentrations chemically react to form calcium phosphate. The normal calcium × phosphate product is estimated to be 60 meq/L; when it exceeds 70 meq/L, precipitation of calcium phosphate crystals in soft tissue is likely. Precipitation in vascular tissue accelerates arteriosclerotic vascular disease.

PTH, secreted by the parathyroid glands, has several actions, the most important of which is to prevent hypocalcemia.

Parathyroid cells sense decreases in the level of serum ionized calcium via the calcium-sensing receptor, which lies in the cell membrane of parathyroid cells. Hypocalcemia leads to decreased binding of calcium to the calcium-sensing receptor, with resultant release of preformed PTH into the circulation. PTH increases the serum calcium level within minutes by increasing renal and intestinal absorption of calcium and by rapidly mobilizing calcium and phosphate from bone (bone resorption). PTH enhances distal tubular calcium reabsorption. PTH also decreases renal phosphate reabsorption and thus increases urine phosphate losses. Urine phosphate loss prevents the solubility product of calcium and phosphate from being exceeded in serum as calcium levels rise in response to PTH (**Figure 14**).

PTH also increases the serum calcium level by upregulation of the 1α-hydroxylase enzyme, which stimulates conversion of vitamin D to its most active form, 1,25-dihydroxy vitamin D; this form of vitamin D increases the percentage of dietary calcium absorbed by the intestine. Vitamin D_3 is derived from dietary sources and by skin exposure to ultraviolet light, which converts cholesterol precursors to vitamin D_3, which in turn is converted in the liver to 25-hydroxy vitamin D. This form, in turn, subsequently undergoes 1α-hydroxylation in the proximal renal tubular cells to become 1,25-dihydroxy vitamin D. Measurement of serum 25-hydroxy vitamin D is the best indicator of total vitamin D body stores because of its long half-life.

Long-term increases in PTH secretion generally result in bone resorption by inhibiting osteoblast function and promoting osteoclast activity. PTH and 1,25-dihydroxy vitamin D both function as important regulators of bone growth and bone remodeling. Testing of parathyroid function includes measuring circulating intact PTH levels by radioimmunoassay.

Calcitonin is secreted by the thyroid parafollicular C cells. The effect of calcitonin on bone metabolism is weak and is clinically significant only in pharmacologic amounts.

KEY POINTS

- Calcium and phosphorus balance is maintained within a narrow physiologic range through the interactions of parathyroid hormone, vitamin D, and, to a lesser extent, calcitonin.
- Measurement of serum levels of 25-hydroxy vitamin D_3 provides the best indicator of total body vitamin D stores.

Hypercalcemia

Hypercalcemia occurs when calcium influx from the gastrointestinal tract and bone overwhelms the ability of the kidneys to excrete calcium.

Clinical Manifestations of Hypercalcemia

Signs and symptoms of hypercalcemia relate both to the degree of serum calcium elevation and to the rapidity of the increase. Mild hypercalcemia (serum calcium level <11.5 mg/dL [2.88 mmol/L]) usually results in few symptoms. Polyuria and polydipsia can occur because of decreased renal concentrating capacity (nephrogenic diabetes insipidus). Dyspepsia can be caused by a calcium-mediated elevation in gastrin secretion that increases gastric acid production. Vague symptoms of depression or mild cognitive impairment also can be present. Symptoms become more obvious when hypercalcemia is moderate (serum calcium level of 11.5 to 14 mg/dL [2.88 to 3.5 mmol/L]) and include anorexia, nausea, apathy, fatigue, muscle weakness, and constipation. Severe hypercalcemia (serum calcium level >14 mg/dL [3.5 mmol/L]) is associated with further progression of the symptoms of moderate disease but also dehydration, abdominal pain, vomiting, lethargy, obtundation, and coma.

Pancreatitis can be a clinical manifestation of hypercalcemia. Depending on its severity and chronicity, hypercalcemia due to hyperparathyroidism can lead to osteopenia, osteoporosis, nephrolithiasis, nephrocalcinosis, azotemia, and soft-tissue calcification (such as chondrocalcinosis and band keratopathy). Dyspepsia and hypertension also occur in patients with hyperparathyroidism. An electrocardiogram may show a shortened QT interval.

Causes of Hypercalcemia

Hypercalcemia is encountered in both inpatient and outpatient settings. The measurement of the serum PTH level plays a vital role in its evaluation. When PTH levels are high or, in some instances, inappropriately normal, the hypercalcemia is said to be PTH mediated.

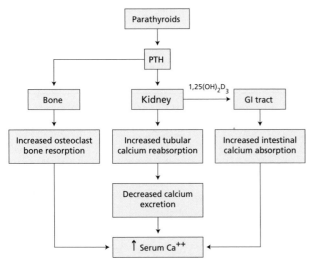

FIGURE 14.
Overview of the metabolic systems maintaining calcium homeostasis.

Ca++ = ionized calcium; GI = gastrointestinal; 1,25(OH)$_2$D$_3$ = 1,25-dihydroxy vitamin D; PTH = parathyroid hormone; ↑ = increased.

Parathyroid Hormone–Mediated Hypercalcemia

PTH-mediated hypercalcemia is referred to as hyperparathyroidism. Primary hyperparathyroidism is the most common form of hypercalcemia in nonhospitalized patients. The peak incidence of hyperparathyroidism is in the fifth and sixth decades of life, with a female to male ratio of 3:2. The most common clinical presentation is asymptomatic mild hypercalcemia.

Secondary hyperparathyroidism occurs when decreased circulating serum calcium levels stimulate secondarily increased secretion of PTH. This commonly occurs in vitamin D deficiency and chronic kidney disease. Although hypercalcemia does not occur in secondary hyperparathyroidism, patients with chronic kidney disease who have hypercalcemia can develop dysregulation of parathyroid function, which results in a condition known as tertiary hyperparathyroidism. Briefly, long-standing secondary hyperparathyroidism leads to four-gland parathyroid hyperplasia; the hyperplastic parathyroid glands are autonomous and no longer respond to physiologic suppression by elevated ionized calcium levels, which causes hypercalcemia to subsequently ensue. The PTH level is greatly elevated in this condition.

Bone manifestations of hyperparathyroidism depend on the degree and duration of hypercalcemia and include osteopenia and osteoporosis, with preferential cortical bone loss. More advanced forms of hyperparathyroid bone disease, such as osteitis fibrosa cystica, also can rarely occur; radiographic manifestations of osteitis fibrosa cystica include periosteal resorption of the digits, irregular demineralization of the skull, and brown tumors of the long bones.

Because patients with hyperparathyroidism have an increased filtered load of calcium, they frequently are hypercalciuric, despite the tendency of PTH to increase renal tubule calcium ion reabsorption. The hypercalciuria can cause nephrolithiasis and, less commonly, nephrocalcinosis. Urinary tract stones in patients with hyperparathyroidism consist of calcium oxalate and may be bilateral. Other clinical manifestations of hyperparathyroidism include hypertension and peptic ulcer disease.

Primary hyperparathyroidism results from a solitary parathyroid adenoma in 80% to 85% of patients with the disorder; in 5%, double adenomas are present. Multigland parathyroid hyperplasia is present in 5% to 15% of patients, usually in familial syndromes (such as multiple endocrine neoplasia types 1 and 2a [MEN1 and MEN2a]). Parathyroid carcinoma occurs in less than 1%.

The diagnosis of hyperparathyroidism requires an elevated serum calcium level with simultaneous demonstration of PTH levels that are elevated (in 80% to 90% of patients) or within normal limits (in 10% to 20%). The serum phosphorus level may be low, and urine calcium excretion may be greater than 400 mg/24 h (10 mmol/24 h).

Other findings of hyperparathyroidism on laboratory study include mild hypophosphatemia (because PTH decreases the renal threshold for phosphate clearance) and a mild hyperchloremic metabolic acidosis (because PTH enhances renal excretion of bicarbonate). Serum levels of 1,25-dihydroxy vitamin D, which are under the direct control of PTH, are in the high or high-normal range, but serum levels of 25-hydroxy vitamin D, which reflect the body's total vitamin D stores, are normal.

Localization of abnormal parathyroid glands preoperatively by means of ultrasonography, technetium Tc 99m sestamibi scintigraphy, or MRI offers the possibility of a less invasive surgical approach. However, the accuracy of these radiologic modalities is variable.

Removal of the abnormal and hyperfunctioning parathyroid tissue results in a long-term cure in 96% of patients with hyperparathyroidism; those with complications, such as kidney stones, overt bone disease, or prior episodes of hypercalcemic crisis, are obvious candidates for surgical correction. Because most patients are asymptomatic and because there is a lack of reliable predictive indices regarding the development of hyperparathyroidism-related clinical problems, other candidates are less easy to identify. Therefore, at international workshops on primary hyperparathyroidism, the following criteria were proposed in 2002 and refined in 2008 as indications for parathyroidectomy in asymptomatic patients; a surgical candidate needs to fulfill any one of the criteria:

1. Serum calcium level greater than 1 mg/dL (0.25 mmol/L) above the upper limit of normal

2. A creatinine clearance (calculated) less than 60 mL/min (0.996 mL/s)

3. Reduction in bone mineral density of the femoral neck, lumbar spine, or distal radius greater than 2.5 standard deviations below peak bone mass (T-score below −2.5)

4. Age younger than 50 years

5. Patients for whom medical surveillance is not desirable or possible

Because of the high prevalence of vitamin D deficiency in patients with primary hyperparathyroidism, the 2008 workshop recommended measuring vitamin D levels in all patients and replenishing levels to normal before making a treatment decision.

Parathyroid surgery remains the single most effective treatment option for hyperparathyroidism. Traditionally, this has meant bilateral exploration of the neck to identify all (typically four) parathyroid glands, assess which ones are abnormal, and remove only the abnormal glands. In experienced hands, this approach has a high rate of successful long-term cure (greater than 96%) and a low rate of surgical complications (less than 1% for hypercalcemia, 2% to 5% for recurrent laryngeal nerve injury, and less than 1% for neck hematoma or infection).

In recent years, parathyroid procedures have been developed that use smaller incisions under sedation and local anesthesia, which allows for outpatient surgery. Minimally invasive parathyroid surgery can include laparoscopic surgery, radioguided parathyroidectomy, or, most frequently, unilateral neck surgery only. Minimally invasive parathyroid surgery is appropriate for patients who have a clearly defined parathyroid abnormality seen on an ultrasound or a sestamibi scan but is indicated only when PTH levels can be monitored intraoperatively. Bilateral neck exploration is mandatory for all other types of parathyroid surgery and for patients with familial or genetic syndromes. Management of hyperparathyroidism not treated surgically should ensure good hydration and, if possible, avoid the use of thiazide diuretics, which can increase serum calcium levels. Ambulation should be encouraged. Calcium intake should be normal (1000 mg/d) because excessive intake may aggravate hypercalcemia, and a low calcium intake may stimulate PTH secretion and aggravate bone disease. Bisphosphonates can be used to improve bone density but have little effect on serum calcium levels in patients with primary hyperparathyroidism.

Familial Forms of Hyperparathyroidism

The literature suggests that up to 10% of patients with primary hyperparathyroidism have hereditary forms. The most common familial form of hyperparathyroidism is a component of MEN1. Primary hyperparathyroidism is almost always present in this disorder (>95% of patients) by age 65 years, but it can be diagnosed in children and even infants. Indications for surgical intervention are generally the same as in other types of hyperparathyroidism. The presence of four-gland hyperplasia mandates a more complete surgery, such as a three-and-one-half parathyroid gland resection or removal of all four glands with reimplantation of one gland into the musculature of the forearm to maintain accessibility and prevent hypoparathyroidism. Pancreatic tumors, present in 30% to 80% of patients with MEN1, are islet cell tumors that most commonly secrete gastrin and cause Zollinger-Ellison syndrome (~ two thirds of patients). The second most common pancreatic tumor is an insulinoma. Pituitary adenomas affect 15% to 50% of patients with MEN1 and are mostly prolactinomas, although tumors causing acromegaly and Cushing disease also occur. Adrenocortical hyperplasia is seen in roughly one third of patients with MEN1.

Hyperparathyroidism (mostly asymptomatic) also occurs in about one half of patients with MEN2a. Because MEN2a is associated with medullary thyroid cancer, timely thyroidectomy is life-saving. Other familial syndromes are rare and include the hyperparathyroidism-jaw tumor syndrome and familial isolated primary hyperparathryroidism.

A careful family history is paramount in recognizing familial forms of primary hyperparathyroidism. Genetic testing usually confirms the diagnosis. Screening of urine for catecholamine overproduction is vital before surgical treatment in familial hyperparathyroidism because of its potential association with pheochromocytoma.

Non–Parathyroid Hormone-Mediated Hypercalcemia

When PTH levels are suppressed, the resultant hypercalcemia is said to be non–PTH mediated. Cancer is the most common cause of non–PTH-mediated hypercalcemia (**Table 28**) and the most frequent cause in hospitalized patients. Humoral hypercalcemia of malignancy and local osteolytic hypercalcemia are the major forms of cancer-associated hypercalcemia.

Humoral hypercalcemia of malignancy results from the systemic effect of a circulating factor produced by neoplastic cells. The hormone most commonly responsible for this syndrome is PTH-related protein. This protein's N terminal shares significant homologic features with PTH. PTH-related protein shares most, if not all, of the metabolic effects of PTH, including osteoclast activation, increased renal tubular calcium reabsorption, and increased renal clearance of phosphorus. Because tumors that produce PTH-related protein (see Table 28) do so in small quantities, patients who have associated hypercalcemia on presentation usually have an extensive tumor burden. Therefore, it is unusual for hypercalcemia to be the presenting feature of cancer. Another form of humoral hypercalcemia of malignancy is caused by the unregulated production of calcitriol, usually by B-cell lymphomas. This type is less common than the one associated with PTH-related protein.

In contrast, local osteolytic hypercalcemia occurs when tumor growth in the skeleton leads to the release of calcium by the elaboration or stimulation of local cytokines and other osteoclast-activating factors. The classic tumor is multiple myeloma. Adenocarcinoma of the breast and certain lymphomas also may be responsible.

TABLE 28 Mechanisms and Causes of Malignancy-Associated Hypercalcemia
Humoral Hypercalcemia of Malignancy
Parathyroid hormone–related protein
Squamous cell carcinoma
Lung
Oral cavity, larynx
Esophagus
Cervix, vulva
Adenocarcinoma
Breast
Ovary
Renal cell carcinoma
Transitional cell carcinoma
T-cell lymphoma
Islet cell neoplasms
Myeloma
Increased 1,25-Dihydroxy Vitamin D
B-cell lymphoma
Local Osteolytic Hypercalcemia
Myeloma
Breast carcinoma
Lymphoma

Other non–PTH-mediated causes of hypercalcemia include granulomatous diseases, such as sarcoidosis or tuberculosis (increased 1,25-dihydroxy vitamin D production). In addition, endocrine disorders, such as thyrotoxicosis (increased bone turnover), primary adrenal insufficiency (decreased vascular volume and calcium clearance), and pheochromocytoma (production of PTH-related protein), occasionally result in hypercalcemia. Prolonged immobilization also is associated with hypercalcemia, usually in young persons with an active skeleton or in older persons with either Paget disease of bone or previously unrecognized hyperparathyroidism. Certain drugs or supplements, including thiazide diuretics, lithium, vitamin D, and vitamin A, can also raise serum calcium levels, and the milk-alkali syndrome results when large amounts of both calcium and alkali are consumed on a long-term basis.

Benign familial hypocalciuric hypercalcemia is a rare familial condition caused by inactivating mutations of the calcium-sensing receptor, which has a major function in regulating calcium metabolism through parathyroid tissue and renal calcium. The disorder is autosomal dominant with high penetrance. There is decreased sensitivity of the calcium-sensing receptor to calcium; therefore, higher calcium levels are required to suppress PTH secretion. Heterozygous patients generally have hypercalcemia, hypocalciuria, and mild hypermagnesemia at presentation. Fractional excretion of calcium is less than 1% despite the hypercalcemia, and the PTH level is normal or slightly elevated. The clinical significance of this disease lies mostly in its mistaken diagnosis as hyperparathyroidism. The commonly performed subtotal parathyroidectomy cannot correct hypercalcemia in this disorder, and patients sometimes undergo multiple surgical procedures. To avoid unnecessary surgery, all patients with possible primary hyperparathyroidism require measurement of urine calcium excretion.

Genetic testing is not routinely available for benign familial hypocalciuric hypercalcemia. In patients without symptoms, a family history should uncover more family members with hypercalcemia; urine calcium excretion is low, with approximately 75% of patients excreting less than 100 mg/24 h (2.5 mmol/24 h). The ratio of calcium clearance to creatinine clearance may be used for diagnosis and is calculated by the following formula:

$$ClCa/ClCr = (Ca_u \times Cr_s)/(Cr_u \times Ca_s)$$

in which ClCa is calcium clearance, ClCr is creatinine clearance, Ca_u is the urine calcium excretion, Cr_s is the serum creatinine level, Cr_u is the urine creatinine excretion, and Ca_s is the serum calcium level. A ratio of 0.01 or less is typically seen in persons with benign familial hypocalciuric hypercalcemia.

Treatment of Acute Hypercalcemia

The need to treat hypercalcemia depends on the degree of hypercalcemia and the presence or absence of clinical symptoms. If the serum calcium level is less than 12 mg/dL (3.0 mmol/L) and the patient has no symptoms, treatment is unnecessary. In patients with moderate calcium elevation (12 to 14 mg/dL [3.0 to 3.5 mmol/L]) without symptoms, treatment can simply be adequate hydration, but in those with moderate calcium elevation and symptoms consistent with hypercalcemia, more aggressive treatment is necessary. Patients with serum calcium levels greater than 14 mg/dL (3.5 mmol/L) should be treated aggressively, regardless of symptoms.

Measures taken to treat hypercalcemia include nonspecific therapies aimed at increasing urine calcium excretion and decreasing intestinal absorption of calcium, therapies specifically aimed at slowing bone resorption, therapies that directly remove calcium from the circulation, and therapies aimed at controlling the underlying disease(s) causing the hypercalcemia. Urine calcium excretion can be attained by inhibition of proximal tubular and loop sodium reabsorption, which is best achieved by volume expansion using intravenous normal saline infusion (1 to 2 L for 1 hour). This will result in a marked increase in sodium, calcium, and water delivery to the loop of Henle. After the hypovolemia has been corrected, adding a loop diuretic (such as furosemide) has been advocated, but the unproved utility and potential adverse effects of this measure (such as hypokalemia and aggravation of hypovolemia) and the availability of bisphosphonate therapy have led to a recent reappraisal of this approach. Volume repletion alone will result in a marked increase in excretion of calcium, water, and other electrolytes in the urine. Water, sodium, potassium, and chloride must be continuously replaced, as should magnesium if the treatment lasts more than 10 hours. Urinary flow should exceed 250 mL/h during this time, and the serum calcium level will start decreasing within 2 to 4 hours. Recurrent hypovolemia should be avoided. Hemodialysis or peritoneal dialysis with low levels of calcium in the dialysis fluid is also very effective for removing calcium from the circulation. These methods are used in patients with renal insufficiency and heart failure when saline infusion is not feasible.

Hypercalcemia due to increased 1,25-dihydroxy vitamin D production in patients with granulomatous diseases (sarcoidosis or lymphoma) can be treated with prednisone for 2 to 5 days. Intestinal calcium absorption can be partially blocked by phosphate-containing drugs that form insoluble calcium phosphate complexes and prevent absorption. Reducing calcium intake to 400 mg/d or less is also beneficial.

When bone resorption is the main source of calcium, inhibiting it lowers the serum calcium level. Drugs used for this purpose include bisphosphonates, calcitonin, gallium nitrate, and plicamycin (formerly mithramycin).

Bisphosphonates powerfully inhibit osteoclast-mediated bone resorption and very effectively lower the serum calcium level. Their maximum effect is seen in 2 to 4 days, and the duration of effect is usually several weeks, varying between patients and depending on the type of bisphosphonate.

Pamidronate, etidronate, alendronate, and zoledronate are the bisphosphonates currently available in the United States, but only pamidronate and zoledronate are approved by the U.S. Food and Drug Administration (FDA) to treat hypercalcemia. Pamidronate is given by intravenous infusion over 4 to 24 hours. The initial dose varies according to the serum calcium level; a subsequent dose should not be given for 7 days. Zoledronate appears to have the longest-lasting effect (1 to 1.5 months) and a faster onset of action. Given in a 15-minute intravenous infusion, it is FDA-approved for use in hypercalcemia of malignancy. Because of the lag in the onset of effect, bisphosphonates should be combined with faster-acting therapeutic modalities, such as intravenous saline infusion and calcitonin injections. The most common adverse effects of bisphosphonates are gastrointestinal. Trials have reported esophageal ulcerations from all bisphosphonates, except zoledronate. A link between atrial fibrillation and either zoledronate or alendronate has also been shown. Osteonecrosis of the jaw is a recently described adverse effect of bisphosphonate therapy. Oversuppression of bone turnover is the most likely primary mechanism for the development of this condition. For further discussion, see MKSAP 15 Hematology and Oncology.

Calcitonin, which can be given subcutaneously or intramuscularly every 12 hours, has a very rapid calcium-lowering action (4-6 hours). However, calcitonin is effective in only 60% to 70% of patients with hypercalcemia, and most of them develop tachyphylaxis in 48 to 72 hours, most likely because of receptor downregulation. Gallium nitrate is potent but nephrotoxic and requires prolonged infusion (usually 5 days); only limited experience with it exists in clinical practice. Plicamycin use is limited by its toxicity, particularly in patients with renal, liver, or bone marrow disease.

KEY POINTS

- Serum parathyroid hormone (PTH) levels are elevated or inappropriately normal in the PTH-mediated causes of hypercalcemia and are suppressed in the non–PTH-mediated causes.

- Primary hyperparathyroidism is the most common cause of hypercalcemia in the outpatient setting; cancer is the most common cause in hospitalized patients.

- Minimally invasive parathyroidectomy with intraoperative measurement of the parathyroid hormone level is becoming the preferred surgical treatment of primary hyperparathyroidism.

- Hyperparathyroidism associated with the multiple endocrine neoplasia syndromes typically involves four-gland hyperplasia, is associated with additional endocrine syndromes, and requires removal of three or more glands for surgical cure.

Hypocalcemia

Causes and Diagnosis of Hypocalcemia

Hypocalcemia varies from a mild asymptomatic biochemical abnormality to a severe life-threatening disorder, depending on its duration, severity, and rapidity of development. The causes of hypocalcemia (**Table 29**) involve either increased loss of calcium from the circulation or insufficient entry of calcium into the circulation.

A low total serum calcium level is usually caused by a low serum albumin level; the ionized calcium level is normal. The most common cause of acquired hypocalcemia is hypoparathyroidism, which often occurs because of ischemic damage to or removal of the parathyroid glands at the time of surgery in the central neck (such as thyroidectomy or resection of a head and neck cancer). This disorder develops in 1% to 2% of patients after a total thyroidectomy for thyroid cancer or benign thyroid disease. Autoimmune hypoparathyroidism occurs as an isolated defect or as part of polyglandular autoimmune syndrome type 1 in association with adrenal insufficiency and mucocutaneous candidiasis. Pseudohypoparathyroidism, another cause of hypocalcemia, comprises a group of disorders whose exact mechanism is thought to involve postreceptor resistance to the effects of PTH.

Congenital causes of hypocalcemia include constitutively activating mutations of the calcium-sensing receptor that reset the calcium-PTH relationship to a lower serum calcium level and hypoplasia or aplasia of the parathyroid glands (DiGeorge syndrome). See Table 29 for other causes of hypocalcemia.

Chronic moderate hypocalcemia can be completely asymptomatic, but severe hypocalcemia directly causes increased neuromuscular irritability. The chief clinical manifestation of hypocalcemia is tetany. Other symptoms include perioral and fingertip paresthesia, spontaneous muscle cramps, and contraction of the respiratory and laryngeal muscles. Alkalosis, hypokalemia, and hypomagnesemia aggravate symptoms of hypocalcemia, and acidosis diminishes them.

The diagnosis of hypocalcemia is suggested by a positive Chvostek sign (unilateral contraction of the facial muscles when the facial nerve is tapped just in front of the ear) and Trousseau sign (carpal spasm after occluding the brachial artery with an inflated blood pressure cuff) and confirmed by the finding of a serum total calcium level less than 8.2 mg/dL (2.05 mmol/L) or an ionized calcium level less than 4.4 mg/dL (1.1 mmol/L). Concomitant renal failure, cell lysis syndromes, hypomagnesemia, hypermagnesemia, and acute pancreatitis should be diagnosed or excluded with appropriate history, physical examination, and laboratory studies; serum magnesium levels less than 1.0 mg/dL (0.413 mmol/L) should be corrected (see later discussion of patients with coexisting impaired kidney function). If none of these conditions is found, intact PTH, 25-hydroxy vitamin D, and 1,25-dihydroxy vitamin D levels need to be measured.

TABLE 29 Causes of Hypocalcemia

Condition	Characteristics

Disorders of vitamin D metabolism (vitamin D deficiency)
  Lack of sunlight
  Dermatologic disorders
  Dietary deficiency
  Malabsorption
  Liver disease
  Renal disease
  Vitamin D–dependent rickets type I (1α-hydroxylase deficiency)
	Laboratory findings of mild hypocalcemia, hypophosphatemia, elevated PTH level, decreased 25-hydroxy vitamin D level, and decreased 1,25-dihydroxy vitamin D level if renal disease is present. Vitamin D deficiency is widespread among housebound and institutionalized elderly and general medical patients with disorders that predispose to altered vitamin D metabolism.

Vitamin D resistance Vitamin D–dependent rickets type II	Laboratory findings of hypocalcemia, hypophosphatemia, elevated PTH level, and elevated 1,25-dihydroxy vitamin D level when treated with vitamin D; vitamin D–receptor defect causes resistance to 1,25-dihydroxy vitamin D_3.

Hypoparathyroidism
  Postsurgical (thyroid, parathyroid, or neck surgery)
  Autoimmune (such as polyglandular autoimmune syndrome)
  Congenital (such as DiGeorge syndrome)
  Infiltrative (such as hemochromatosis, sarcoidosis)
	Laboratory findings of hypocalcemia, hyperphosphatemia, and a low or inappropriately normal PTH level; postsurgical hypoparathyroidism is the most common form.

PTH resistance Pseudohypoparathyroidism	Laboratory findings of hypocalcemia, hyperphosphatemia, and an elevated PTH level with a normal 25-hydroxy vitamin D level; pseudohypoparathyroidism type 1a is an autosomal dominant disorder marked by resistance to multiple hormones and Albright hereditary osteodystrophy (short stature, obesity, round facies, brachymetacarpia, and mental deficiency).

Hypomagnesemia
  Chronic diuretic use
  Alcoholism
  Diarrhea
  Malabsorption
  Certain drugs (amphotericin B, aminoglycosides, cisplatin)
	Laboratory findings of hypomagnesemia and hypocalcemia with a low, normal, or high PTH level; hypomagnesemia causes impaired PTH secretion and PTH resistance with impaired tissue responsiveness to PTH.

Medications
  Those altering vitamin D metabolism (phenytoin, phenobarbital, isoniazid, theophylline, rifampin, 5-fluorouracil plus leucovorin)
  Those causing intravascular binding (phosphate, foscarnet, EDTA, citrated blood products)
  Bisphosphonates
	Laboratory findings of hypocalcemia and low 25-hydroxy vitamin D or 1,25-dihydroxy vitamin D level (with agents that alter vitamin D metabolism); hypocalcemia can develop rapidly with use of some medications, especially if given intravenously.

Extravascular deposition
  Pancreatitis
  Hungry-bone syndrome
  Rhabdomyolysis
  Tumor lysis syndrome
  Osteoblastic metastases
	Laboratory findings of hypocalcemia and hyper- or hypophosphatemia; in pancreatitis, hypocalcemia results from the deposition of calcium in the form of calcium soaps. Hyperphosphatemia suggests rhabdomyolysis or tumor lysis syndrome with release of phosphate from the bone, whereas hypophosphatemia is seen in hungry-bone syndrome or in osteoblastic metastases.

Sepsis	Laboratory findings of hypocalcemia and low PTH and 1,25-dihydroxy vitamin D levels; most likely mediated by the action of inflammatory cytokines on the parathyroid glands, kidneys, and bone.
Acute respiratory alkalosis	Laboratory findings of a normal total serum calcium level but a low ionized calcium level (increased calcium binding to albumin in the serum with resultant reduction in serum ionized calcium level).
Artifactual hypoglycemia with hypoalbuminemia	Laboratory findings of a low total serum calcium level and a normal ionized calcium level (reduced protein binding lowers total serum calcium level but ionized fraction remains normal).

EDTA = ethylenediaminetetraacetic acid; PTH = parathyroid hormone.

A measurement of the 25-hydroxy vitamin D level is more informative in most patients with hypocalcemia than is a measurement of the 1,25-dihydroxy vitamin D level because vitamin D deficiency causes hypocalcemia and stimulates PTH secretion, which in turn stimulates renal conversion of 25-hydroxy vitamin D to 1,25-dihydroxy vitamin D. Low dietary intake, poor absorption of vitamin D, and lack of production of 25-hydroxy vitamin D in the skin will result in its low serum level. The level will also be low in patients on phenytoin, those with nephrotic syndrome (loss of vitamin

D–binding protein), and those with hepatobiliary disease. 1,25-Dihydroxy vitamin D levels will be low despite normal or high 25-hydroxy vitamin D levels in patients with renal insufficiency, deficiency of the renal 1α-hydroxylase enzyme, and hypoparathyroidism. High levels of 1,25-dihydroxy vitamin D are seen in hereditary vitamin D–resistant rickets.

Therapy for Hypocalcemia

Patients with acute symptomatic hypocalcemia (serum total calcium level usually <7.0 mg/dL [1.75 mmol/L] and ionized calcium usually <3.2 mg/dL [0.8 mmol/L]) should be treated promptly with intravenous calcium. Calcium gluconate is preferred over calcium chloride because tissue necrosis is less if extravasated. The first 100 to 200 mg of elemental calcium (1 to 2 g of calcium gluconate) should be given over 10 to 20 minutes. Faster administration can result in cardiac dysfunction, a prolonged QT interval, and even cardiac arrest. This treatment should be followed by a slow calcium infusion at 0.5 to 1.5 mg/kg/h, with infusion continued until the patient is receiving effective dosages of oral calcium and vitamin D. Infused calcium should be diluted in saline or dextrose solution to avoid vein irritation. The infusion solution should contain no bicarbonate or phosphate because both can form insoluble calcium salts. If bicarbonate or phosphate administration is necessary, a separate intravenous line should be used.

Coexisting hypomagnesemia should be corrected, but great care must be taken in patients with impaired renal function because they cannot excrete excess magnesium. Magnesium is given by infusion in the form of magnesium sulfate. In patients with severe hyperphosphatemia (as in tumor lysis syndrome, rhabdomyolysis, or chronic renal failure), treatment is focused on correcting the hyperphosphatemia. Acute hyperphosphatemia usually resolves in patients with intact renal function. Phosphorus excretion may be aided by saline infusion (used cautiously because it can lead to worsening of hypocalcemia) and administration of acetazolamide, a carbonic anhydrase inhibitor. Hemodialysis is often necessary in patients who have symptomatic hypocalcemia and hyperphosphatemia, especially if renal function is impaired. Chronic hyperphosphatemia should be managed by a low-phosphate diet and use of phosphate binders with meals.

Chronic hypocalcemia due to hypoparathyroidism is treated by administration of oral calcium and, if unsuccessful, vitamin D supplementation. The serum calcium level should be targeted to approximately 8.0 mg/dL (2.0 mmol/L). Most patients will be entirely asymptomatic at this level, and further elevation will lead to hypercalciuria, renal stones, nephrocalcinosis, and renal failure because of the lack of PTH effect on the renal tubules.

Calcium carbonate is inexpensive but may be poorly absorbed, especially in elderly patients and those with achlorhydria. If oral calcium preparations alone cannot achieve adequate calcium repletion, vitamin D should be added. Appropriate doses of calcium and vitamin D are established by gradual titration. When the target serum calcium level is achieved, urine calcium excretion needs to be measured. If hypercalciuria is detected, a thiazide diuretic can be added, which will result in diminished calciuria but may further increase the serum calcium level. Phosphorus levels should also be controlled. If the serum phosphorus level is greater than 6.0 mg/dL (1.94 mmol/L) at a time when calcium is satisfactory, an unabsorbable phosphate binder should be added to the regimen.

Once therapeutic goals are achieved, the patient should be monitored every 3 to 6 months for serum calcium and phosphorus levels and for urine calcium excretion.

KEY POINTS

- The most common cause of acquired hypocalcemia is surgical excision of or vascular injury to the parathyroid glands during neck surgery.
- Acute symptomatic hypocalcemia should be treated with intravenous calcium gluconate.
- In hypoparathyroidism, the serum calcium level should be maintained in the low-normal range to prevent hypercalciuria, renal stones, and renal failure.

Metabolic Bone Disease

Two common metabolic bone disorders are osteoporosis and Paget disease of bone. Both have generalized symptoms that may not be clinically apparent in all patients.

Osteoporosis

Osteoporosis is a skeletal disorder characterized by compromised bone strength that predisposes a person to an increased risk of fracture. This definition recognizes that other factors also influence bone quality, such as the microarchitecture of bone. However, measurement of bone mineral density remains the most useful clinical tool available for diagnosing osteoporosis. In the United States, more than 44 million people have osteoporosis or osteopenia (low bone mass). Potentially modifiable risk factors for osteoporosis include:

- Low dietary calcium intake
- Inadequate physical activity
- Low body weight
- Cigarette smoking
- Alcohol
- Excessive exercise (causing functional amenorrhea)

Nonmodifiable risk factors include:

- Increasing age
- Female sex
- Race (white or Asian)
- Previous fragility fracture

- Family history of fragility fracture in a first-degree relative
- Impaired mobility

The presence of one or more of these risk factors warrants measurement of bone mineral density.

World Health Organization Criteria

The World Health Organization Working Group defines osteoporosis (and osteopenia) according to measurements of bone mineral density obtained on dual-energy x-ray absorptiometry (DEXA). DEXA scan results are typically reported as T-scores, or the number of standard deviations above or below the mean bone mineral density of young healthy adults. Osteoporosis is defined as a T-score of 2.5 standard deviations or more below the normal peak values for bone mineral density. Established or severe osteoporosis is present when there is a history of at least one or more fragility fractures in conjunction with a T-score below –2.5. Osteopenia is defined as a T-score between –1.0 and –2.5, and normal bone density is present if the T-score is above –1. These criteria were initially established for the assessment of osteoporosis in white women. Bone mineral density reports after DEXA also may include a Z-score, which is the number of standard deviations by which the patient differs from the mean for his or her age group; a Z-score has greater clinical utility in younger persons. The World Health Organization definition of osteoporosis only considers measurement of bone density, with no component of bone quality.

Prediction of Fracture Risk

Declining bone mineral density is a continuous risk factor for fracture. For each standard deviation below the age-adjusted mean measured at any site, there is an approximately 1.5-fold increase in the relative risk of any type of fracture. A decrease of one standard deviation in lumbar spine bone mineral density results in a 2.3-fold increase in relative risk (95% CI, 1.9-2.8) for vertebral fractures. Likewise, a standard deviation decrease of one in hip bone mineral density increases the age-adjusted risk of hip fracture by a factor of 2.6-fold (95% CI, 2.0-3.5).

Preexisting vertebral fractures in postmenopausal women are associated with a fourfold increase in the risk of a further vertebral fracture, independent of bone mineral density. However, when previous vertebral fractures are present with low bone mineral density measurements, the predictive risk of future vertebral fracture and fractures at other sites is further increased. The risk of hip fracture is increased independent of bone mineral density in the setting of a maternal history of hip fracture, increasing age, predisposing conditions leading to falls, previous fractures, and estrogen deficiency states. **Table 30** shows indications for bone mineral density testing.

Evaluation

In the evaluation of osteoporosis, causative medical conditions should be considered (**Table 31**). The use of markers of bone

TABLE 30 Indications for Measurement of Bone Mineral Density

Women age ≥65 years and men age ≥70 years (regardless of risk factors)
Postmenopausal women age <65 years and men age <70 years who have at least one risk factor for osteoporosis (other than menopause in women)
Women or men who have fractures on presentation
Women or men who are considering therapy for osteoporosis and for whom bone mineral densitometry test results would influence this decision
Radiographic findings suggestive of osteoporosis or vertebral deformity
Corticosteroid therapy for more than 3 months
Primary hyperparathyroidism
Treatment for osteoporosis (to monitor therapeutic response)

formation and bone resorption is limited by their circadian rhythms and large intra- and interassay variability. Bone biopsy is rarely indicated, except in patients with unusual skeletal lesions or renal osteodystrophy and in young patients with severe osteoporosis or a fracture without an obvious cause.

Prevention

Prevention of bone loss in postmenopausal women should be considered when the T-score is below –1 and risk factors are present. Preventive measures include adequate calcium and vitamin D intake, exercise, smoking cessation, fall prevention, limitation of alcohol and caffeine intake, and use of medications (such as bisphosphonates and raloxifene). The recommended goal for calcium intake depends on sex and age

TABLE 31 Causes of Secondary Osteoporosis[a]

Endocrine disorders: hyperparathyroidism, Cushing syndrome, hypogonadism, hyperthyroidism, prolactinoma, acromegaly, osteomalacia
Hematopoietic disorders: multiple myeloma, sickle-cell disease, thalassemia minor, leukemia, lymphoma, polycythemia vera
Connective tissue disorders: osteogenesis imperfecta, homocystinuria
Renal disease: chronic renal failure, renal tubular acidosis, hypercalciuria
Nutritional: malabsorption, total parenteral nutrition
Gastrointestinal disorders: gastrectomy, primary biliary cirrhosis, celiac disease
Medications: corticosteroids, anticonvulsants, heparin
Genetic: Turner syndrome, Klinefelter syndrome

[a]Not an all-inclusive list.

(**Table 32**). Adults younger than 50 years need 400 to 800 U/d of vitamin D, and adults age 50 years and older need 800 to 1000 U/d. Patients with severe vitamin D deficiency should receive 50,000 U of ergocalciferol three times weekly for 5 weeks, after which their serum 25-hydroxy vitamin D level should be rechecked to ensure that it has normalized.

Indications for Therapy

The American College of Physicians has published guidelines for the pharmacologic therapy of low bone density or osteoporosis to prevent fractures. High-quality evidence supports the pharmacologic treatment of men and women who have known osteoporosis and of those who have experienced fragility fractures (a spontaneous fracture or a fracture due to a fall from a standing height or less). Moderate-quality evidence supports a recommendation that physicians consider pharmacologic treatment of men and women who are at risk of developing osteoporosis.

Therapy for Postmenopausal Women

Drug therapies approved by the FDA to treat osteoporosis are shown in **Table 33**.

Bisphosphonates are the first-line drugs for treating osteoporosis in postmenopausal women. Alendronate and risedronate reduce the risk of both vertebral and nonvertebral fractures. Whether there are differences in fracture protection among the bisphosphonates is uncertain. All most likely produce greater relative and absolute fracture risk reductions in women with more severe osteoporosis. The recent FDA approval of annual intravenous zoledronate for the treatment of female osteoporosis was based on the results of a randomized, double-blind, placebo-controlled, multinational study

that enrolled 7736 women, age 65 to 89 years, who had osteoporosis. Over 3 years, zoledronate significantly reduced the incidence of new vertebral fractures and hip fractures compared with placebo; all participants also received daily supplementation with elemental calcium and vitamin D. Ibandronate was first approved by the FDA in a daily oral tablet formulation for the treatment and prevention of postmenopausal osteoporosis; a once-monthly oral therapy was subsequently approved. An intravenous formulation was then approved on the basis of the results of the Dosing Intravenous Administration (DIVA) study.

The selective estrogen-receptor modulator raloxifene is most often used in postmenopausal women with low bone

TABLE 32 Optimal Calcium Requirements

Group	Optimal Daily Calcium Intake (mg)
Men	
25-65 y	1000
>65 y	1500
Women	
25-50 y	1000
Pregnant and nursing	1200-1500
>50 y (postmenopausal)	1500
On estrogen	1000
Not on estrogen	1500
>65 y	1500

Adapted from Optimal Calcium Intake. NIH Consensus Statement Online 1994;12(4):1-31 (Table 1 — Optimal Calcium Requirements). Available at http://consensus.nih.gov/1994/1994optimalcalcium097html.htm.

TABLE 33 U.S. Food and Drug Administration–Approved Medications for Osteoporosis and Approved Indications

Medication	Postmenopausal Osteoporosis		Osteoporosis in Men	Corticosteroid-Induced Osteoporosis	
	Prevention	Treatment	Treatment	Prevention	Treatment
Estrogens	Yes	No	No	No	No
Calcitonin	No	Yes[a]	No	No	No
Raloxifene	Yes	Yes	No	No	No
Alendronate[b]	Yes	Yes	Yes	No	Yes
Risedronate[c]	Yes	Yes	Yes	Yes	Yes
Teriparatide	No	Yes	Yes	No	No
Ibandronate[d]	Yes	Yes	No	No	No
Zoledronate[e]	Yes	Yes	Yes	Yes	Yes

[a]More than 5 years after menopause.

[b]Oral daily or weekly dosing.

[c]Oral daily, weekly or monthly dosing.

[d]Oral daily or monthly dosing; intravenous dosing every 3 months.

[e]Intravenous dosing once yearly.

mass or younger postmenopausal women with osteoporosis who are at a greater risk of spine fracture than hip fracture. Raloxifene prevents bone loss and reduces the risk of vertebral fractures, but its effectiveness in reducing other fractures is uncertain. This drug is approved for treatment and prevention of osteoporosis in postmenopausal women, for reduction in risk of invasive breast cancer in postmenopausal women with osteoporosis, and for reduction in risk of invasive breast cancer in postmenopausal women without osteoporosis who are at high risk for invasive breast cancer.

Teriparatide (recombinant human parathyroid hormone [1-34]) is reserved for treating patients at high risk of fracture, including those with very low bone mineral density (T-score below −3.0) with a previous vertebral fracture and contraindications to bisphosphonate use. This therapy improves bone mineral density, stimulates new bone formation, and reduces the risk of new vertebral and nonvertebral fractures. Dosage requirements (such as daily subcutaneous injections) may limit its use. Teriparatide is an anabolic agent, whereas the other osteoporosis drugs are antiresorptive agents.

The United States Preventive Services Task Force advises against using estrogen or estrogen plus progestin for the prevention of chronic diseases, including osteoporosis, after menopause, citing data from the Women's Health Initiative that showed at least a trend toward an increased risk of breast cancer, coronary heart disease, stroke, venous thromboembolism, dementia and cognitive decline, and urinary incontinence with such use. Calcitonin is not a first-line drug for postmenopausal osteoporosis treatment; its fracture efficacy is low, and its effects on bone mineral density are less than those of other agents. This drug is not recommended for treating bone pain, except that from acute vertebral compression fractures.

Data are inadequate to make definitive recommendations about combination or serial antiresorptive and anabolic drug therapy, although one study showed that concurrent teriparatide and bisphosphonate therapy was no better than teriparatide alone. During therapy, treatment goals and medications should be reevaluated on an ongoing basis through periodic medical examinations and follow-up bone mineral density testing. An appropriate interval for repeat bone mineral density testing is 2 years. The treatment of osteoporosis needs to be long-term in most women.

Osteoporosis in Men

Approximately 2 million American men have osteoporosis, and another 12 million are at risk for the disease. The primary potentially modifiable risk factors for osteoporosis in men include:

- Physical inactivity
- Cigarette smoking
- Low dietary calcium
- BMI of 20 to 25 (or lower)

- Weight loss greater than 10%
- Corticosteroid use
- Alcoholism

The primary potentially nonmodifiable risk factors include:

- Age greater than 70 years
- Previous fragility fracture
- Androgen deprivation therapy (usually not modifiable)
- Spinal cord injury

To preserve bone health, the recognition and treatment of any underlying medical condition affecting bone health are necessary. Medications that cause bone loss should be identified, evaluated, and changed (if possible), and unhealthy habits, such as smoking, excessive alcohol intake, and inactivity, should be altered. Men younger than 65 years need 1000 mg/d of calcium and 400 to 800 U/d of vitamin D, and men age 65 years and older need at least 1500 mg/d of calcium and 800 to 1000 U/d of vitamin D. Engagement in a regular regimen of weight-bearing exercises in which bone and muscles work against gravity (such as walking, jogging, racquet sports, stair climbing, and team sports) should be encouraged; notably, lifting weights or using resistance machines appears to help preserve bone density.

The FDA has approved three antiresorptive medications (alendronate, risedronate, and zoledronate) and the anabolic agent teriparatide to treat male osteoporosis. When osteoporosis is due to hypogonadism, testosterone replacement therapy is encouraged.

The loss of bone mineral density with androgen deprivation therapy for prostate cancer is well recognized, with significant loss occurring within 12 months of therapy initiation. The annual loss of bone mineral density associated with androgen deprivation therapy is roughly 2% to 8% per year at the lumbar spine and 1.8% to 6.5% at the hip; the loss appears to continue indefinitely while treatment continues, and there is no recovery after therapy stops. Of men surviving at least 5 years after the diagnosis of prostate cancer who are treated with androgen deprivation therapy, 19.4% have a fracture compared with 12.6% of men not so treated, which is equivalent to one additional fracture for every 28 men treated with androgen deprivation therapy.

Because vitamin D deficiency exacerbates the development of osteoporosis, vitamin D status should be evaluated before commencing androgen deprivation therapy. The use of bisphosphonates (zoledronate, pamidronate, and alendronate) in men treated with androgen deprivation therapy has been shown to prevent bone loss in prospective studies and to increase bone mineral density in one randomized controlled trial. However, bisphosphonates have not been shown to prevent fractures in men with prostate cancer.

Corticosteroid-Induced Osteoporosis

Corticosteroids enhance bone resorption and decrease bone formation directly through their action on osteoblasts and osteoclasts and indirectly by inhibiting calcium absorption. Corticosteroids inhibit the replication of the osteoblastic lineage, decrease the genesis of new osteoblastic cells, and induce apoptosis. Although the degree of corticosteroid-induced bone loss is related to the total cumulative dosage, bone loss is highest (up to 30% in some studies) in the initial months of treatment. Initial loss is followed by slower, continuous bone loss. The extent of bone loss depends on the dosage and duration of therapy. The typical risk factors for osteoporosis may have an independent and additive effect. The risk of fragility fractures may be higher among postmenopausal women taking corticosteroids.

Diagnostic thresholds based on bone mineral density have not been established for corticosteroid-induced osteoporosis, and established diagnostic guidelines for postmenopausal women do not apply in this case. At similar bone mineral density levels, patients on corticosteroids appear to have a higher risk of fracture than those not taking such medications. However, patients who have received corticosteroid therapy for 3 months should undergo bone mineral density measurement; therapeutic intervention is recommended if the T-score is less than −1.0. An initial (baseline) bone mineral density measurement should be obtained when patients initiate long-term (more than 6 months) corticosteroid therapy, and monitoring can be repeated as often as every 6 months to detect bone loss. In patients receiving antiresorptive agents, annual measurements are likely sufficient.

Preventive measures must begin at the initiation of corticosteroid therapy. Bisphosphonates have been shown in controlled clinical trials to be the antiresorptive agents of choice for the treatment of corticosteroid-induced osteoporosis.

Osteomalacia

Causes

Osteomalacia in adults and rickets in children are mineralization disorders in which the structural integrity of bone is reduced because of a deficient supply of calcium to the growth plate and bone surface (inadequate osteoid mineralization). Osteomalacia is an abnormality of bone, and rickets is an abnormality of the growth plate. Causes of osteomalacia include a very low dietary calcium intake, calcium malabsorption due to a bowel disorder (such as celiac disease), and secondary malabsorption due to vitamin D deficiency caused by a lack of exposure to sunlight. Rickets is clinically more evident in children than osteomalacia is in adults because of a greater calcium requirement for skeletal growth. Osteomalacia and rickets caused by phosphate deficiency are discussed later.

Clinical Features

Proximal myopathy occurs in both adults and children with mineralization disorders, especially when vitamin D deficiency is prominent. Bone pain may be due to stress fractures that fail to heal (Looser zones), often in the pelvis and medial side of the femur.

Diagnostic Workup

Biochemical testing should include measurements of ionized calcium, which may be low or normal; PTH, which may be high (secondary hyperparathyroidism) or normal; and vitamin D, which is generally low. An elevated level of serum alkaline phosphatase is typically present. However, given that bone alkaline phosphatase levels increase with age, it is essential to differentiate pathologic and physiologic changes.

Management

Treatment of osteomalacia consists of calcium supplementation combined with vitamin D replacement. Although dietary calcium is effective, consuming the required quantity of calcium in tablet form as calcium carbonate or the better-absorbed calcium citrate is easier. Vitamin D replacement with ergocalciferol is appropriate, even if sunlight is available. Calcitriol, the active form of vitamin D, is used if renal function is compromised.

Phosphate Deficiency–Induced Mineralization Disorders

Osteomalacia and rickets also can result from a deficient supply of phosphate to the bone surface and growth plate, respectively. Because dietary phosphorus, unlike calcium, is rarely deficient, phosphate deficiency is generally due to excess excretion in the urine. In adults, this can result from oncogenic osteomalacia (also known as tumor-induced osteomalacia), which is caused by typically benign, but occasionally malignant, mesenchymal tumors that secrete factors (such as fibroblast growth factor 23) leading to phosphate wasting and a phenotype similar to X-linked hypophosphatemic rickets in adults and children. Another cause of excess phosphorus secretion is autosomal dominant hypophosphatemic rickets, which typically presents in childhood.

A family history is essential to rule out inherited forms of hypophosphatemic osteomalacia. The clinical features of the disorder are similar to those of osteomalacia secondary to vitamin D deficiency. Laboratory studies typically show a low serum phosphorus level and increased renal phosphorus excretion. Serum levels of markers of bone turnover, such as serum alkaline phosphatase and osteocalcin, are usually elevated. The serum calcium level is relatively normal, except in patients who develop hypocalcemia as a result of phosphate therapy, which can result in secondary hyperparathyroidism. If cancer-induced osteomalacia is suspected, bone scanning that uses a radiolabeled bisphosphonate tracer (which is deposited in areas of increased bone turnover), MRI, or CT may be needed to locate the tumor. **Table 34** shows typical findings on laboratory study of the major acquired types of osteomalacia.

The aim of treatment is to supply sufficient amounts of phosphorus to mineralizing surfaces to maintain bone structure. This is achieved with regular doses of oral phosphate and calcitriol. In tumor-induced osteomalacia, surgical removal of tumors leads to prompt biochemical remission.

Paget Disease of Bone

Paget disease is a localized disorder of osteoclast overactivity, which leads to the formation of mechanically ineffective woven or repaired, rather than lamellar, bone. This process results in the bending of long bones, with compensatory periosteal expansion and cortical thickening. Some variants of the disease are caused by a mutation in the sequestosome gene. A previously postulated slow virus origin remains controversial. Persons affected by the disease are frequently, but not exclusively, of northern European background. The condition is progressive throughout life but usually does not cause symptoms until middle age or later life.

Clinical Features and Evaluation

Paget disease is often asymptomatic, with typical radiographic findings. When symptoms are present, they include localized deformity, bone pain, and fracture, including stress fracture. Careful examination of affected areas, noting deformity, temperature of the overlying skin, and localized bone pain suggestive of stress fracture, is important. Paraplegia, deafness, and high-output heart failure occasionally occur.

Biochemical evaluation is directed at measuring markers of bone formation (serum alkaline phosphatase and osteocalcin levels) and resorption (urine deoxypyridinoline-to-creatinine ratio). The most useful diagnostic test is measurement of the serum alkaline phosphatase level, which can be very high but occasionally is within the reference range. Bone scans are the most sensitive means of detecting sites of Paget disease of bone. Scans are nonspecific and can be positive in nonpagetic areas that have degenerative changes or metastatic disease in the skeleton. Plain radiographs of bones noted to be positive on a bone scan should be obtained to provide the most specific information; changes noted on the radiograph are usually characteristic to the point of being pathognomonic.

Treatment

Paget disease should be treated if symptoms are present or if lytic involvement of the vertebrae, skull, weight-bearing bones, or areas adjacent to major joints occurs. Symptomatic treatment with analgesics may be all that is required. However, with the development of powerful, effective, and safe bisphosphonates, therapy to prevent long-term deformity is now possible with alendronate, risedronate, or zoledronate.

KEY POINTS

- Osteoporosis is present when the T-score is below –2.5 on bone mineral densitometry.
- Oral alendronate, oral risedronate, and subcutaneous teriparatide reduce the risk of both vertebral and nonvertebral fractures in patients with osteoporosis; annual intravenous administration of zoledronate significantly reduces the risk of both vertebral and hip fractures in women.
- Osteomalacia is characterized by decreased bone mineralization and low or normal ionized calcium, normal or high parathyroid hormone, and low vitamin D levels.
- Paget disease should be treated if symptoms are present or if lytic involvement of the vertebrae, skull, weight-bearing bones, or areas adjacent to major joints occurs; bisphosphonates are the therapeutic agents of choice for Paget disease.

TABLE 34 Biochemical Findings in Osteomalacia

Indices	Osteomalacia		
	Nutritional	Oncogenic	Acidotic
Serum			
Calcium	Decreased or low normal	Normal	Normal or decreased
25-Hydroxy vitamin D	Decreased	Normal	Normal
1,25-Dihydroxy vitamin D	Decreased, normal, or increased	Decreased	Normal or decreased
PTH	Increased	Normal or increased	Normal or increased
Alkaline phosphatase	Increased	Increased	Increased
Urine			
Calcium	Decreased	Normal	Normal or increased
Phosphorus	Normal	Increased	Normal
Aminoaciduria	—	Occasionally present	Present

PTH = parathyroid hormone.

Bibliography

Black DM, Delmas PD, Eastell R, et al; HORIZON Pivotal Fracture Trial. Once-yearly zoledronic acid for treatment of postmenopausal osteoporosis. N Engl J Med. 2007;356(18):1809-1822. [PMID: 17476007]

Holick MF. High prevalence of vitamin D inadequacy and implications for health. Mayo Clin Proc. 2006;81(3):353-373. [PMID: 16529140]

Holick MF. Vitamin D deficiency. N Engl J Med. 2007;357(3):266-281. [PMID: 17634462]

Israeli RS, Ryan CW, Jung LL. Managing bone loss in men with locally advanced prostate cancer receiving androgen deprivation therapy. J Urol. 2008;179(2):414-423. [PMID: 18076933]

MacLean C, Newberry S, Maglione M, et al. Systematic review: comparative effectiveness of treatments to prevent fractures in men and women with low bone density or osteoporosis. Ann Intern Med. 2008;148(3):197-213. [PMID: 18087050]

Pennisi P, Trombetti A, Rizzoli R. Glucocorticoid-induced osteoporosis and its treatment. Clin Orthop Relat Res. 2006;443:39-47. [PMID: 16462424]

Shepard MM, Smith JW 3rd. Hypercalcemia. Am J Med Sci. 2007;334(5):381-385. [PMID: 18004092]

Shoback D. Update in osteoporosis and metabolic bone disorders. J Clin Endocrinol Metab. 2007;92(3):747-753. [PMID: 17341572]

Sitges-Serra A, Bergenfelz A. Clinical update: sporadic primary hyperparathyroidism. Lancet. 2007;370(9586):468-470. [PMID: 17693163]

Udelsman R, Pasieka JL, Sturgeon C, Young JE, Clark OH. Surgery for asymptomatic primary hyperparathyroidism: proceedings of the third international workshop. J Clin Endocrinol Metab. 2009;94(2):366-372. [PMID: 19193911]

Whyte MP. Clinical practice. Paget's disease of bone. N Engl J Med. 2006;355(6):593-600. [PMID: 16899779]

Self-Assessment Test

This self-assessment test contains one-best-answer multiple-choice questions. Please read these directions carefully before answering the questions. Answers, critiques, and bibliographies immediately follow these multiple-choice questions. The American College of Physicians is accredited by the Accreditation Council for Continuing Medical Education (ACCME) to provide continuing medical education for physicians.

The American College of Physicians designates MKSAP 15 Endocrinology and Metabolism for a maximum of 18 *AMA PRA Category 1 Credits*™. Physicians should only claim credit commensurate with the extent of their participation in the activity. Separate answer sheets are provided for each book of the MKSAP program. Please use one of these answer sheets to complete the Endocrinology and Metabolism self-assessment test. Indicate in Section H on the answer sheet the actual number of credits you earned, up to the maximum of 18, in ¼-credit increments. (One credit equals one hour of time spent on this educational activity.)

Use the self-addressed envelope provided with your program to mail your completed answer sheet(s) to the MKSAP Processing Center for scoring. Remember to provide your MKSAP 15 order and ACP ID numbers in the appropriate spaces on the answer sheet. The order and ACP ID numbers are printed on your mailing label. If you have *not* received these numbers with your MKSAP 15 purchase, you will need to acquire them to earn CME credits. E-mail ACP's customer service center at custserv@acponline.org. In the subject line, write "MKSAP 15 order/ACP ID numbers." In the body of the e-mail, make sure you include your e-mail address as well as your full name, address, city, state, ZIP code, country, and telephone number. Also identify where you have made your MKSAP 15 purchase. You will receive your MKSAP 15 order and ACP ID numbers by e-mail within 72 business hours.

CME credit is available from the publication date of July 31, 2009, until July 31, 2012. You may submit your answer sheets at any time during this period.

Self-Scoring Instructions:
Endocrinology and Metabolism

Compute your percent correct score as follows:

Step 1: Give yourself 1 point for each correct response to a question.

Step 2: Divide your total points by the total number of questions: 116.

The result, expressed as a percentage, is your percent correct score.

	Example	Your Calculations
Step 1	97	
Step 2	97 ÷ 116	÷ 116
% Correct	84%	%

Item 1

A 76-year-old woman is evaluated in the emergency department for a 2-month history of fatigue, anorexia, thirst, polydipsia, and polyuria. Squamous cell lung cancer was diagnosed 6 months ago; the patient has declined surgery and chemotherapy. She takes no medications.

On physical examination, temperature is 37.5 °C (99.5 °F), blood pressure is 90/60 mm Hg, pulse rate is 118/min, respiration rate is 22/min, and BMI is 18. The patient appears cachectic. The remaining general physical examination findings are normal.

Laboratory studies:

Blood urea nitrogen	70 mg/dL (25.0 mmol/L)
Calcium	13.5 mg/dL (3.38 mmol/L)
Creatinine	2.9 mg/dL (256.4 µmol/L)
Parathyroid hormone	Undetectable

Aggressive volume replacement with intravenous normal saline is initiated.

Which of the following drugs is likely to provide the most sustained benefit in decreasing this patient's calcium level?

(A) Calcitonin
(B) Cinacalcet
(C) Prednisone
(D) Zoledronate

Item 2

A 78-year-old woman who resides in a nursing home is seen for management of her diabetes mellitus. The patient's blood glucose log shows levels ranging between 40 and 400 mg/dL (2.2 and 22.2 mmol/L). She otherwise feels well. She has been on insulin for more than 25 years after first taking oral agents for several years following her initial diagnosis. The patient has hypothyroidism treated with levothyroxine and remote history of Graves disease treated with radioactive iodine. Her diabetes is currently treated with neutral protamine Hagedorn (NPH) insulin, 25 units twice daily; the dosage has been gradually increased over the past 3 weeks.

The only pertinent finding on physical examination is her lean body habitus (BMI of 19.3).

Results of routine laboratory studies are all within the normal range. An anti–glutamic acid decarboxylase antibody titer is positive.

Which of the following is the most likely diagnosis?

(A) Late-onset autoimmune diabetes of adulthood
(B) Maturity-onset diabetes of the young
(C) Type 1 diabetes mellitus
(D) Type 2 diabetes mellitus

Item 3

A 47-year-old woman is evaluated for difficult-to-control hypertension. She was previously treated for hypokalemia.

On physical examination, temperature is 36.0 °C (96.8 °F), blood pressure is 178/100 mm Hg, pulse rate is 58/min, respiration rate is 16/min, and BMI is 29. No abdominal bruit is detected. Funduscopic examination shows mild arteriolar narrowing.

Laboratory studies:

Electrolytes	
Sodium	143 meq/L (143 mmol/L)
Potassium	3.5 meq/L (3.5 mmol/L) (after replacement therapy)
Chloride	101 meq/L (101 mmol/L)
Bicarbonate	33 meq/L (33 mmol/L)
Aldosterone	
Baseline	23 ng/dL (635 pmol/L)
3 Days after high salt intake	15 ng/dL (414 pmol/L)
Renin activity	
Baseline	<0.1 ng/mL/h (0.1 µg/L/h)
3 Days after high salt intake	<0.1 ng/mL/h (0.1 µg/L/h)
Aldosterone to renin activity ratio	>50

Which of the following is the most appropriate next step in management?

(A) Adrenalectomy
(B) Bilateral adrenal vein catheterization
(C) CT of the adrenal glands
(D) Duplex ultrasonography of the renal arteries

Item 4

A 28-year-old man is evaluated for a 2-month history of recurrent confusion, palpitations, and diaphoresis occurring whenever he misses breakfast. The symptoms are relieved with eating. His medical history is otherwise unremarkable, and he takes no medications.

On physical examination, vital signs are normal, and BMI is 26. The results of the general physical examination are normal.

Results of laboratory studies show a fasting plasma glucose level of 52 mg/dL (2.9 mmol/L) and an insulin level of 18 µU/mL (129.9 pmol/L) (normal range, 2 to 20 µU/mL [14.4 to 144.3 pmol/L]).

Which of the following is the most appropriate next step in diagnosis?

(A) CT of the abdomen
(B) Endoscopic ultrasonography of the pancreas
(C) Home glucose monitoring
(D) Octreotide scan
(E) Supervised 72-hour fast in the hospital

Item 5

A 26-year-old woman is evaluated for a 4-month history of amenorrhea. Menses began at age 13 years. At age 18 years, the patient was placed on an oral contraceptive pill to control heavy bleeding. She discontinued the oral contraceptive pill 4 months ago because she and her husband want to become pregnant, and she has had no menses since then. There is no family history of infertility or premature menopause.

On physical examination, vital signs are normal, and BMI is 24. There is no acne, hirsutism, or galactorrhea. Examination of the thyroid gland and visual field testing yield normal findings. Pelvic examination findings are also normal. An office pregnancy test is negative.

Laboratory studies:

Follicle-stimulating hormone	2 mU/mL (2 U/L)
Prolactin	17 ng/mL (17 µg/L)
Thyroid-stimulating hormone	1.1 µU/mL (1.1 mU/L)
Thyroxine (T$_4$), free	1.0 ng/dL (12.9 pmol/L)

Which of the following is the most appropriate next diagnostic test?

(A) Measurement of the plasma dehydroepiandrosterone sulfate level
(B) Measurement of serum estradiol level
(C) MRI of the pituitary gland
(D) Progestin withdrawal challenge

Item 6

A 54-year-old man is evaluated for increasing fatigue and loss of libido. He reports no headache, diplopia, visual loss, rhinorrhea, or changes in thirst, urination, or weight. The patient underwent transsphenoidal surgery 6 years ago to remove a nonfunctioning pituitary adenoma; results of postoperative pituitary testing were normal. He had stereotactic irradiation to treat the residual tumor 3 months after surgery. He has no pertinent family history and takes no medications. An MRI performed 18 months ago showed no growth of the residual pituitary tumor.

Physical examination reveals a pale man. Blood pressure is 106/70 mm Hg, pulse rate is 60/min, respiration rate is 14/min, and BMI is 27.4. Other findings are unremarkable.

Results of routine hematologic and serum chemistry studies are normal, except for a hemoglobin level of 11.8 g/dL (118 g/L).

Which of the following is the most likely diagnosis?

(A) Diabetes insipidus
(B) Hydrocephalus
(C) Hypopituitarism
(D) Regrowth of the adenoma

Item 7

A 75-year-old man is admitted to the intensive care unit with sepsis associated with pneumonia, hypoxemic respiratory failure requiring ventilator support, and hypotension. He is treated appropriately with volume resuscitation, vasopressors, and antibiotic therapy and is extubated 5 days later.

On physical examination, blood pressure is 110/75 mm Hg, pulse rate is 88/min, and respiration rate is 16/min. Examination of the neck reveals a thyroid gland of normal size and without nodules. There are no tremors in the extremities.

Because results of admission laboratory studies showed mild hyponatremia, additional blood tests are performed to evaluate the hyponatremia.

Laboratory studies:

Thyroid-stimulating hormone	0.23 µU/mL (0.23 mU/L)
Thyroxine (T$_4$), free	0.9 ng/dL (11.6 pmol/L)
Triiodothyronine (T$_3$), free	0.4 ng/L (0.6 pmol/L)
Cortisol (8 AM)	30 µg/dL (828 nmol/L) (normal range, 5-25 µg/dL [138-690 nmol/L])

Which of the following is the most appropriate next step in management?

(A) Brain MRI
(B) Levothyroxine
(C) Liothyronine
(D) Repeat thyroid function tests in 4 to 8 weeks
(E) Ultrasonography of the thyroid gland

Item 8

A 72-year-old man comes to the office for a follow-up evaluation. He has had type 2 diabetes mellitus for 13 years. Over the past 5 years, his hemoglobin A$_{1c}$ value has slowly risen to 9.8%, and his fasting blood glucose levels at home have frequently exceeded 180 mg/dL (10.0 mmol/L). He has been adherent to recommended lifestyle changes. The patient is currently on metformin, 1000 mg twice daily, and extended-release glipizide, 20 mg/d. He has hypertension treated with candesartan and hydrochlorothiazide and hyperlipidemia treated with atorvastatin.

Results of physical examination are normal.

Which of the following is the best next step in therapy?

(A) Add exenatide
(B) Add insulin glargine
(C) Add pioglitazone
(D) Add sitagliptin
(E) Double his dosage of glipizide

Item 9

A 25-year-old man is evaluated for a 2-year history of infertility. He and his wife have been unable to conceive since marrying 2 years ago. Analysis of a semen sample provided 3 weeks ago during an infertility evaluation showed azoospermia. The patient has a strong libido and no history of erectile dysfunction. He has no other medical problems and exercises regularly. There is no family history of delayed puberty or endocrine tumors.

On physical examination, the patient appears very muscular. Temperature is normal, blood pressure is 142/85 mm Hg, pulse rate is 55/min, respiration rate is 14/min, and BMI is 22. Visual fields are full to confrontation. There is extensive acne but no gynecomastia or galactorrhea. Testes volume is 4 mL (normal, 18-25 mL) bilaterally. The penis appears normal.

Laboratory studies:
Follicle-stimulating hormone	<0.1 mU/mL (0.1 U/L)
Luteinizing hormone	<0.1 mU/mL (0.1 U/L)
Prolactin	12 ng/mL (12 µg/L)
Testosterone, total	<50 ng/dL (1.7 nmol/L)

An MRI of the pituitary gland shows normal findings.

Which of the following is the most likely diagnosis?

(A) Anabolic steroid abuse
(B) Nonfunctioning pituitary macroadenoma
(C) Primary testicular failure
(D) Prolactinoma

Item 10

A 23-year-old woman comes to the office for follow-up. The patient has a 5-year history of hypothyroidism and has been on a stable dose of levothyroxine for the past 3 years. She is now 6 weeks pregnant with her first child.

Physical examination findings are noncontributory.

Results of laboratory studies 1 month ago showed a serum thyroid-stimulating hormone (TSH) level of 2.9 µU/mL (2.9 mU/L) and a free thyroxine level of 1.4 ng/dL (18.1 pmol/L).

Which of the following is the most appropriate management?

(A) Add iodine therapy
(B) Measure her free triiodothyronine (T_3) level
(C) Recheck her serum TSH level
(D) Continue current management

Item 11

A 45-year-old woman is seen for routine follow-up. She has type 2 diabetes mellitus, diagnosed 5 years ago; initial treatment included metformin and glimepiride. A daily injection of insulin glargine was added to her regimen 1 year ago. At present, her hemoglobin A_{1c} value is 8.1%. Mean blood glucose values derived from the past 4 days of the patient's blood glucose log, which includes preprandial (Pre) and postprandial (Post) values, are shown.

Meal	Pre (mg/dL [mmol/L])	Post (mg/dL [mmol/L])
Breakfast	105 (5.8)	186 (10.3)
Lunch	169 (9.4)	258 (14.3)
Supper	146 (8.1)	—

Her mean bedtime blood glucose level is 278 mg/dL (15.4 mmol/L).

Which of the following changes should be made to this patient's medication regimen?

(A) Add exenatide
(B) Increase the insulin glargine dosage
(C) Start insulin pump therapy
(D) Stop glimepiride and add mealtime insulin aspart

Item 12

A 60-year-old-woman is evaluated for headache and aching pain in her hips and knees that has gradually become more severe over the past 3 years. She reports that she has had to increase her shoe size twice over the past 2 years. The patient takes no medications.

On physical examination, blood pressure is 142/90 mm Hg, pulse rate is 76/min, respiration rate is 16/min, and BMI is 25. Other findings include an unusually prominent forehead, a heavy brow ridge, a broad nose, accentuated nasolabial folds, a large tongue, and large, thick hands and feet.

Laboratory studies show a serum growth hormone (GH) level of 18.7 ng/mL (18.7 µg/L) and an insulin-like growth factor 1 (IGF-1) level of 543 ng/mL (543 µg/L) (normal range, 190-300 ng/mL [190-300 µg/L]).

An MRI shows a 1.7-cm pituitary tumor with minimal parasellar extension.

The patient undergoes transsphenoidal surgery, after which her GH level remains mildly elevated at 4.2 ng/mL (4.2 µg/L) and her IGF-1 level remains elevated at 402 ng/mL (402 µg/L).

Which of the following additional therapies is most likely to normalize her GH and IGF-1 levels over the next year?

(A) Cabergoline
(B) Craniotomy
(C) Radiation therapy
(D) Somatostatin analogue

Item 13

A 21-year-old woman is evaluated for a 7-year history of oligomenorrhea and slowly progressive hirsutism. Menses began at age 14 years and were always irregular. She has gained weight at a rate of approximately 4.5 kg (10 lb) per year. Her facial hair has become progressively thicker since age 18 years, and she now menstruates only three to four times per year. She is sexually active but does not want to become pregnant at this time. Family history is noncontributory, and she takes no medications.

On physical examination, vital signs are normal, and BMI is 28. Prominent terminal hairs are noted on the upper lip and chin, with some on the upper cheeks and chest; there is thick hair from the pubis to the umbilicus. Results of a pelvic examination and Pap smear are normal.

Laboratory studies:
Dehydroepiandrosterone sulfate	4.3 µg/mL (11.6 µmol/L)

Human chorionic gonadotropin	Negative for pregnancy
17-Hydroxyprogesterone	105 ng/dL (3.15 nmol/L) (normal, <400 ng/dL [12.0 nmol/L])
Prolactin	11 ng/mL (11 µg/L)
Testosterone, total	84 ng/dL (2.9 nmol/L)
Thyroid-stimulating hormone	1.4 µU/mL (1.4 mU/L)

A progestin withdrawal challenge with medroxyprogesterone acetate results in a temporary resumption of menses.

Which of the following is the most appropriate next step in management?

(A) Measurement of free testosterone level

(B) Prednisone therapy

(C) Spironolactone and oral contraceptive therapy

(D) Transvaginal ovarian ultrasonography

Item 14

A 45-year-old man is evaluated for a 3-month history of fatigue, constipation, and polyuria. He also has a 5-year history of hypertension. Current medications are losartan and diltiazem.

Physical examination findings, including vital signs, are normal.

Laboratory studies:

Calcium	11.4 mg/dL (2.85 mmol/L)
Creatinine	1.1 mg/dL (97.2 µmol/L)
Glucose, fasting	88 mg/dL (4.9 mmol/L)
Phosphorus	2.2 mg/dL (0.71 mmol/L)
Thyroid-stimulating hormone	1.2 µU/mL (1.2 mU/L)

Measurement of which of the following levels should be done next?

(A) Calcitonin

(B) 25-Hydroxy vitamin D

(C) Parathyroid hormone

(D) Parathyroid hormone–related protein

Item 15

A 65-year-old woman is seen in the office after a CT scan obtained in the emergency department for suspected renal colic incidentally revealed an adrenal nodule.

On physical examination, temperature is 36.5 °C (97.7 °F), blood pressure is 128/74 mm Hg, pulse rate is 88/min, respiration rate is 16/min, and BMI is 30. All other examination findings are normal. There is no evidence of masculinization.

The previously obtained CT scan of the abdomen reveals a 2.5-cm right adrenal mass with an attenuation value of 10 Hounsfield units; the liver and kidneys appear normal. Findings on a chest radiograph are also normal.

In addition to an overnight 1-mg dexamethasone suppression test, which of the following is the most reasonable next step in the evaluation of this patient?

(A) Determination of the serum aldosterone to plasma renin activity ratio

(B) Determination of the serum aldosterone to plasma renin activity ratio and measurement of plasma dehydroepiandrosterone sulfate level

(C) Measurement of morning serum cortisol and plasma dehydroepiandrosterone sulfate levels

(D) Measurement of plasma metanephrine level

Item 16

A 35-year-old woman comes to the office for her annual physical examination. The patient says she feel well. She has no pertinent personal or family medical history and takes no medications.

On physical examination, vital signs are normal. Palpation of the thyroid gland suggests the presence of a nodule. All other findings of the general physical examination are normal.

Laboratory studies show a thyroid-stimulating hormone level of 1.3 µU/mL (1.3 mU/L) and a free thyroxine (T$_4$) level of 1.3 ng/dL (16.8 pmol/L).

An ultrasound of the thyroid gland reveals a normal-sized gland with a 2-cm hypoechoic right midpole nodule.

Which of the following is the most appropriate next step in management?

(A) Fine-needle aspiration biopsy of the nodule

(B) Measurement of anti-thyroperoxidase and anti–thyroglobulin antibody titers

(C) Neck CT with contrast

(D) Thyroid scan with technetium

(E) Trial of levothyroxine therapy

Item 17

A 51-year-old man is evaluated for a 9-month history of chronic abdominal pain. He has a long-standing history of alcoholism and has been admitted to the hospital several times in the past 8 years for gastrointestinal bleeding and acute pancreatitis. A review of symptoms is positive only for a 5.5-kg (12.1-lb) weight loss over the past year. He currently takes no medications.

Vital signs are normal, and BMI is 23. Physical examination reveals a scaphoid-appearing abdomen with normal bowel sounds and diffuse abdominal tenderness to palpation without guarding.

His fasting plasma glucose level is 175 mg/dL (9.7 mmol/L), and a repeat fasting plasma glucose level is 182 mg/dL (10.1 mmol/L).

A CT scan of the abdomen reveals diffuse pancreatic calcifications.

Which of the following is the best categorization of this patient's diabetes mellitus?

(A) Late-onset autoimmune diabetes of adulthood

(B) Secondary diabetes

(C) Type 1 diabetes

(D) Type 2 diabetes

Item 18

A 24-year-old woman is admitted to the hospital for a supervised fast to evaluate persistent fasting hypoglycemia. The patient lives with her parents. She has no pertinent personal medical history and takes no medications. Family history is notable for type 2 diabetes mellitus in her mother. Five hours into the test, she develops diaphoresis, vocal slurring, and confusion. The test is stopped, and the symptoms resolve with intravenous administration of glucose.

Laboratory studies (blood obtained during the fast):

C-peptide	2.6 ng/mL (0.86 nmol/L) (normal range, 0.5-2.5 ng/ml [0.2-0.8 nmol/L])
Glucose	32 mg/dL (1.8 mmol/L)
Insulin	22 µU/mL (158.8 pmol/L) (normal range, 2-20 µU/mL [14.4-144.3 pmol/L])
Proinsulin	Pending

Which of the following should be done next?

(A) CT scan of abdomen

(B) Endoscopic ultrasonography of the pancreas

(C) Measurement of serum calcium level and assessment of anterior pituitary function

(D) Measurement of serum levels of sulfonylureas

(E) MRI of the abdomen

Item 19

A 55-year-old woman is evaluated in the surgical recovery room for tetany. Two hours ago, she had a single large parathyroid adenoma removed. Preoperative skeletal radiographs showed subperiosteal bone resorption of the distal phalanges, femoral and spinal osteopenia, and osteoporosis in the radius.

She is treated with intravenous calcium and improves.

Laboratory studies (before calcium therapy):

Albumin	4.2 g/dL (42 g/L)
Calcium	6.0 mg/dL (1.5 mmol/L)
Phosphorus	1.8 mg/dL (0.58 mmol/L)
Parathyroid hormone	20 pg/mL (20 ng/L)

Which of the following is the most likely diagnosis?

(A) Hungry bone syndrome

(B) Osteomalacia

(C) Permanent hypoparathyroidism

(D) Vitamin D deficiency

Item 20

A 55-year-old man with recently diagnosed pheochromocytoma is evaluated prior to surgical removal in 10 days. His only medication is amlodipine.

On physical examination, the patient appears anxious. Temperature is 36.0 °C (96.8 °F), blood pressure is 172/96 mm Hg, pulse rate is 98/min, respiration rate is 16/min, and BMI is 23. Results of funduscopic, cardiovascular, and neurologic examinations are normal.

An electrocardiogram shows sinus rhythm at a rate of 100/min. There is no evidence of ischemia.

Which of the following is the most appropriate next step in management?

(A) Add chlorthalidone

(B) Add metoprolol

(C) Add prazosin

(D) Hospitalize and begin intravenous phentolamine

(E) Hospitalize and begin intravenous sodium nitroprusside

Item 21

A 68-year-old woman is re-evaluated after laboratory studies show a fasting plasma glucose level of 113 mg/dL (6.3 mmol/L). She has a maternal family history of type 2 diabetes mellitus.

On physical examination, blood pressure is 142/88 mm Hg and BMI is 29. Other vital signs and examination findings are normal.

She undergoes an oral glucose tolerance test, during which her 2-hour plasma glucose level increases to 135 mg/dL (7.5 mmol/L).

Additional laboratory studies:

Hemoglobin A_{1c}	5.8%
LDL-cholesterol	110 mg/dL (2.85 mmol/L)
HDL-cholesterol	48 mg/dL (1.24 mmol/L)
Triglyceride	172 mg/dL (1.94 mmol/L)

Which of the following is the most appropriate treatment recommendation to control her glucose level?

(A) Acarbose administration

(B) Diet and exercise

(C) Metformin administration

(D) Ramipril administration

(E) Rosiglitazone administration

Item 22

A 28-year-old woman is evaluated for a 2-year history of infertility and a 4-year history of amenorrhea and galactorrhea. She has no other relevant personal or family medical history and takes no medications.

On physical examination, vital signs are normal. Bilateral expressible galactorrhea is noted.

Results of laboratory studies are normal except for a serum prolactin level of 239 ng/mL (239 µg/L).

An MRI of the pituitary gland shows a 1.4-cm hypodense lesion compatible with a macroadenoma.

She is treated with cabergoline, and her prolactin level returns to the normal range. A repeat MRI shows that the tumor had decreased to 7 mm in maximum diameter. She calls 1 week later after she learns that she is approximately 2 months pregnant; she has discontinued taking cabergoline.

The patient should be counseled about which of the following potential complications related to her prolactinoma?

(A) Fetal malformation
(B) Premature delivery
(C) Prolactinoma enlargement
(D) Sheehan syndrome
(E) Stillbirth

Item 23

A 38-year-old man is evaluated for a 2-year history of fatigue, erectile dysfunction, and arthralgias of the knees. He also has hypercholesterolemia. Family history is remarkable for type 2 diabetes mellitus in his paternal uncle and nonalcoholic cirrhosis in his father. Current medications include pravastatin and acetaminophen.

On physical examination, temperature is normal, blood pressure is 110/65 mm Hg, pulse rate is 98/min, respiration rate is 14/min, and BMI is 31. Visual fields are full to confrontation. The patient has a dark complexion and gynecomastia; there is no galactorrhea. Testes volume is 5 mL (normal, 18-25 mL) bilaterally. The right knee is slightly swollen and tender.

Laboratory studies:

Alanine aminotransferase	80 U/L
Aspartate aminotransferase	60 U/L
Glucose, fasting	135 mg/dL (7.5 mmol/L)
Luteinizing hormone	0.4 mU/mL (0.4 U/L)
Testosterone, total (AM)	
Initial measurement	120 ng/dL (4.2 nmol/L)
Repeat measurement	130 ng/dL (4.5 nmol/L)

An MRI of the sella turcica shows normal findings.

Which of the following is the most appropriate next test for this patient?

(A) CT of the adrenal glands
(B) Measurement of urine free cortisol excretion over 24 hours
(C) Serum calcium and parathyroid hormone measurement
(D) Transferrin saturation measurement

Item 24

A 19-year-old woman is evaluated for a 2-month history of increasing fatigue and polyuria. Medical history is remarkable for a prolactinoma treated with cabergoline. Her father has a history of kidney stones.

On physical examination, vital signs are normal, and BMI is 21. All other findings are unremarkable.

Laboratory studies:

Calcium	12 mg/dL (3.0 mmol/L)
Creatinine	0.8 mg/dL (70.7 µmol/L)

Parathyroid hormone	260 pg/mL (260 ng/L)
Prolactin	15 ng/mL (15 µg/L)

Which of the following is the most likely diagnosis?

(A) Autoimmune polyglandular syndrome type 1
(B) Multiple endocrine neoplasia type 1
(C) Multiple endocrine neoplasia type 2
(D) Osteosclerotic myeloma

Item 25

A 35-year-old woman comes to the office for a follow-up evaluation. The patient has a 5-year history of hypothyroidism for which she takes levothyroxine; the dosage has been stable for the past 2 years, and her thyroid-stimulating hormone level has been within the target range of 1 to 3 µU/mL (1 to 3 mU/L). She has been otherwise healthy except for iron deficiency anemia for which she started taking ferrous sulfate 3 months ago. She has been on the same low-dose oral contraceptive pills since delivering her last child 3 years ago. The patient exercises 45 minutes 4 days per week. Current medications are levothyroxine (75 µg/d), ferrous sulfate (325 mg/d), and ethinyl estradiol with norgestimate (once daily), all on awakening.

On physical examination, vital signs are normal, and BMI is 24.4. The thyroid gland is slightly enlarged and smooth, without nodules.

Results of laboratory studies show a serum thyroid-stimulating hormone level of 12.5 µU/mL (12.5 mU/L) and a free thyroxine (T_4) level of 0.9 ng/dL (11.6 pmol/L).

Which of the following changes to her medication regimen should be recommended?

(A) Add desiccated thyroid hormone
(B) Increase the levothyroxine dosage to 125 µg
(C) Increase the levothyroxine dosage to 125 µg and add liothyronine, 25 µg
(D) Substitute a progestin-only pill for ethinyl estradiol and norgestimate
(E) Take the levothyroxine on an empty stomach

Item 26

A 78-year-old man is evaluated in the hospital for poor glycemic control before undergoing femoral-popliteal bypass surgery. He has been on the vascular surgery ward for 3 weeks with a nonhealing foot ulcer. The patient has an extensive history of arteriosclerotic cardiovascular disease, including peripheral vascular disease, and a 20-year-history of type 2 diabetes mellitus. His most recent hemoglobin A_{1c} value, obtained 2 months before admission, was 8.9%. His diabetes regimen consists of glipizide, 40 mg/d. While in the hospital, his plasma glucose levels have generally been in the 200 to 250 mg/dL (11.1 to 13.9 mmol/L) range. He is eating well.

In addition to stopping glipizide, which of the following is the most appropriate treatment for this patient?

(A) Basal insulin and rapid-acting insulin before meals

(B) Insulin infusion

(C) Neutral protamine Hagedorn (NPH) insulin twice daily

(D) Sliding scale regular insulin

Item 27

A 45-year-old woman is evaluated for a 6-month history of weakness, menstrual irregularities, hirsutism, insomnia, and emotional lability. She also reports an 8.0-kg (17.6-lb) weight gain during this period. She was previously healthy. She takes no medications.

On physical examination, temperature is 36.0 °C (96.8 °F), blood pressure is 172/90 mm Hg, pulse rate is 78/min, respiration rate is 16/min, and BMI is 32. The patient has a rounded, plethoric face with increased supra-clavicular and dorsal fat pads. There are areas of unexplained ecchymoses over the upper and lower extremities. Abdominal examination reveals purple striae. She has proximal muscle weakness.

Results of routine laboratory studies are normal except for a serum potassium level of 3.4 meq/L (3.4 mmol/L).

Which of the following is the most appropriate next test for this patient?

(A) Cosyntropin stimulation test

(B) High-dose dexamethasone suppression test

(C) Measurement of morning serum cortisol level

(D) Measurement of 24-hour urine free cortisol excretion

Item 28

A 72-year-old woman comes to the office for a follow-up evaluation of osteoporosis. She has a history of vertebral compression fractures. For the past 5 years, the patient has been taking oral formulations of elemental calcium, 1500 mg/d; ergocalciferol, 800 U/d; and alendronate, 70 mg once weekly. She is adherent to her therapy.

On physical examination, the patient appears frail. Vital signs are normal, and BMI is 19. There is obvious kyphosis. Mild tenderness in the region of the prior compression fractures is noted.

Laboratory studies:

Calcium	9.5 mg/dL (2.4 mmol/L)
Phosphorus	3.8 mg/dL (1.2 mmol/L)
Parathyroid hormone	33 pg/mL (33 ng/L)
Thyroid-stimulating hormone	1.8 µU/mL (1.8 mU/L)
25-Hydroxy vitamin D	35 ng/mL (87 nmol/L)
Urine calcium	315 mg/24 h (7.9 mmol/24 h)

Results of a bone mineral density study show T-scores of −3.8 in the spine and −3.7 in the hip, compared with scores obtained 3 years ago of −3.4 and −3.3, respectively.

Which of the following is the best next step in management?

(A) Add teriparatide

(B) Change to high-dose ergocalciferol

(C) Discontinue the alendronate and start teriparatide

(D) Substitute intravenous zoledronate for the alendronate

Item 29

A 24-year-old woman is evaluated for a 5-week history of polyuria and polydipsia (both of which were of sudden onset), a 3-month history of mild fatigue, a 7-month history of galactorrhea, and a 1-year history of secondary amenorrhea. She has been drinking between 7.5 and 9.5 liters of water daily and has been awakening three to five times per night to urinate; she is always thirsty at these times. The patient reports normal growth and development; she experienced menarche at age 12 years. Approximately 6 months ago, her ophthalmologist diagnosed uveitis. She takes no medications.

Physical examination reveals a short, mildly overweight woman. Blood pressure is 118/74 mm Hg, pulse rate is 78/min, and BMI is 27.1. Bilateral expressible galactorrhea and axillary lymphadenopathy are noted. Breast development and pubic hair are normal.

Laboratory studies:

Sodium	146 meq/L (146 mmol/L)
Osmolality	
Plasma	305 mosm/kg
Urine	84 mosm/kg
Prolactin	48.2 ng/mL (48.2 µg/L)
Thyroxine (T_4), free	1.2 ng/dL (15.5 pmol/L)

An MRI shows a normal pituitary gland but a thickened pituitary stalk.

Which of the following is the best next step in diagnosis?

(A) Biopsy of the stalk lesion

(B) Chest radiography

(C) Inferior petrosal sinus sampling

(D) Measurement of anti–single-stranded DNA antibodies

Item 30

A 52-year-old man is evaluated in the surgical intensive care unit for carpopedal spasm and tetany. He underwent a thyroidectomy and a modified radical neck dissection for follicular thyroid cancer 2 days ago and was extubated this morning. The patient reports perioral and fingertip paresthesias.

On physical examination, vital signs are normal. A thyroidectomy scar and carpopedal spasms are noted. A Chvostek sign is elicited.

Laboratory studies:

Albumin	4.5 g/dL (45 g/L)
Calcium	6.9 mg/dL (1.7 mmol/L)
Phosphorus	3.9 mg/dL (1.3 mmol/L)

Which of the following is the most appropriate acute treatment for this patient?

(A) Intravenous calcitriol

(B) Intravenous calcium gluconate

(C) Oral calcium

(D) Oral calcium and vitamin D

Item 31

A homeless man is brought by ambulance to the emergency department. He was found unconscious in an abandoned, unheated house by city workers. The temperature has been below freezing for the past 24 hours. No medications were found on the patient.

Physical examination reveals an obese, poorly arousable older man. Temperature is 33.3 °C (92.0 °F), blood pressure is 120/90 mm Hg, pulse rate is 50/min, and BMI is 34. His pupils are equal, round, and reactive to light. Examination of the neck reveals a well-healed surgical scar at the base. His lungs are clear to auscultation. Distant heart sounds are heard on cardiac examination. There is 2+ edema bilaterally in the lower legs. Neurologic examination shows bilateral ankle jerk reflexes with delayed tendon relaxation recovery.

Laboratory studies:

Creatinine	1.5 mg/dL (132.6 µmol/L)
Electrolytes	
Sodium	130 meq/L (130 mmol/L)
Potassium	3.8 meq/L (3.8 mmol/L)
Chloride	101 meq/L (101 mmol/L)
Bicarbonate	27 meq/L (27 mmol/L)
Thyroid-stimulating hormone	Pending
Thyroxine, free	Pending
Arterial blood gas studies (ambient air)	
pH	7.31
P_{CO_2}	55 mm Hg
P_{O_2}	60 mm Hg
Oxygen saturation	90%

Blood, urine, and sputum cultures are obtained.

Findings on chest radiography are within normal limits. Electrocardiography reveals sinus bradycardia with low voltage throughout.

In addition to beginning intravenous normal saline and passively warming the patient, which of the following is the most appropriate next step in management?

(A) Intravenous levothyroxine

(B) Intravenous levothyroxine and intravenous hydrocortisone

(C) Intravenous levothyroxine, intravenous hydrocortisone, and empiric antibiotics

(D) Review of results of thyroid-stimulating hormone and free thyroxine (T_4) level measurements

Item 32

A 66-year-old man is seen for follow-up evaluation of hypogonadism that was first diagnosed 6 months ago. He has been on testosterone enanthate, 200 mg by injection every 2 weeks, ever since and has noticed an improvement in stamina and libido. He takes no other medications.

On physical examination, vital signs are normal. There is normal beard growth. Testes volume is 12 mL (normal, 18-25 mL) bilaterally. Rectal examination shows a slightly enlarged prostate without nodules. All other general physical examination findings are normal.

Laboratory studies:

	Baseline	After 3 months (1 day before testosterone injection)	After 6 months (1 day before testosterone injection)
Hematocrit	39%	40%	41%
Prostate-specific antigen (PSA)	0.5 ng/mL (0.5 µg/L)	2 ng/mL (2 µg/L)	6 ng/mL (6 µg/L)
Testosterone, total	150 ng/dL (5.2 nmol/L)	300 ng/dL (10.4 nmol/L)	400 ng/dL (13.9 nmol/L)

Which of the following is the most appropriate treatment for this patient?

(A) Administer the testosterone enanthate every 3 weeks

(B) Stop the testosterone enanthate and refer for prostate biopsy

(C) Stop the testosterone enanthate for 2 weeks and then repeat the PSA measurement

(D) Substitute topical testosterone for the testosterone enanthate

Item 33

A 68-year-old woman comes to the office for a follow-up evaluation. She has had type 2 diabetes mellitus for the past 13 years and has experienced two early-morning hypoglycemic episodes in the past 3 months. Although her self-monitoring of fasting blood glucose levels over the past 6 months has consistently shown results in the 110 to 140 mg/dL (6.1 to 7.8 mmol/L) range, her hemoglobin A_{1c} value during this same period has exceeded 8.5%. Her current diabetes regimen consists of metformin, 850 mg three times daily, and insulin detemir, 38 units at night. She has no other medical problems.

Which of the following is the most appropriate next step in management?

(A) Add exenatide to her regimen

(B) Check her serum fructosamine level

(C) Increase the insulin detemir dosage

(D) Measure 2-hour postprandial glucose levels

Item 34

A 34-year-old man is evaluated for a 1-year history of impotence. He reports mild fatigue but no headaches or visual symptoms. Personal and family medical histories are noncontributory. He takes no medications.

Physical examination reveals an obese man. Blood pressure in 132/80 mm Hg, pulse rate is 80/min, respiration rate is 16/min, and BMI is 32.3. He has normal secondary sexual characteristics.

Laboratory studies:

Prolactin	11,420 ng/mL (11,420 µg/L)
Testosterone	134 ng/dL (4.6 nmol/L)
Thyroid-stimulating hormone	0.6 µU/mL (0.6 mU/L)
Thyroxine (T$_4$), free	0.52 ng/dL (6.7 pmol/L)
Cortisol (8 AM)	4.3 µg/dL (118.7 nmol/L) (normal range, 5-25 µg/dL [138-690 nmol/L])

An MRI shows a 3.2- × 1.7- × 2.8-cm macroadenoma invading the cavernous sinus and wrapping around the right carotid artery. Results of visual field testing are normal.

In addition to treating the hypopituitarism, which of the following is the most appropriate initial therapy for this patient?

(A) Cabergoline
(B) Pituitary surgery via a craniotomy
(C) Radiation therapy
(D) Somatostatin analogue
(E) Transsphenoidal surgery

Item 35

A 39-year-old woman is seen in the office for follow-up of Cushing syndrome.

Laboratory studies:

Adrenocorticotropic hormone	45 pg/mL (9.9 pmol/L)
24-Hour urine free cortisol	318 µg/24 h (876.3 nmol/24 h)
Morning cortisol (8 AM)	
After 1 mg of dexamethasone the night before	15.6 µg/dL (430.6 nmol/L) (normal, <5 µg/dL [138 nmol/L])
After 8 mg of dexamethasone the night before	9.5 µg/dL (262.2 nmol/L) (normal, <5 µg/dL [138 nmol/L])

An MRI of the pituitary gland shows a 1.1-cm microadenoma on the left side. A CT of the chest shows normal findings.

Which of the following is the most appropriate next step in management?

(A) Bilateral adrenalectomy
(B) Ketoconazole treatment
(C) Pituitary adenomectomy
(D) Pituitary radiation therapy

Item 36

A 60-year-old man is evaluated for slowly worsening bone pain in the lower extremities. He reports no other symptoms and takes no medications.

On physical examination, vital signs are normal. Bilateral bowing of the legs is noted, as is increased warmth anteriorly over the shins. All other findings are normal.

Results of laboratory studies are normal except for an alkaline phosphatase level of 450 U/L.

A bone scan shows increased areas of radiotracer uptake, visualized as "hot spots" in the skull, left femoral shaft, and right and left tibias. A radiograph of the left femur is shown.

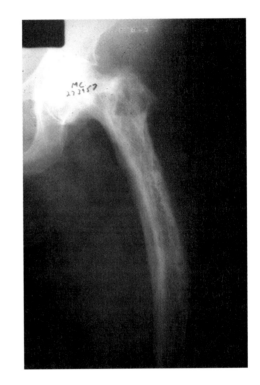

In addition to NSAIDs, which of the following is the most appropriate treatment for this patient?

(A) Alendronate
(B) Calcitonin
(C) Calcium
(D) Teriparatide

Item 37

A 35-year-old woman is evaluated for a 6-month history of fatigue. She reports no abdominal pain or diarrhea. The patient has a history of unexplained osteopenia and hypothyroidism due to Hashimoto disease; the hypothyroidism is treated with levothyroxine. Her dosage has steadily increased over the past 2 years to her current dosage of 0.3 mg/d without normalization of her serum thyroid hormone levels; she takes the levothyroxine on awakening. Other medications include a daily calcium tablet and multivitamin, both taken at noon. She is adherent to her medical program.

On physical examination, blood pressure is 126/90 mm Hg, pulse rate is 60/min, respiration rate is 14/min, and BMI is 24.5; weight is 59.1 kg (130 lb). Neck examination reveals a small firm goiter.

Laboratory studies:

Hemoglobin	11.0 g/dL (110 g/L)
Mean corpuscular volume	75 fL
Albumin	3.7 g/dL (37 g/L)
Thyroid-stimulating hormone	13.6 µU/mL (13.6 mU/L)
Thyroxine (T_4), free	1.0 ng/dL (12.9 pmol/L)

Which of the following is the most appropriate next step in management?

(A) Add liothyronine
(B) Change to a different brand of levothyroxine
(C) Move the calcium tablet and vitamin dosing to bedtime
(D) Screen for celiac disease

Item 38

A 20-year-old man is hospitalized after sustaining a pelvic fracture in an automobile accident. One month into his hospitalization, the patient notes nausea and anorexia. Before the injury, he was in good health and took no medications. Family history is unremarkable. Current medications are enoxaparin and hydromorphone.

Physical examination reveals an alert, oriented, and thin patient. Blood pressure is 128/78 mm Hg, pulse rate is 88/min, and respiration rate is 16/min. Thyroid examination reveals no goiter, and the lungs are clear to auscultation. The patient is immobilized in bed and a pelvic external fixation device is in place. Neurologic examination findings are unremarkable.

Laboratory studies:

Albumin	4.4 g/dL (44 g/L)
Calcium	12.6 mg/dL (3.15 mmol/L)
Creatinine	1.6 mg/dL (141.4 µmol/L)
Phosphorus	4.1 mg/dL (1.3 mmol/L)
Parathyroid hormone	7.1 pg/mL (7.1 ng/L)
Thyroid-stimulating hormone	0.3 µU/mL (0.3 mU/L)
Thyroxine (T_4), free	1.1 ng/dL (14.2 pmol/L)
1,25-Dihydroxy vitamin D	35.2 pg/mL (84.5 pmol/L)
25-Hydroxy vitamin D	38 ng/mL (95 nmol/L)

Which of the following is the most likely cause of his hypercalcemia?

(A) Acute kidney injury
(B) Fracture-related hypercalcemia
(C) Humoral hypercalcemia of malignancy
(D) Hypercalcemia of immobilization

Item 39

A 32-year-old man is evaluated for a 5-month history of poor libido, constant fatigue, and erectile dysfunction. The patient has chronic pain from a motor vehicle accident 3 years ago in which he sustained back trauma. Although the pain is largely controlled with sustained-release oral morphine and his functional status is good, his quality of life is poor because of the fatigue and lack of sex drive. He takes no other medications.

On physical examination, vital signs are normal, and BMI is 35. Visual fields are full to confrontation. There is no gynecomastia. Testes volume is 15 mL (normal, 18–25 mL) bilaterally. The penis appears normal.

Laboratory studies:

Cortisol (8 AM)	20 µg/dL (552 nmol/L) (normal range, 5-25 µg/dL [138-690 nmol/L])
Follicle-stimulating hormone	0.2 mU/mL (0.2 U/L)
Insulin-like growth factor 1	Normal
Luteinizing hormone	0.1 mU/ml (0.1 U/L)
Prolactin	12 ng/mL (12 µg/L)
Sex hormone binding globulin	Normal
Testosterone, total	167 ng/dL (5.8 nmol/L)
Thyroid-stimulating hormone	1.6 µU/mL (1.6 mU/L)
Thyroxine (T_4), free	1.7 ng/dL (21.9 pmol/L)

An MRI of the pituitary gland shows normal findings.

Which of the following is the most likely diagnosis?

(A) Anabolic steroid abuse
(B) Opioid-induced hypogonadism
(C) Primary hypogonadism
(D) Normal gonadal function

Item 40

A 67-year-old woman is transferred to the cardiothoracic intensive care unit (ICU) after undergoing repair of an abdominal aortic aneurysm. She has a 12-year history of type 2 diabetes mellitus. Her blood glucose level on arrival at the ICU is 289 mg/dL (16.0 mmol/L). Although no longer on a cardiopulmonary bypass pump, she remains intubated and on vasopressors.

Which of the following is the best treatment to control her blood glucose level during her ICU stay?

(A) Insulin glargine, once daily
(B) Intravenous insulin infusion
(C) Neutral protamine Hagedorn (NPH) insulin, twice daily
(D) Regular insulin administered on a sliding scale

Item 41

A 38-year-old woman is evaluated for a 3-month history of increased sweating, increased appetite, and a 7.3-kg (16-lb) weight loss. The patient also reports a 4-month history of amenorrhea, before which time she felt "completely healthy." Medical history is otherwise unremarkable, and she takes no medications.

Physical examination shows a thin, restless woman with smooth, fine, moist skin and fine hair. Blood pressure is 108/60 mm Hg, pulse rate is 96/min, respiration rate is 14/min, and BMI is 18.1. Mild lid lag is noted, but no proptosis, diplopia, or conjunctival injection are detected. Her thyroid gland is soft and enlarged approximately two-fold. There is a mild, fine tremor of the outstretched hands. Reflexes are brisk.

Laboratory studies:

Thyroid-stimulating hormone	2.4 µU/mL (2.4 mU/L)
Thyroxine (T_4), free	2.7 ng/dL (34.8 pmol/L)
Triiodothyronine (T_3), total	387 ng/dL (5.96 nmol/L)

Which of the following is the most appropriate next test to perform on this patient?

(A) MRI of the pituitary gland
(B) Thyroid anti–peroxidase antibody test
(C) Thyroid radioactive iodine uptake determination
(D) Thyroid scan
(E) Thyroid-stimulating immunoglobulin measurement

Item 42

A 78-year-old man is evaluated in the emergency department for a 1-week history of weakness, fatigue, nausea, and anorexia. Medical history is remarkable for recurrent squamous cell carcinoma of the lung treated with surgery and chemotherapy.

On physical examination, temperature is 37.2 °C (99.0 °F), blood pressure is 90/60 mm Hg, pulse rate is 100/min, and respiration rate is 20/min. Confusion, skin tenting, and bitemporal wasting are noted.

Laboratory studies:

Blood urea nitrogen	30 mg/dL (10.7 mmol/L)
Calcium	13.5 mg/dL (3.38 mmol/L)
Creatinine	1.9 mg/dL (167.96 µmol/L)
Phosphorus	2.4 mg/dL (0.78 mmol/L)

Which of the following is the most appropriate next step in treatment for this patient?

(A) 0.45% saline infusion
(B) 0.45% saline infusion and furosemide
(C) 0.9% saline infusion
(D) 0.9% saline infusion and furosemide

Item 43

A 71-year-old man is evaluated in the emergency department for new dyspnea on exertion. He has a 15-year history of type 2 diabetes mellitus and has had a number of changes in his medications over the past 12 weeks to improve glycemic control. His dosage of metformin has been increased to 1000 mg/d, glyburide to 10 mg/d, and pioglitazone to 45 mg/d. Within the past week, bedtime insulin glargine was initiated.

On physical examination, blood pressure is 140/90 mm Hg, pulse rate is 90/min, and respiration rate is 20/min. Jugular venous distention, an S_3, basilar pulmonary crackles, and 3+ pitting edema at the ankles are noted.

Besides the initiation of insulin glargine, which of the following most likely contributed to these findings?

(A) Increased glyburide dosage
(B) Increased metformin dosage
(C) Increased pioglitazone dosage
(D) Medication-associated hypoglycemia

Item 44

A 55-year-old man is evaluated for a 5-year history of progressively increasing fatigue and loss of energy. He has had a 6.8-kg (15-lb) weight gain during this period. He reports decreased libido, occasional erectile dysfunction, and daytime somnolence. He says his wife has told him that he snores during the night. Type 2 diabetes mellitus was diagnosed last year. Current medications are metformin and glipizide.

On physical examination, vital signs are normal, and BMI is 27. There is normal beard growth and no gynecomastia. Testes volume is 18 mL (normal, 18-25 mL) bilaterally. The penis appears normal.

Laboratory studies:

Follicle-stimulating hormone	2 mU/mL (2 U/L)
Luteinizing hormone	3 mU/mL (3 U/L)
Prolactin	10 ng/mL (10 µg/L)
Testosterone, total	160 ng/dL (5.6 nmol/L)
Thyroid-stimulating hormone	1.7 µU/mL (1.7 mU/L)
Thyroxine (T_4), free	1.0 ng/dL (12.9 pmol/L)

An MRI of the pituitary gland shows normal findings.

Which of the following is the best next step in management?

(A) Sleep study
(B) Testosterone replacement therapy
(C) Vardenafil treatment
(D) Visual field testing
(E) Reassurance

Item 45

A 49-year-old man is evaluated in the emergency department for acute chest pain. He has a history of hypertension for which he takes amlodipine daily, hyperlipidemia for which he takes atorvastatin daily, and gout for which he takes an NSAID as needed. Several family members have type 2 diabetes mellitus, and the patient recalls being told once that his blood glucose level was "borderline."

An acute ST-elevation myocardial infarction is diagnosed, and the patient is admitted and then treated with emergency stenting, which results in complete relief of his chest pain. After the procedure, he is alert, and his vital signs are normal. A random plasma glucose level obtained in the emergency department is 161 mg/dL (8.9 mmol/L). Laboratory studies on blood obtained the next morning show a fasting plasma glucose level of 131 mg/dL (7.3 mmol/L).

Which of the following is the most appropriate next step in management?

(A) Initiation of a sulfonylurea
(B) Initiation of metformin
(C) Intravenous infusion of insulin
(D) Measurement of the fasting plasma glucose level after discharge

Item 46

A 55-year-old man is evaluated for a 4-month history of weight loss, heat intolerance, tremor, and hyperdefecation and a 1-week history of dry eyes that are sensitive to light and frequently injected. He reports no blurred or double vision but does relate having been previously diagnosed with a "thyroid condition" and having a severe allergic reaction to methimazole therapy. The patient currently takes no medications.

On physical examination, blood pressure is 140/88 mm Hg, pulse rate is 120/min, respiration rate is 18/min, and BMI is 22. Pupils are equal, round, and reactive to light and accommodation; extraocular movements are intact. Mild bilateral conjunctival injection and periorbital edema are noted. There is no chemosis, but some slight lid lag and proptosis are present. Examination of the neck reveals a smooth thyroid gland that is three times its normal size. Cardiac examination shows tachycardia and a regular rhythm. There is a 3+ upper extremity tremor bilaterally.

Laboratory studies show a serum thyroid-stimulating hormone level of 0.01 µU/mL (0.01 mU/L) and a serum free thyroxine (T$_4$) level of 3.8 ng/dL (49.0 pmol/L).

Which of the following is the most appropriate treatment for this patient?

(A) Immediate thyroidectomy
(B) Orbital decompression surgery
(C) Prednisone and radioactive iodine ablation
(D) Radioactive iodine ablation alone

Item 47

A 44-year-old woman is noted to have osteopenia on a chest radiograph, which is confirmed on subsequent bone density testing. She is otherwise asymptomatic. The patient is premenopausal, is a nonsmoker, and drinks one to two glasses of wine per week. Personal medical history is noncontributory, and there is no family history of osteoporosis. Current medications are calcium carbonate, 600 mg twice daily, and ergocalciferol, 400 U twice daily.

On physical examination, vital signs are normal, and BMI is 21. There is no neck mass, thyromegaly, or spinal tenderness. All other findings are also normal.

Laboratory studies:

Albumin	4.0 g/dL (40 g/L)
Calcium	9.5 mg/dL (2.4 mmol/L)
Phosphorus	3.1 mg/dL (1.0 mmol/L)
Parathyroid hormone	79 pg/mL (79 ng/L)
25-Hydroxy vitamin D	9 ng/mL (22.5 nmol/L)

Which of the following is the most appropriate treatment for this patient?

(A) Calcitriol
(B) Calcium acetate therapy
(C) Gluten-free diet
(D) High-dose ergocalciferol
(E) Parathyroidectomy

Item 48

A 34-year-old woman is seen for follow-up after results of laboratory studies confirm hypercortisolism.

Laboratory studies:

Adrenocorticotropic hormone	50 pg/mL (11 pmol/L)
Urine free cortisol	288 µg/24 h (793.6 nmol/24 h)
Cortisol (8 AM)	
After 1 mg of dexamethasone the night before	12.9 µg/dL (356.0 nmol/L) (normal, <5 µg/dL [138.0 nmol/L])
After 8 mg of dexamethasone the night before	6.5 µg/dL (179.4 nmol/L) (normal, <5 µg/dL [138.0 nmol/L])

A CT scan of the abdomen reveals bilateral adrenal hyperplasia; a CT scan of the chest shows normal findings. Results of a pituitary MRI are normal.

Which of the following is the most appropriate next diagnostic test?

(A) Cosyntropin stimulation test
(B) Inferior petrosal sinus catheterization and sampling
(C) Positron-emission tomography
(D) Selective bilateral adrenal vein catheterization

Item 49

A 20-year-old woman is evaluated because of concerns about her thyroid status. Her family history is positive for Hashimoto disease in her mother and sister and for Graves disease in her older brother.

On physical examination, vital signs are normal, and BMI is 25. Examination of her neck reveals a firm, slightly enlarged thyroid gland.

Laboratory studies:

Thyroid-stimulating hormone	1.1 µU/mL (1.1 mU/L)
Thyroxine (T$_4$), free	1.5 ng/dL (19.4 pmol/L)
Anti–thyroglobulin antibodies	Positive
Anti–thyroid peroxidase (TPO) antibodies	Positive

Which of the following is the most appropriate next step in management?

(A) Levothyroxine therapy

(B) Serial anti-TPO and anti–thyroglobulin antibody titers

(C) Thyroid function tests, annually

(D) Ultrasonography of the thyroid gland

Item 50

A 64-year-old man is admitted to the hospital because of anorexia, nausea, episodes of hypoglycemia, and progressive renal insufficiency. His serum creatinine level has increased to 4.6 mg/dL (406.6 µmol/L) from his previous value 3 months ago of 1.4 mg/dL (123.8 µmol/L). He has had type 2 diabetes mellitus for more than 10 years and currently is on a glyburide and metformin regimen. His glycemic control has been improving over the past 4 months, with fasting blood glucose levels ranging between 150 and 180 mg/dL (8.3 and 10.0 mmol/L), but over the past month, he has had several hypoglycemic episodes. His medical history is also notable for hypertension treated with irbesartan and furosemide.

On admission, his random plasma glucose level is 83 mg/dL (4.6 mmol/L) and hemoglobin A_{1c} value is 7.0%. His diabetes medications are discontinued, and a nephrology consultation is obtained.

His nutritional intake improves over the next 3 days, and his fasting plasma glucose levels increase, with values again ranging from 150 to 180 mg/dL (8.3 to 10.0 mmol/L).

Which of the following antihyperglycemic regimens is most appropriate for this patient?

(A) Restart the glyburide only

(B) Restart the metformin only

(C) Restart the glyburide and metformin

(D) Start premixed insulin 70/30 once daily

(E) Start sitagliptin

Item 51

A 78-year-old woman is evaluated for a 6-month history of progressive weakness, fatigue, and myalgia. She has been a nursing-home resident for the past 3 years. Medical history is remarkable for hypertension and a cerebrovascular accident with residual deficit. Current medications are aspirin, enalapril, hydrochlorothiazide, and atorvastatin.

On physical examination, vital signs are normal, and BMI is 22. The patient walks with a hemiplegic gait. Right-sided hemiparesis is noted.

Laboratory studies:

Albumin	3.9 g/dL (39 g/L)
Alkaline phosphatase	190 U/L
Calcium	8.5 mg/dL (2.1 mmol/L)
Phosphorus	2.4 mg/dL (0.78 mmol/L)
Parathyroid hormone	100 pg/mL (100 ng/L)

Measurement of which of the following substances is the most appropriate next diagnostic test?

(A) Alkaline phosphatase isoenzymes

(B) 1,25-Dihydroxy vitamin D

(C) 25-Hydroxy vitamin D

(D) Osteocalcin

Item 52

A 30-year-old woman is evaluated for a 3-year history of amenorrhea and a 1-year history of galactorrhea.

Vital signs are normal. Physical examination reveals bilateral expressible galactorrhea.

Laboratory studies show a serum prolactin level of 31.2 ng/mL (31.2 µg/L). Other serum chemistry measurements are normal, as are results of serum free thyroxine (T_4) and thyroid-stimulating hormone measurements.

An MRI shows a 1.1-cm hypodense area compatible with a pituitary adenoma.

The patient is placed on bromocriptine, 2.5 mg twice daily. After 2 months, her prolactin level decreases to 19 ng/mL (19 µg/L), her galactorrhea ceases, and regular menstruation resumes.

At a follow-up visit 1 year later, she reports headaches that have progressively worsened over a 3-month period and increasing fatigue.

Repeat laboratory studies show a serum prolactin measurement of 13.5 ng/mL (13.5 µg/L). A repeat MRI scan shows a 1.2- × 1.6-cm mass in the sella turcica with considerable suprasellar extension.

Which of the following is the most appropriate next step in management?

(A) Add a long-acting-release somatostatin analogue

(B) Increase the dosage of bromocriptine

(C) Recommend stereotactic radiation therapy

(D) Recommend transsphenoidal surgery

(E) Substitute cabergoline for the bromocriptine

Item 53

A 58-year-old woman with a recent diagnosis of a lung nodule is evaluated for metastatic disease with a ^{18}F-fluoro-2-deoxy-D-glucose positron emission tomography (FDG-PET) scan. Results show no lung focus but do reveal focal uptake in the right lobe of the thyroid gland. The patient has no history of a thyroid disorder. Family history is positive for two sisters with hypothyroidism.

On physical examination, vital signs are normal. Examination of the neck shows a normal-sized thyroid gland without palpable nodules; there is no lymphadenopathy.

Serum thyroid-stimulating hormone level is 2.0 µU/mL (2.0 mU/L).

An ultrasound of the thyroid gland confirms an 8-mm right upper pole thyroid nodule.

Which of the following should be done next?

(A) Fine-needle aspiration biopsy of the nodule

(B) Radiodine scan

(C) Repeat FDG-PET scan in 6 months

(D) Thyroidectomy

Item 54

An asymptomatic 72-year-old woman is evaluated after results of screening laboratory studies show hypercalcemia. Her only medication is calcium carbonate.

On physical examination, vital signs are normal and BMI is 24. There are no masses palpable in the neck.

Laboratory studies:

Albumin	4.2 g/dL (42 g/L)
Calcium, total	10.9 mg/dL (2.73 mmol/L)
Creatinine	1.0 mg/dL (88.4 µmol/L)
Parathyroid hormone	178 pg/mL (178 ng/L)
Urine calcium	120 mg/24 h (3 mmol/24 h)

A technetium Tc 99m sestamibi scan and ultrasound of the neck both show a 1.5-cm enlarged mass in the right tracheoesophageal groove. Results of dual-energy x-ray absorptiometry show T scores of –2.2 in the femoral neck and –1.5 in the lumbar spine.

Which of the following is the most appropriate next step in management?

(A) Biopsy of the neck mass

(B) Measurement of the 1,25-dihydroxy vitamin D level

(C) Measurement of the 25-hydroxy vitamin D level

(D) Parathyroidectomy

Item 55

A 47-year-old woman is evaluated for lightheadedness on standing. The patient has nearly lost consciousness on several occasions when she stood rapidly. She also reports difficulty with night vision, early satiety, and occasional urinary incontinence. She has a 30-year history of type 1 diabetes mellitus complicated by hypertension, peripheral neuropathy, retinopathy, and nephropathy. The patient uses an insulin pump and also takes lisinopril and aspirin.

On physical examination, blood pressure is 110/70 mm Hg while seated and 90/60 mm Hg while standing and pulse rate is 94/min independent of position. All other findings are normal.

Results of standard laboratory studies are normal.

An electrocardiogram shows nonspecific ST-T wave changes and absent heart rate variability with respiration.

Which of the following is the most appropriate next diagnostic test?

(A) Adrenocorticotropic hormone stimulation test

(B) Echocardiography

(C) Exercise stress test

(D) 24-Hour arrhythmia monitoring

Item 56

A 47-year-old woman is hospitalized for pyelonephritis. The patient has a 6-year history of primary adrenal insufficiency and has been doing well on therapy with oral hydrocortisone and fludrocortisone. She reports missing two doses of the hydrocortisone today because of nausea. She is started on rapid infusion of intravenous saline and ceftriaxone.

On physical examination, temperature is 38.9 °C (102.0 °F), blood pressure is 92/58 mm Hg supine and 76/50 mm Hg sitting, pulse rate is 98/min supine and 112/min sitting, respiration rate is 19/min, and BMI is 26.

Results of laboratory studies reveal a serum sodium level of 125 meq/L (125 mmol/L) and a serum potassium level of 5.5 meq/L (5.5 mmol/L).

Which of the following should be administered next?

(A) Baseline dosage of oral hydrocortisone and fludrocortisone

(B) Double dosage of intravenous hydrocortisone and fludrocortisone

(C) Infusion of 3% saline

(D) Stress dosage of intravenous hydrocortisone

Item 57

A 66-year-old man is seen for his annual physical examination. The patient feels well and has no current symptoms. He takes no medications.

On physical examination, vital signs are normal. All other general physical examination findings, including those from a prostate examination, are normal.

Laboratory studies:

Alanine aminotransferase	30 U/L
Aspartate aminotransferase	28 U/L
Alkaline phosphatase	350 U/L
Bilirubin, total	0.9 mg/dL (15.4 µmol/L)
Calcium	9.0 mg/dL (2.25 mmol/L)
Phosphorus	4.0 mg/dL (1.3 mmol/L)
Prostate-specific antigen	1.2 ng/mL (1.2 µg/L)
25-Hydroxy vitamin D	42 ng/mL (104.8 nmol/L)

A radionuclide bone scan reveals increased uptake in the skull and left tibia. Radiographs show lytic erosions in the skull and a lytic flame-shaped lesion in the metaphysis of the left tibia.

Which of the following is the most likely diagnosis?

(A) Bony metastases

(B) Osteomalacia

(C) Osteoporosis

(D) Paget disease of bone

Item 58

A pregnant 23-year-old woman is evaluated in the office for a 3-week history of progressive generalized headaches and severe progressive weakness. She is at 30 weeks' gestation and has lost 0.9 kg (2.0 lb) over the past month. She has a history of Hashimoto disease with hypothyroidism and no history of irregular menses. Current medications include levothyroxine, 112 µg/d, and prenatal vitamins.

Physical examination reveals a clinically euthyroid woman. Blood pressure is 92/60 mm Hg, pulse rate is

92/min, and BMI is 24.9. Her thyroid is mildly enlarged and firm. Other physical examination findings, including results of visual field testing and funduscopic examination, are normal. Neurologic examination findings are also normal.

Laboratory studies:

Adrenocorticotropic hormone	<5 pg/mL (1.1 pmol/L)
Cortisol (8 AM)	4.2 µg/dL (115.9 nmol/L) (normal range, 5-25 µg/dL [138-690 nmol/L])
Prolactin	124 ng/mL (124 µg/L)
Thyroid-stimulating hormone	1.3 µU/mL (1.3 mU/L)
Thyroxine (T_4), free	1.6 ng/dL (20.6 pmol/L)

An MRI shows a diffusely enhancing, symmetric 1.5-cm lesion extending above the sella turcica and impinging the optic chiasm. A subsequent formal visual field examination shows normal results.

Which of the following is the most likely diagnosis?

(A) Craniopharyngioma
(B) Lymphocytic hypophysitis
(C) Pituitary tumor apoplexy
(D) Prolactinoma

Item 59

A 48-year-old man comes to the office for mild blurring of his central vision bilaterally. He has had type 1 diabetes mellitus for 24 years. Recent hemoglobin A_{1c} values have ranged between 7.1% and 7.8%. A retinal examination performed 12 months ago showed background changes with some hard exudates and a few microaneurysms. The patient also has hypertension, which is well controlled with lisinopril, hydrochlorothiazide, and amlodipine. His medication regimen also includes insulin detemir, 18 units in the morning and 16 units in the evening, and insulin glulisine, 3 to 6 units before meals.

General physical examination shows normal vital signs, including a blood pressure of 120/70 mm Hg. Mild loss of vibratory sensation in the feet is noted.

The patient is referred for an immediate retinal examination, which reveals macular edema and new neovascularization.

Which of the following is the most appropriate next step in management?

(A) Addition of aspirin
(B) Addition of atorvastatin
(C) Decrease in the insulin dosage
(D) Panretinal photocoagulation

Item 60

A 32-year-old woman is evaluated for recent anxiety and insomnia. She is slightly overweight and has a family history of hypothyroidism. Three years ago, she tested positive for anti–thyroid peroxidase antibodies and anti–thyroglobulin antibodies. Her thyroid-stimulating hormone level was normal 1 year ago. Current medications include a daily multivitamin and an over-the-counter preparation for weight loss.

On physical examination, vital signs are normal, and BMI is 28. Examination of the neck shows a small, smooth, palpable thyroid gland. Other examination findings are normal.

Laboratory studies show a thyroid-stimulating hormone level of 0.1 µU/mL (0.1 mU/L) and a free thyroxine (T_4) level of 1.5 ng/dL (19.4 pmol/L).

Which of the following is the best next step in management?

(A) Check the thyroid-stimulating immunoglobulin and thyrotropin-binding inhibitory immunoglobulin titers
(B) Recheck the anti–thyroid peroxidase and anti–thyroglobulin antibody titers
(C) Repeat the thyroid function tests 6 weeks after stopping the metabolism enhancer
(D) Schedule thyroid ultrasonography

Item 61

A 34-year-old woman is evaluated for a 6-month history of rapidly progressive hirsutism, a 3-month history of acne and weight gain, and a 2-month history of irregular menses. She also notes that her voice has deepened over the past month. The patient has not menstruated for the past 2 months despite having normal menses previously. Family history is unremarkable. She takes no medications.

On physical examination, vital signs are normal, and BMI is 26. There are coarse hairs on the upper and lower lips, chin, and sides of her face. Acne is present on her face and back. She has no galactorrhea. Pelvic examination reveals an enlarged clitoris.

Laboratory studies:

Follicle-stimulating hormone	2 mU/mL (2 U/L)
Human chorionic gonadotropin	Negative
Luteinizing hormone	1.2 mU/mL (1.2 U/L)
Prolactin	17 ng/mL (17 µg/L)
Testosterone, total	326 ng/dL (11.3 nmol/L)
Thyroid-stimulating hormone	1.1 µU/mL (1.1 mU/L)

Which of the following is the most appropriate next diagnostic test?

(A) CT of the abdomen and pelvis
(B) Measurement of the serum estradiol level
(C) Measurement of the serum free testosterone level
(D) Progestin withdrawal challenge

Item 62

A 32-year-old asymptomatic woman is evaluated for hypercalcemia that was discovered on a routine screening examination. She has a history of three kidney stones, all passing spontaneously; her last episode was 9 months ago.

Physical examination findings, including vital signs, are normal.

Laboratory studies:

Calcium	12.0 mg/dL (3.0 mmol/L)
Phosphorus	1.9 mg/dL (0.61 mmol/L)
Creatinine	0.9 mg/dL (79.6 µmol/L)
	(no change from 3 years ago)
Parathyroid hormone	190 pg/mL (190 ng/L)

A dual-energy x-ray absorptiometry scan shows normal bone mineral density at the left femoral neck and in the total lumbar spine. A sestamibi scan of the parathyroid glands shows a right inferior parathyroid adenoma.

Which of the following is the most appropriate treatment for this patient?

(A) Calcitonin
(B) Cinacalcet
(C) Pamidronate
(D) Parathyroidectomy

Item 63

A 43-year-old man is evaluated for drug-resistant hypertension. Hypertension was diagnosed 1 year ago and has been difficult to control despite maximum dosages of lisinopril, metoprolol, and nifedipine. The patient reports feeling well.

On physical examination, temperature is 36.5 °C (97.7 °F), blood pressure is 146/92 mm Hg, pulse rate is 88/min, respiration rate is 17/min, and BMI is 27. The general physical examination and funduscopic examination are unremarkable.

Laboratory studies:

Electrolytes	
Sodium	143 meq/L (143 mmol/L)
Potassium	3.3 meq/L (3.3 mmol/L)
Chloride	101 meq/L (101 mmol/L)
Bicarbonate	33 meq/L (33 mmol/L)
Creatinine	1.0 mg/dL (88.4 µmol/L)
Random (spot) urine potassium	Inappropriately high
Urinalysis	Normal

Which of the following is the most appropriate next diagnostic test for this patient?

(A) CT of the adrenal glands
(B) Determination of serum aldosterone to plasma renin activity ratio
(C) Digital subtraction renal angiography
(D) Measurement of plasma metanephrine and normetanephrine levels

Item 64

An 83-year-old woman who has had type 2 diabetes mellitus for 25 years comes to the office for routine care. She also has a history of hypertension, dyslipidemia, and coronary artery disease. Her current antihyperglycemic regimen includes glipizide, pioglitazone, and insulin glargine, 24 units at bedtime. Fasting blood glucose levels at home range between 110 and 150 mg/dL (6.1 and 8.3 mmol/L), and her most recent hemoglobin A$_{1c}$ value was 7.2%. Other medications include metoprolol, lisinopril, and simvastatin.

Physical examination shows a blood pressure of 108/72 mm Hg, a pulse rate of 76/min, and a respiration rate of 16/min. Background retinopathy, a left femoral bruit, and mild loss of light-touch sensation in the feet are noted.

Results of laboratory studies show an LDL-cholesterol level of 65 mg/dL (1.7 mmol/L).

Which of the following is the most appropriate treatment for this patient?

(A) Add exenatide to her regimen
(B) Add metformin to her regimen
(C) Continue her current regimen
(D) Stop the pioglitazone

Item 65

A 56-year-old man is evaluated in the office for a persistent headache that began 1 week ago when he struck his head in a fall from a ladder. A CT scan obtained in the emergency department at that time showed no subdural hematoma but did show a pituitary adenoma. A subsequent MRI confirmed a 1.1-cm hypodense area in the pituitary that was compatible with a pituitary adenoma and did not abut the optic chiasm. He has had no symptoms compatible with Cushing syndrome or acromegaly and has normal sexual function. He takes no medications.

On physical examination, blood pressure is 128/74 mm Hg, pulse rate is 76/min, respiration rate is 14/min, and BMI is 25.3. There is no clinical evidence of either Cushing syndrome or acromegaly. The patient has normal secondary sexual characteristics.

Laboratory studies:

Insulin-like growth factor 1	383 ng/mL (383 µg/L) (normal for age)
Prolactin	13.2 ng/mL (13.2 µg/L)
Testosterone	485 ng/dL (16.8 nmol/L)
Thyroxine (T$_4$), free	1.2 ng/dL (15.5 pmol/L)

Which of the following is the most appropriate management of his pituitary adenoma?

(A) Gamma knife irradiation
(B) Initiation of cabergoline
(C) Initiation of a somatostatin analogue
(D) Repeat MRI in 1 year
(E) Transsphenoidal surgery

Item 66

A 24-year-old woman is evaluated for irregular menses and infertility. She reports having had normal puberty but having irregular menses until she started taking an oral contraceptive pill. She has been unable to become pregnant since marrying 1 year ago despite regular intercourse and discontinuing the oral contraceptive pill; during the past year, she has menstruated three times. The patient has never had acne or facial hair. She was a track athlete in high school and college and still enjoys distance running, typically running 50 miles per week. There is no family history of infertility or an endocrine disorder.

On physical examination, blood pressure is 100/68 mm Hg, pulse rate is 52/min, and BMI is 16. Visual fields are full to confrontation. The patient has small breasts without galactorrhea and no facial hair or acne. Pubic hair is normal.

Laboratory studies:

Human chorionic gonadotropin	Negative for pregnancy
Prolactin	16 ng/mL (16 µg/L)
Follicle stimulating hormone	2 mU/mL (2 U/L)
Thyroid-stimulating hormone	1.2 µU/mL (1.2 mU/L)

Which of the following is the most appropriate next step in management?

(A) Clomiphene therapy
(B) Pelvic ultrasonography
(C) Progestin withdrawal challenge
(D) Weight gain and decreased exercise

Item 67

An 18-year-old woman is evaluated for tachycardia, nervousness, decreased exercise tolerance, and weight loss of 6 months' duration. She has otherwise been healthy. Her sister has Graves disease. She takes no medications.

On physical examination, blood pressure is 128/78 mm Hg, pulse rate is 124/min, respiration rate is 16/min, and BMI is 19.5. There is no proptosis. An examination of the neck reveals a smooth thyroid gland that is greater than 1.5 times the normal size. Cardiac examination reveals regular tachycardia with a grade 2/6 early systolic murmur at the base. Her lungs are clear to auscultation.

Laboratory studies:

Human chorionic gonadotropin	Negative
Thyroid-stimulating hormone	<0.01 µU/mL (0.01 mU/L)
Thyroxine (T_4), free	5.5 ng/dL (71.0 pmol/L)
Triiodothyronine (T_3), free	9.1 ng/L (14 pmol/L)

Which of the following is the most appropriate treatment regimen at this time?

(A) Atenolol only
(B) Methimazole only
(C) Atenolol and methimazole
(D) Radioactive iodine and methimazole

Item 68

A 24-year-old woman is evaluated for a 6-month history of weakness, fatigue, diaphoresis, tremor, and oligomenorrhea. She has had an unintentional 6.8-kg (15-lb) weight loss during this same period. She has a history of bipolar affective disorder. Her only medication is lithium.

On physical examination, temperature is 37.2 °C (99.0 °F), blood pressure is 122/85 mm Hg, pulse rate is 118/min, respiration rate is 14/min, and BMI is 20. Bilateral proptosis is noted. Examination of the neck reveals a diffuse goiter. There is a tremor of both hands, and both palms are sweaty.

Laboratory studies:

Albumin	4.0 g/dL (40 g/L)
Calcium	11.1 mg/dL (2.78 mmol/L)
Phosphorus	4.5 mg/dL (1.5 mmol/L)
Parathyroid hormone	10 pg/mL (10 ng/L)
Thyroid-stimulating hormone	<0.001 µU/mL (0.001 mU/L)
Thyroxine (T_4), free	2.3 ng/dL (29.7 pmol/L)
Triiodothyronine (T_3), total	350 ng/dL (5.39 nmol/L)

Which of the following is the most likely cause of her hypercalcemia?

(A) Lithium
(B) Primary hyperparathyroidism
(C) Secondary hyperparathyroidism
(D) Thyrotoxicosis

Item 69

A 65-year-old woman is evaluated for a 3-week history of fatigue, nausea, and poor appetite. In the week before symptom onset, she had acute bronchitis with productive cough and fever. The patient has a 2-year history of osteoarthritis of the knees that requires intra-articular corticosteroid injections every 3 to 4 months; her last injection was 3 months ago. Her only other medication is acetaminophen.

On physical examination, the patient looks tired. Temperature is 37.5 °C (99.5 °F), blood pressure is 112/58 mm Hg, pulse rate is 92/min, respiration rate is 17/min, and BMI is 32. The patient has cushingoid features and central obesity. There are multiple ecchymoses on the upper and lower extremities. Decreased axillary and pubic hair is noted. There is bony hypertrophy and small effusions of the knees bilaterally but no evidence of warmth or erythema.

Laboratory studies:

Adrenocorticotropic hormone (AM)	9 pg/mL (1.98 pmol/L)
Cortisol (8 AM)	
Initial measurement	1.4 µg/dL (38.6 nmol/L) (normal range, 5-25 µg/dL [138-690 nmol/L])
After cosyntropin stimulation	9.0 µg/dL (248.4 nmol/L)
Follicle-stimulating hormone	40 mU/mL (40 U/L)
Luteinizing hormone	35 mU/mL (35 U/L)
Prolactin	14 ng/mL (14 µg/L)
Thyroid-stimulating hormone	3.1 µU/mL (3.1 mU/L)
Thyroxine (T_4), free	1.2 ng/dL (15.5 pmol/L)

Which of the following is the most likely cause of this patient's current symptoms?

(A) Adrenal adenoma

(B) Exogenous corticosteroids

(C) Pituitary microadenoma

(D) Primary adrenal insufficiency

Item 70

A 49-year-old woman is evaluated for recurrent urinary tract infections. Over the past 6 months, she has had four urinary tract infections. She has a 35-year history of poorly controlled type 1 diabetes mellitus. Home blood glucose readings range between 150 and 300 mg/dL (8.3 and 16.7 mmol/L), and hemoglobin A_{1c} values are typically greater than 8.7%. A review of systems is notable for orthostatic dizziness and intermittent episodes of constipation and diarrhea. She describes frequent urination of small volumes, difficulty initiating urination, and nearly constant urinary dribbling. Current medications include nighttime insulin glargine and multiple daily injections of insulin lispro.

On physical examination, blood pressure is 140/86 mm Hg supine and 120/78 mm Hg standing, and pulse rate is 104/min both supine and standing. Results of the general physical examination are otherwise noncontributory. On neurologic examination, she cannot feel a 10-g Semmes-Weinstein monofilament and has no vibratory sensation below the knees.

Her serum creatinine level has recently increased from 1.5 mg/dL (132.6 µmol/L) to 2.3 mg/dL (203.3 µmol/L).

Which of the following is the best next step in management?

(A) Begin chronic suppressive ciprofloxacin therapy

(B) Begin oxybutynin

(C) Measure postvoid urinary residual volumes

(D) Order pelvic CT

Item 71

A 34-year-old woman comes for a follow-up evaluation. At an initial visit 4 weeks ago, she had fatigue, weight gain, and increased menstrual flow. At that time, results of laboratory studies included a thyroid-stimulating hormone (TSH) level of 50 µU/mL (50 mU/L), a free thyroxine (T_4) level of 0.5 ng/dL (6.5 pmol/L), and the presence of anti–thyroperoxidase and anti–thyroglobulin antibodies, and she was started on levothyroxine, 75 µg/d. Her history is notable for pernicious anemia treated with oral vitamin B_{12}, 1000 µg daily.

Physical examination reveals a young woman with fully gray hair. Blood pressure is 94/58 mm Hg, pulse rate is 75/min, respiration rate is 12/min, and BMI is 25.7. There is a slight increase in the pigment of the mucous membranes, and the thyroid gland is slightly enlarged and smooth. Cardiopulmonary examination findings are normal.

Results of repeat laboratory studies now show a TSH level of 7.1 µU/mL (7.1 mU/L) and free T_4 level of 1.5 ng/dL (19.4 pmol/L).

Which of the following is the most appropriate next step in management?

(A) Increase the levothyroxine dosage

(B) Measure the glutamic acid decarboxylase antibody level

(C) Measure the thyroid-stimulating immunoglobulin titer

(D) Perform a cosyntropin stimulation test

Item 72

A 48-year-old man is evaluated in the office for a 1-year history of progressive fatigue. He also reports occasional constipation. Twelve years ago, the patient underwent transsphenoidal surgery to remove a clinically nonfunctioning pituitary adenoma. Because of persistent tumor postoperatively, he underwent a 5-week course of conventional irradiation. He subsequently developed hypogonadism and was started on a transdermal testosterone preparation. An MRI scan obtained 2 years ago showed a partially empty sella turcica. Six months ago, he was found to have an elevated LDL-cholesterol level. Current medications include testosterone, transdermally, and pravastatin.

Physical examination shows a man with a sallow complexion who otherwise looks healthy. Blood pressure is 134/86 mm Hg, pulse rate is 64/min, respiration rate is 16/min, and BMI is 28.1. The remainder of the general physical examination, including examination of the thyroid gland, is unremarkable.

Laboratory studies:

Testosterone, total	428 ng/dL (14.9 nmol/L)
Thyroid-stimulating hormone	0.7 µU/mL (0.7 mU/L)
Cortisol (8 AM)	16.8 µg/dL (463.7 nmol/L) (normal range, 5-25 µg/dL [138-690 nmol/L])

Which of the following tests should be ordered next?

(A) Adrenocorticotropic hormone stimulation test

(B) Free testosterone level measurement

(C) Free thyroxine (T_4) level measurement

(D) Oral glucose tolerance test with measurement of growth hormone level

Item 73

A 67-year-old woman is seen for a follow-up visit. Three weeks ago, she had a predawn episode of hypoglycemia on the way to the bathroom that caused her to fall, fracturing her hip. The patient has had type 2 diabetes mellitus for more than 20 years and has repeatedly had mild hypoglycemic episodes since the diagnosis. Although well tolerated to this point, these episodes have become increasingly frequent over the past 6 months. Her current medications are neutral protamine Hagedorn (NPH) insulin, 20 units, and regular insulin, 5 units, both injected before breakfast and supper. A review of her glucose log shows blood glucose readings ranging between 70 and 150 mg/dL (3.9 and 8.3 mmol/L) when fasting and 50 and 250 mg/dL (2.8 and 13.9 mmol/L) during the day. Her last measured hemoglobin A_{1c} value was 7.8%.

Which of the following changes should be made to her diabetes regimen?

(A) Change her medications to oral metformin and sitagliptin

(B) Change her medications to insulin glargine and insulin lispro

(C) Decrease the dosages of NPH and regular insulin by 10%

(D) Increase her caloric intake

Item 74

A 32-year-old man is evaluated for increasing shortness of breath, fatigue, anorexia, and polyuria. He has a history of hypertension. His only medication is lisinopril.

On physical examination, temperature is normal, blood pressure is 120/80 mm Hg, pulse rate is 98/min, respiration rate is 22/min, and BMI is 30. Lungs are clear to auscultation.

Laboratory studies:

Calcium	12.0 mg/dL (3.0 mmol/L)
Phosphorus	4.4 mg/dL (1.4 mmol/L)
Parathyroid hormone	Undetectable
1,25-Dihydroxy vitamin D	Elevated
25-Hydroxy vitamin D	Low

A chest radiograph shows bilateral hilar lymphadenopathy with prominent interstitial markings. Mediastinal biopsy shows granulomas consistent with sarcoidosis.

Which of the following is the best initial treatment for this patient?

(A) Calcitonin

(B) Pamidronate

(C) Plicamycin

(D) Prednisone

Item 75

A 34-year-old woman is evaluated for amenorrhea and infertility. Her last menses occurred 4 months ago, before which her menses were regular. The patient has two children, age 3 and 6 years. She had a spontaneous abortion 6 months ago and underwent dilation and curettage 1 month later. There was no withdrawal bleeding while she was on an oral contraceptive pill for 2 months after the procedure. A recent progestin withdrawal challenge with medroxyprogesterone acetate did not produce withdrawal bleeding. There is no relevant family history. She takes no other medications.

On physical examination, vital signs are normal, and BMI is 30. No acne or hirsutism is detected. All other examination findings are normal.

Laboratory studies:

Follicle-stimulating hormone	6 mU/mL (6 U/L)
Prolactin	15 ng/mL (15 µg/L)
Thyroid-stimulating hormone	3 µU/mL (3 mU/L)
Thyroxine (T_4), free	1.3 ng/dL (16.8 pmol/L)
Pregnancy test	Negative

Which of the following is the most appropriate next diagnostic test?

(A) Hysteroscopy

(B) Karyotype

(C) Measurement of serum 17-hydroxyprogesterone level

(D) Transvaginal pelvic ultrasonography

Item 76

A 76-year-old woman is reevaluated after results of thyroid function tests performed 2 weeks ago are abnormal. The patient otherwise feels well. She has a history of hypertension, atrial fibrillation, gastroesophageal reflux disease, and depression. Current medications are metoprolol, amiodarone, warfarin, omeprazole, and sertraline.

On physical examination, blood pressure is 125/65 mm Hg, pulse rate is 83/min, and respiration rate is 15/min. The thyroid gland is smooth and of normal size. Cardiac examination reveals an irregularly irregular rhythm. Deep tendon reflexes are normal.

Laboratory studies:

Thyroid-stimulating hormone	6.5 µU/mL (6.5 mU/L)
Thyroxine (T_4), free	2.4 ng/dL (31.0 pmol/L)
Triiodothyronine (T_3), free	0.8 ng/L (1.2 pmol/L)

Which of the following medications is most likely responsible for the laboratory results?

(A) Amiodarone

(B) Metoprolol

(C) Omeprazole

(D) Sertraline

Item 77

A 30-year-old woman is evaluated in the hospital for paresthesias of the fingers and mouth that started 2 days after she underwent a difficult total thyroidectomy for Graves disease. Her only medication is atenolol.

On physical examination, vital signs are normal except for a respiration rate of 24/min. Trousseau and Chvostek signs are present.

Laboratory studies:

Albumin	4.1 g/dL (41 g/L)
Calcium	7.5 mg/dL (1.88 mmol/L)
Phosphorus	3.8 mg/dL (1.2 mmol/L)
Parathyroid hormone	6 pg/mL (6 ng/L)

Which of the following is the most likely cause of the hypocalcemia?

(A) Hyperventilation

(B) Hypoparathyroidism

(C) Pseudohypoparathyroidism

(D) Pseudo-pseudohypoparathyroidism

Item 78

A 55-year-old man is evaluated for new-onset type 2 diabetes mellitus. The patient also reports a chronic productive cough and poor exercise tolerance. Six months ago, he had normal results on physical examination and normal laboratory values, including glucose, lipids, and electrolytes. He has a 40-pack-year smoking history. There is no pertinent family history. The patient takes no medications.

On physical examination, temperature is 36.5 °C (97.7 °F), blood pressure is 172/92 mm Hg, pulse rate is 90/min, respiration rate is 21/min, and BMI is 24.5. Mucous membranes and nail beds are hyperpigmented. There is temporal muscle wasting and proximal muscle weakness in the upper and lower extremities. He does not have a dorsal fat pad, moon facies, or purple striae.

Laboratory studies:

Electrolytes

Sodium	146 meq/L (146 mmol/L)
Potassium	2.4 meq/L (2.4 mmol/L)
Chloride	101 meq/L (101 mmol/L)
Bicarbonate	33 meq/L (33 mmol/L)
Adrenocorticotropic hormone (ACTH)	365 pg/mL (80.3 pmol/L)
Cortisol (8 AM)	58 µg/dL (1601 nmol/L) (normal range, 5-25 µg/dL [138-690 nmol/L])

Which of the following is the most likely cause of this patient's findings?

(A) Adrenal adenoma

(B) Adrenal carcinoma

(C) Cushing disease

(D) Ectopic ACTH secretion

Item 79

A 54-year-old woman undergoes transsphenoidal surgery to remove a nonfunctioning pituitary macroadenoma. The patient develops polyuria and polydipsia postoperatively, and urine output is 8 L/day; central diabetes insipidus is diagnosed. After she is treated with desmopressin, urine output decreases. Four days after her operation, she is discharged with instructions to take desmopressin nasal spray, one puff (10 µg) twice daily, and hydrocortisone, 20 mg on arising in the morning. After a few days at home, her appetite becomes normal again and she begins eating her normal amount of food and resumes her years-long habit of drinking 8 glasses (64 oz) of water daily. One month after discharge, her husband brings her to the emergency department after she becomes progressively more somnolent and incoherent over a 3-hour period.

She has been taking no medications except for the desmopressin and hydrocortisone.

Physical examination reveals an awake but confused woman. Blood pressure is 132/80 mm Hg, pulse rate is 88/min, respiration rate is 16/min, and BMI is 24. Skin turgor is normal, mucous membranes are moist, and there is no edema. Other than confusion, findings from the remainder of the general physical and neurologic examinations are normal.

Laboratory results reveal a serum sodium level of 116 meq/L (116 mmol/L).

Which of the following is the most likely cause of the hyponatremia?

(A) Cerebral salt-wasting syndrome

(B) Cortisol deficiency

(C) Excessive water ingestion

(D) Syndrome of inappropriate antidiuretic hormone secretion

Item 80

A 35-year-old woman is evaluated for diaphoresis, a 3.6-kg (8.0-lb) weight loss, and elevated blood glucose levels 6 weeks after delivering her second child. She has an 18-year history of type 1 diabetes mellitus, which has been successfully treated with an insulin pump for the past 8 years. Her glycemic control during this period has been outstanding, with an average hemoglobin A_{1c} value of 6.2%. Although her diabetes was well controlled during most of the gestation, the insulin dosage needed to be increased by almost 50% to maintain glycemic control. Postpartum, the patient reduced the insulin dosage to her prepregnancy baseline requirements, but this step has been inadequate to control her blood glucose level.

On physical examination, vital signs are normal. Tachycardia, tremor, hyperreflexia, and a wide pulse pressure are noted.

Results of a complete blood count and metabolic panel are normal.

Measurement of which of the following is most likely to diagnose the cause of her deteriorating control of her blood glucose level?

(A) Antitransglutaminase antibody titers

(B) Hemoglobin A_{1c} value

(C) Postprandial glucose level

(D) Thyroid-stimulating hormone level

(E) Urine free cortisol level

Item 81

An asymptomatic 65-year old woman comes to the office for a new patient visit.

On physical examination, vital signs are normal. Her thyroid gland is enlarged and nodular. All other findings are normal.

Results of laboratory studies show a thyroid-stimulating hormone level of 1.6 µU/mL (1.6 mU/L) and a free thyroxine (T_4) level of 1.1 ng/dL (14.2 pmol/L).

An ultrasound of the thyroid gland shows a symmetrically enlarged thyroid with four solid nodules in the following locations and of the following sizes: right upper pole, 0.8 cm; right midpole, 2.0 cm; left midpole, 0.9 cm; and left lower pole, 0.7 cm. No microcalcifications or increased central intranodular blood flow is noted in any of the nodules.

Which of the following is the most appropriate next step in management?

(A) Fine-needle aspiration biopsy of all four thyroid nodules
(B) Fine-needle aspiration biopsy of the dominant right midpole nodule only
(C) Levothyroxine therapy and repeat ultrasound in 6 months
(D) Thyroid scan

Item 82

A 23-year-old man is evaluated for a 2-year history of infertility. He also reports declining libido. Growth and development have been normal, except for scant beard growth. Medical history is unremarkable, and he takes no medications. He and his wife have been married for 2 years and have not been able to conceive. His wife already has been tested, and no cause of infertility was found in her. Family history is noncontributory.

On physical examination, vital signs are normal. BMI is 22. The patient's sense of smell is normal, and visual fields are full to confrontation. There is 2-cm bilateral gynecomastia. The testes are firm and 4 mL (normal, 18-25 mL) in volume bilaterally. The penis appears normal in size.

Laboratory studies:

Follicle-stimulating hormone	76 mU/mL (76 U/L)
Luteinizing hormone	45 mU/mL (45 U/L)
Prolactin	8 ng/mL (8 µg/L)
Testosterone, total (AM)	90 ng/dL (3.1 nmol/L)

Which of the following is the most appropriate next step?

(A) Measure his serum estradiol level
(B) Measure his serum free testosterone level
(C) Obtain an MRI of the pituitary gland
(D) Obtain the patient's karyotype
(E) Schedule a testicular biopsy

Item 83

A 54-year-old woman with a 6-year history of type 2 diabetes mellitus is evaluated for suboptimal glycemic control. Her current hemoglobin A_{1c} value is 8.1%. Her diabetes regimen consists of metformin, 1000 mg twice daily, and glimepiride, 4 mg/d; the patient declines all injection therapy at this time. She has no other medical problems.

There are no abnormalities in cardiovascular, kidney, or liver function.

In addition to reinforcing lifestyle modifications, which of the following is most likely to maximally improve her glycemic control?

(A) Add acarbose
(B) Add exenatide
(C) Add pioglitazone
(D) Increase the glimepiride dosage
(E) Increase the metformin dosage

Item 84

A 56-year-old woman is evaluated for a 2-year history of chronic low back pain. She also has had a 2-cm (0.8-in) height loss during this period. Medical history is remarkable for chronic obstructive pulmonary disease requiring intermittent high doses of prednisone. Current medications are albuterol and ipratropium bromide inhalers; prednisone, 20 mg/d; vitamin D, 800 U/d; and calcium, 1500 mg/d.

On physical examination, temperature is normal, blood pressure is 135/80 mm Hg, pulse rate is 100/min, respiration rate is 24/min, and BMI is 28. Breath sounds are distant with an occasional wheeze. There is back tenderness. Neurologic examination findings are unremarkable.

Laboratory studies show normal serum calcium, phosphorus, parathyroid hormone, and vitamin D levels.

A radiograph of the spine shows a compression fracture of the T8 vertebra. A dual-energy x-ray absorptiometry scan reveals a T-score of –2.2 in the lumbosacral spine and –2.5 in the left hip.

Which of the following is the best treatment for this patient?

(A) Calcitonin
(B) Increased dosage of vitamin D (to 1000 U/d)
(C) Raloxifene
(D) Risedronate

Item 85

A 56-year-old woman is evaluated for a 6-month history of bilateral carpal tunnel syndrome and a 3-year history of dull aches in her knees and hips. She says that she has had to increase the size of her gloves and shoes twice over the past 2 years. She takes no medications.

On physical examination, blood pressure is 146/88 mm Hg, pulse rate is 74/min, respiration rate is 16/min, and BMI is 27. Other findings include frontal bossing, a broad nose, accentuated nasolabial folds, a large tongue, and large, thick hands and feet.

Results of laboratory studies, including a complete blood count and a standard serum chemistry panel, are normal.

Which of the following is the best initial step in diagnosis?

(A) Measurement of the growth hormone level
(B) Measurement of the insulin-like growth factor 1 level
(C) MRI of the pituitary gland
(D) Octreotide scan

Item 86

A 59-year-old woman with type 2 diabetes mellitus is evaluated for suboptimal glycemic control. The patient is obese. Her hemoglobin A_{1c} value has occasionally been greater than 9.0% during the past 9 months. Her current medication regimen is metformin, 2000 mg/d, and pioglitazone, 45 mg/d. She was previously treated with glyburide but experienced a severe hypoglycemic episode, which prompted the change to her current regimen. She is extremely reluctant to try another sulfonylurea and refuses insulin therapy because she is fearful of hypoglycemia.

Which of the following is the most reasonable modification to make to her medication regimen?

(A) Add acarbose

(B) Add exenatide

(C) Substitute nateglinide for metformin

(D) Substitute rosiglitazone for pioglitazone

(E) Substitute sitagliptin for pioglitazone

Item 87

A 62-year-old man is evaluated after an adrenal mass is found on a CT scan of the abdomen. The scan was obtained during the evaluation of abdominal pain of 1 week's duration; the pain has since subsided, and he has had no other symptoms. The patient reports feeling healthy. Personal and family medical history is noncontributory. He takes no medications.

On physical examination, vital signs and results of the general physical examination are normal.

Laboratory studies:

Electrolytes	
Sodium	139 meq/L (139 mmol/L)
Potassium	4.1 meq/L (4.1 mmol/L)
Chloride	97 meq/L (97 mmol/L)
Bicarbonate	29 meq/L (29 mmol/L)
Cortisol (8 AM)	
Initial measurement	13.8 µg/dL (380.9 nmol/L) (normal, 5-25 µg/dL [138-690 nmol/L])
After 1 mg of dexamethasone the night before	1.1 µg/dL (30.4 nmol/L) (normal, <5 µg/dL [138 nmol/L])
Metanephrines	Normal

The previously obtained CT scan shows a right adrenal mass that measures 2.5 cm in its longest dimension and has an attenuation value of 9 Hounsfield units.

Which of the following is the most appropriate next step in management?

(A) Metaiodobenzylguanidine (MIBG) scan

(B) Positron emission tomography

(C) Repeat testing in 12 months

(D) Right adrenalectomy

Item 88

A 72-year-old man is evaluated for a 2-week history of low back pain. The patient has a history of alcoholism but stopped drinking alcohol 10 years ago. He also has stage 3 chronic kidney disease and a 50-pack-year smoking history. Current medications are hydrochlorothiazide, ramipril, and a multivitamin.

On physical examination, vital signs are normal. Lumbar lordosis, decreased mobility and spasm of the paravertebral muscles, and tenderness to palpation at L4-L5 are noted. Neurologic screening examination findings are normal.

Laboratory studies:

Calcium	9.0 mg/dL (2.25 mmol/L)
Creatinine	2.1 mg/dL (185.6 µmol/L)
Phosphorus	3.2 mg/dL (1.0 mmol/L)
Parathyroid hormone	50 pg/mL (50 ng/L)
Testosterone	400 ng/dL (13.9 nmol/L)
25-Hydroxy vitamin D	34 ng/mL (85 nmol/L)
Estimated glomerular filtration rate	40 mL/min/1.73 m^2

A radiograph of the lumbosacral spine shows a compression fracture of L4. A dual-energy x-ray absorptiometry scan shows a T-score of –3.0 in the lumbosacral spine and –3.2 in the left hip.

Which of the following is the best treatment for this patient?

(A) Alendronate

(B) Calcitonin

(C) Teriparatide

(D) Testosterone

Item 89

A 23-year-old woman with type 1 diabetes mellitus is admitted to the hospital with a diagnosis of community-acquired pneumonia and lethargy. Before admission, her insulin pump therapy was discontinued because of confused mentation.

On physical examination, temperature is 37.5 °C (99.5 °F), blood pressure is 108/70 mm Hg, pulse rate is 100/min, and respiration rate is 24 min. There are decreased breath sounds in the posterior right lower lung. Neurologic examination reveals altered consciousness.

Laboratory studies:

Blood urea nitrogen	38 mg/dL (13.6 mmol/L)
Creatinine	1.4 mg/dL (123.8 µmol/L)
Electrolytes	
Sodium	130 meq/L (130 mmol/L)
Potassium	5.0 meq/L (5.0 mmol/L)
Chloride	100 meq/L (100 mmol/L)
Bicarbonate	16 meq/L (16 mmol/L)
Glucose	262 mg/dL (14.5 mmol/L)
Urine ketones	Positive

Which of the following is the most appropriate next step in management?

(A) Add insulin glargine

(B) Add neutral protamine Hagedorn (NPH) insulin

(C) Implement a sliding scale for regular insulin

(D) Start an insulin drip

Item 90

A 43-year-old man is evaluated for persistent fatigue and poor libido. He first had these symptoms, along with vision loss, 2 years ago; an MRI obtained at that time showed a 3- × 3-cm pituitary mass displacing the optic chiasm. He was placed on cabergoline therapy, which immediately restored normal vision, but his symptoms of hypogonadism persisted. His only medication is cabergoline.

On physical examination, vital signs are normal, and BMI is 21. The only notable physical examination abnormality is the finding of soft testes, with a volume of 8 mL (normal, 18-25 mL) bilaterally.

Laboratory studies:

Follicle-stimulating hormone	<0.1 mU/mL (0.1 U/L)
Luteinizing hormone	<0.1 mU/mL (0.1 U/L)
Prolactin	10 ng/mL (10 µg/L)
Testosterone, total	104 ng/dL (3.61 nmol/L)
Thyroid-stimulating hormone	1.0 µU/mL (1.0 mU/L)

A repeat MRI now shows marked shrinkage of the tumor, and some normal pituitary gland is visible at the right superior aspect of the tumor.

Which of the following is the most appropriate treatment for this patient?

(A) Discontinuation of cabergoline

(B) Increased cabergoline dosage

(C) Retesting in 1 year

(D) Testosterone replacement therapy

Item 91

A 28-year-old woman is evaluated in the office for a 3-year history of amenorrhea. The patient has been otherwise healthy. She is sexually active and is not interested in becoming pregnant in the near future. Her personal and family medical histories are noncontributory. She takes no medications.

Examination reveals normal vital signs; BMI is 24. No galactorrhea is detected. Findings from the remainder of the examination, including visual field testing by confrontation, are normal.

Laboratory studies show a serum prolactin level of 48.3 ng/mL (48.3 µg/L). Results of thyroid, adrenal, and hepatic function testing are normal, and a pregnancy test is negative.

An MRI shows a 4-mm hypointense area in the pituitary gland that is compatible with a microadenoma.

Which of the following is the most appropriate next step in management?

(A) Bromocriptine

(B) Oral contraceptives

(C) Stereotactic radiation therapy

(D) Transsphenoidal surgery

(E) Reassurance

Item 92

A 26-year-old woman is evaluated for a 5-day history of constipation, fatigue, and weight gain. Two months ago, she began experiencing nervousness, heat intolerance, and weight loss but says these symptoms abated after 6 weeks. The patient delivered a healthy infant 14 weeks ago. After thyroid function tests performed 8 weeks postpartum revealed a thyroid-stimulating hormone (TSH) level of 0.02 µU/mL (0.02 mU/L) and a free thyroxine (T_4) level of 3.5 ng/dL (45.2 pmol/L), she was placed on atenolol, 25 mg/d.

On physical examination, blood pressure is 115/70 mm Hg, pulse rate is 50/min, respiration rate is 14/min, and BMI is 23.3. No proptosis or inflammatory changes are noted on ocular examination. Examination of the neck reveals no tenderness or bruits; the thyroid gland cannot be palpated.

Which of the following is the best next step in management?

(A) Methimazole

(B) Repeat measurement of TSH and free T_4 levels

(C) Thyroid scan and 24-hour radioactive iodine uptake test

(D) Thyroid ultrasonography

Item 93

An 18-year-old man is evaluated for hyperglycemia. Type 1 diabetes mellitus was diagnosed 4 years ago. Hemoglobin A_{1c} levels have been worsening over the past 6 months, increasing from 7.5% 6 months ago to 8.0% 3 months ago to 8.5% now. His current insulin regimen consists of a breakfast dose of neutral protamine Hagedorn (NPH) insulin, 20 units, and regular insulin, 8 to 15 units, and a supper dose of NPH insulin, 10 units, and regular insulin, 6 to 12 units.

The patient's glucose log is shown below.

Timing	Blood Glucose Measurement
8 AM (fasting)	220-300 mg/dL (12.2-16.7 mmol/L)
12 PM (noon)	150-180 mg/dL (8.3-10.0 mmol/L)
6 PM (postprandial)	130-160 mg/dL (7.2-8.9 mmol/L)
10 PM (bedtime)	110-150 mg/dL (6.1-8.3 mmol/L)

Which of the following is the most appropriate treatment for this patient?

(A) Add a bedtime dose of regular insulin

(B) Increase the dosage of NPH insulin at supper

(C) Increase the dosage of regular insulin at supper

(D) Move the supper dose of NPH insulin to bedtime

Item 94

A 70-year-old woman is evaluated for worsening gastro-esophageal reflux disease with heartburn. She first noticed this symptom 1 month ago when she began taking alendronate, 70 mg orally once weekly, for osteoporosis. Current medications are alendronate, calcium, and ergocalciferol.

A dual-energy x-ray absorptiometry scan reveals a T-score of –3.0 in the lumbar spine and –2.5 in the left hip.

After the alendronate is discontinued, which of the following is now the most appropriate treatment for this patient?

(A) Calcitonin

(B) Intravenous ibandronate

(C) Intravenous zoledronate

(D) Raloxifene

Item 95

A 52-year-old woman is evaluated in the emergency department for what she describes as the "worst headache of her life." The pain started at 3 AM; she has been nauseated since that time and has vomited once. She also says the vision in her left eye seems decreased. An incidental 1.1-cm pituitary adenoma was diagnosed 2 years ago, at which time she had normal pituitary function and no visual field defects. An MRI obtained 1 year ago showed no new changes.

Physical examination reveals a woman in obvious distress from the headache. Temperature is 37.7 °C (99.9 °F), blood pressure is 90/50 mm Hg, pulse rate is 104/min, and respiration rate is 16/min. Her neck is stiff, and she cannot see the left lateral portion of her visual field. Results of the remainder of the general physical and neurologic examinations are normal.

Results of laboratory studies are pending.

Which of the following is the most appropriate immediate next step in management?

(A) Begin bromocriptine

(B) Begin hydrocortisone

(C) Obtain an MRI of the sella turcica

(D) Refer for transsphenoidal surgery

Item 96

A 32-year-old man is evaluated for poor libido and fatigue, both of which have gradually worsened over the past 18 months. He reports occasional hot flushes and declining performance at work; he frequently falls asleep during dinner. The patient had normal puberty and has fathered two children. He takes no medications.

On physical examination, the patient appears sallow. Vital signs are normal, and BMI is 24. Visual fields are full to confrontation. There is trace gynecomastia but no galactorrhea. Testes volume is 8 mL (normal, 18-25 mL) bilaterally. The penis appears normal.

Laboratory studies:

Follicle-stimulating hormone	0.3 mU/mL (0.3 U/L)
Insulin-like growth factor 1	64 ng/mL (64 µg/L) (normal range, 180-360 ng/mL [180-360 µg/L])
Luteinizing hormone	0.2 mU/mL (0.2 U/L)
Prolactin	32 ng/mL (32 µg/L)
Testosterone, total	130 ng/dL (4.5 nmol/L)
Thyroid-stimulating hormone	0.6 µU/mL (0.6 mU/L)
Thyroxine (T$_4$), free	0.7 ng/dL (9.0 pmol/L)

Which of the following is the most appropriate next step in management?

(A) Cabergoline therapy

(B) Levothyroxine therapy

(C) MRI of the pituitary gland

(D) Testicular ultrasonography

(E) Testosterone replacement therapy

Item 97

A 59-year-old man is evaluated for recently discovered spontaneous hypokalemia and hypertension. The patient had normal blood pressure at a visit 1 year ago. He has no symptoms and takes no medications.

On physical examination, temperature is 36.9 °C (98.4 °F), blood pressure is 148/96 mm Hg, pulse rate is 58/min, respiration rate is 18/min, and BMI is 25. Examination findings are otherwise unremarkable.

The serum potassium level is 2.9 meq/L (2.9 mmol/L) with increased urine potassium losses. After correction of the hypokalemia, the serum aldosterone level is 28.7 ng/dL (792 pmol/L) and the serum aldosterone to plasma renin activity ratio is 287. The serum aldosterone level is not suppressible with a high-sodium diet.

A CT scan of the adrenal glands shows minimal bilateral enlargement, with no identifiable masses or nodules.

Which of the following is the most appropriate initial treatment?

(A) Bilateral adrenalectomy

(B) Lisinopril

(C) Spironolactone

(D) Triamterene

Item 98

A 26-year-old woman comes to the office for her annual physical examination. She reports feeling well and has no symptoms. Family history is notable for hypercalcemia in her mother and maternal grandfather; both underwent parathyroidectomy but remained mildly hypercalcemic after surgery. The patient's only medication is a daily multivitamin.

All general physical examination findings, including vital signs, are normal.

Laboratory studies:

Calcium	11.0 mg/dL (2.75 mmol/L)
Creatinine	0.7 mg/dL (61.9 µmol/L)
Parathyroid hormone (PTH)	42 pg/mL (42 ng/L)

A renal ultrasound shows no kidney stones.

Measurement of which of the following is the most appropriate next diagnostic test?

(A) Serum 1,25 dihydroxy vitamin D level
(B) Serum 25-hydroxy vitamin D level
(C) Serum PTH-related protein level
(D) Urine calcium to creatinine clearance ratio

Item 99

A 35-year-old woman comes for a new patient evaluation. She works as a pharmacist. The patient reports a 1-week history of insomnia, fatigue, and palpitations. She has chronically struggled with her weight and has become progressively concerned about weight gain since the birth of her first child 2 months ago. There is no relevant family history.

Physical examination reveals an overweight, tired-looking woman. Blood pressure is 128/64 mm Hg, pulse rate is 91/min, respiration rate is 16/min, and BMI is 29. There is no proptosis. The thyroid gland is nonpalpable. Cardiac examination reveals tachycardia and a regular rhythm. Neurologic examination shows tremors of both hands.

Laboratory studies:

Erythrocyte sedimentation rate	17 mm/h
Thyroid-stimulating hormone	0.01 µU/mL (0.01 mU/L)
Thyroxine (T_4), free	3.6 ng/dL (46.4 pmol/L)

A thyroid scan shows no perceptible uptake by the thyroid gland; results of a radioactive iodine uptake test show 1% uptake.

Which of the following should be done next?

(A) Begin methimazole
(B) Begin prednisone
(C) Measure serum thyroglobulin level
(D) Measure serum triiodothyronine (T_3) level

Item 100

A 38-year-old man with a 24-year history of type 1 diabetes mellitus comes to the office for a follow-up evaluation. The patient has proliferative retinopathy that required bilateral laser photocoagulation 2 years ago. He also has diabetic nephropathy, peripheral neuropathy, and hypertension. Current medications are insulin glargine, insulin aspart, hydrochlorothiazide, lisinopril, diltiazem, atorvastatin, and aspirin.

On physical examination, blood pressure is 138/84 mm Hg, pulse rate is 72/min, and BMI is 24.2. Fundu - scopic examination shows scars from the laser treatment. Results of cardiopulmonary and abdominal examinations are normal. There is 2+ edema in the ankles to the midcalf.

The patient is unable to detect vibration in the toes up to the malleoli and cannot feel a monofilament on his toes. Achilles tendon reflexes are absent.

Laboratory studies:

Potassium	5.8 meq/L (5.8 mmol/L)
Creatinine	2.1 mg/dL (185.6 µmol/L)
Urine albumin-to-creatinine ratio	723 mg/g

Which of the following medication changes is most appropriate?

(A) Add amlodipine
(B) Add metoprolol
(C) Substitute furosemide for hydrochlorothiazide
(D) Substitute irbesartan for lisinopril

Item 101

A 55-year-old woman is evaluated for a 6-month history of recurrent episodes of palpitations, sweating, and headaches. Medical history is otherwise unremarkable. She takes no medications.

On physical examination, the patient appears anxious. Temperature is 36.9 °C (98.4 °F), blood pressure is 158/96 mm Hg, pulse rate is 88/min, respiration rate is 18/min. and BMI is 30. Findings from a general physical examination, including examination of the thyroid gland, are otherwise unremarkable.

Laboratory studies:

Epinephrine	320 ng/L (1747 pmol/L)
Norepinephrine	1980 ng/L (11,704 pmol/L)
Metanephrines	124 pg/mL (0.64 nmol/L) (normal range, 12-61 pg/mL [0.06-0.32 nmol/L])
Normetanephrines	798 pg/mL (4.47 nmol/L) (normal range, 18-112 pg/mL [0.10-0.63 nmol/L])
Thyroid-stimulating hormone	1.2 µU/mL (1.2 mU/L)
Urine	
Norepinephrine	3215 µg/24 h (19,001 nmol/d) (normal range, 0-140 µg/24 h [0-827 nmol/d])
Metanephrines	575 µg/24 h (2915 nmol/d) (normal range, 35-460 µg/24 h [177-2332 nmol/d])
Normetanephrines	4350 µg/24 h (23,751 nmol/d) (normal range, 110-1050 µg/24 h [601-5733 nmol/d])
Vanillylmandelic acid	12.3 mg/24 h (62.1 µmol/d)

A CT scan of the adrenal glands shows no adrenal masses.

Which of the following is the most appropriate next test for this patient?

(A) Adrenalectomy
(B) Bilateral adrenal vein sampling

(C) Metaiodobenzylguanidine (MIBG) scan

(D) MRI scan from base of skull to pelvis

Item 102

A 48-year-old man comes to the office after lunch for a routine physical examination. The patient is asymptomatic but overweight. Although he has no pertinent personal medical history, he has a strong family history of diabetes mellitus. He currently takes no medications.

Results of physical examination are normal. BMI is 29.2.

Results of routine laboratory studies show a random plasma glucose level of 158 mg/dL (8.8 mmol/L).

Which of the following terms best describes his current glycemic status?

(A) Impaired fasting glucose

(B) Impaired glucose tolerance

(C) Metabolic syndrome

(D) Type 2 diabetes mellitus

(E) Noncategorizable

Item 103

A 23-year-old woman is evaluated after having no menses for 6 months. She began menstruating at age 12 years, and menses have always been regular. The patient reports no recent weight gain, voice change, or facial hair growth; she says she may even have lost some weight recently and tends to feel warm. She is not sexually active. There is no family history of infertility or premature menopause.

On physical examination, temperature is normal, blood pressure is 115/72 mm Hg, pulse rate is 66/min, respiration rate is 14/min, and BMI is 22. She has no acne, hirsutism, or galactorrhea. Her thyroid gland is slightly enlarged. Visual field testing yields normal results.

Results of standard laboratory studies are normal, including thyroid-stimulating hormone and free thyroxine (T_4) levels; a human chorionic gonadotropin level is negative for pregnancy.

Which of the following is the most appropriate first step in evaluation?

(A) Hysterosalpingography

(B) Measurement of serum follicle-stimulating hormone and prolactin levels

(C) Measurement of total serum testosterone level

(D) Pelvic ultrasonography

Item 104

A 65-year-old man comes to the office for routine follow-up. He says he is feeling well. The patient has a history of a 2-cm thyroid cancer with two positive cervical lymph nodes that was treated with a total thyroidectomy and radioactive iodine therapy 1 year ago. Six months ago, results of laboratory studies showed a stimulated thyroglobulin level of less than 0.2 ng/mL (0.2 µg/L) and no thyroglobulin antibodies, and a

neck ultrasound showed no evidence of any residual disease. The patient takes levothyroxine, 188 µg/d. Other medications include atenolol, 50 mg/d, for hypertension.

On physical examination, vital signs are normal, and BMI is 27.9. Examination of the neck reveals a well-healed surgical scar at its base. No cervical lymphadenopathy or mass is noted. The patient has a slight bilateral upper extremity tremor.

Results of laboratory studies show a thyroid-stimulating hormone level of 0.3 µU/mL (0.3 mU/L) and a free thyroxine (T_4) level of 1.96 ng/dL (25.3 pmol/L).

Which of the following is the most appropriate next step in management?

(A) Decrease the dosage of levothyroxine

(B) Increase the dosage of levothyroxine

(C) Make no changes to the medication regimen

(D) Measure the triiodothyronine (T_3) level

Item 105

A 32-year-old woman is evaluated for a 3-month history of fatigue, nausea, poor appetite, and salt craving. She also reports a 6.0-kg (13.2-lb) weight loss over this same period.

On physical examination, temperature is normal, blood pressure is 92/62 mm Hg supine and 78/58 mm Hg sitting, pulse rate is 88/min supine and 110/min sitting, respiration rate is 16/min, and BMI is 25. Her skin is tanned, and hyperpigmentation is noted in the gum line.

Laboratory studies:

Electrolytes	
Sodium	127 meq/L (127 mmol/L)
Potassium	5.9 meq/L (5.9 mmol/L)
Chloride	101 meq/L (101 mmol/L)
Bicarbonate	24 meq/L (24 mmol/L)
Adrenocorticotropic hormone	155 pg/mL (34.1 pmol/L)
Cortisol (8 AM)	8 µg/dL (220.8 nmol/L) (normal range, 5-25 µg/dL [138-690 nmol/L])

Which of the following is the most appropriate next diagnostic test?

(A) Cosyntropin stimulation test

(B) Insulin-induced hypoglycemia test

(C) Measurement of morning salivary cortisol level

(D) 24-Hour urine free cortisol measurement

Item 106

An obese 44-year-old woman is evaluated for persistent hyperglycemia. For the past 3 months, she has followed a strict regimen of diet and exercise in an attempt to control her hyperglycemia. Home blood glucose monitoring has shown preprandial levels between 120 and 160 mg/dL (6.7 and 8.9 mmol/L) and occasional postprandial levels exceeding 200 mg/dL (11.1 mmol/L). She has a history of hypertension and hyperlipidemia. Current medications include lisinopril, hydrochlorothiazide, and pravastatin.

Vital signs and physical examination findings are normal, except for a BMI of 30.

The serum creatinine level is 0.8 mg/dL (70.7 μmol/L), and the urine is negative for microalbuminuria.

Which of the following is the most appropriate next step in treatment to improve her glycemic control?

(A) Continue the diet and exercise for an additional 3 months
(B) Begin exenatide
(C) Begin glimepiride
(D) Begin metformin
(E) Begin pioglitazone

Item 107

A 55-year-old woman is evaluated for new-onset fever, productive cough, palpitations, and hyperdefecation. The patient has Graves disease treated with methimazole. She has been nonadherent to her medication regimen, not having refilled her methimazole prescription 6 weeks ago.

On physical examination, temperature is 39.4 °C (102.9 °F), blood pressure is 140/85 mm Hg, pulse rate is 138/min, and respiration rate is 16/min. Examination of the neck reveals a smoothly symmetrical thyroid gland that is three time its normal size. Auscultation of the lungs reveals crackles in the left lower lobe. Cardiac examination shows tachycardia and a regular rhythm.

Laboratory studies:

Leukocyte count	14,300/μL (14.3 × 10^9/L)
Alanine aminotransferase	100 U/L
Aspartate aminotransferase	75 U/L
Alkaline phosphatase	135 U/L
Thyroid-stimulating hormone	<0.1 μU/mL (0.1 mU/L)
Thyroxine (T$_4$), free	4.4 ng/dL (56.8 pmol/L)
Triiodothyronine (T$_3$), free	7.8 ng/L (12 pmol/L)

A chest radiograph shows a left lower lobe infiltrate. Electrocardiography reveals sinus tachycardia.

Ceftriaxone and azithromycin are begun.

Which of the following is the most appropriate next step in management?

(A) Atenolol
(B) Propranolol, propylthiouracil, and hydrocortisone
(C) Thyroid ablation with radioactive iodine
(D) Thyroid scan with a radioactive iodine uptake test

Item 108

A 20-year-old man is admitted to a rehabilitation hospital 2 months after sustaining head trauma in a motor vehicle accident. As he begins his rehabilitation program, he becomes increasingly fatigued as he exercises. The patient takes no medications.

Physical examination reveals a pale, mentally alert young man. Blood pressure is 102/74 mm Hg, pulse rate is 60/min, respiration rate is 14/min, and BMI is 23. He

has normal secondary sexual characteristics. Other examination findings are normal.

Results of routine hematologic and serum chemistry studies are normal, except for a hemoglobin level of 11.7 g/dL (117 g/L).

An MRI of the brain shows only changes that are compatible with his trauma with no interval change suggesting deterioration.

Which of the following is the most critical test for this patient?

(A) Measurement of morning (8 AM) serum cortisol level
(B) Measurement of serum growth hormone level
(C) Measurement of serum luteinizing hormone level
(D) Measurement of serum thyroid-stimulating hormone level

Item 109

A 45-year-old man is evaluated for recent onset of cold intolerance and constipation. He also reports a 2.3 kg (5.0-lb) weight gain over the past 3 months. The patient has an 8-year history of bipolar disorder successfully treated with lithium, 300 mg three times daily. Family history is notable for a mother and sister with Graves disease. His only other medication is sertraline for depression.

On physical examination, blood pressure is 130/88 mm Hg, pulse rate is 58/min, respiration rate is 14/min, and BMI is 23.7. Examination of the neck shows a thyroid gland that is smooth and 1.5 times the normal size. There is no edema of the extremities.

Laboratory studies:

Thyroid-stimulating hormone	8.9 μU/mL (8.9 mU/L)
Thyroxine (T$_4$), free	0.9 ng/dL (11.6 pmol/L)
Anti–thyroid peroxidase antibody	100 U/mL (normal range, 0-20 U/mL)

Which of the following is the most appropriate next step in management?

(A) Add levothyroxine
(B) Add liothyronine
(C) Check the anti–thyroglobulin antibody titer
(D) Discontinue lithium
(E) Give iodine supplementation

Item 110

A 58-year-old man is evaluated for possible osteoporosis. He recently underwent removal of a 1.6-cm nonfunctioning pituitary adenoma and was placed on levothyroxine therapy.

On physical examination, vital signs are normal. Examination of the neck reveals no palpable goiter. The testes are small and soft.

Laboratory studies:

Follicle-stimulating hormone	<1.0 mU/mL (1.0 U/L)
Luteinizing hormone	<1.0 mU/mL (1.0 U/L)

Testosterone   50 ng/dL (1.7 nmol/L)
Thyroxine (T_4), free   1.2 ng/dL (15.5 pmol/L)

A dual-energy x-ray absorptiometry scan shows T-scores of –2.5 in the left hip and –2.6 in the lumbar spine.

In addition to calcium and vitamin D supplementation, which of the following is the most appropriate initial treatment for this patient?

(A) Bromocriptine
(B) Calcitonin
(C) Decreased dosage of levothyroxine
(D) Testosterone

Item 111

A 38-year-old woman is evaluated after an adrenal mass is discovered on a CT scan obtained because of abdominal pain. The patient reports a 4.0-kg (8.8-lb) weight gain over the past year but no other symptoms. She has no history of diabetes mellitus, palpitations, headaches, or sweating and no pertinent family history. She takes no medications.

On physical examination, temperature is 36.9 °C (98.4 °F), blood pressure is 148/96 mm Hg, pulse rate is 88/min, respiration rate is 18/min, and BMI is 34. General physical examination findings are normal.

Laboratory studies:
Electrolytes
  Sodium   144 meq/L (144 mmol/L)
  Potassium   3.9 meq/L (3.9 mmol/L)
  Chloride   97 meq/L (97 mmol/L)
  Bicarbonate   29 meq/L (29 mmol/L)
Adrenocorticotropic   10 pg/mL (2.2 pmol/L)
  hormone
Aldosterone to renin   8.7
  activity ratio
Cortisol (8 AM)
  Initial measurement   19.8 µg/dL (546 nmol/L) (normal range, 5-25 µg/dL [138-690 nmol/L])
  After 1 mg of   11.1 µg/dL (306 nmol/L) dexamethasone (normal, <5 µg/dL the night before [138 nmol/L])
Metanephrines   Normal
Urine free cortisol   95 µg/24 h (261.8 nmol/24 h)

The previously obtained CT scan shows a left adrenal mass that measures 2.5 cm in its longest dimension and has an attenuation value of 12 Hounsfield units; the right adrenal gland appears small.

Which of the following is the most appropriate next step in management?

(A) Adrenal vein catheterization
(B) Left adrenalectomy
(C) MRI of the pituitary gland
(D) Repeat biochemical testing in 6 months

Item 112

A 44-year-old woman comes for a new patient evaluation. She reports amenorrhea, loss of libido, and fatigue that have persisted since the birth of her youngest child 7 years ago. She remembers having a difficult delivery and requiring blood transfusions when she last gave birth. She takes no medications.

Physical examination reveals a pale but otherwise healthy-looking woman. Blood pressure is 92/60 mm Hg, pulse rate is 60/min, and BMI is 21.2. No galactorrhea is expressible.

Laboratory studies:
Sodium   133 meq/L (133 mmol/L)
Follicle-stimulating   1.4 mU/mL (1.4 U/L)
  hormone
Insulin-like growth   84 ng/mL (84 µg/L) (normal factor 1 range, 101-267 ng/mL [101-267 µg/L])
Luteinizing hormone   1.8 mU/mL (1.8 U/L)
Prolactin   2.3 ng/mL (2.3 µg/L)
Thyroxine (T_4), free   0.6 ng/dL (7.7 pmol/L)
Cortisol (8 AM)   4.7 µg/dL (129.7 nmol/L) (normal range, 5-25 µg/dL [138-690 nmol/L])
Urine pregnancy test   Negative

Which of the following is the most appropriate initial treatment of this patient?

(A) Estrogen and progesterone, cyclically
(B) Free water restriction
(C) Growth hormone
(D) Hydrocortisone
(E) Levothyroxine

Item 113

A 55-year-old man is evaluated for a 1-year history of weight gain, insomnia, fatigue, and diminished libido. The patient has an 18-month history of polymyalgia rheumatica treated with prednisone, with dosages ranging from 5 to 10 mg/d. Family history is noncontributory. He takes no other medications.

On physical examination, temperature is 36.9 °C (98.4 °F), blood pressure is 140/86 mm Hg, pulse rate is 68/min, respiration rate is 18/min, and BMI is 30. The patient has a rounded, plethoric face. Bilateral gynecomastia is noted. The testes are soft in consistency but normal in size.

Laboratory studies:
Adrenocorticotropic   4 pg/mL (0.88 pmol/L)
  hormone
Cortisol (AM)   0.8 µg/dL (22.1 nmol/L) (normal range, 5-25 µg/dL [138-690 nmol/L])
Dehydroepiandrosterone   0.08 µg/mL (0.22 µmol/L)
  sulfate
Follicle-stimulating   1.1 mU/mL (1.1 U/L)
  hormone
Luteinizing hormone   0.5 mU/mL (0.5 U/L)
Prolactin   8.0 ng/mL (8.0 µg/L)

Testosterone	127 ng/dL (4.4 nmol/L)
Thyroid-stimulating hormone	1.5 µU/mL (1.5 mU/L)
Thyroxine (T_4), free	1.9 ng/dL (24.5 pmol/L)

Which of the following is the most likely cause of this patient's hypogonadism?

(A) Klinefelter syndrome
(B) Pituitary microadenoma
(C) Prednisone therapy
(D) Primary testicular failure

Item 114

A 58-year-old man is evaluated for a 2-year history of gradually progressive fatigue and erectile dysfunction with reduced libido. A screening total testosterone measurement was 250 ng/dL (8.7 nmol/L).

On physical examination, vital signs are normal, and BMI is 28. Visual fields are full to confrontation. There is no gynecomastia. Testes volume is 18 mL (normal, 18-25 mL) bilaterally.

Which of the following is the most appropriate management option for this patient?

(A) Begin a trial of sildenafil
(B) Begin testosterone therapy
(C) Measure his serum estradiol level
(D) Measure his serum free testosterone level

Item 115

A 20-year-old woman is evaluated for new-onset fatigue and weight gain. She has a 5-year history of hypothyroidism for which she takes levothyroxine, 75 µg/d in the morning on an empty stomach, and has been on a stable dosage for the past 2 years; her most recent thyroid-stimulating hormone (TSH) level obtained 6 months ago was 1.0 µU/mL (1.0 mU/L). Other medications are an oral contraceptive pill, started 3 months ago and taken in the morning, and a multivitamin with iron, taken at bedtime.

On physical examination, blood pressure is 110/74 mm Hg, pulse rate is 54/min, and BMI is 23.4. The thyroid gland is slightly enlarged and smooth, without nodules.

Laboratory studies now show a TSH level of 15.3 µU/mL (15.3 mU/L) and a free thyroxine (T_4) level of 0.9 ng/dL (11.6 pmol/L).

Which of the following is the most appropriate change to this patient's treatment regimen?

(A) Discontinue the multivitamin
(B) Increase the levothyroxine dosage
(C) Start desiccated thyroid hormone
(D) Take the oral contraceptive pill at bedtime

Item 116

A 35-year-old man is evaluated for hypoglycemia. He has had type 1 diabetes mellitus for 21 years and has experienced four severe episodes of hypoglycemia in the past 2 months, two of which resulted in loss of consciousness and visits to the emergency department. These episodes have occurred both overnight and during the day. He says he can no longer feel the hypoglycemia developing. He uses a blood glucose meter eight to ten times each day, and his average blood glucose level over the past month is 95 mg/dL (5.3 mmol/L); his most current hemoglobin A_{1c} value is 5.8%. His diabetes regimen consists of insulin glargine, 22 units at night, and insulin lispro, four to eight units before meals.

Vital signs are normal. Physical examination findings are normal, with no evidence of peripheral or autonomic neuropathy.

Which of the following is the most appropriate treatment?

(A) Add metformin
(B) Change the insulin glargine to insulin detemir
(C) Change the insulin lispro to regular insulin
(D) Decrease the dosage of both insulins

Answers and Critiques

Item 1   Answer: D

Educational Objective: Treat humoral hypercalcemia of malignancy.

This patient should receive an intravenous infusion of zoledronate. Malignancy is the most common cause of non-parathyroid hormone (PTH)–mediated hypercalcemia and the most frequent cause of hypercalcemia in hospitalized patients. Malignancy-associated hypercalcemia is differentiated into two forms: local osteolytic hypercalcemia and humoral hypercalcemia of malignancy. Local osteolytic hypercalcemia occurs when tumor growth in the skeleton leads to the release of calcium by the elaboration or stimulation of local cytokines and other osteoclast-activating factors. The classic associated tumor is multiple myeloma, although adenocarcinoma of the breast and certain lymphomas may also be responsible. Humoral hypercalcemia of malignancy results from the systemic effect of a circulating factor produced by neoplastic cells. The hormone most commonly responsible for this syndrome is PTH-related protein (PTHrP). This peptide's *N*-terminal shares substantial homologic features with PTH. Tumors that elaborate PTHrP are most commonly squamous cell carcinomas, such as those of the lung (as in this patient), esophagus, or head and neck. PTHrP levels can be measured, but this is rarely needed to establish the diagnosis of humoral hypercalcemia of malignancy.

Bisphosphonates powerfully inhibit osteoclast-mediated bone resorption. They very effectively lower the serum calcium level, with their maximum effect seen in 2 to 4 days. Their duration of effect is usually several weeks and varies between patients and between types of bisphosphonate. Zoledronate appears to have the longest-lasting effect (1-1.5 months) and a faster onset of action than other bisphosphonates; it is approved for use in patients with hypercalcemia of malignancy by the U.S. Food and Drug Administration.

Because of the lag in the onset of effect, bisphosphonates should be combined with faster-acting therapeutic modalities, such as aggressive volume replacement with normal saline infusion and possibly calcitonin injections. However, calcitonin has a short-lived effect on hypercalcemia because of tachyphylaxis and therefore should only be used as an interim step.

Cinacalcet is a calcimimetic agent that occupies the calcium sensing receptor and lowers serum calcium levels in patients with primary and tertiary hyperparathyroidism associated with chronic kidney disease. It is not effective and not approved for use in malignancy-associated hypercalcemia.

Increased calcitriol production associated with activated macrophages (granulomatous diseases and lymphomas) can be diminished by using corticosteroids. However, prednisone does not lower PTHrP levels and therefore is not useful in humoral hypercalcemia of malignancy.

> **KEY POINT**
> - Vigorous volume replacement and bisphosphonate administration is the treatment of choice for malignancy-associated acute hypercalcemia.

Bibliography

Lumachi F, Brunello A, Roma A, Basso U. Medical treatment of malignancy-associated hypercalcemia. Curr Med Chem. 2008; 15(4):415-421. [PMID: 18288996]

Item 2   Answer: A

Educational Objective: Diagnose late-onset autoimmune diabetes of adulthood.

This patient most likely has late-onset autoimmune diabetes of adulthood (LADA). Diabetes mellitus is categorized into several types. Most affected patients have type 2 diabetes, and a minority (5% to 10%) have type 1 diabetes. Patients with type 2 diabetes are usually overweight, if not frankly obese. Type 1 diabetes results from autoimmune destruction of pancreatic beta cells and results in absolute insulin deficiency, whereas type 2 is marked by insulin resistance and relative insulin deficiency. Type 1 diabetes is classically seen in younger patients, usually in children, teens, and young adults. However, type 1 diabetes can be diagnosed at any age. When diagnosed in older persons, especially those in whom hyperglycemia was once controlled with oral agents, this form of diabetes is referred to as LADA. In persons with LADA, beta cell destruction over time leads to the requirement for insulin therapy, as in type 1 diabetes. LADA typically occurs in leaner persons after glycemic control has become more labile and there is clear insulin dependency. Autoimmune markers (anti–islet cell autoantibodies) are present, including anti-glutamic acid decarboxylase antibody, the detection of which can confirm the diagnosis.

Maturity-onset diabetes of the young is typically diagnosed in adolescents or young adults and usually is marked by mild hyperglycemia, often with a strong family history of diabetes.

> **KEY POINT**
> - Diabetes mellitus in older, lean patients with anti–islet cell autoantibodies is termed late-onset autoimmune diabetes of adulthood.

Bibliography

Fourlanos S, Perry C, Stein MS, Stankovich J, Harrison LC, Colman PG. A clinical screening tool identifies autoimmune diabetes in adults. Diabetes Care. 2006;29(5):970-975. [PMID: 16644622]

Item 3　　Answer:　C

Educational Objective: Manage primary hyperaldosteronism.

The most appropriate next step is CT of the patient's adrenal glands, with and without contrast. This patient has severe and difficult-to-control hypertension associated with laboratory findings characteristic of primary hyperaldosteronism. She had spontaneous, unprovoked hypokalemia and has metabolic alkalosis. The evaluation of unexplained hypertension and unprovoked hypokalemia begins with measurement of the plasma renin activity and aldosterone level. A serum aldosterone to plasma renin activity ratio greater than 20 and a serum aldosterone level greater than 15 ng/dL (414 pmol/L) strongly suggest primary hyperaldosteronism. On follow-up testing, the patient has an elevated serum aldosterone level that was not suppressed by high salt intake; plasma renin activity was suppressed. These are the biochemical features of primary hyperaldosteronism. After hyperaldosteronism is confirmed, a search for the anatomic or pathologic cause should begin. CT of the adrenal glands is the appropriate initial step in identifying the anatomic cause of the disease.

Aldosterone-producing adenomas respond to unilateral adrenalectomy. Within the first postoperative year, 67% of patients are normotensive and 90% are normokalemic. Medical therapy is the treatment of choice for adrenal hyperplasia. Neither partial nor complete adrenalectomy is indicated, however, until the anatomic and pathologic features have been defined by a CT scan.

Although bilateral adrenal vein catheterization and sampling can be helpful in defining the source of excessive aldosterone secretion (unilateral versus bilateral), the procedure is invasive, is technically difficult, and should not be performed before a CT scan is obtained.

Duplex ultrasonography of the renal arteries is used to investigate the possibility of renal artery stenosis. Such testing is not indicated in this patient, nor would it be helpful. The biochemical features of her case (suppressed plasma renin activity but elevated serum aldosterone level) practically rule out the possibility of renal artery stenosis.

KEY POINT

- Primary hyperaldosteronism is characterized by an elevated serum aldosterone level that is not suppressed by high salt intake and is associated with suppressed plasma renin activity; the anatomic/pathologic cause of the disease is determined by a CT scan.

Bibliography

Funder JW, Carey RM, Fardella C, et al; Endocrine Society. Case detection, diagnosis, and treatment of patients with primary aldosteronism: an Endocrine Society clinical practice guideline. J Clin Endocrinol Metab. 2008;93(9):3266-3281. [PMID: 18552288]

Item 4　　Answer:　E

Educational Objective: Evaluate a suspected insulinoma.

This patient most likely has an insulin-producing tumor and should be admitted to the hospital for a supervised 72-hour fast. Because symptoms of hypoglycemia are nonspecific, it is important to clearly document the presence of an abnormally low level of blood glucose. The biochemical diagnosis of insulinoma is made when the fasting glucose level falls below 45 mg/dL (2.5 mmol/L), accompanied by inappropriate hyperinsulinemia (insulin level higher than 5-6 μU/mL [36.1-43.3 pmol/L]), after exogenous factors have been eliminated. To best evaluate the patient for insulinoma, a prolonged fast (up to 72 hours) under strict medical observation is often necessary. Serum glucose, insulin, C-peptide, and proinsulin levels are measured at 4- to 6-hour intervals throughout the supervised fast. The fast is discontinued once the glucose value falls below 45 mg/dL (2.5 mmol/L) with associated symptoms of hypoglycemia and appropriate blood tests (measurement of plasma glucose, insulin, and C-peptide levels) are obtained. More than 95% of patients with insulinoma will have hypoglycemia within 72 hours. Insulin and C-peptide levels will generally be elevated, as will the proinsulin level, which suggests a greater tumor release of immature insulin.

Once the diagnosis of insulinoma is confirmed biochemically, imaging studies of the pancreas are obtained, beginning with an abdominal CT scan. Although these typically benign lesions are usually too small to be detected on a CT scan, this imaging modality is an important first step to exclude larger lesions or lesions already metastatic to the liver. If there are no significant findings, further evaluation may include endoscopic ultrasonography, MRI, hepatic venous sampling with arterial calcium stimulation, arteriography, and intraoperative ultrasound. Octreotide scans are usually not helpful for small, localized tumors. After the lesion is identified, surgical resection should follow.

The measurement of glucose should involve whole blood or plasma samples, collected in specialized tubes that inhibit glycolysis. "Fingerstick" capillary readings using home glucose meters are inaccurate in the hypoglycemic range, and results should be interpreted cautiously.

KEY POINT

- The supervised 72-hour fast is the gold standard for diagnosing insulinoma.

Bibliography

Khoo TK, Service FJ. Hyperinsulinemic hypoglycemia. Endocr Pract. 2007;13(4):424-426. [PMID: 17669722]

Item 5   Answer: D

Educational Objective: Evaluate secondary amenorrhea.

The next step in the evaluation of this patient with secondary amenorrhea after stopping her oral contraceptive pill is a progestin withdrawal challenge. At one time, the use of oral contraceptives was thought to be associated with an increased risk of developing amenorrhea once the oral contraceptive pill was discontinued. Studies have since shown that the incidence of amenorrhea and other endocrinologic findings in women who discontinue oral contraceptive use is no different from that in women with spontaneous amenorrhea. Therefore, women who stop oral contraceptive use are evaluated in the same way as women who have secondary amenorrhea and have never used oral contraceptives.

This patient has an unremarkable personal and family medical history and no evidence of androgen excess. Results of her screening laboratory studies are negative for thyroid disorders, ovarian dysfunction, and hyperprolactinemia. Given these data, the differential diagnosis of this patient's secondary amenorrhea includes anatomic defects and chronic anovulation, with or without estrogen. The differential diagnosis can be narrowed most effectively with a progestin withdrawal challenge. Menses after challenge excludes anatomic defects and chronic anovulation without estrogen. Therefore, a progestin withdrawal challenge is the most appropriate next step.

Polycystic ovary syndrome (PCOS) affects 6% of women of child-bearing age and typically presents with oligomenorrhea and signs of androgen excess (hirsutism, acne, and, occasionally, alopecia). Insulin resistance is a major feature of the disorder, as is overweight and obesity (although only 50% of women with PCOS are obese). Typically, testosterone and dehydroepiandrosterone sulfate levels are mildly elevated, and the luteinizing hormone to follicle-stimulating hormone ratio is greater than 2:1. Measurement of dehydroepiandrosterone sulfate is rarely clinically useful.

Positive withdrawal bleeding after the progestin withdrawal challenge suggests an estradiol level of greater than 40 pg/mL (146.8 pmol/L) and thus obviates the need for measurement of serum estradiol levels.

An MRI of the pituitary gland is unnecessary at this point because her follicle-stimulating hormone, prolactin, and thyroid levels are all normal.

> ### KEY POINT
> - **Menstrual flow on progestin withdrawal indicates relatively normal estrogen production and a patent outflow tract, which limits the differential diagnosis of secondary amenorrhea to chronic anovulation with estrogen present.**

Bibliography

Practice Committee of the American Society for Reproductive Medicine. Current evaluation of amenorrhea. Fertil Steril. 2006;86(5 Suppl 1):S148-S155. [PMID: 17055812]

Item 6   Answer: C

Educational Objective: Diagnose hypopituitarism as a late consequence of pituitary irradiation.

This patient's symptoms are most likely caused by hypopituitarism. Any kind of radiation therapy, including stereotactic radiation therapy, to the area of the pituitary and hypothalamus can cause deficiencies of anterior pituitary hormones during the subsequent 10 (or more) years. Although such deficiencies are seen most commonly with radiation therapy directed to a pituitary tumor, they also occur with radiation therapy for other tumors in this area, such as a nasopharyngeal carcinoma. Cortisol deficiency could occur with such irradiation and be the cause of his symptoms, as could hypothyroidism or hypogonadism.

Diabetes insipidus is unlikely in this patient. Surgery to the pituitary sometimes causes diabetes insipidus, which can be associated with hypernatremia, but this disorder usually manifests within the first day or so after surgery; this patient had normal results on testing postoperatively. In addition, radiation therapy typically does not cause damage to the posterior pituitary and, therefore, has not been associated with either diabetes insipidus or the syndrome of inappropriate antidiuretic hormone secretion.

Neither transsphenoidal surgery nor irradiation causes hydrocephalus, and the patient has no other symptoms of the disorder, such as headache, behavior or personality changes, or neurologic signs. Therefore, this diagnosis is unlikely.

Although radiation therapy works slowly, it is generally quite effective. In one study of nonfunctioning adenomas treated with stereotactic irradiation, adenoma volume decreased or remained stable in over 90% of patients, whereas new hypopituitarism developed in approximately 20% of patients during the 3.5-year follow-up period. Therefore, regrowth of the adenoma is less likely to be causing the patient's symptoms than the development of new hypopituitarism.

> ### KEY POINT
> - **Hypopituitarism is a common late finding after irradiation of pituitary adenomas.**

Bibliography

Darzy KH, Shalet SM. Hypopituitarism following radiation therapy. Pituitary. 2009;12(1):40-50. [PMID: 18270844]

Item 7   Answer: D

Educational Objective: Evaluate abnormal results on thyroid function tests in a patient with a nonthyroidal illness.

This patient should have repeat thyroid function tests in 4 to 8 weeks. With his history of a recent severe illness, the results of his thyroid function tests (low thyroid-stimulating hormone [TSH] and free triiodothyronine [T_3] levels and a low-normal free thyroxine [T_4] level) are most consistent with changes from a nonthyroidal illness (collectively known as euthyroid sick syndrome). The classic pattern consists of low TSH and free T_3 levels with a free T_4 level in the normal to low-normal range (or even frankly low with a prolonged illness). Reverse T_3 levels are elevated (if measured), but because results of this measurement typically take several weeks to obtain, reverse T_3 level results are seldom used clinically. The best next step is to allow the patient to recover for 4 to 8 weeks and then repeat the thyroid function tests. If results of these tests are not normal after recovery, further work-up can commence.

Brain MRI is not appropriate for this patient because no clinical finding suggests pituitary dysfunction. Furthermore, if evaluation of the pituitary gland were required, MRI of the sella turcica would be most appropriate.

There are no data showing that T_4 or T_3 replacement therapy is beneficial for nonthyroidal illness. Therefore, initiation of levothyroxine or liothyronine is inappropriate for this patient.

Thyroid ultrasonography does not help determine changes in thyroid function and thus is not useful for this patient.

KEY POINT

- Severe illness can cause euthyroid sick syndrome, which is associated with abnormal results on thyroid function tests that often normalize after recovery; neither levothyroxine nor liothyronine is indicated for treatment of the thyroid function changes seen with such nonthyroidal illness.

Bibliography

Adler SM, Wartofsky L. The nonthyroidal illness syndrome. Endocrinol Metab Clin North Am. 2007;36(3):657-672, vi. [PMID: 17673123]

Item 8   Answer: B

Educational Objective: Treat poorly controlled type 2 diabetes mellitus.

Insulin glargine should be added to this patient's regimen. Type 2 diabetes mellitus is associated with progressive beta cell dysfunction, resulting in deterioration of endogenous insulin secretory capacity over time. This leads to secondary failure rates of previously successful oral pharmacologic therapy and, ultimately, the need for insulin therapy in most patients with diabetes.

This patient has poor glycemic control, despite combination therapy with metformin and extended-release glipizide (a sulfonylurea), and thus requires insulin. The standard method of initiating insulin therapy is to begin with a single daily injection of a basal insulin, such as insulin glargine, insulin detemir, or neutral protamine Hagedorn (NPH) insulin; this approach minimizes the risk of hypoglycemia. Starting doses in the 0.2 to 0.3 U/kg range will be well tolerated in most patients, with future titration based on the results of home glucose monitoring. Dose changes are typically made in increments of 2 to 4 units every few days or weekly until the fasting glucose level is consistently in the range of 70 to 130 mg/dL (3.9 to 7.2 mmol/L). The addition of insulin glargine or insulin detemir to this patient's regimen should result in a substantial reduction in his hemoglobin A_{1c} value. Randomized studies of stepped therapy in type 2 diabetes showed that most patients were able to achieve target hemoglobin A_{1c} goals of 7% using a combination of oral antihyperglycemic agents and basal insulin therapy. If such a reduction is not achieved and postprandial hyperglycemia occurs, the addition of a mealtime rapid-acting insulin analogue or the substitution of a premixed insulin should be recommended.

Adding the injectable agent exenatide or another oral agent to this patient's medication regimen is unlikely to reduce his hemoglobin A_{1c} value sufficiently. When added to a combination oral regimen, exenatide has been shown to reduce hemoglobin A_{1c} values by only 1% and the oral agents pioglitazone and sitagliptin by 1% or less.

In most studies of patients with diabetes, increasing the sulfonylurea dosage beyond the half maximal dosage has resulted in little to no improvement in glycemic control. Therefore, doubling this patient's dosage of glipizide is unlikely to be effective.

KEY POINT

- In patients who have persistent fasting hyperglycemia despite combination oral agents, the addition of insulin, typically a basal formulation, will improve glycemic control.

Bibliography

Nathan DM, Buse JB, Davidson MB, et al. Medical management of hyperglycemia in type 2 diabetes: a consensus algorithm for the initiation and adjustment of therapy: a consensus statement of the American Diabetes Association and the European Association for the Study of Diabetes. Diabetes Care. 2009;32(1):193-203. [PMID: 18945920]

Item 9   Answer: A

Educational Objective: Diagnose androgen abuse.

This patient is most likely abusing anabolic steroids and possibly other performance-enhancing drugs. Anabolic steroid abuse should be suspected in a muscular man with normal libido, normal erectile function, atrophic testes, infertility, and low gonadotropin and testosterone levels. Fertility can be restored with abstinence from androgens and with gonadotropin injections.

A patient such as this one who has low levels of testosterone and gonadotropins might ordinarily be classified as having secondary hypogonadotropic hypogonadism. However, despite his low testosterone level, there is clinical evidence of adequate circulating androgens, including good muscle mass, normal libido, and erectile function. Therefore, despite the low testosterone and gonadotropin levels, pituitary macroadenoma and prolactinoma are unlikely diagnoses because they cannot explain the patient's clinical findings. An MRI of the sella turcica to exclude a pituitary tumor is unnecessary.

Common causes of primary testicular failure include Klinefelter syndrome, HIV infection, uncorrected cryptorchidism, previous use of cancer chemotherapeutic agents, irradiation, surgical orchiectomy, and previous infectious orchitis. Although each of these entities is a cause of low testosterone levels, each is also associated with elevated levels of gonadotropins (hypergonadotropic hypogonadism). Primary testicular failure is not a tenable diagnosis in this patient given the findings on clinical evaluation and the suppression of both follicle-stimulating hormone and luteinizing hormone levels.

KEY POINT

- **Anabolic steroid abuse should be suspected in a muscular man with atrophic testes, normal libido, normal erectile function, and a low testosterone level.**

Bibliography

Karila T, Hovatta O, Seppälä T. Concomitant abuse of anabolic androgenic steroids and human chorionic gonadotrophin impairs spermatogenesis in power athletes. Int J Sports Med. 2004;25(4):257-263. [PMID: 15162244]

Item 10   Answer: C

Educational Objective: Manage hypothyroidism during pregnancy.

The most appropriate next step is to recheck this patient's serum thyroid-stimulating hormone (TSH) level. Because a fetus depends on maternal thyroid hormone for the first 10 to 12 weeks of gestation, the thyroid levels of pregnant women with hypothyroidism should be carefully monitored. Recent guidelines recommend that TSH and total thyroxine (T_4) levels be monitored throughout pregnancy because standard free T_4 levels are not as accurate in pregnant patients. The total T_4 level should be kept stable at approximately 1.5 times the normal range, and the TSH level should be kept in the lower range of normal. Because of estrogen elevation during pregnancy, thyroid-binding globulin (TBG) levels increase. However,

without an increase in the dosage of levothyroxine, free T_4 levels may decrease as more T_4 becomes bound by TBG. After delivery, TBG levels decrease, as do thyroid hormone requirements.

Because the patient's TSH level was already borderline high 1 month ago, it should be rechecked. If the TSH level is any higher now, an increase in the levothyroxine dosage is warranted. Pregnant patients with hypothyroidism may require an increase in their levothyroxine dosage of approximately 35% to 50% as early as the first trimester.

Although maternal iodine replacement has been successfully used in countries with prevalent iodine deficiency, its use in patients who are iodine sufficient can be associated with catastrophic results, such as a fetal goiter. Because significant iodine deficiency in the United States is rare, iodine therapy in pregnant U.S. women is not indicated.

Measurement of the free triiodothyronine (T_3) level is not useful in the evaluation of hypothyroidism because T_3 levels typically remain within the reference range until the point of severe hypothyroidism. This pattern is unaltered by pregnancy.

Continuing the current management is inappropriate because undertreatment of maternal hypothyroidism can have a potentially negative effect on fetal neurocognitive development.

KEY POINT

- **Because the fetus is dependent on maternal thyroid hormone during the first trimester, guidelines for the treatment of hypothyroidism during pregnancy recommend that the total thyroxine (T_4) level be kept stable at 1.5 times the normal range and the thyroid-stimulating hormone level be kept in the lower range of normal.**

Bibliography

Abalovich M, Amino N, Barbour LA, et al. Management of thyroid dysfunction during pregnancy and postpartum: an Endocrine Society clinical practice guideline. J Clin Endocrinol Metab. 2007;92(8 Suppl):S1-S47. [PMID: 17948378]

Item 11   Answer: D

Educational Objective: Treat a patient with postprandial hyperglycemia who requires mealtime insulin therapy.

This patient's medication regimen should be altered by stopping the glimepiride and initiating mealtime insulin aspart. Patients with type 2 diabetes mellitus experience progressive beta cell dysfunction, which eventually results in the requirement of insulin in most patients. Insulin therapy is typically begun with a single injection of a basal insulin, such as insulin glargine or insulin detemir, or two injections of neutral protamine Hagedorn (NPH) insulin. Over time, insulin secretion becomes progressively deficient, and postprandial glucose excursions can no longer be addressed by increasing the basal insulin dose. Such a scenario requires the addition of a rapid-acting insulin analogue before meals. Insulin lispro, insulin aspart, and insulin glulisine are typically used in this setting in dosages sufficient to prevent the glucose level from increasing more than 40 to 60 mg/dL (2.2 to 3.3 mmol/L) with each meal. Once this more intensive insulin regimen is initiated, ongoing use of a sulfonylurea, such as glimepiride, is no longer required.

Exenatide does reduce postprandial glucose levels and may be effective in doing so for this patient. However, this injectable glucagon-like peptide-1 mimetic is not approved for use in conjunction with insulin and so is not appropriate for this patient.

Increasing this patient's insulin glargine dosage will not address her prandial insulin requirements because glargine is a basal insulin and does not control postprandial glycemic peaks.

Continuous subcutaneous insulin infusion using an insulin pump is becoming a viable treatment option for patients with type 2 diabetes. Patients who may benefit from an insulin pump include those who have not been able to achieve glycemic goals on an intensified insulin regimen of multiple daily injections; have unacceptable rates of hypoglycemia when following insulin injection regimens that combine intermediate- or long-acting insulin (NPH, glargine) with prandial insulin; have a marked dawn phenomenon (increase in blood glucose levels during the early morning hours [4 AM-8 AM]); or have erratic lifestyles (travel, shift work). Insulin pump therapy is premature at this juncture because this patient has not had a trial of an intensified insulin regimen of multiple daily injections.

> **KEY POINT**
> - The addition of rapid-acting insulin analogues at mealtimes decreases postprandial glycemic excursions.

Bibliography
Dailey GE. Using prandial insulin to achieve glycemic control in type 2 diabetes. J Fam Pract. 2007;56(9):735-742. [PMID: 17764645]

Item 12   Answer: D
Educational Objective: Treat acromegaly.

The most appropriate treatment to normalize this patient's growth hormone (GH) and insulin-like growth factor 1 (IGF-1) levels over the next year is use of a somatostatin analogue. The goal of treatment in patients with acromegaly is to normalize anterior pituitary function and GH secretion, control tumor growth, and treat systemic complications. Transsphenoidal surgical resection is typically the treatment of choice. Medical treatment is often also required because many of these tumors are too large at presentation to be completely excised by surgery. In patients with such tumors, medical therapy is indicated.

This patient should be treated with a somatostatin analogue, such as octreotide or lanreotide. These drugs can normalize GH and IGF-1 levels in approximately 50% of patients when given adjunctively after pituitary surgery. They also commonly decrease tumor size.

Cabergoline normalizes GH and IGF-1 levels in only 10% to 20% of patients. Because this drug is cheaper and easier to administer than the somatostatin analogues, it may be worth trying initially as medical therapy, but only with the understanding that it is unlikely to succeed.

When transsphenoidal surgery is unable to cure a patient with a pituitary tumor, a second surgery, such as craniotomy, does so in only approximately 25% of patients. Because craniotomy also has substantial morbidity, it would rarely be used in a patient such as this one.

Radiation therapy may normalize GH and IGF-1 levels, but only after an extended period of time. With conventional radiation therapy, hormone levels in approximately two thirds of patients normalize in approximately 10 years; with gamma knife stereotactic radiation therapy, the time is reduced to 4 years. Neither type of radiation therapy would have a normalizing effect on these levels within 1 year.

> **KEY POINT**
> - In patients with pituitary tumors who are not cured by surgery, hormone levels often normalize with use of somatostatin analogues.

Bibliography
Ben-Shlomo A, Melmed S. Acromegaly. Endocrinol Metab Clin North Am. 2008;37(1):101-122, viii. [PMID: 18226732]

Item 13   Answer: C
Educational Objective: Manage hirsutism in a patient with polycystic ovary syndrome.

This patient with classic polycystic ovary syndrome (PCOS) is a good candidate for therapy with spironolactone and an oral contraceptive. PCOS affects 6% of women of childbearing age and typically presents with oligomenorrhea and signs of androgen excess (hirsutism, acne, and occasionally alopecia). Insulin resistance is a major feature of the disorder, as are overweight and obesity, although only 50% of affected women are obese. Typically, there is a mild elevation in testosterone and dehydroepiandrosterone sulfate levels and a luteinizing hormone to follicle-stimulating hormone ratio of greater than 2:1. Diagnosis requires two of the three following features: (1) ovulatory dysfunction, (2) laboratory or clinical evidence of hyperandrogenism, and (3) ultrasonographic evidence of polycystic ovaries. This patient has ovulatory dysfunction and clinical evidence of hyperandrogenism. Because her chief symptom is hirsutism and she does not want to become pregnant, spironolactone is the drug of choice. This drug should be combined with an oral contraceptive to prevent vaginal spotting and ter-atogenism, should she become pregnant.

Because the patient has an only mildly elevated total testosterone level and clinical evidence of hyperandro-genism, measurement of her serum free testosterone level will add nothing to the diagnosis or management of her disorder.

This patient's normal 17-hydroxyprogesterone level excludes nonclassic 21-hydroxylase deficiency as a diagno-sis. Therefore, corticosteroid (prednisone) therapy is not indicated.

This patient's total testosterone level (84 ng/dL [2.9 nmol/L]), although somewhat high, is not high enough to raise concerns about a tumor. Typically, the serum testos-terone level in patients with PCOS rarely exceeds 150 ng/dL (5.2 nmol/L); higher levels warrant a search for an adrenal or ovarian tumor. Therefore, a transvaginal ovarian ultrasound is not needed either to establish the diagnosis of PCOS or to establish the presence of an ovarian tumor.

KEY POINT

- **In patients with hirsutism and polycystic ovary syndrome who do not wish to become preg-nant, the most appropriate initial therapy is spironolactone and an oral contraceptive pill.**

Bibliography

Carmina E, Rosato F, Jannì A, Rizzo M, Longo RA. Extensive clini-cal experience: relative prevalence of different androgen excess dis-orders in 950 women referred because of clinical hyperandro-genism. J Clin Endocrinol Metab. 2006;91(1):2-6. [PMID: 16263820]

Item 14　　Answer:　C

Educational Objective: Evaluate hypercalcemia.

This patient's parathyroid hormone (PTH) level should be determined next. Primary hyperparathyroidism is the most common cause of hypercalcemia in the outpatient setting. The first step in the diagnosis of hypercalcemia is determi-nation of the PTH level with an assay for intact PTH. If the PTH level is high or "inappropriately" normal, primary hyperparathyroidism is the diagnosis. If the PTH level is suppressed, a search for other entities that cause hypercal-cemia must be conducted.

Calcitonin is secreted by thyroid parafollicular C cells. This serum level is elevated in patients with medullary thy-roid cancer or C-cell hyperplasia. Calcitonin tends to lower the calcium level by enhancing cellular uptake, renal excre-tion, and bone formation. The effect of calcitonin on bone metabolism is weak and only relevant in pharmacologic amounts. Measurement of serum calcitonin is not indicated in a patient with hypercalcemia.

One of the ways in which PTH increases the serum cal-cium level is by upregulation of the 1α-hydroxylase enzyme, which stimulates conversion of vitamin D to its most active form, 1,25-dihydroxy vitamin D. This form of vitamin D increases the percentage of dietary calcium absorbed by the intestine. Body stores of vitamin D are assessed by measuring the 25-hydroxy vitamin D level, which has a long half-life. Measurement of this patient's 25-hydroxy vitamin D and 1,25-dihydroxy vitamin D levels may be appropriate if the parathyroid hormone level is sup-pressed or if further evaluation suggests concomitant vita-min D deficiency and hyperparathyroidism (a frequent association, particularly in elderly patients). At this time, however, such measurement is not indicated.

Humoral hypercalcemia of malignancy results from the systemic effect of a circulating factor produced by neoplas-tic cells. The hormone most commonly responsible for this syndrome is parathyroid hormone–related protein (PTHrP). This peptide's *N*-terminal shares many homo-logic features with PTH and most, if not all, of the meta-bolic effects of PTH. Tumors that elaborate PTHrP are most commonly squamous cell carcinomas, such as those of the lung, esophagus, and head and neck. This patient has no evidence of cancer, which makes measurement of the PTHrP level inappropriate at this time. The diagnosis of humoral hypercalcemia of malignancy can often be made in the absence of PTHrP measurements if a compatible malig-nancy, hypercalcemia, and suppressed parathyroid hor-mone level are present.

KEY POINT

- **The most common cause of hypercalcemia in the outpatient setting is hyperparathyroidism.**

Bibliography

Moe SM. Disorders involving calcium, phosphorus, and magnesium. Prim Care. 2008;35(2):215-237, v-vi. [PMID: 18486714]

Item 15　　Answer:　D

Educational Objective: Evaluate an incidentally discovered adrenal mass.

In addition to an overnight 1-mg dexamethasone suppres-sion test, the most reasonable next diagnostic step is mea-surement of the plasma metanephrine level. Clinically inap-parent adrenal masses are discovered in 0.4% to 6.9% of imaging studies performed during evaluation of nonadrenal disorders. Most adrenal nodules are hormonally silent and have no malignant potential. As many as 30%, however, secrete cortisol, aldosterone, androgens, or catecholamines. After a complete history and physical examination, the hor-monal activity of the incidentaloma should be determined.

Subclinical Cushing syndrome should first be excluded with an overnight 1-mg dexamethasone sup-pression test. A screening test for pheochromocytoma (by measurement of the plasma metanephrine level) is also rec-ommended by most experts, even if the patient is nor-motensive. The rationale for screening is that patients with pheochromocytoma may only be intermittently hyperten-sive. Other experts recommend screening only if the adrenal nodule is vascular, which suggests the presence of pheochromocytoma, or if the patient has other symptoms suggestive of pheochromocytoma, such as hypertension, tachycardia, or palpitations.

In patients with hypertension who have an incidentally discovered adrenal nodule, screening for hypercortisolism and pheochromocytoma is essential, as is measurement of serum aldosterone and plasma renin activity. Obtaining the serum aldosterone to plasma renin activity ratio is not indicated, however, in normotensive patients and thus is not necessary in this patient.

Adrenal androgens, such as dehydroepiandrosterone sulfate, should only be assessed in masculinized female patients, just as the estrogen level should be measured in feminized male patients. They should not be assessed in this patient.

KEY POINT

- **All patients with an incidentally discovered adrenal nodule should be evaluated for hypercortisolism (and, possibly, pheochromocytoma); if such patients are hypertensive, hypercortisolism, pheochromocytoma, and an elevated serum aldosterone to plasma renin activity ratio should be excluded.**

Bibliography

Young WF Jr. Clinical practice. The incidentally discovered adrenal mass. N Engl J Med. 2007;356(6):601-610. [PMID: 17287480]

Item 16   Answer: A

Educational Objective: Manage a solitary thyroid nodule.

Fine-needle aspiration biopsy is the most appropriate next step in the evaluation of this patient. Whereas screening for thyroid nodules with ultrasonography is not recommended, ultrasonography is an excellent modality for assessing the thyroid gland when anatomic abnormalities are suspected clinically. Ultrasonography allows identification of nodules, whether palpable or not, and of nodule characteristics, such as echogenicity, vascular pattern, and presence of calcifications. Fine-needle aspiration is the mainstay in the evaluation of such thyroid nodules in euthyroid patients and has an excellent sensitivity and specificity for detecting cancer. Ultrasonography-guided fine-needle aspiration would be preferred in this patient because the nodule was not definitively palpated on examination.

Nodules can harbor malignancy regardless of the presence or absence of autoimmune disease. Therefore, determination of anti–thyroperoxidase antibody and anti–thyroglobulin antibody titers in this patient is unlikely to be helpful.

Ultrasonography is superior to CT in the evaluation of thyroid nodules, except when there is a goiter with substantial substernal extension. This patient has no such goiter. Because the thyroid nodule has been verified on an ultrasound, further imaging is unnecessary before obtaining a tissue sample.

Thyroid scanning has no role in the initial workup of thyroid nodules because both benign and malignant nodules tend to be hypofunctional or "cold" on a thyroid scan. Thyroid scanning may be helpful when the thyroid-stimulating hormone (TSH) level is suppressed (which this patient's is not) to assess for a hyperfunctioning ("hot") nodule that does not require fine-needle aspiration biopsy. Hyperfunctioning nodules are rarely malignant.

Suppression of the TSH level with levothyroxine has fallen out of favor in the management of benign nodular thyroid disease because most randomized prospective trials have shown no net reduction in nodule size, and concerns are increasing about the adverse effects of iatrogenic thyrotoxicosis. Suppressive therapy is generally now reserved for patients with a cancer diagnosis.

KEY POINT

- **Fine-needle aspiration is the mainstay in evaluation of nontoxic thyroid nodules.**

Bibliography

Cooper DS, Doherty GM, Haugen BR, et al; American Thyroid Association Guidelines Taskforce. Management guidelines for patients with thyroid nodules and differentiated thyroid cancer. Thyroid. 2006;16(2):109-142. [PMID: 16420177]

Item 17   Answer: B

Educational Objective: Diagnose secondary diabetes related to pancreatic insufficiency.

Diabetes mellitus is generally categorized as type 1, type 2, gestational, and secondary diabetes. This patient's diabetes is the last type, which consists of a group of unrelated conditions that are associated with hyperglycemia through effects on either insulin availability or insulin sensitivity. These include various endocrine disorders, such as Cushing syndrome and acromegaly; several pancreatic conditions, such as acute and chronic pancreatitis and pancreatic cancer; drug-induced hyperglycemia; and several genetic syndromes. This patient has a history of ethanol abuse and chronic abdominal pain, which may be related to chronic pancreatitis. The most common cause of chronic pancreatitis in western industrialized countries is chronic alcohol abuse, which accounts for 50% or more of all cases. The presence of pancreatic calcifications on radiographs confirms the diagnosis. Although plain films of the abdomen will show pancreatic calcifications in some patients, most patients will require abdominal CT scans to exclude other causes of pain.

Patients with pancreatic disease causing secondary diabetes may still respond to oral sulfonylureas, and a trial of such a drug is appropriate. If there has been enough loss of beta cell mass, however, insulin therapy may be required. Because of glucagon deficiency, patients with diabetes related to pancreatic insufficiency may be predisposed to hypoglycemia.

Late-onset autoimmune diabetes of adulthood is a possibility in this patient, given his age (51 years), his lean body habitus, and the insidious onset of diabetes. However, it would be much less common than secondary diabetes in this man with confirmed chronic pancreatitis.

This patient's clinical presentation is atypical for type 1 diabetes, which usually has an acute or subacute onset and is characterized by polyuria, polydipsia, polyphagia, and weight loss.

Most patients with type 2 diabetes are obese or at least have abdominal obesity (high waist-to-hip ratio). This patient is of normal body weight, and his scaphoid-appearing abdomen makes type 2 diabetes even less likely.

KEY POINT

- **Secondary causes of diabetes mellitus should be considered in any patient who presents with atypical features.**

Bibliography

Nair RJ, Lawler L, Miller MR. Chronic pancreatitis. Am Fam Physician. 2007;76(11):1679-1688. [PMID: 18092710]

Item 18   Answer: D

Educational Objective: Diagnose surreptitious use of a sulfonylurea leading to hypoglycemia.

This patient's serum levels of sulfonylureas should be measured. In patients with hypoglycemia who do not have diabetes mellitus, inadvertent or surreptitious use of oral hypoglycemic agents or insulin must first be excluded. Exogenous insulin administration is best confirmed by measuring insulin and glucose levels, with simultaneous measurement of C-peptide to confirm endogenous insulin secretion. In a patient whose hypoglycemia results from insulin injections, C-peptide levels are suppressed. However, if hypoglycemia results from the use of insulin secretagogues, such as sulfonylureas or meglitinides, C-peptide levels are inappropriately elevated, as with this patient. This finding may mimic that seen in patients with an insulinoma, so measurement of serum sulfonylurea levels is essential in distinguishing surreptitious use of a sulfonylurea from an insulinoma.

A CT scan of the abdomen is often the first step in the evaluation of a suspected insulinoma, but insulinomas are often too small to be detected on a CT scan. Other imaging modalities include MRI and endoscopic ultrasonography. However, each of these imaging procedures is premature until surreptitious use of oral hypoglycemic agents is excluded as a possible cause of this patient's hypoglycemia.

Some patients with pancreatic islet cell tumors have a familial syndrome known as multiple endocrine neoplasia type 1 (MEN1). MEN1 involves islet cell tumors of the pancreas, parathyroid glands, and anterior pituitary gland.

Screening for this disorder by measuring the serum calcium level and assessing anterior pituitary function might be appropriate in a patient with an insulinoma but not before the diagnosis of insulinoma is established.

KEY POINT

- **In nondiabetic patients with hypoglycemia, inadvertent or surreptitious use of oral hypoglycemic agents or insulin must be considered; sulfonylurea ingestion causes elevations in both insulin and C-peptide levels, and insulin injection suppresses C-peptide levels.**

Bibliography

Kwong PY, Teale JD. Screening for sulphonylureas in the investigation of hypoglycaemia. J R Soc Med. 2002;95(8):381-385. [PMID: 12151486]

Item 19   Answer: A

Educational Objective: Diagnose hungry bone syndrome.

This patient most likely has hungry bone syndrome. Hypocalcemia frequently occurs after removal of a hyperfunctioning parathyroid adenoma because of suppressed secretion of parathyroid hormone (PTH) by the remaining parathyroid tissue. The associated hypoparathyroidism is usually transient because the healthy parathyroid glands recover function quickly, generally within 1 week, even after long-term suppression. Transient postoperative hypocalcemia may be exaggerated or prolonged in patients, such as this one, who had marked preexisting hyperparathyroid bone disease. In these patients, the surgically induced reduction of previously elevated serum levels of PTH results in an increased movement of serum calcium and phosphorus into "hungry bones" for the purpose of remineralization. Treatment with calcium and a short-acting vitamin D metabolite may be required until the bones heal.

Both osteomalacia and vitamin D deficiency cause secondary hyperparathyroidism with elevated PTH levels. This patient's normal serum PTH level argues against these diagnoses.

Permanent hypoparathyroidism in patients treated for primary hyperparathyroidism is rare, developing in approximately 1% of these patients. The incidence of permanent hypoparathyroidism is greatly increased with repeated neck surgery for recurrent or persistent hyperparathyroidism, with subtotal parathyroidectomy for parathyroid hyperplasia, or with neck surgery performed by inexperienced surgeons.

KEY POINT

- **Hungry bone syndrome with severe hypocalcemia and hypophosphatemia can occur after removal of a parathyroid adenoma in patients with significant hyperparathyroid bone disease.**

Bibliography

Angeli A, Dovio A. The hungry bone: expected and unexpected. Ann Ital Med Int. 2004;19(3):IV-VI. [PMID: 15529940]

Item 20　　Answer:　C

Educational Objective: Manage a pheochromocytoma preoperatively.

The most appropriate next step is to initiate therapy with an α-blocker, either a long-acting, noncompetitive antagonist, such as phenoxybenzamine, or a short-acting antagonist, such as prazosin, doxazosin, or terazosin. Recent data indicate that many centers use a short-acting α-blocker instead of phenoxybenzamine because the latter can be associated with more prolonged postoperative hypotension. Preoperative preparation with α-adrenergic blockade reduces the incidence of intraoperative hypertensive crisis and postoperative hypotension. The primary goal is to maintain blood pressure in the range of 140 to 150/90 mm Hg. Preoperative medical therapy should be instituted once the diagnosis is reached and before surgical resection.

Adding a diuretic, such as chlorthalidone, to the medical regimen of a patient with pheochromocytoma as treatment of hypertension is a poor choice because the typical patient with pheochromocytoma is vasoconstricted and volume depleted and the addition of a diuretic will only worsen, not improve, his or her condition.

β-Blockade with metoprolol to control tachycardia is appropriate only after α-adrenergic blockade has been instituted to prevent unopposed α-adrenergic stimulation. The use of β-blockade alone will result in blocking the vasodilating effects of circulating catecholamines, which can lead to severe hypertension and be fatal.

Acute hypertensive crisis may occur before or during an operation and is typically treated intravenously with sodium nitroprusside, phentolamine, or nicardipine. This patient has no evidence of hypertensive crisis at this point, and hospitalization and treatment of his blood pressure with intravenous medications is not necessary.

KEY POINT

- α-Adrenergic blockers are the treatment of choice to prepare patients with pheochromocytoma for adrenalectomy; β-blockers should not be used in patients with suspected or confirmed pheochromocytoma until and unless α-adrenergic blockers have been used.

Bibliography

Pacak K. Preoperative management of the pheochromocytoma patient. J Clin Endocrinol Metab. 2007;92(11):4069-4079. [PMID: 17989126]

Item 21　　Answer:　B

Educational Objective: Treat prediabetes to prevent development of type 2 diabetes mellitus.

This patient with impaired fasting glucose (IFG), defined as a fasting plasma glucose level in the range of 100 to 125 mg/dL (5.6 to 6.9 mmol/L), should begin a program of intensive lifestyle change, including 30 minutes of exercise most days of the week and a calorie-restricted diet, to achieve weight reduction on the order of 7% of body weight.

According to a consensus statement on the prevention of diabetes from the American Diabetes Association and the European Association for the Study of Diabetes, diet and exercise is the recommended approach for patients with either IFG or impaired glucose tolerance (IGT), the prediabetic states. In the Diabetes Prevention Program (DPP), the relative risk reduction (RRR) in the incidence of diabetes in patients with IGT who were assigned to intensive lifestyle change was 58%.

Pharmacologic therapy with glucose-lowering drugs is not indicated for this patient with isolated IFG. In pharmacologic studies of diabetes prevention, acarbose therapy resulted in only a 25% RRR, which is inferior to that obtained with diet and exercise.

Metformin therapy is associated with a RRR of 31%, which is also inferior to the 58% RRR obtained with diet and exercise. The consensus panel has recommended that metformin therapy be considered in patients with both IFG and IGT, who constitute a higher risk group. This patient does not have IGT (fasting plasma glucose level of 140 to 199 mg/dL [7.7 to 11.0 mmol/L] at the 2-hour mark of an oral glucose tolerance test) and so should not receive metformin.

Modulators of the renin-angiotensin axis, such as ramipril and other angiotensin-converting enzyme inhibitors, were once thought to contribute to diabetes prevention, but the Diabetes Reduction Assessment with Ramipril and Rosiglitazone Medication (DREAM) study disproved this.

Rosiglitazone and pioglitazone have been associated, respectively, with 62% and 81% RRRs in the incidence of diabetes. However, the consensus panel has not endorsed their routine pharmacologic use in patients with prediabetes because of their costs and adverse effects, including edema, increased fracture risk in women, and possible increased cardiovascular morbidity.

KEY POINT

- Patients with prediabetes should be advised to adopt a program of lifestyle change to prevent progression to type 2 diabetes mellitus.

Bibliography

Knowler WC, Barrett-Connor E, Fowler SE, et al; Diabetes Prevention Program Research Group. Reduction in the incidence of type 2 diabetes with lifestyle intervention or metformin. N Engl J Med. 2002;346(6):393-403. [PMID: 11832527]

Item 22 Answer: C

Educational Objective: Anticipate the problems for which a pregnant woman with prolactinomas is at risk.

For women with prolactinomas, dopamine agonists are stopped once pregnancy is achieved. Dopamine agonists are reinstituted when breast feeding is completed. Approximately 30% of patients with macroprolactinomas will experience clinically significant enlargement of their prolactinomas during pregnancy. If this occurs, options include reinstitution of dopamine agonists, surgery, or delivery, depending on fetal viability. In contrast, only approximately 3% of women with microadenomas will experience such enlargement. Tumor enlargement is due both to the elimination of the dopamine agonist that had been controlling tumor size and to the stimulatory effect of the high estrogen status of pregnancy.

Follow-up studies of women who became pregnant after using cabergoline or bromocriptine have shown no increased risk of fetal malformations, premature deliveries, or stillbirth. Therefore, the patient is unlikely to encounter any of these problems.

Sheehan syndrome is the development of hypopituitarism postpartum because of a pituitary infarction, usually in association with an obstetric hemorrhage. This syndrome is quite rare, even in patients with pituitary adenomas, and thus is unlikely to develop in this patient.

KEY POINT

- **Macroprolactinomas can enlarge during pregnancy.**

Bibliography

Molitch ME. Pituitary disorders during pregnancy. Endocrinol Metab Clin North Am. 2006;35(1):99-116, vi. [PMID: 16310644]

Item 23 Answer: D

Educational Objective: Identify hemochromatosis as a cause of hypogonadism.

This patient most likely has hemochromatosis and thus should have his transferrin saturation level measured to establish the diagnosis. Hereditary hemochromatosis is an autosomal-recessive disorder characterized by increased intestinal absorption of iron and iron deposition in multiple organs, including the liver, pancreas, heart, joints, thyroid, and hypothalamus. This patient's family history of liver disease and diabetes mellitus in male members of his family, his arthritis, and his elevated aminotransferase levels, low total testosterone level, and low luteinizing hormone level support the diagnosis of hemochromatosis. The endocrinopathies of hemochromatosis typically include diabetes mellitus, hypogonadotropic hypogonadism, and adrenal insufficiency. His laboratory study results confirm the presence of diabetes (elevated fasting glucose level) and hypogonadism (low testosterone and luteinizing hormone

levels). His resting tachycardia and low blood pressure suggest the possibility of adrenal insufficiency, which can be life-threatening and so should be evaluated.

Although CT of the adrenal glands is essential in the evaluation of adrenocorticotropic hormone–independent hypercortisolism, it has no role in the initial diagnosis of hypocortisolism and is not indicated in this patient.

A 24-hour urine free cortisol measurement is a screening test for hypercortisolism and is not indicated for a patient with suspected hypocortisolism. Instead, basal and cosyntropin-stimulated cortisol measurements would be more appropriate as initial testing.

Measurement of serum calcium and parathyroid hormone levels is likewise not indicated because the patient does not have symptoms of hypercalcemia, and hemochromatosis does not typically involve the parathyroid glands.

KEY POINT

- **The endocrinopathies of hemochromatosis typically include diabetes mellitus, hypogonadotropic hypogonadism, and adrenal insufficiency.**

Bibliography

McDermott JH, Walsh CH. Hypogonadism in hereditary hemochromatosis. J Clin Endocrinol Metab. 2005;90(4):2451-2455. [PMID: 15657376]

Item 24 Answer: B

Educational Objective: Diagnose mutiple endocrine neoplasia type 1.

This patient most likely has multiple endocrine neoplasia type 1 (MEN1). MEN1 is characterized by tumors of the parathyroid, pituitary, and pancreatic islet cells (the three "P"s). Typically, MEN1-associated hyperparathyroidism is caused by a double adenoma or multigland hyperplasia. Rarely, carcinoid tumors, lipomas, and tumors of the adrenal cortex have been described. MEN1 is inherited in an autosomal or sporadic manner, but it may not always be possible to differentiate between the two if the parents are unknown or have died before developing symptoms. Molecular genetic studies have identified the gene that causes MEN1—*MENIN*—and have labeled it a tumor suppressor gene.

MEN2 is characterized by medullary carcinoma of the thyroid gland in combination with pheochromocytoma and parathyroid adenomas (MEN2a) or with a pheochromocytoma, ganglioneuromas, and a marfanoid habitus (MEN2b). MEN2 is inherited as an autosomal dominant trait with a high degree of penetrance and is caused by mutations in the *RET* proto-oncogene. This patient has a pituitary tumor and no clinical evidence of thyroid or adrenal tumors, which rules out MEN2.

Autoimmune polyglandular syndrome type 1 (APS1) is an inherited autosomal recessive disorder with a 25% incidence among siblings of patients with the disease. APS1 is characterized by the triad of chronic mucocutaneous candidiasis, autoimmune hypoparathyroidism, and adrenal insufficiency. This patient has hyperparathyroidism, not hypoparathyroidism, which makes APS1 unlikely.

Osteosclerotic myeloma, or POEMS syndrome, consists of Polyneuropathy, Organomegaly, Endocrinopathy, Monoclonal protein (M spike) on serum protein electrophoresis, and Skin abnormalities. This syndrome is associated with several endocrinopathies in the setting of lymphoproliferative disorders and presumed B-cell dysfunction. Hypogonadism appears to be the most common endocrine abnormality. This clinical and biochemical description is not consistent with this patient's findings.

KEY POINT

- **Multiple endocrine neoplasia type 1 is characterized by tumors of the pancreas and the parathyroid and pituitary glands.**

Bibliography

Piecha G, Chudek J, Wiecek A. Multiple endocrine neoplasia type 1. Eur J Intern Med. 2008;19(2):99-103. [PMID: 18249304]

Item 25   Answer: E

Educational Objective: Treat hypothyroidism in the context of drug interaction.

Levothyroxine is best taken on an empty stomach either 1 hour before or 2 to 3 hours after any food or other medication. The patient has a newly elevated thyroid-stimulating hormone (TSH) level after the level was in the target range for 2 years on a stable dose of levothyroxine. Her oral contraceptive pills have been unchanged for 3 years. The only change to her medical regimen is the initiation of ferrous sulfate therapy. Over-the-counter supplements, such as iron, calcium, multivitamins (which contain both iron and calcium), and psyllium, are all known to bind levothyroxine in the gut and negatively affect its absorption. This problem should not occur if she takes the levothyroxine at least 1 hour before the ferrous sulfate.

Desiccated thyroid hormone contains variable amounts of thyroxine (T_4) and triiodothyronine (T_3) and therefore is not recommended for routine use.

Changes in the estrogen level can raise thyroxine-binding globulin levels, and an increase in the levothyroxine dosage would be needed to keep free T_4 levels stable. Because this patient has been on a stable dosage of estrogen for 3 years with stable TSH levels, neither changing her levothyroxine dosage nor switching her oral contraceptive to a progestin-only pill is indicated. Furthermore, increasing the levothyroxine dosage by 50 µg a day is excessive. Finally, the body of evidence to date shows no clinical advantage of combined levothyroxine-liothyronine therapy over traditional levothyroxine treatment.

KEY POINT

- **Levothyroxine is best taken on an empty stomach either 1 hour before or 2 to 3 hours after any food or other medication.**

Bibliography

Grozinsky-Glasberg S, Fraser A, Nahshoni E, Weizman A, Leibovici L. Thyroxine-triiodothyronine combination therapy versus thyroxine monotherapy for clinical hypothyroidism: meta-analysis of randomized controlled trials. J Clin Endocrinol Metab. 2006;91(7):2592-2599. [PMID: 16670166]

Item 26   Answer: A

Educational Objective: Manage insulin therapy in a hospitalized patient with suboptimal glycemic control.

This patient has uncontrolled diabetes mellitus during an acute medical illness requiring hospitalization. Although there are no data demonstrating improved clinical outcomes with better glycemic control in patients on general hospital wards, such treatment likely improves outcomes in the intensive care unit. Accordingly, national consensus guidelines recommend attempting to improve glycemic control in all hospitalized patients (premeal glucose level <140 mg/dL [7.8 mmol/L] and random glucose level <180 mg/dL [10.0 mmol/L]). Thus, a basal-bolus insulin regimen consisting of a long- or intermediate-acting insulin and a rapid-acting insulin analogue before meals is recommended for this hospitalized patient with diabetes mellitus. Such an approach allows for a more easily titratable regimen and can conveniently be held during diagnostic testing or procedures when nutritional intake is interrupted.

Insulin infusions are difficult to administer outside the intensive care unit in most hospitals; therefore, initiating one is not the best treatment for this patient and may not even be necessary to obtain good glycemic control.

A regimen of neutral protamine Hagedorn (NPH) insulin twice daily will likely improve glycemic control but is not as easily titratable as a basal-bolus correction and does not provide for premeal coverage to prevent postprandial glucose spikes.

Sliding scale regular insulin has been associated with increased hyperglycemic and hypoglycemic excursions and has been found to result in inferior glycemic control compared with a basal-bolus correction regimen in hospitalized patients. Initiating this approach is therefore inappropriate.

KEY POINT

- **There are no data demonstrating improved clinical outcomes after treatment to achieve better glycemic control in patients on general hospital wards, but such treatment has been shown to improve outcomes in critically ill patients in the intensive care unit.**

Bibliography

Umpierrez GE, Smiley D, Zisman A, et al. Randomized study of basal-bolus insulin therapy in the inpatient management of patients with type 2 diabetes (RABBIT 2 trial). Diabetes Care. 2007;30(9):2181-2186. [PMID: 17513708]

Item 27   Answer: D

Educational Objective: Evaluate suspected Cushing syndrome.

Measuring this patient's 24-hour urine free cortisol excretion is the most appropriate next test. She has clinical features of Cushing syndrome, including weight gain, round or "moon" facies and a "buffalo hump," violaceous striae and incidental bruising, hirsutism, and menstrual irregularity. The unprovoked hypokalemia also supports that diagnosis. The value of measuring serum or salivary cortisol in the late evening (11:00 PM or later) is based on the finding that the normal evening nadir in cortisol production is preserved in obese and depressed patients but not in those with Cushing syndrome. Many consider obtaining a 24-hour urine free cortisol level as the most reliable screening test. Patients with Cushing syndrome excrete three- to five-times higher amounts of free cortisol than do those without the syndrome. Others favor the overnight dexamethasone suppression test as most reliable and convenient; the 1-mg overnight dexamethasone suppression test documents the nonsuppressibilty of cortisol by exogenous corticosteroids. Generally, most authorities recommend either of these tests in patients suspected of having Cushing syndrome.

The cosyntropin stimulation test is used to determine the adrenal reserve by measuring the response to a standard dose of synthetic adrenocorticotropic hormone. The test does not detect Cushing syndrome but, rather, adrenal insufficiency and is therefore not indicated for this patient.

The high-dose (8 mg) dexamethasone suppression test is used to determine the possible cause of Cushing syndrome by assessing the degree of suppression achieved by the higher dose of dexamethasone. This test is not indicated unless the evaluation demonstrates excess cortisol production or inability to suppress cortisol production with the low-dose dexamethasone screening test.

Although this patient's morning serum cortisol level is likely to be elevated, this finding does not provide any additional information to what is provided by the elevated evening cortisol level.

KEY POINT

- **The best two screening tests for Cushing syndrome are measurement of 24-hour urine free cortisol excretion and the 1-mg overnight dexamethasone suppression test.**

Bibliography

Findling JW, Raff H. Cushing's syndrome: important issues in diagnosis and management. J Clin Endocrinol Metab. 2006; 91(10):3746-3753. [PMID: 16868050]

Item 28   Answer: C

Educational Objective: Treat severe osteoporosis with teriparatide.

The most appropriate management for this patient's severe osteoporosis is to discontinue the alendronate and start teriparatide (recombinant human parathyroid hormone [1-34]). This patient has adequate calcium and vitamin D intake; therefore, her bisphosphonate therapy is not working adequately. Teriparatide, one of the few available therapies that stimulates new bone formation, is given via daily subcutaneous injection for a recommended duration of 1 to 2 years. Teriparatide can significantly decrease the incidence of both vertebral and nonvertebral fractures. Because animal studies have shown an increased risk of osteosarcoma, this agent should be avoided in patients with Paget disease of bone, previous radiation therapy involving the skeleton, or a history of skeletal cancer. Teriparatide should be considered in patients who are intolerant of other medications, are not responding to first-line therapy, or have the greatest fracture risk. Trials, however, have shown no benefit of concurrent teriparatide and bisphosphonate therapy, so adding teriparatide to her current regimen is inappropriate. This patient should stop taking alendronate, which may actually attenuate the benefit of teriparatide therapy by unknown mechanisms. Prior treatment with alendronate also seems to diminish the increases in bone mineral density usually caused by teriparatide, particularly in the first 6 months.

Because this patient is not vitamin D deficient, high-dose ergocalciferol is not indicated.

There is no evidence that this patient is malabsorbing the oral alendronate or is not adherent to this therapy. Therefore, intravenous bisphosphonate therapy is not indicated and is unlikely to provide the same benefit as teriparatide.

KEY POINT

- **Progressive osteoporosis in a patient on bisphosphonate therapy who has adequate calcium and vitamin D intake is an indication to change the medication to teriparatide.**

Bibliography

Obermayer-Pietsch BM, Marin F, McCloskey EV, et al; EUROFORS Investigators. Effects of two years of daily teriparatide treatment on BMD in postmenopausal women with severe osteoporosis with and without prior antiresorptive treatment. J Bone Miner Res. 2008;23(10):1591-1600. [PMID: 18505369]

Item 29   Answer: B

Educational Objective: Evaluate diabetes insipidus.

A chest radiograph should be obtained in this patient to assist in diagnosis. When hypopituitarism is accompanied by diabetes insipidus or hyperprolactinemia, hypothalamic causes should be suspected. She has diabetes insipidus (polyuria, polydipsia, hypernatremia, serum hypo-osmolality, and hyposmolar urine) and mild hyperprolactinemia with a thickened pituitary stalk on an MRI of the pituitary gland. These findings are compatible with infiltrative disease of the pituitary stalk and hypothalamus; sarcoidosis should be suspected. A chest radiograph may show hilar lymphadenopathy, which can then be biopsied. Another diagnostic possibility is Langerhans cell histiocytosis. Interstitial lung disease may show up on a chest radiograph with either of these possibilities.

Although biopsy of the stalk lesion is the most direct way of obtaining a diagnosis, it is also the most invasive and potentially hazardous method. The finding of sarcoidosis or histiocytosis in another organ is sufficient to make a diagnosis of infiltrative disease of the pituitary stalk and hypothalamus.

Inferior petrosal sinus sampling is only performed in patients with Cushing syndrome to differentiate pituitary from ectopic secretion of adrenocorticotropic hormone. It provides no useful information in this patient's case.

The presence of anti–single-stranded DNA (anti-ssDNA) antibodies is sometimes used to support a diagnosis of systemic lupus erythematosus (SLE). However, these antibodies are not specific for SLE. Therefore, measurement of anti-ssDNA antibodies has limited usefulness for diagnosing SLE and no usefulness for diagnosing sarcoidosis or Langerhans cell histiocytosis.

KEY POINT

- **A thickened pituitary stalk in association with diabetes insipidus usually indicates infiltrative types of hypothalamic disease, such as sarcoidosis and Langerhans cell histiocytosis.**

Bibliography

Bihan H, Christozova V, Dumas JL, et al. Sarcoidosis: clinical, hormonal, and magnetic resonance imaging (MRI) manifestations of hypothalamic-pituitary disease in 9 patients and review of the literature. Medicine (Baltimore). 2007;86(5):259-268. [PMID: 17873755]

Item 30   Answer: B

Educational Objective: Treat acute symptomatic hypocalcemia.

During neck surgery, excision or vascular compromise of the parathyroid glands can lead to hypoparathyroidism with hypocalcemia and hyperphosphatemia. Patients with acute symptomatic hypocalcemia (serum calcium level <7.0 mg/dL [1.75 mmol/L] and ionized calcium level <3.2 mg/dL [0.8 mmol/L]) should be treated promptly with intravenous (IV) calcium, and calcium gluconate is generally preferred over calcium chloride because it causes less tissue necrosis if extravasated. Administration is best done through a central venous line. The infusion solution should generally not contain bicarbonate or phosphorus because these substances can form insoluble calcium salts.

If bicarbonate or phosphorus administration is necessary, a separate IV line should be used. Coexisting hypomagnesemia should also be treated with magnesium replacement. Oral calcium and oral vitamin D should be started thereafter, but usually not until the tetany has resolved.

An intravenous injection of calcitriol is indicated in the treatment of hypocalcemia in patients undergoing chronic renal dialysis, which this patient is not. Such therapy has been shown to significantly reduce elevated parathyroid hormone levels, with improvement in renal osteodystrophy.

Oral calcium is used for therapy of less severe hypocalcemia or chronic hypocalcemia. Dosages between 1.5 and 3.0 g/d of elemental calcium may be required. Numerous preparations of calcium are available.

Oral vitamin D also is used as therapy in chronic hypocalcemia. A short-acting preparation of vitamin D (calcitriol) and very-long-acting preparations, such as vitamin D_2 (ergocalciferol), are available. Therapy with ergocalciferol is not useful in patients with hypoparathyroidism because 25-hydroxy vitamin D cannot be converted to 1,25-dihydroxy vitamin D because of a lack of parathyroid hormone action. In hypoparathyroidism, calcitriol is the preferred modality of therapy. The goal of therapy is to keep the patient asymptomatic and the serum calcium level between 8.5 and 9.2 mg/dL (2.1 to 2.3 mmol/L). Higher calcium levels are associated with hypercalciuria and a risk of nephrolithiasis, nephrocalcinosis, and renal failure.

KEY POINT

- **Patients with acute symptomatic hypocalcemia should be treated promptly with intravenous calcium.**

Bibliography

Kraft MD, Btaiche IF, Sacks GS, Kudsk KA. Treatment of electrolyte disorders in adult patients in the intensive care unit. Am J Health Syst Pharm. 2005;62(16):1663-1682. [PMID: 16085929]

Item 31   Answer: C

Educational Objective: Manage myxedema coma.

The most appropriate next step in management is to give this patient intravenous levothyroxine, intravenous hydrocortisone, and empiric antibiotics. The patient has mental status changes, hypothermia, hyponatremia, hypoxia, and hypercapnia—all classic symptoms of new-onset myxedema coma. In addition, his neck scar is consistent with prior thyroidectomy, but he most likely has not been taking thyroid replacement therapy. His thyroid-stimulating hormone and free thyroxine (T_4) levels should be promptly obtained to confirm the diagnosis. However, given that myxedema coma is a life-threatening condition, immediate therapy before the results of the thyroid studies are returned should be instituted to support the patient.

Hydrocortisone therapy is standard for patients with myxedema coma because, in some cases, adrenal insufficiency is also present. Although infection is the most common precipitant of myxedema coma, it is easily over-looked because patients with severe hypothyroidism are less likely to have a fever or develop substantial leukocytosis. Therefore, after blood, urine, and sputum cultures are obtained, patients with myxedema coma should also be treated with empiric broad-spectrum antibiotics until culture results are shown to be negative. Finally, given his prior thyroidectomy and likely nonadherence to thyroid replacement therapy, this patient should receive levothyroxine immediately. Intravenous levothyroxine is preferred over oral treatment because gastrointestinal absorption may be impaired by the intestinal edema associated with a myxedematous state.

KEY POINT

- In patients with myxedema coma, immediate therapy should be instituted until thyroid hormone levels can be normalized, and potential underlying precipitants should be identified and addressed.

Bibliography

Wartofsky L. Myxedema coma. Endocrinol Metab Clin North Am. 2006(4):687-698. [PMID: 17127141]

Item 32   Answer: B

Educational Objective: Treat hypogonadism.

This patient should be taken off the testosterone enanthate and referred for a prostate biopsy. Testosterone replacement therapy requires follow-up to monitor for adverse events. Testosterone treatment can cause polycythemia due to increased hemoglobin levels, can induce or exacerbate sleep apnea syndrome, and may uncover previously occult prostate cancer. No evidence indicates that testosterone replacement causes prostate cancer. However, androgens can exacerbate preexisting prostate cancer and should not be administered to men with a history of prostate cancer. It is not known whether long-term testosterone administration in older men will unmask microscopic foci of prostate cancer. This uncertainty is the main reason for periodic measurements of prostate-specific antigen (PSA) levels in men receiving testosterone replacement therapy. Men with hypogonadism often have a low PSA level that typically increases less than twofold on therapy and then stabilizes by 6 months after therapy has begun. A continued, greater than twofold rise in PSA level, such as this patient has, is concerning for prostate cancer exacerbated by the testosterone therapy. Therefore, this patient's testosterone replacement therapy should be discontinued until definitive urologic evaluation can rule out prostate cancer.

If the evaluation is negative for cancer, testosterone replacement therapy can resume. However, the trough testosterone level should ideally be 200 to 250 ng/dL (6.9 to 8.7 nmol/L). Therefore, if testosterone replacement is resumed in this patient, either the dosage should be lowered or the dosing interval increased.

Taking the patient off testosterone enanthate for 2 weeks and then remeasuring his PSA level or substituting topical testosterone for the testosterone enanthate will not address his potential cancer risk and thus are not the most appropriate treatments.

KEY POINT

- Men with hypogonadism often have a low prostate-specific antigen level that doubles with therapy and then stabilizes by 6 months after therapy initiation; a greater increase should prompt discontinuation of therapy and evaluation for prostate cancer.

Bibliography

Rhoden EL, Morgentaler A. Risks of testosterone-replacement therapy and recommendations for monitoring. N Engl J Med. 2004;350(5):482-492. [PMID: 14749457]

Item 33   Answer: D

Educational Objective: Manage diabetic postprandial hyperglycemia in a patient with elevated hemoglobin A_{1c} values but acceptable fasting blood glucose levels.

This patient requires measurement of her 2-hour postprandial blood glucose levels. A common clinical scenario in diabetes management is the patient whose hemoglobin A_{1c} values are suboptimal despite fasting blood glucose monitoring results suggesting good glycemic control. Several possible explanations for this phenomenon exist, including a falsely altered hemoglobin A_{1c} value in the setting of hemoglobinopathy or hemolytic anemia; however, there is no reason to suspect a blood disorder in this patient. The most common cause is elevated postprandial blood glucose levels. The possibility of postprandial hyperglycemia should be assessed by measuring blood glucose levels 2 hours after meals several times each week. If elevated blood glucose levels are noted postprandially, the addition of a mealtime rapid-acting insulin analogue, such as insulin aspart, insulin lispro, or insulin glulisine, is appropriate. These insulin preparations, which have peak action within 30 to 90 minutes and a duration of action of 2 to 4 hours, successfully modulate the postprandial rise in glucose.

Although adding exenatide to insulin may reduce postprandial hyperglycemia, it would not reveal the reason for the discrepancy between the fasting blood glucose levels and the hemoglobin A_{1c} values. Exenatide is approved by the U.S. Food and Drug Administration for use in combination with metformin, with a sulfonylurea, or with a combination of metformin and a sulfonylurea but not with insulin.

When a hemoglobinopathy or a hemolytic anemia is responsible for incorrect hemoglobin A_{1c} readings, another biochemical measure of long-term glucose levels, such as fructosamine or glycated albumin, can be used instead of hemoglobin A_{1c}. Because these conditions are unlikely in this patient, measurement of her serum fructosamine level is inappropriate.

Basal insulin analogues, such as insulin glargine and insulin detemir, are effective agents to control fasting glucose levels and, in most circumstances, hemoglobin A_{1c} values. However, they cannot reduce postprandial glucose excursions. Additionally, increasing the dosage of insulin detemir may increase the incidence of overnight hypoglycemia without addressing postprandial glucose spikes.

KEY POINT

- When the hemoglobin A_{1c} value is higher than that suggested by the fasting glucose readings, the postprandial glucose level should be checked.

Bibliography

Dailey G. Assessing glycemic control with self-monitoring of blood glucose and hemoglobin A_{1c} measurements. Mayo Clin Proc. 2007;82(2):229-235. [PMID: 17290732]

Item 34   Answer: A

Educational Objective: Treat an invasive macroprolactinoma.

In addition to levothyroxine and hydrocortisone therapy, this patient should initially be treated with cabergoline. Hypogonadism is a common presenting symptom of hyperprolactinemia and results from prolactin inhibition of gonadotropin-releasing hormone neurons that leads to suppression of the hypothalamic-pituitary-gonadal axis. Evidence of additional hormone deficiency may be the result of mass effect. Results of this patient's laboratory evaluation are compatible with hypothyroidism and impaired adrenal function.

Because prolactin is under inhibitory control by hypothalamic dopamine, prolactinomas respond to dopamine agonists, which cause a reduction in prolactin synthesis and secretion and a decrease in cellular proliferation. Dopamine agonists are effective for patients with small and large prolactinomas, and cabergoline is more efficacious and better tolerated than bromocriptine. Cabergoline causes a normalization of prolactin levels in greater than 90% of patients and also a significant reduction in prolactinoma size in nearly 90%. If the large tumor has caused hypopituitarism, a restoration of normal pituitary function may also occur.

Radiation therapy is rarely performed for prolactinomas because of the high efficacy rates of dopamine agonists. Irradiation is reserved for those patients who cannot tolerate or do not respond to dopamine agonists or surgery.

Somatostatin analogues have not been shown to have substantial prolactin-lowering or tumor-shrinking effects in patients with prolactinomas and would not be used in such patients.

Surgery through the cranium or via a transsphenoidal route cannot cure a tumor that is wrapped around the carotid artery. In any case, surgery is reserved for the few patients who cannot tolerate or respond to dopamine agonists.

KEY POINT

- Dopamine agonists are preferred as the initial treatment of patients with prolactinomas because of their very high efficacy.

Bibliography

Casanueva FF, Molitch ME, Schlechte JA, et al. Guidelines of the Pituitary Society for the diagnosis and management of prolactinomas. Clin Endocrinol (Oxf). 2006;65(2):265-273. [PMID: 16886971]

Item 35   Answer: C

Educational Objective: Manage Cushing syndrome.

This patient with biochemical features of adrenocorticotropic hormone (ACTH)–dependent Cushing syndrome should be referred to an experienced pituitary neurosurgeon for adenomectomy. In patients with documented hypercortisolism, elevated or normal ACTH levels indicate a pituitary or neoplastic (ectopic) source, whereas suppressed ACTH concentrations indicate a primary adrenal source. Partial suppression of cortisol secretion was achieved in this patient with dexamethasone administration. This finding suggests an ACTH-secreting pituitary microadenoma as the cause of the Cushing syndrome, which was confirmed by the MRI scan showing a pituitary microadenoma; Cushing syndrome caused by a pituitary tumor is known as Cushing disease. The most appropriate next step is removal of the pituitary microadenoma by pituitary adenomectomy. Selective excision of the pituitary tumor can cure Cushing disease in most patients (66% to 89%) and preserves pituitary function.

Bilateral adrenalectomy is an appropriate option in patients with ectopic ACTH secretion and an occult or metastatic tumor. Adrenalectomy provides immediate removal of the abnormal cortisol-producing tissue. However, in patients with an accessible pituitary tumor, resection of the tumor results in much less morbidity than does bilateral adrenalectomy.

Ketoconazole inhibits several steps in the steroidogenesis pathway and can be used to lower cortisol secretion. However, this drug is used not as a definitive therapy for hypercortisolism but instead as an interim therapy for patients with severe Cushing syndrome. Ketoconazole is also used in patients with recurrent or inoperable ACTH-secreting tumors and is often given as an interim therapy for patients undergoing radiation therapy because the beneficial effect of radiation treatment may be delayed. Given this patient's overwhelming evidence of an ACTH-secreting pituitary tumor and the high likelihood of success with surgical resection, ketoconazole is not indicated.

Conventional radiation therapy leads to the normalization of urine free cortisol production in over 80% of patients, usually within 2 years. Radiation therapy is reserved for patients who cannot tolerate surgery or as a secondary treatment when pituitary surgery has failed. It is not the best option for this patient.

KEY POINT

- Patients with adrenocorticotropic hormone–dependent Cushing syndrome who have a demonstrable pituitary adenoma on MRI scan should undergo pituitary adenomectomy.

Bibliography
Findling JW, Raff H. Cushing's syndrome: important issues in diagnosis and management. J Clin Endocrinol Metab. 2006;91(10): 3746-3753. [PMID: 16868050]

Item 36   Answer: A
Educational Objective: Treat a patient with uncomplicated Paget disease of bone with bisphosphonate therapy.

This patient with uncomplicated Paget disease should be treated with alendronate. Paget disease is a focal disorder of bone remodeling that leads to greatly accelerated rates of bone turnover, disruption of the normal architecture of bone, and sometimes gross deformities of bone (such as enlargement of the skull and bowing of the femur or tibia). Most patients with Paget disease are asymptomatic. The diagnosis is often suspected from radiographs obtained for other reasons or from an isolated elevation of the serum alkaline phosphatase level. There is no cure for Paget disease, but bisphosphonates (such as alendronate, risedronate, tiludronate, pamidronate, zoledronate, and etidronate) decrease the accelerated rate of osteoclastic bone resorption. Treatment of symptomatic patients should also include other modalities, such as analgesics, NSAIDs, canes, shoe lifts, hearing aids, and surgery.

Calcitonin also can be effective in the treatment of Paget disease when administered as a subcutaneous or intramuscular injection. Calcitonin nasal spray, however, is not effective because of its low bioavailability. Whereas suppression of disease activity may last for several years after bisphosphonate administration, the response to calcitonin is generally short-lived once the calcitonin has been discontinued. Additionally, resistance to the effects of calcitonin can result from the formation of neutralizing antibodies. Therefore, calcitonin should be reserved for patients with primarily lytic disease or those in whom a rapid response is required, such as patients with high-output cardiac failure or symptomatic disease of the spine or those who are having elective surgery on pagetic bone.

Calcium supplementation does not provide any suppression of pagetic disease activity, nor does it provide any symptomatic relief. Therefore, this treatment is inappropriate for this patient.

Teriparatide (recombinant human parathyroid hormone [1-34]) is an anabolic agent that builds new bone. The drug is administered daily by subcutaneous injection. Although approved for treatment of osteoporosis, teriparatide is contraindicated in patients with Paget disease of bone.

KEY POINT

- Uncomplicated Paget disease of bone is treated with bisphosphonate therapy.

Bibliography
Whyte MP. Clinical practice. Paget's disease of bone. N Engl J Med. 2006;355(6):593-600. [PMID: 16899779]

Item 37   Answer: D
Educational Objective: Manage suspected levothyroxine malabsorption.

This patient should be screened for celiac disease. She takes a very high dosage of levothyroxine and still has inadequate levels of thyroid hormone. A normal replacement dose is typically 1.6 µg/kg/d; this patient is taking nearly 5 µg/kg/d. Hashimoto disease is the most common cause of hypothyroidism in the United States. Because she has one autoimmune disorder, she is at risk for additional autoimmune disorders, including celiac disease. Celiac disease has recently been found to be a cause of unexpectedly high dosing requirements for levothyroxine in some patients with Hashimoto disease. Another clue that she has celiac disease is the unexplained osteopenia and microcytic anemia. The diagnosis of celiac disease in patients with iron deficiency anemia or manifestations of fat-soluble vitamin deficiency (coagulopathy, osteoporosis) is becoming more common; such features may be the sole manifestations of early disease.

Because the thyroid directly releases 20% of the body's triiodothyronine (T_3), with the remainder generated through peripheral conversion of thyroxine (T_4), it has been proposed that an ideal replacement regimen for hypothyroidism would contain both levothyroxine and liothyronine. However, studies have found no benefit to combining these drugs in the treatment of hypothyroidism. Finally, this patient likely has malabsorption, and treating the cause of the levothyroxine malabsorption is preferred to adding another thyroid preparation or changing thyroid preparations.

Taking calcium or an iron-containing multivitamin concurrently with levothyroxine is a cause of levothyroxine malabsorption. This patient, however, is already separating her medications by several hours (morning and noon); further separation of the doses will not improve her absorption of levothyroxine.

KEY POINT

- Patients with hypothyroidism due to Hashimoto disease who require unusually high doses of levothyroxine should be screened for celiac disease.

Bibliography

Hadithi M, de Boer H, Meijer JW, et al. Coeliac disease in Dutch patients with Hashimoto's thyroiditis and vice versa. World J Gastroenterol. 2007;13(11):1715-1722. [PMID: 17461476]

Item 38   Answer: D

Educational Objective: Diagnose hypercalcemia caused by immobilization.

This patient has hypercalcemia most likely caused by his immobilization. Patients with high bone turnover, such as young patients and patients with Paget disease of bone, are more likely to develop hypercalcemia of immobilization, and serum calcium levels should be monitored in immobilized patients to check for the disease. Given this patient's young age and near-complete immobilization because of his pelvic fracture, he is at high risk for the disorder. Hypercalcemia associated with immobilization is most likely due to increased osteoclastic activity. Acute therapy includes saline infusion for volume repletion. Bisphosphonate therapy has also been used to decrease osteoclastic activity.

The patient's serum creatinine elevation is a result rather than the cause of his hypercalcemia and will resolve with volume resuscitation. Furthermore, acute kidney injury does not cause hypercalcemia.

Although the patient had sustained fractures, such trauma in itself is not generally associated with hypercalcemia.

No malignancy has been identified in this patient, and humoral hypercalcemia of malignancy is rarely due to an occult tumor.

KEY POINT

- Serum calcium levels should be monitored in immobilized patients to check for the development of hypercalcemia of immobilization, which is more likely to occur in patients with high bone turnover, such as young patients and patients with Paget disease.

Bibliography

Massagli TL, Cardenas DD. Immobilization hypercalcemia treatment with pamidronate disodium after spinal cord injury. Arch Phys Med Rehabil. 1999;80(9):998-1000. [PMID: 10488998]

Item 39   Answer: B

Educational Objective: Diagnose opioid-induced hypogonadism.

This patient most likely has opioid-induced hypogonadism. In most cases, adults with acquired hypogonadism have a central (pituitary or hypothalamic) component. It is often difficult to determine if their low testosterone level is primarily hypothalamic or pituitary in origin, so both are classified as secondary hypogonadism. The most common cause is pituitary tumors; other causes include trauma and infiltrative diseases (such as hemochromatosis). In addition, many patients develop hypogonadism due to acquired factors that act centrally, including drugs, chronic illnesses, malnutrition, obesity, and aging.

This patient has a history of chronic pain for which he continuously takes opioids. Therefore, the most likely diagnosis is opioid-induced hypogonadism. Many drugs, including opioids, can cause androgen deficiency by their inhibitory effects at one or more levels of the hypothalamic-pituitary-testicular axis. Other commonly implicated drugs include alcohol, corticosteroids, cocaine, and ketoconazole. If he absolutely needs to continue his pain medication, a trial of testosterone replacement therapy, with the usual safety monitoring, may be useful to determine if his symptoms and quality of life improve.

This patient's symptoms are very different from those of anabolic steroid abuse (aggression, increased muscular mass, acne, normal libido) and make that diagnosis unlikely.

Given his low testosterone and gonadotropin levels and his symptoms of poor libido, constant fatigue, and erectile dysfunction, this patient does not have primary hypogonadism or normal gonadal function.

KEY POINT

- In a patient with symptoms of hypogonadism who is on chronic opioid therapy, opioid-induced hypogonadism should be suspected.

Bibliography

Schneider J. Hypogonadism in men treated with chronic opioids. Arch Phys Med Rehabil. 2008;89(7):1414. [PMID: 18586148]

Item 40   Answer: B

Educational Objective: Treat a hospitalized patient in the intensive care unit with intensive glycemic control.

The intensive control of glucose levels in hospitalized patients during critical illness has garnered substantial attention over the past decade. Several randomized clinical trials have shown a benefit to patient morbidity and mortality with stringent glycemic control. Whereas the precise target remains controversial, the bulk of the data suggests that treating to achieve glucose levels between 140 and 180 mg/dL (7.8 and 10.0 mmol/L) may be optimal. In the setting of an intensive care unit (ICU), this is best and most safely achieved through the use of intravenous insulin. Intravenous delivery of insulin allows for more rapid titration and does not rely on subcutaneus absorption, which may be diminished or delayed in patients with cardiogenic shock or other critical illnesses associated with poor peripheral circulation.

If it appears that ongoing insulin is required once this patient is ready for transfer to a general ward, she should be transitioned to an injectable regimen involving long- or intermediate-acting and rapid-acting insulins. Oral agents can be restarted before discharge as long as renal function is normal and no contraindications exist.

Insulin glargine, the dosage of which is typically adjusted every 2 to 3 days until optimal glycemic control is achieved, cannot quickly guarantee adequate control during the 1 to 2 days that this patient is likely to be in the ICU. For similar reasons, using neutral protamine Hagedorn (NPH) insulin twice daily is unlikely to be the best treatment.

Although the dosage of regular insulin can be adjusted more frequently when administered on a sliding scale, this approach to glycemic control is considered inadequate because insulin is provided only when hyperglycemia becomes established. This method is not proactive enough to result in acceptable glycemic control during an ICU stay.

KEY POINT

- Intensive glycemic control is best achieved in the intensive care unit with an intravenous insulin infusion.

Bibliography

NICE-SUGAR Study Investigators, Finfer S, Chittock DR, et al. Intensive versus conventional glucose control in critically ill patients. N Engl J Med. 2009;360(13):1283-1297. [PMID: 19318384]

Item 41   Answer: A

Educational Objective: Evaluate a suspected thyroid-stimulating hormone–secreting tumor.

This patient should undergo MRI of the pituitary gland to detect a possible thyroid-stimulating hormone (TSH)–secreting tumor. This patient clinically has hyperthyroidism, and testing shows clearly elevated levels of free thyroxine (T_4) and total triiodothyronine (T_3). However, her serum TSH level is not suppressed, as it is in almost all causes of hyperthyroidism. This incongruity raises the possibility of a TSH-secreting pituitary adenoma as the cause of her hyperthyroidism.

Antiperoxidase antibodies are usually present in patients with autoimmune thyroid disease, such as Hashimoto disease. The presence or absence of such antibodies in this patient with a probable TSH-secreting pituitary adenoma, however, would not be diagnostically helpful.

A determination of thyroid radioactive iodine uptake helps to quantitate hyperactivity in the thyroid gland and may help differentiate thyroiditis from Graves disease. In this patient, the uptake would not be useful in the differential diagnosis because the patient most likely has a TSH-secreting pituitary adenoma and not a primary thyroid gland disorder.

A thyroid scan is useful in showing functional morphology of a gland. Although a thyroid scan is likely to show diffuse hyperfunction in this patient, it would not be useful in the differential diagnosis because the most likely cause of this patient's symptoms is not primary thyroid disease but a TSH-secreting pituitary adenoma.

Patients with Graves disease have an unregulated production of T_4 and T_3 because of the presence of autoantibodies, such as thyroid-stimulating immunoglobulin, against the TSH receptor, but these autoantibodies are not always present at all time points. In this patient, the titer of such antibodies is likely to be low because the cause of this patient's hyperthyroidism is not likely to be Graves disease.

KEY POINT

- In a patient with hyperthyroidism, the finding of an inappropriately normal level of thyroid-stimulating hormone suggests a pituitary cause of the hyperthyroidism.

Bibliography

Beck-Peccoz P, Persani L. Thyrotropinomas. Endocrinol Metab Clin North Am. 2008;37(1):123-134. [PMID: 18226733]

Item 42   Answer: C

Educational Objective: Treat acute hypercalcemia.

This patient should receive volume replacement with normal (0.9%) saline. Measures undertaken to treat hypercalcemia can be divided into four categories:

1. Nonspecific therapies aimed at increasing renal calcium excretion and decreasing intestinal absorption of calcium
2. Therapies specifically aimed at slowing bone resorption
3. Therapies that directly remove calcium from the circulation
4. Therapies aimed at controlling the underlying diseases causing hypercalcemia

Increased excretion of calcium can be achieved by inhibition of proximal tubular and loop sodium reabsorption, which is best achieved by aggressive volume expansion with intravenous normal saline infusion.

An infusion of 0.45% saline will be less effective than 0.9% saline in both restoring volume and delivering sodium to the proximal tubule, which is necessary for increased urinary excretion of calcium.

Furosemide therapy after aggressive intravenous saline infusion has been suggested as the next step in the emergency management of hypercalcemia. However, a review of the evidence for the use of furosemide in the medical management of hypercalcemia yielded only case reports published before the introduction of bisphosphonates, the use of which is supported by multiple randomized controlled trials. Therefore, furosemide should no longer be recommended as part of the management of hypercalcemia.

KEY POINT

- In the treatment of acute hypercalcemia, the first step is aggressive volume expansion with intravenous normal saline.

Bibliography

LeGrand SB, Leskuski D, Zama I. Narrative review: furosemide for hypercalcemia: an unproven yet common practice. Ann Intern Med. 2008;149(4):259-263. [PMID: 18711156]

Item 43   Answer: C

Educational Objective: Diagnose new heart failure in a patient on thiazolidinedione therapy.

This patient's recently increased pioglitazone dosage most likely contributed to his diagnosis of heart failure. Edema, a recognized adverse effect of thiazolidinedione (TZD) therapy, occurs in 5% to 10% of all treated patients and in up to 20% of patients treated concurrently with insulin. Exacerbation of preexisting heart failure can result. However, there is no evidence of any direct negative effect of TZDs on cardiac function. The pathogenesis of fluid retention and potential heart failure with TZD therapy relates to this drug class's tendency to increase renal sodium retention, which typically resolves with discontinuation of the TZD. The U.S. Food and Drug Administration states that pioglitazone and rosiglitazone are contraindicated in patients with advanced heart failure (New York Heart Association class III or IV) and are not recommended in any patient with symptomatic heart failure (class II).

Sulfonylurea drugs, such as glyburide, can cause weight gain (not due to fluid retention) and hypoglycemia. These medications are metabolized by the liver and cleared by the kidneys and therefore should be used cautiously in patients with impaired hepatic or renal function. Sulfonylureas, however, do not cause heart failure, and the increased glyburide dosage is not responsible for this patient's dyspnea.

Metformin is currently contraindicated only in patients with decompensated heart failure, especially when renal function is abnormal or threatened. Metformin therapy, however, is not associated with a direct negative inotropic effect, and the increased dosage is an unlikely cause of this patient's symptoms.

There is no history of recent hypoglycemia. Also, hypoglycemia would not be expected to lead to heart failure.

KEY POINT

- **Thiazolidinedione use is not recommended in patients with New York Heart Association (NYHA) class II heart failure and is contraindicated in those with NYHA class III and IV heart failure.**

Bibliography

Lago RM, Singh PP, Nesto RW. Congestive heart failure and cardiovascular death in patients with prediabetes and type 2 diabetes given thiazolidinediones: a meta-analysis of randomised clinical trials. Lancet. 2007;370(9593):1129-1136. [PMID: 17905165]

Item 44   Answer: A

Educational Objective: Manage a low testosterone level.

This patient has hypogonadotropic hypogonadism with normal MRI findings and no other evidence of hypopituitarism. This presentation suggests an isolated defect in the hypothalamic-pituitary-gonadal axis. The history of snoring and daytime somnolence suggests sleep apnea, despite his relatively normal BMI. Because luteinizing hormone and testosterone pulses are increased during deep sleep, sleep disorders can reduce testosterone production sufficiently to cause hypogonadism. Sleep apnea has been associated with hypogonadism and can be reversed by application of continuous positive-airway pressure. Therefore, determining whether he has sleep apnea with a sleep study is critical and must precede initiation of testosterone therapy. In fact, testosterone replacement therapy can worsen sleep apnea, another reason to pursue the sleep study first.

Vardenafil treatment is premature because the patient's erectile dysfunction is mild compared with his fatigue. Vardenafil will only treat the erectile dysfunction and not address his other problems and health needs.

Visual field testing is unnecessary because MRI findings are normal, which excludes a pituitary tumor as the cause of his hypogonadism.

Reassurance alone is inappropriate because this patient is symptomatic. His possible sleep apnea can cause numerous health problems if not detected and treated.

KEY POINT

- **Sleep apnea has been associated with hypogonadism and can be reversed by application of continuous positive-airway pressure.**

Bibliography

Rosner W, Auchus RJ, Azziz R, Sluss PM, Raff H. Position statement: Utility, limitations, and pitfalls in measuring testosterone: an Endocrine Society position statement. J Clin Endocrinol Metab. 2007;92(2):405-413. [PMID: 17090633]

Item 45   Answer: D

Educational Objective: Manage mild hyperglycemia in a patient with a myocardial infarction with outpatient follow-up for diabetes mellitus.

This patient should have his fasting plasma glucose level measured several weeks after discharge. Cardiovascular disease is extremely common in patients with diabetes mellitus. Even in patients without recognized diabetes who have a myocardial infarction, such as this man, there is still an increased incidence of glycemic abnormalities, which range from impaired fasting glucose to impaired glucose tolerance to previously undiagnosed diabetes. However, the optimal treatment approach for such patients has not been established. It cannot be predicted if a new elevation in the blood glucose level in a hospitalized patient will improve on discharge or is a sign of diabetes or prediabetes. Hospitalized patients frequently experience stress hyperglycemia because of counterregulatory hormonal surges, which frequently complicate an acute illness. Therefore, the best next step in managing this patient's mild hyperglycemia is to measure his fasting plasma glucose level (or perform an oral glucose tolerance test) several weeks after discharge. If diabetes or prediabetes is established, treatment can then be initiated.

Treatment with a sulfonylurea, metformin, or insulin is premature because it is not yet known if this patient's hyperglycemia will persist after discharge.

An intravenous infusion of insulin is unlikely to provide any benefit in the setting of such mild hyperglycemia because his blood glucose level is already at target.

KEY POINT

- Patients with hyperglycemia while hospitalized should be retested for glucose abnormalities after recovery from their illness.

Bibliography

Inzucchi SE. Clinical practice. Management of hyperglycemia in the hospital setting. N Engl J Med. 2006;355(18):1903-1911. [PMID: 17079764]

Item 46   Answer: C
Educational Objective: Treat Graves ophthalmopathy.

This patient should receive prednisone and radioactive iodine ablation concomitantly. He has active Graves disease and mild Graves ophthalmopathy. Because he also has a history of a severe allergic reaction to methimazole, a retrial of antithyroidal drugs is not recommended. Although thyroidectomy is a viable treatment for hyperthyroidism resulting from Graves disease, patients are typically first made euthyroid with antithyroidal drugs preoperatively, which is not an option with this patient.

Graves disease is complicated by Graves ophthalmopathy in approximately 5% to 10% of patients. Graves ophthalmopathy is an autoimmune disease of the retro-orbital tissues that may present with proptosis and periorbital edema. Patients may report irritation in the eyes, tearing, ocular pain, and changes in vision. Vision loss may occur. A persistent thyrotoxic or hypothyroid state appears to exacerbate eye disease activity, so patients should be made euthyroid as soon as possible. However, the use of radioactive iodine to treat hyperthyroidism can exacerbate thyroid-associated eye disease, especially in patients with significant preexisting ophthalmopathy at the time of ablation. Prednisone can mitigate this negative effect. A periablative course of prednisone is thus appropriate in patients with mild ophthalmopathy who are being considered for ablation therapy.

Orbital decompression surgery is reserved for patients with severe ophthalmopathy that has not responded to medical treatment. Furthermore, the patient would first need to be made euthyroid before any such surgery. Decompression surgery is thus inappropriate in this patient.

KEY POINT

- Radioactive iodine should be avoided as treatment in patients with significant thyroid-associated eye disease but can be used in patients with mild ophthalmopathy if concomitant prednisone therapy is used.

Bibliography

Bartalena L, Baldeschi L, Dickinson AJ, et al. Consensus statement of the European group on Graves' orbitopathy (EUGOGO) on management of Graves' orbitopathy. Thyroid. 2008;18(3):333-346. [PMID: 18341379]

Item 47   Answer: D
Educational Objective: Treat secondary hyperparathyroidism.

The most appropriate treatment for this patient is high-dose ergocalciferol, rather than the low dose she is currently taking. She has a low vitamin D level, low-normal serum calcium and phosphorus levels, and an elevated parathyroid hormone level. She has secondary hyperparathyroidism due to vitamin D deficiency. This is among the most common causes of secondary hyperparathyroidism and is best treated with high-dose ergocalciferol therapy. A typical treatment regimen is 50,000 units weekly for 6 weeks followed by retesting to assess the need for maintenance therapy.

Calcitriol, or 1,25-dihydroxycholecalciferol, is a vitamin D_3 analogue. It is most useful in patients with decreased synthesis of calcitriol, as occurs in hypoparathyroidism and chronic renal failure. Calcitriol therapy would not replete the body stores of vitamin D because it is given in very low doses because of its enhanced potency, compared with ergocalciferol, and so is inappropriate treatment for this patient.

Adding calcium acetate to her regimen is unlikely to be helpful. She is not absorbing the calcium carbonate she already takes because of her vitamin D deficiency.

Celiac disease should be considered when patients have symptoms or signs that could result from malabsorption of micronutrients, such as unexplained deficiencies of folate, iron, and vitamins D, E, A, and K. A gluten-free diet is a treatment for celiac disease, but treatment is premature until this disorder is confirmed with proper diagnostic testing.

Parathyroidectomy is the appropriate treatment of primary, not secondary, hyperparathyroidism caused by vitamin D deficiency. Her parathyroid hormone level is elevated as a means of maintaining normal serum calcium levels through bone resorption, in the face of poor calcium absorption from the gastrointestinal tract. Effective treatment with ergocalciferol will result in increased absorption of calcium and normalization of the parathyroid hormone level.

- **Vitamin D deficiency is best treated with high-dose ergocalciferol therapy to replace total body stores of vitamin D.**

Bibliography

Holick MF. Vitamin D deficiency. N Engl J Med. 2007;357(3):266-281. [PMID: 17634462]

Item 48   Answer: B

Educational Objective: Evaluate a patient with suspected Cushing syndrome.

The most appropriate next diagnostic test for this patient is inferior petrosal sinus catheterization and sampling. She has clinical and biochemical features of adrenocorticotropic hormone (ACTH)–dependent Cushing syndrome. The cause of the ACTH hypersecretion is either a pituitary adenoma or an ectopic source, such as a carcinoid tumor. In this patient, partial suppression was achieved with dexamethasone administration, which suggests an ACTH-secreting pituitary microadenoma. However, a pituitary MRI was negative for a microadenoma. Notably, MRI findings are normal in 40% to 50% of patients with documented ACTH-secreting pituitary adenomas. This makes it difficult to differentiate an ACTH-secreting adenoma from ectopic ACTH secretion because there is already significant overlap between these two entities regarding their biochemical features and responsiveness to dexamethasone suppression.

A good way to confirm a central source of ACTH secretion in patients with normal findings on pituitary MRIs is bilateral inferior petrosal sinus catheterization and sampling. In this procedure, ACTH levels are measured in blood samples obtained simultaneously from both sides of the sinus before and after corticotropin-releasing hormone stimulation. This test is technically difficult and should only be performed at experienced centers.

A cosyntropin stimulation test is not indicated (or likely to be helpful) in patients suspected of having Cushing syndrome. The latter test assesses the ability of the adrenal glands to respond to exogenous ACTH and would therefore be useful in patients suspected of having adrenal insufficiency.

A positron-emission tomographic scan might be helpful in localizing a malignant source of excess ACTH secretion. However, a cancerous adenoma is less likely in this patient with partial suppression of cortisol after a high-dose dexamethasone suppression test.

Selective bilateral adrenal vein catheterization is inappropriate in this patient because a primary adrenal cause of the hypercortisolism has already been ruled out by the nonsuppressed ACTH level. Furthermore, bilateral adrenal hyperplasia is most consistent with adrenal glands that are stimulated by excessive ACTH release.

- **Bilateral petrosal sinus catheterization should be performed in patients with biochemically established adrenocorticotropic hormone–dependent Cushing syndrome who have negative findings on pituitary MRIs and chest CT scans.**

Bibliography

Findling JW, Raff H. Cushing's syndrome: important issues in diagnosis and management. J Clin Endocrinol Metab. 2006;91(10): 3746-3753. [PMID: 16868050]

Item 49   Answer: C

Educational Objective: Determine the risk of hypothyroidism in a patient with Hashimoto disease.

This patient should have annual thyroid function tests. She has a strong family history of autoimmune thyroid disease and positive thyroid antibodies on testing. However, her current thyroid-stimulating hormone and free thyroxine (T_4) levels indicate that she is euthyroid. According to one study, patients with Hashimoto disease who are currently euthyroid carry an approximately 4% per year risk of developing hypothyroidism. Therefore, serial thyroid function tests should be performed at least annually to check the thyroid status of such patients.

Because the patient is presently euthyroid, levothyroxine therapy is premature. Should she develop hypothyroidism in the future, levothyroxine would be indicated.

Once anti–thyroid peroxidase and anti–thyroglobulin antibodies have been found to be positive, there is little to be gained from rechecking the values serially.

On an ultrasound, the thyroid gland of patients with Hashimoto disease often appears very heterogeneous. This heterogeneity can lead to the erroneous identification of a nodule, which would lead to unnecessary testing. Therefore, ultrasonography is best reserved for patients with a possible structural abnormality, such as a nodule found on palpation.

- **Patients with Hashimoto disease can have normal thyroid hormone levels but are at increased risk for hypothyroidism in the future.**

Bibliography

Vanderpump MP, Tunbridge WM, French JM, et al. The incidence of thyroid disorders in the community: a twenty-year follow-up of the Whickham Survey. Clin Endocrinol (Oxf). 1995;43(1):55-68. [PMID: 7641412]

Item 50   Answer: E

Educational Objective: Manage glycemic control in a patient with type 2 diabetes who develops progressive renal dysfunction.

This patient should be started on sitagliptin, a dipeptidyl peptidase-IV (DPP-IV) inhibitor that is frequently used in patients with chronic kidney disease. Inhibiting the degradation of DPP-IV increases glucagon-like peptide-1 levels and thereby leads to increased insulin secretion and decreased glucagon secretion. When used as monotherapy or in combination with metformin or thiazolidinediones, sitagliptin does not cause hypoglycemia. Sitagliptin is metabolized in the liver but excreted largely unchanged in the urine, and the dosage needs to be reduced by 50% to 75% in patients with renal insufficiency. As monotherapy, sitagliptin is associated with hemoglobin A_{1c} reductions in the range of 0.6% to 0.8%. Other secretagogues, such as glimepiride or the nonsulfonylurea secretagogue repaglinide, could also be tried. Notably, in many patients with diabetes mellitus and kidney failure, glycemic control improves spontaneously, as it did in this patient, because of altered insulin clearance caused by the kidney failure.

This patient's recent hypoglycemia is most likely due to his glyburide therapy. Glyburide has the longest duration of action of the sulfonylureas. Accordingly, the drug is inappropriate for patients with renal disease, either alone or in combination with another agent.

Metformin is contraindicated in men with a serum creatinine level greater than 1.5 mg/dL (132.6 µmol/L) or women with a level greater than 1.4 mg/dL (123.8 µmol/L). When the glomerular filtration rate is reduced, circulating concentrations of metformin can accumulate, which increases the risk of lactic acidosis.

If an insulin formulation is used, there is an increased risk of hypoglycemia. Starting premixed insulin 70/30 is therefore not the best option for this patient with recent episodes of hypoglycemia. However, cautious insulin therapy may be required if sitagliptin does not result in an adequate reduction of the hemoglobin A_{1c} value.

KEY POINT

- The half-life of certain sulfonylureas, such as glyburide, is prolonged and the clearance of metformin is altered in patients with kidney failure, which make both drugs inappropriate for routine use in patients with diabetes mellitus and kidney disease.

Bibliography

Amiel SA, Dixon T, Mann R, Jameson K. Hypoglycaemia in type 2 diabetes. Diabet Med. 2008;25(3):245-254. [PMID: 18215172]

Item 51   Answer: C

Educational Objective: Evaluate suspected vitamin D deficiency.

The most appropriate next diagnostic step is to measure this patient's serum level of 25-hydroxy vitamin D. She is at high risk of vitamin D deficiency, which is characterized by mild hypocalcemia, mild hypophosphatemia, increased alkaline phosphatase and parathyroid hormone levels, and a decreased serum 25-hydroxy vitamin D level. Measurement of 25-hydroxy vitamin D (calcidiol) is more informative

than measurement of 1,25-dihydroxy vitamin D (calcitriol) in most patients with hypocalcemia because vitamin D deficiency causes hypocalcemia and stimulates parathyroid hormone secretion, which in turn stimulates renal conversion of 25-hydroxy vitamin D to 1,25-dihydroxy vitamin D. Low dietary intake, poor absorption of vitamin D, and lack of production in the skin will result in a low serum 25-hydroxy vitamin D level. This serum level will also be low in patients taking phenytoin, those with nephrotic syndrome (loss of vitamin D–binding protein), and those with hepatobiliary disease. Whereas 25-hydroxy vitamin D has a long half-life, 1,25-dihydroxy vitamin D is more short-lived and therefore not a good measure of vitamin D status. 1,25-Dihydroxy vitamin D levels will be low despite normal or high 25-hydroxy vitamin D levels in patients with renal insufficiency, deficiency of renal 1α-hydroxylase (vitamin D–dependent rickets type 1), or hypoparathyroidism.

Measurement of the patient's serum alkaline phosphatase isoenzyme level does not specifically help diagnose vitamin D deficiency and is probably unnecessary in this patient at high risk for vitamin D deficiency, hypocalcemia, and hypophosphatemia.

Measurement of the osteocalcin level assesses bone formation. The level is elevated in disorders that increase the metabolic turnover of bone, such as Paget disease and osteomalacia. The serum level of osteocalcin is not a specific marker of vitamin D deficiency and is not indicated.

KEY POINT

- Vitamin D deficiency is characterized by a low-normal to mildly suppressed serum calcium level, mild hypophosphatemia, increased alkaline phosphatase and parathyroid hormone levels, and a decreased 25-hydroxy vitamin D level; measurement of the 25-hydroxy vitamin D level best assesses body stores of the vitamin.

Bibliography

Mosekilde L. Vitamin D and the elderly. Clin Endocrinol (Oxf). 2005;62(3):265-281. [PMID: 15730407]

Item 52   Answer: D

Educational Objective: Treat a clinically nonfunctioning adenoma.

This patient likely has a clinically nonfunctioning pituitary adenoma that was originally suspected to be a prolactinoma. The most appropriate treatment for such an adenoma is surgery.

She was first treated with the dopamine agonist bromocriptine, which is an accepted treatment for prolactinomas, and seemed to respond well. After 1 year of this therapy, however, she developed headaches and fatigue, and her tumor has increased in size.

The key feature of her initial presentation was the combination of a mildly elevated prolactin level in the face of a 1.1-cm lesion. A patient with a prolactinoma of that size would more likely have a prolactin level in the range of 150 to 400 ng/mL (150 to 400 μg/L); the serum level of prolactin generally parallels the size of a prolactinoma. The increase in prolactin levels due to the hypothalamic or stalk dysfunction caused by a nonfunctioning pituitary adenoma is usually mild to moderate, with levels rarely rising above 150 ng/mL (150 μg/L). Thus, it is reasonable to do at least one MRI for surveillance of a patient treated initially with a dopamine agonist for a suspected prolactinoma, even when prolactin levels respond readily. This is especially true when there is a discrepancy between the prolactin level and the size of the lesion.

Somatostatin analogues, such as octreotide, only rarely reduce the size of nonfunctioning adenomas. Starting a long-acting-release somatostatin analogue is therefore inappropriate for this patient.

Increasing the dosage of bromocriptine or substituting cabergoline for the bromocriptine is unlikely to benefit this patient. Although dopamine agonists can lower elevated prolactin levels caused by nonfunctioning adenomas, they are much less likely to control tumor size.

Radiation therapy, whether conventional or stereotactic, is a third-line therapy that is used when there is no response to surgical or medical treatments.

> **KEY POINT**
> - **Nonfunctioning pituitary adenomas and other mass lesions can cause mild hyperprolactinemia because of hypothalamic or stalk dysfunction.**

Bibliography

Molitch ME. Nonfunctioning pituitary tumors and pituitary incidentalomas. Endocrinol Metab Clin North Am. 2008;37(1):151-171. [PMID: 18226735]

Item 53   Answer: A

Educational Objective: Evaluate an incidentaloma discovered on a positron emission tomography scan.

This patient should undergo fine-needle aspiration biopsy of the identified right upper pole thyroid nodule to rule out cancer. The widespread use of imaging procedures often results in unexpected results that may need further evaluation. An incidental finding of increased focal metabolic activity in a thyroid gland on an ^{18}F-fluoro-2-deoxy-D-glucose positron emission tomography (FDG-PET) scan needs additional evaluation because of the increased risk of thyroid cancers. In two studies of FDG-PET scans done for nonthyroidal disorders, unexpected focal uptake was discovered in approximately 2% of the thyroid glands, and approximately 30% to 40% of these glands proved to have papillary cancer. Diffuse ^{18}FDG uptake, on the other hand, does not seem to be associated with an increased risk of cancer.

A radiodine scan can detect a nodule but will not provide further information on whether it is benign or malignant and therefore will not aid in the management of this patient's disorder.

Repeating the FDG-PET scan in 6 months is not the best choice when the risk of malignancy is so high and prompt fine-needle aspiration biopsy is indicated.

A thyroidectomy may be appropriate if thyroid cancer is confirmed but is not indicated before a diagnosis is established.

> **KEY POINT**
> - **Incidentally found focal thyroid uptake on ^{18}F-fluoro-2-deoxy-D-glucose positron emission tomography requires evaluation and biopsy of the nodule for cancer, whereas diffuse thyroid uptake is usually a benign process.**

Bibliography

Choi JY, Lee KS, Kim HJ, et al. Focal thyroid lesions incidentally identified by integrated ^{18}F-FDG PET/CT: clinical significance and improved characterization. J Nucl Med. 2006;47(4):609-615. [PMID: 16595494]

Item 54   Answer: C

Educational Objective: Manage primary hyperparathyroidism with concomitant vitamin D deficiency.

Measurement of this patient's 25-hydroxyvitamin D level is the most appropriate next step in management. Primary hyperparathyroidism is the most common cause of asymptomatic hypercalcemia in the outpatient setting; a single parathyroid adenoma is the cause in 85% of patients. In uncomplicated hyperparathyroidism, hypercalcemia causes an increase in the filtered load of calcium. This increase overwhelms the ability of parathyroid hormone to stimulate reabsorption of calcium in the renal tubule with resultant hypercalciuria. Vitamin D deficiency is common, especially in older patients, and can mask the severity of primary hyperparathyroidism. In such patients, the parathyroid hormone level is disproportionately elevated compared with the serum calcium level, and urine calcium excretion is often normal, as with this patient. The 25-hydroxyvitamin D level reflects total body stores of vitamin D and is thus the most appropriate to measure; the 1,25-dihydroxy vitamin D level is influenced more by parathyroid hormone and phosphorus levels and by renal function.

The optimal approach to the treatment of hyperparathyroidism is controversial. The National Institutes of Health (NIH) recommends parathyroidectomy for patients with asymptomatic primary hyperparathyroidism and any one of the following four criteria:

1. Serum calcium concentration greater than 1 mg/dL (0.25 mmol/L) above the normal range

2. Creatinine clearance reduced to less than 60 mL/min

3. Bone mineral density T score less than −2.5 at any site or a previous fragility fracture

4. Age younger than 50 years

Urine calcium is often measured but by itself is not a criterion for parathyroidectomy because the development of kidney stones does not correlate with the urine calcium level. Because this patient does not meet any of the NIH criteria, immediate surgery may not be required. However, vitamin D status should be clarified by measurement of the 25-hydroxy vitamin D level; if the level is abnormal, it should be corrected to prevent long-term bone problems. If the serum calcium level and urine calcium excretion increase substantially with supplementation of vitamin D, parathyroidectomy would then be necessary.

This patient's clinical presentation of asymptomatic hypercalcemia, an elevated parathyroid hormone level, and an enlarged mass in the right tracheoesophageal groove is most consistent with a single parathyroid adenoma. A needle biopsy of the mass is not needed to confirm the diagnosis. It would be prudent to stop her calcium carbonate therapy for a few months while vitamin D is supplemented in the face of her hyperparathyroidism.

KEY POINT

- **Vitamin D deficiency can mask the severity of primary hyperparathyroidism.**

Bibliography

Silverberg SJ. Vitamin D deficiency and primary hyperparathyroidism. J Bone Miner Res. 2007;22 Suppl 2:V100-V104. [PMID: 18290710]

Item 55   Answer: C

Educational Objective: Evaluate a patient with diabetes mellitus and autonomic neuropathy for silent ischemia.

This patient should next have an exercise stress test. She has characteristic symptoms of diabetic autonomic neuropathy, including early satiety due to gastroparesis, poor night vision due to pupillary dysfunction, and urinary incontinence. Diabetic autonomic neuropathy is clinically challenging to manage and an important indicator of patients who are at very high risk for cardiovascular disease and sudden death. Cardiovascular neuropathies may result in orthostatic hypotension, absent normal variation of the heart rate with breathing, tachycardia, and sudden death. Patients with diabetes who have cardiovascular manifestations of diabetic autonomic neuropathy should thus undergo further testing, such as an exercise stress test, to exclude exercise-induced silent ischemia. The treatment of orthostatic hypotension in this patient will be particularly difficult because of the need to use an angiotensin-converting enzyme inhibitor, which can predispose patients to orthostatic hypotension, for the treatment of diabetic nephropathy. To treat orthostatic hypotension, fludrocortisone and midodrine are usually the drugs of first choice. Patients being treated with these drugs should be closely monitored for supine hypertension, abnormal potassium levels, and fluid retention.

Orthostatic hypotension is a manifestation of adrenal insufficiency, but this diagnosis would be associated with compensatory tachycardia, hyperkalemia, and hyponatremia. Furthermore, adrenal insufficiency cannot explain the patient's other symptoms, which are most consistent with autonomic neuropathy. Therefore, an adrenocorticotropic hormone stimulation test is not indicated.

There is currently no indication for echocardiography. Echocardiography is useful in the evaluation of heart failure–related structural heart disease but is unlikely to provide useful management information in a patient with multiple manifestations of autonomic neuropathy.

In patients who have frequent episodes of presyncope or syncope and are at risk for an arrhythmia, 24-hour monitoring for arrhythmia is recommended. However, this patient clearly has orthostatic dizziness, not presyncope, so 24-hour arrhythmia monitoring is not indicated.

KEY POINT

- **The clinical manifestations of cardiovascular neuropathy include orthostatic hypotension, absent normal variation of the heart rate with breathing, resting tachycardia, and sudden death; the diagnosis of diabetic autonomic cardiovascular neuropathy should prompt testing to exclude silent ischemia.**

Bibliography

Vinik AI, Ziegler D. Diabetic cardiovascular autonomic neuropathy. Circulation. 2007;115(3):387-397. [PMID: 17242296]

Item 56   Answer: D

Educational Objective: Treat adrenal insufficiency during stress by adjusting the corticosteroid replacement dosage.

Given her fever and hypotension, this patient with known primary adrenal insufficiency should receive a stress dosage of intravenous hydrocortisone. Generally, patients with adrenal insufficiency are educated to increase their corticosteroid dosage during stressful events, such as an infection. When they do not, symptoms of adrenal insufficiency occur. Some patients, such as this one, develop nausea and vomiting that limit the use of orally administered corticosteroids. In such patients, corticosteroids should be administered parenterally. Cortisol replacement with corticosteroids and restoration of intravascular volume with normal saline are vital to treatment of acute adrenal insufficiency. Stress-level dosages of corticosteroids are considered to be 10-times the normal daily replacement dosage. For most patients, this is equivalent to 100 mg of hydrocortisone daily, best administered as 25 mg every 6 hours. For a minor stress (such as a common cold), doubling of the oral dosage of hydrocortisone for 2 days is recommended; for moderate stresses (such as a limited surgical procedure), tripling the dosage for 2 to 3 days is adequate. Once the dosage of hydrocortisone is over 60 mg per day, fludrocortisone is unnecessary because that dose of hydrocortisone has adequate mineralocorticoid activity.

Although this patient requires close observation, making no changes to her therapeutic regimen (maintaining baseline dosages) would be inappropriate, given the need for a higher dosage of the corticosteroid during this stressful event.

Fludrocortisone is a mineralocorticoid that is required in most patients with chronic primary adrenal insufficiency. Treatment with fludrocortisone is usually not necessary in a hospitalized patient receiving normal saline and high dosages of hydrocortisone, which has mineralocorticoid activity. This therapy will maintain vascular volume and suppress vasopressin, which is responsible for the hyponatremia. Fludrocortisone therapy alone is insufficient for a patient with chronic adrenal insufficiency who is experiencing physiologic stress.

Hyponatremia is a common feature of adrenal insufficiency and is easily corrected with hydrocortisone and normal saline to restore plasma volume. Administering 3% saline to correct the low sodium level is therefore inappropriate.

> **KEY POINT**
>
> - Patients with adrenal insufficiency who have nausea and vomiting should be given parenteral rather than oral corticosteroids, especially during stress.

Bibliography

Arafah BM. Hypothalamic pituitary adrenal function during critical illness: limitations of current assessment methods. J Clin Endocrinol Metab. 2006;91(10):3725-3745. [PMID: 16882746]

Item 57   Answer: D

Educational Objective: Diagnose Paget disease of bone.

This patient with a highly elevated alkaline phosphatase level most likely has Paget disease of bone. The cardinal features of Paget disease of bone are pain, fractures, and deformity. However, at least two thirds of patients with Paget disease of bone are asymptomatic. Hence, the diagnosis is made in many patients while they are being evaluated for an isolated elevation of the alkaline phosphatase level. Bone scans are the most sensitive means of detecting sites of Paget disease of bone. These scans, however, are nonspecific and can be positive in nonpagetic areas that have degenerative changes or metastatic disease in the skeleton. Plain radiographs of bones noted to be positive on bone scan provide the most specific information because changes noted on the radiograph are usually characteristic to the point of being pathognomonic. Changes that occur in the early stages of Paget disease include erosions of the skull, osteoporosis circumscripta, and pagetic lesions in the long

bones that begin in the metaphysis and migrate down the shaft as a V-shaped absorptive front. Over years, trabeculae become coarse and thickened, and bone may be enlarged or bowed. The serum alkaline phosphatase level is usually increased, sometimes to very high levels, and the serum calcium and phosphorus levels are usually normal.

Bony metastasis from prostate cancer usually presents as osteoblastic lesions. In this asymptomatic patient with a normal prostate-specific antigen level and normal findings on prostate examination, the likelihood of prostate cancer is negligible.

Rickets in children and osteomalacia in adults are mineralization disorders due to a deficient supply of calcium to the growth plate and bone surface. The ionized calcium level may be low or normal, the parathyroid hormone level may be high (secondary hyperparathyroidism) or normal, and the vitamin D level is generally low. An increased level of serum alkaline phosphatase is usually detected; however, as bone alkaline phosphatase levels increase with age, pathologic and physiologic changes become indistinguishable.

Osteoporosis is defined as a silent skeletal disorder characterized by low bone mass predisposing a person to an increased risk of fracture. Radiographic findings are usually noted when advanced osteoporosis is present and include rarefaction of bone, vertebral compression fractures, or other bone fractures. The serum calcium, phosphorus, and alkaline phosphatase levels are usually normal.

> **KEY POINT**
>
> - Most patients with Paget disease of bone are asymptomatic and have unexplained elevation of the serum alkaline phosphatase level at presentation.

Bibliography

Ralston SH, Langston AL, Reid IR. Pathogenesis and management of Paget's disease of bone. Lancet. 2008;372(9633):155-163. [PMID: 18620951]

Item 58   Answer: B

Educational Objective: Diagnose lymphocytic hypophysitis in a pregnant woman.

This patient most likely has lymphocytic hypophysitis, a rare cause of hypopituitarism. In lymphocytic hypophysitis, a pituitary mass that mimics an adenoma is typically seen on an MRI. Diffuse enhancement of a symmetrically enlarged pituitary gland on MRI is also characteristic. This disorder, which usually develops intrapartum, is a destructive process thought to have an autoimmune basis. Adrenocorticotropic hormone (ACTH) deficiency occurs in two thirds of patients with such lesions and is a major cause of death in patients with lymphocytic hypophysitis. In this patient, the progressive severe fatigue and weight loss suggest ACTH deficiency. Thyroid-stimulating hormone deficiency occurs in 60% of patients with this disorder, and other hormonal deficits are of lower frequency. The only way to diagnose the lesions of lymphocytic hypophysitis with certainty is by biopsy, but in this patient, the clinical diagnosis can be made with reasonable certainty.

Expectant management will usually suffice for lymphocytic hypophysitis because the size of most lesions decreases after delivery. Serial visual field testing is indicated. If field defects do develop, surgical debulking may be necessary.

Craniopharyngiomas do occur in this patient's age group, but they are much less common than adenomas, and there have been only three reports of a change in size during pregnancy. An MRI would typically show an irregular cystic lesion with an enhancing wall, not the symmetric sellar lesion seen with this patient. Usually, craniopharyngiomas also cause panhypopituitarism and diabetes insipidus, neither of which was seen in this patient before her pregnancy.

Pituitary tumor apoplexy, which is usually due to hemorrhage into a prior tumor, has a dramatic presentation, with sudden onset of severe headache, stiff neck, and (often) a decreased level of consciousness. This patient's MRI is also not compatible with hemorrhage.

Nonsecreting (clinically nonfunctioning) and prolactin-secreting pituitary adenomas are by far the most common sellar lesions in women of this patient's age. Nonsecreting adenomas generally do not enlarge and cause symptoms during pregnancy. Prolactinomas can enlarge during pregnancy. A review of the literature showed that of 457 women with microprolactinomas who became pregnant, only 12 (2.6%) developed symptomatic tumor enlargement; of 142 pregnant women with macroadenomas, 45 (31%) developed symptomatic tumor enlargement. Key features in this patient's presentation that exclude prolactinoma are that she had been well until 3 weeks ago, had regular menses before pregnancy, and was able to become pregnant. Additionally, prolactin levels in patients with lymphocytic hypophysitis are usually less than 200 ng/mL (200 μg/L) but in patients with a macroprolactinoma are generally greater than 500 ng/mL (500 μg/L).

KEY POINT

- Lymphocytic hypophysitis usually presents during the latter part of pregnancy and is commonly associated with adrenocorticotropic hormone deficiency.

Bibliography

Rivera JA. Lymphocytic hypophysitis: disease spectrum and approach to diagnosis and therapy. Pituitary. 2006;9(1):35-45. [PMID: 16703407]

Item 59   Answer: D

Educational Objective: Manage a patient's proliferative diabetic retinopathy and macular edema with laser therapy.

Panretinal photocoagulation is the most appropriate next step in management for this patient. Diabetic retinopathy is a well-recognized microvascular complication of type 1 diabetes mellitus and is one of the leading causes of visual loss in adults in the United States. Diabetic retinopathy is classified as nonproliferative (with hard exudates, microaneurysms, and minor hemorrhages), which is not associated with visual decline, and proliferative (with "cotton-wool spots" and neovascularization), which is associated with loss of vision. Changes in retinal blood flow occur after several years of diabetes. These changes cause retinal ischemia, which in turn promotes growth factors that stimulate proliferation of new blood vessels. This process leads to scarring and fibrosis. Fibrous tissue can put traction on the retina, which can cause retinal detachment with resultant vision loss. New vessels can also become more permeable and leak serum, which causes macular edema. Tight glycemic control has been shown to decrease the incidence and progression of retinopathy. Blood pressure reduction appears to exert as great a beneficial effect on retinopathy as glycemic control. Once proliferative retinopathy or macular edema is established, vision can be preserved by appropriately timed laser photocoagulation.

Randomized clinical trials have detected no beneficial effect of aspirin on the incidence or progression of proliferative retinopathy or visual loss. On the other hand, other studies have not demonstrated harm to the optic system of patients who must take aspirin for cardiovascular protection.

Although lipid-lowering drugs, such as atorvastatin, have been associated in some studies with reduced rates of retinopathy, they cannot alter the course of established retinopathy and are not indicated in this patient.

Abrupt rapid improvement in glycemic control has been associated with modest worsening of diabetic retinopathy in early studies, but there is no evidence that allowing control to deteriorate by reducing the intake of insulin will improve retinopathy. This patient's glycemic control has been stable, so his insulin regimen should not be changed.

KEY POINT

- Laser photocoagulation of the retina can help preserve vision in patients with proliferative diabetic retinopathy and/or macular edema.

Bibliography

Frank RN. Diabetic retinopathy. N Engl J Med. 2004;350(1):48-58. [PMID: 14702427]

Item 60   Answer: C

Educational Objective: Manage hypothyroidism in a patient taking an over-the-counter metabolism enhancer.

The patient has a mildly suppressed thyroid-stimulating hormone (TSH) level with symptoms consistent with excess thyroid hormone. The positive family history of hypothyroidism and the fact that the patient tested positive for anti–thyroid peroxidase (TPO) and anti–thyroglobulin (TG) antibodies is concerning for the possible presence of autoimmune thyroid disease, such as Graves disease. The most appropriate management step is first to discontinue all supplements. Although thyroid hormone–containing medications are regulated by the U.S. Food and Drug Administration, over-the-counter supplements are not, and some may contain either thyroid hormone or related products. Thyroid function tests should be repeated after 4 to 6 weeks to allow for clearance of any hormone that may have been present in the product.

Thyroid-stimulating immunoglobulins (TSIs) and thyrotropin-binding inhibitory immunoglobulins (TBII) are classically present in Graves disease. Patients with a family history of autoimmune thyroid disease are at increased risk for developing Hashimoto thyroiditis or thyrotoxicosis from Graves disease. However, TSI and TBII titers are expensive tests and not necessary at this point in the diagnostic work-up of this patient.

Repeating the anti–TPO and anti–TG antibody titers will not add any new useful information and so is inappropriate as the next step in management. Anti-TPO antibodies may be positive in patients with Hashimoto thyroiditis, Graves disease, and postpartum and sporadic thyroiditis, although this finding is not generally needed to make the diagnosis, and a positive antibody test does not differentiate between these disorders. Anti-TG antibody is often positive in patients with thyroiditis. Both of these antibody tests were positive when the patient was asymptomatic; repeating the tests now when the patient is symptomatic will not help clarify the diagnosis.

Thyroid ultrasonography is most helpful in the diagnosis of morphologic disorders of the thyroid gland, such as nodules, but is not likely to be helpful in the diagnosis of functional disorders, such as hyperthyroidism.

KEY POINT

- **Exogenous thyroid hormone can suppress thyroid-stimulating hormone levels.**

Bibliography

Bauer BA, Elkin PL, Erickson D, Klee GG, Brennan MD. Symptomatic hyperthyroidism in a patient taking the dietary supplement tiratricol. Mayo Clin Proc. 2002;77(6):587-590. [PMID: 12059130]

Item 61   Answer: A

Educational Objective: Evaluate possible causes of hirsutism.

This woman with rapid virilization and a high serum testosterone level should undergo CT of the abdomen and pelvis to evaluate for an adrenal or ovarian tumor. Her normal menses have stopped, and she has rapidly developed progressive hirsutism, acne, and a deepened voice, all associated with an unambiguously very high testosterone level. Such a high level (>200 ng/dL [6.9 nmol/L]) is suggestive of a tumor of the adrenal glands or ovaries, and such tumors can be best detected on an imaging study.

Polycystic ovary syndrome (PCOS) is the most common etiology of hirsutism with oligomenorrhea. This form of hirsutism normally starts at puberty or several years later and is slowly progressive. Furthermore, the serum testosterone level in women with PCOS rarely exceeds 150 ng/dL (5.2 nmol/L), so higher values warrant a search for an adrenal or ovarian tumor with an abdominal and pelvic CT scan.

Evaluation of menstrual or ovarian function by measurement of the patient's serum estradiol level or by a progestin withdrawal challenge is often useful in women with secondary amenorrhea. However, the entities diagnosed by either low estradiol levels or the progestin withdrawal challenge cannot account for this patient's rapid virilization.

Measuring the serum free testosterone level has little value in this patient because her elevated total serum testosterone level is associated with unequivocal clinical markers of hyperandrogenemia. To confirm this finding with measurement of a free testosterone level is unnecessary and will not alter the subsequent evaluation.

KEY POINT

- **A very high testosterone level (>200 ng/dL [6.9 nmol/L]) in a woman with rapidly progressive hirsutism suggests the presence of an adrenal or ovarian tumor, which requires evaluation with an abdominal and pelvic CT scan.**

Bibliography

Moreno S, Montoya G, Armstrong J, et al. Profile and outcome of pure androgen-secreting adrenal tumors in women: experience of 21 cases. Surgery. 2004;136(6):1192-1198. [PMID: 15657575]

Item 62   Answer: D

Educational Objective: Treat primary hyperparathyroidism, recognizing the indications for surgery.

This patient should undergo parathyroidectomy to treat her primary hyperparathyroidism. Primary hyperparathyroidism commonly presents as asymptomatic hypercalcemia. The diagnosis of hyperparathyroidism requires an elevated serum calcium level with a simultaneous parathyroid hormone level that is elevated or inappropriately within normal limits. Removal of the abnormal and hyperfunctioning parathyroid tissue results in a long-term cure of primary hyperparathyroidism in 96% of patients. The optimum approach to asymptomatic patients has not always been clear. The following criteria have been proposed as indications for parathyroidectomy in asymptomatic persons:

1. Serum calcium level greater than 1 mg/dL (0.25 mmol/L) above the upper limit of normal

2. Reduction in creatinine clearance of greater than 30% compared with age-matched controls

3. Reduction in bone mineral density of the femoral neck, lumbar spine, or distal radius of more than 2.5 standard deviations below peak bone mass for age-matched controls (Z-score)

4. Age younger than 50 years

5. Patients for whom medical surveillance is not desirable or possible

The Consensus Development Conference on the Management of Asymptomatic Primary Hyperparathyroidism, sponsored by the National Institutes of Health, proposed the following two additional criteria:

1. Presence of any complications (such as nephrolithiasis or overt bone disease)

2. An episode of hypercalcemic crisis

Hence, because of the patient's serum calcium level, young age, and history of kidney stones, the correct therapy is minimally invasive parathyroidectomy.

Calcitonin is an antiresorptive agent that inhibits osteoclastic activity and thereby lowers serum calcium levels. However, calcitonin has no role in this patient with an identified parathyroid adenoma.

Cinacalcet, a calcimimetic agent that can lower calcium levels in patients with hyperparathyroidism, has been approved by the U.S. Food and Drug Administration (FDA) as therapy of tertiary hyperparathyroidism associated with chronic kidney disease but not as therapy in patients with primary hyperparathyroidism.

Pamidronate is a bisphosphonate that works as an antiresorptive agent by inactivating osteoclasts. Given intravenously, pamidronate has been used successfully as therapy of hypercalcemia in patients with humoral hypercalcemia of malignancy. However, it is inappropriate for this patient who has primary hyperparathyroidism.

KEY POINT

- Patients with asymptomatic hyperparathyroidism may benefit from parathyroidectomy if they meet certain criteria, such as a calcium level greater than 1 mg/dL (0.25 mmol) above normal, evidence of osteoporosis, decreased creatinine clearance, and age less than 50 years.

Bibliography

Bilezikian JP, Potts JT Jr, Fuleihan Gel-H, et al. Summary statement from a workshop on asymptomatic primary hyperparathyroidism: a

perspective for the 21st century. J Clin Endocrinol Metab. 2002;87(12):5353-5361. [PMID: 12466320]

Item 63   Answer: B

Educational Objective: Evaluate suspected hyperaldosteronism with the appropriate biochemical screening test.

This patient has drug-resistant hypertension, unprovoked hypokalemia, and probable metabolic alkalosis; he also has an inappropriately high urine potassium level. In this setting, primary hyperaldosteronism is a very likely cause of his hypertension and hypokalemia, especially given his age. The best screening test for primary hyperaldosteronism is a determination of the ratio of serum aldosterone (in ng/dL) to plasma renin activity (in ng/mL/min). A ratio greater than 20, particularly when the serum aldosterone level is greater than 15 ng/dL (414 pmol/L), is consistent with the diagnosis of primary hyperaldosteronism.

After biochemical confirmation of hyperaldosteronism, localization procedures are appropriate to differentiate aldosterone-producing adenomas, which are amenable to surgical resection, from bilateral hyperplasia, which is medically treated. Given the high incidence of incidental adrenal lesions, however, imaging studies, such as CT of the adrenal glands, should not be performed before autonomous production of aldosterone is confirmed through biochemical testing.

This patient does not fit the demographic or clinical profile of a patient with renovascular hypertension, and thus evaluating the renal arteries with digital subtraction renal angiography is not indicated. Renovascular hypertension due to fibromuscular disease of the renal arteries usually presents in patients younger than 35 years, and azotemia is rarely present. Atherosclerotic renovascular hypertension is more common in patients older than 55 years and is frequently associated with vascular disease in other vessels; azotemia is often present.

This patient did not have any symptoms or signs suggestive of a pheochromocytoma (palpitations, headache, tremor, diaphoresis). Therefore, screening for a pheochromocytoma with measurement of the plasma metanephrine and normetanephrine levels is inappropriate, especially when there is a more likely cause suggested by the electrolyte abnormalities.

KEY POINT

- Patients with hypertension should be screened for primary hyperaldosteronism if they are young, have hypokalemia, or have difficult-to-control blood pressure; such screening includes determination of the serum aldosterone to plasma renin activity ratio, with a ratio greater than 20 strongly suggesting the diagnosis.

Bibliography

Funder JW, Carey RM, Fardella C, et al. Case detection, diagnosis, and treatment of patients with primary aldosteronism: an Endocrine Society clinical practice guideline. J Clin Endocrinol Metab. 2008;93(9):3266-3281. [PMID: 18552288]

Item 64   Answer: C

Educational Objective: Treat older patients with diabetes mellitus at risk for cardiovascular disease.

This 83-year-old woman with type 2 diabetes mellitus should continue her current treatment regimen. She has a hemoglobin A_{1c} value of 7.2%, which is close to her target value. Strong evidence suggests a reduction of morbidity and mortality by tight control of blood pressure in elderly patients with diabetes, but the evidence is less convincing for tight glycemic control. Intensifying her glycemic control is unlikely, therefore, to have any benefit and may result in episodes of hypoglycemia, which should be avoided in elderly patients at high risk of cardiovascular events. Accordingly, the most rational approach is to continue her current diabetes regimen and maintain good control of blood pressure and lipids.

Exenatide is not approved for use in combination with insulin and so should not be administered to this patient who is already on a regimen that includes insulin glargine.

Metformin can be problematic if added to the diabetes regimen of older patients because of the expected drop in the glomerular filtration rate with aging. Metformin should not be prescribed if the serum creatinine level is greater than 1.5 mg/dL (132.6 μmol/L) in men or 1.4 mg/dL (123.8 μmol/L) in women. Many experts recommend assessment of renal function by obtaining a 24-hour creatinine clearance in the elderly (age >80 years) before prescribing metformin. The renal clearance of metformin is decreased approximately 30% when the creatinine clearance is below 60 mL/min.

Because thiazolidinediones, such as pioglitazone, can cause fluid retention and peripheral edema, these medications should be avoided in patients with New York Heart Association functional class III or IV heart failure. There is no reason, however, to stop the pioglitazone in this patient.

KEY POINT

- **Intensive glycemic control, especially when applied late in the disease course, appears not to reduce the incidence of cardiovascular disease in elderly patients with diabetes mellitus.**

Bibliography

ADVANCE Collaborative Group, Patel A, MacMahon S, Chalmers J, et al. Intensive blood glucose control and vascular outcomes in patients with type 2 diabetes. N Engl J Med. 2008;358(24):2560-2572. [PMID: 18539916]

Item 65   Answer: D

Educational Objective: Manage an incidentally found pituitary adenoma.

This patient should undergo a repeat MRI in 1 year. Incidentally found pituitary adenomas are very common, having been reported in 10% of healthy persons, and usually cause no symptoms. Patients with incidentally found pituitary adenomas have now been followed without intervention in several series. Patients with microadenomas (<1 cm in diameter) have only an approximately 10% risk of tumor enlargement, whereas those with macroadenomas have only an approximately 20% risk of tumor enlargement. Annual follow-up MRIs (or sooner if new symptoms develop) are appropriate to detect the small percentage of tumors that grow.

Irradiation would only be used in patients whose tumors have failed to be controlled with surgery or conventional medical therapy and thus would be inappropriate for this patient.

Cabergoline is used primarily in patients with prolactinomas. Although some studies have suggested that it controls regrowth of nonsecreting tumors after surgery, use of this drug has not become standard therapy for such tumors. It would be inappropriate for this patient.

Somatostatin analogues would only be indicated if the patient had acromegaly, which he does not. Even then, surgery should be the initial therapy tried.

Transsphenoidal surgery would be indicated if there were a visual disturbance that could be attributed to the tumor, hypopituitarism, or hypersecretion of any of the pituitary hormones (except prolactin). Surgery might be indicated if there is evidence of tumor growth 1 year later.

KEY POINT

- **Patients with pituitary incidentalomas should be followed with periodic MRI scans and receive no intervention as long as they have no visual field defects, hypopituitarism, headaches, hormone oversecretion, or evidence of tumor growth on subsequent surveillance MRI scans.**

Bibliography

Molitch ME. Nonfunctioning pituitary tumors and pituitary incidentalomas. Endocrinol Metab Clin North Am. 2008;37(1):151-171. [PMID: 18226735]

Item 66   Answer: D

Educational Objective: Manage amenorrhea with infertility.

This patient should stop or reduce exercising and gain some weight to restore normal menses and fertility. Hypothalamic amenorrhea (or oligomenorrhea, in this patient's case) involves disordered gonadotropin release and may be the result of a tumor or infiltrative lesion (such as lymphoma or sarcoidosis) but more commonly is functional.

The usual functional causes are stress, excessive loss of body weight or fat, excessive exercise, or some combination thereof; BMI is typically less than 17. Diagnosis of functional hypothalamic amenorrhea is one of exclusion, and the minimal evaluation includes a pregnancy test and measurement of serum prolactin, thyroid-stimulating hormone, and follicle-stimulating hormone levels to rule out prolactinoma, thyroid problems, and ovarian failure, respectively. If a functional etiology is still suspected, decreased exercise, improved nutrition, and attention to emotional needs are helpful adjuncts to restore normal menses and fertility.

Although clomiphene can be used to induce ovulation and pelvic ultrasonography can be used to assess reproductive anatomy, the pretest probability of functional hypothalamic amenorrhea is sufficiently high that conservative treatment should be recommended first.

If results of the initial laboratory assessment are normal, the next step in evaluation of patients with amenorrhea is the progestin withdrawal challenge. Menstrual flow on progestin withdrawal indicates relatively normal estrogen production and a patent outflow tract. However, this patient already has occasional menses, so even if she does have progestin withdrawal bleeding, the test result would be of limited value.

KEY POINT

- Functional hypothalamic amenorrhea, which is usually caused by excessive loss of body weight or fat or excessive exercise, is a diagnosis of exclusion.

Bibliography

Chan JL, Mantzoros CS. Role of leptin in energy-deprivation states: normal human physiology and clinical implications for hypothalamic amenorrhoea and anorexia nervosa. Lancet. 2005;366 (9479):74-85. [PMID: 15993236]

Item 67   Answer: C

Educational Objective: Treat Graves disease.

The most appropriate medical regimen for this patient with Graves disease is atenolol and methimazole. To control her tachycardia, a β-blocker, such as atenolol, is indicated. Given the clinical and laboratory findings, this patient is also moderately hyperthyroid. To treat her hyperthyroidism, either methimazole or propylthiouracil can be used. Methimazole, which generally has fewer side effects and results in quicker achievement of the euthyroid state than propylthiouracil, is preferred in most patients. Recent data indicate that propylthiouracil may carry a higher risk of adverse liver effects; its use should probably be limited to the treatment of hyperthyroidism in patients who are pregnant, are experiencing thyroid storm, or are allergic to methimazole.

Atenolol alone would only address this patient's adrenergic symptoms and not reduce her thyroid hormone levels, and methimazole alone would not address her tachycardia.

Radioactive iodine therapy preceded or followed by adjunctive therapy with an antithyroidal drug is occasionally used to treat Graves disease. The drug is given in an attempt to decrease the risk of a transient worsening of the thyrotoxicosis after thyroid ablation. Because antithyroidal drugs render the thyroid radioresistant, they must be stopped for several days before and after giving the radioactive iodine. This therapy is generally reserved for patients with severe thyrotoxicosis or comorbidities, neither of which this patient has. Antithyroidal drug–related leukopenia (and even agranulocytosis) can occur, so a complete blood count is indicated in patients who develop a high fever or sore throat while on an antithyroidal medication.

KEY POINT

- Methimazole has fewer side effects and results in quicker achievement of the euthyroid state than does propylthiouracil in patients with hyperthyroidism.

Bibliography

Nakamura H, Noh JY, Itoh K, Fukata S, Miyauchi A, Hamada N. Comparison of methimazole and propylthiouracil in patients with hyperthyroidism caused by Graves' disease. J Clin Endocrinol Metab. 2007;97(6):2157-2162. [PMID: 17389704]

Item 68   Answer: D

Educational Objective: Diagnose thyrotoxicosis as the cause of hypercalcemia.

This patient's hypercalcemia is most likely caused by thyrotoxicosis. Mild hypercalcemia is found in approximately 10% of patients with thyrotoxicosis. As with this patient, the parathyroid hormone (PTH) level is below or in the low range of normal, and the serum phosphorus level is typically in the upper range of normal. Thyroid hormone has direct bone-resorbing properties that cause a high-turnover state; if left untreated, progression to osteoporosis often occurs. Therapy of the hypercalcemia should aim at attainment of biochemical euthyroidism, whether by antithyroid drug therapy, radioactive iodine therapy, or thyroidectomy.

Exposure to lithium shifts the set point for inhibition of PTH secretion to the right. Clinically, this results in hypercalcemia and an elevated level of PTH, which this patient does not have. Most patients with therapeutic lithium levels for bipolar affective disorder have a slight increase in the serum calcium level, and up to 10% become mildly hypercalcemic with PTH levels that are high normal or slightly elevated.

Primary hyperparathyroidism involves an elevated or inappropriately normal PTH level in the face of hypercalcemia. This patient's low-normal PTH level is not consistent with this condition.

Secondary hyperparathyroidism refers to an elevation of the PTH level that occurs in response to hypocalcemia or hyperphosphatemia, neither of which this patient has. This disorder is commonly seen in patients with chronic kidney disease or vitamin D deficiency.

Bibliography

Giovanella L, Suriano S, Ceriani L. Graves' disease, thymus enlargement, and hypercalcemia. N Engl J Med. 2008;358(10):1078-1079. [PMID: 18322294]

Item 69   Answer: B

Educational Objective: Identify chronic corticosteroid therapy as the cause of central adrenal insufficiency.

This patient has central adrenal insufficiency. Use of systemic corticosteroids is the most common cause of central adrenal insufficiency, with supraphysiologic dosages of exogenous corticosteroids causing disruption of hypothalamic/pituitary adrenocorticotropic hormone (ACTH) production. Consequently, the adrenal cortex atrophies. When subsequently challenged by stress, the hypothalamus and pituitary gland are unable to stimulate adequate adrenal production of cortisol. This central effect of exogenous corticosteroids can occur after only 3 weeks of suppressive therapy. The patient appears to have developed Cushing syndrome as a result of chronic systemic exposure to the intra-articular injections of corticosteroids. Despite her cushingoid features, however, she has clinical and biochemical evidence of adrenal insufficiency. Her low-normal serum ACTH level and her partial response to cosyntropin stimulation indicate that she has central (secondary) adrenal insufficiency. Patients with adrenal insufficiency often decompensate during concurrent illnesses. Because the rest of her pituitary function is normal, another cause of her loss of ACTH secretion is unlikely.

An adrenal adenoma could cause a suppressed ACTH level, cushingoid features, and central obesity, but her symptoms suggest glucocorticoid deficiency. Furthermore, an adrenal adenoma would cause an elevated, not suppressed, cortisol level.

A nonfunctioning pituitary adenoma is extremely unlikely in light of the isolated ACTH deficiency and the timing of symptom onset—3 months after exogenous corticosteroid administration. A functioning pituitary adenoma might produce excessive ACTH, but in that case both the ACTH and cortisol levels would be elevated, not suppressed as they are in this patient.

Primary adrenal insufficiency (Addison disease) is typically associated with low cortisol production and elevated ACTH levels.

Bibliography

Henzen C, Suter A, Lerch E, Urbinelli R, Schorno XH, Briner VA. Suppression and recovery of adrenal response after short-term, high-dose glucocorticoid treatment. Lancet. 2000;355(9203):542-545. [PMID: 10683005]

Item 70   Answer: C

Educational Objective: Evaluate autonomic dysfunction related to long-standing diabetes mellitus.

The most appropriate next step in management for this patient is to measure her postvoid urinary residual volumes. Diabetic neuropathy, a disorder that typically occurs in patients with a long history of diabetes mellitus, has various manifestations and may affect both the somatosensory and autonomic nervous systems. Symptoms of autonomic dysfunction include gastroparesis, constipation and/or diarrhea, orthostatic hypotension, and an atonic bladder. This patient with long-standing diabetes and established peripheral neuropathy is at risk for a neurogenic bladder, which can manifest as recurrent urinary tract infections and overflow incontinence. Measuring postvoid urinary residual volumes or obtaining a bladder ultrasonogram will determine whether high urinary residual volumes are present. If they are, prokinetic drugs (such as bethanechol chloride) can be given, or an intermittent urinary self-catheterization regimen can be initiated. Regular and complete bladder emptying will help reduce the incidence of urinary tract infection and possibly reverse or improve the patient's renal insufficiency.

Chronic suppressive antibiotic therapy with ciprofloxacin may create resistant bacterial strains. More importantly, such therapy will not address the urinary stasis that may be present because of her bladder dysfunction.

Anticholinergic agents, such as oxybutynin, inhibit contraction of both the normal and unstable bladder. Oxybutynin is highly effective in the treatment of detrusor instability (overactive bladder). However, oxybutynin is contraindicated in patients with an atonic bladder and would likely exacerbate this patient's problems.

This patient's history and examination findings do not suggest the presence of malignancy, so pelvic CT is not the appropriate next step in management. A CT scan would likely reveal nothing but an enlarged bladder and, possibly, hydronephrosis if contrast is used, and the contrast material could worsen renal function.

- Autonomic neuropathy typically occurs in patients with long-standing diabetes mellitus and can manifest as a neurogenic bladder, which can lead to chronic urinary tract infections, urinary retention, and incontinence.

Bibliography

Boulton AJ. Diabetic neuropathy: classification, measurement and treatment. Curr Opin Endocrinol Diabetes Obes. 2007;14(2):141-145. [PMID: 17940432]

Item 71   Answer: D

Educational Objective: Manage adrenal insufficiency in a patient with hypothyroidism.

Performing a cosyntropin stimulation test is the most appropriate next step in management. This patient has hypotension, increased pigmentation, and evidence of two other autoimmune disorders (pernicious anemia and Hashimoto disease). Therefore, adrenal insufficiency is very probable and can be confirmed by such a test. The combination of autoimmune adrenal insufficiency and other autoimmune endocrine disorders is referred to as the polyglandular autoimmune (PGA) syndrome, of which type 2 is the most common form. Nearly 50% of patients with type 2 PGA syndrome have autoimmune adrenal insufficiency on presentation, and another 20% have autoimmune adrenalitis with autoimmune thyroid disease or type 1 diabetes mellitus. Other common associations include pernicious anemia and autoimmune ovarian failure.

The patient's thyroid hormone replacement should be withheld until her adrenal function has been checked because treatment of her hypothyroidism alone may increase the clearance of cortisol, which could increase the severity of the cortisol deficiency and provoke an adrenal crisis. Increasing the thyroid hormone dose is likely to exacerbate cortisol deficiency and thus is contraindicated. Once adrenal insufficiency is confirmed, glucocorticoid replacement should be initiated before restarting or adjusting the levothyroxine therapy.

The glutamic acid decarboxylase antibody level is frequently elevated in the preclinical period of type 1 diabetes mellitus. A positive test may help estimate her risk of developing type 1 diabetes but should have no effect on immediate management in this patient with probable adrenal insufficiency.

Patients with Graves disease have an unregulated production of thyroxine (T_4) and triiodothyronine (T_3) because of the presence of autoantibodies against the thyroid-stimulating hormone receptor, which results in hypertrophy of the gland and autonomous production of thyroid hormone. Because this patient does not have Graves disease, checking her thyroid-stimulating immunoglobulin titer is unlikely to be useful.

- Thyroid hormone replacement can worsen symptoms or even precipitate an adrenal crisis in patients with underlying adrenal insufficiency.

Bibliography

Graves L 3rd, Klein RM, Walling AD. Addisonian crisis precipitated by thyroxine therapy: a complication of type 2 autoimmune polyglandular syndrome. South Med J. 2003:96(8):824-827. [PMID: 14515930]

Item 72   Answer: C

Educational Objective: Evaluate suspected central hypothyroidism.

The most appropriate test for this patient is measurement of his free thyroxine (T_4) level. He has symptoms of fatigue and constipation and a recent elevated LDL-cholesterol level, all of which are compatible with hypothyroidism. Progressive loss of pituitary hormones is to be expected after pituitary irradiation and needs to be monitored. He has already demonstrated loss of gonadotropins, and testosterone replacement has been started. When there is central hypothyroidism, the thyroid-stimulating hormone (TSH) level will not be elevated, as would be expected with primary hypothyroidism. As with this patient, the TSH level may not be abnormally low either. The best way to diagnose central hypothyroidism is by measuring the level of the peripheral hormone T_4. Similarly, thyroid hormone treatment is monitored and adjusted by measuring free T_4 rather than TSH levels.

An adrenocorticotropic hormone (ACTH) stimulation test is primarily helpful for diagnosing intrinsic adrenal disease. If the baseline cortisol level is near the normal level, as with this patient, the response to an ACTH stimulation test will certainly be normal, regardless of the cause of symptoms. Continued monitoring of cortisol levels is warranted, however, because of the progressive nature of the damage that irradiation causes.

Given that this patient, who is only mildly overweight, now has a normal total testosterone level, it is very likely that his free testosterone level will also be normal and thus does not have to be measured. A discrepancy in the levels can occur in obese men in whom the sex hormone–binding globulin (SHBG) level is decreased, which causes a decrease in the total testosterone level. SHBG may increase with age, so that measurement of free testosterone levels may be helpful when assessing gonadal function in older patients.

The patient may well be growth hormone deficient. However, the appropriate stimulation test would determine insulin-induced hypoglycemia and not glucose-induced hyperglycemia.

Bibliography

Toogood AA, Stewart PM. Hypopituitarism: clinical features, diagnosis, and management. Endocrinol Metab Clin North Am. 2008; 37(1):235-261. [PMID: 18226739]

Item 73   Answer: B

Educational Objective: Treat hypoglycemia related to insulin therapy.

Basal and rapid-acting insulin analogues, when dosed properly, reduce the risk of hypoglycemia. Current choices of long- or intermediate-acting basal insulins include insulin glargine, insulin detemir, and neutral protamine Hagedorn (NPH) insulin. The optimal basal insulin should be peakless and have a 24-hour duration of action. Both insulin glargine and, to a lesser extent, insulin detemir meet these requirements. NPH insulin, on the other hand, does not and is usually administered twice daily because its duration of action typically extends only 12 to 18 hours with a peak of activity at 4 to 8 hours after administration, which can precipitate hypoglycemic episodes at other times. In one study, the risk of hypoglycemia was significantly higher during the overnight hours in patients taking NPH insulin versus insulin glargine at bedtime. An ideal prandial insulin has a brisk peak and a short overall duration of action to properly cover postprandial glucose excursions. Such pharmacokinetics are found with the rapid-acting insulin analogues lispro, aspart, and glulisine. In contrast, regular insulin has a duration of action of 6 to 8 hours and so is not an optimal prandial product.

She should be encouraged to switch to a regimen of four injections of insulin per day, with a once daily injection of a basal insulin, such as insulin glargine, and mealtime injections of a rapid-acting analogue, such as insulin lispro.

Patients with advanced type 2 diabetes mellitus who are on insulin should not be transferred to oral agents because the need for insulin suggests an already significant insulin deficiency that oral agents are unlikely to overcome. Glycemic control would inevitably deteriorate.

Decreasing the dosage of NPH and regular insulin may diminish her overnight hypoglycemic episodes but would also result in higher blood glucose levels. Therefore, this change in the patient's diabetes regimen is not appropriate.

Increasing caloric intake to combat hypoglycemia is rarely indicated. Ideally, the insulin regimen should be adjusted on the basis of the patient's nutritional intake, not vice-versa.

Bibliography

Hirsch IB. Insulin analogues. N Engl J Med. 2005;352(2):174-183. [PMID: 15647580]

Item 74   Answer: D

Educational Objective: Treat hypercalcemia associated with sarcoidosis.

This patient should be treated with prednisone. He most likely has sarcoidosis because of the presence of hilar lymphadenopathy, interstitial lung disease, and hypercalcemia. The underlying mechanism of hypercalcemia in sarcoidosis involves the granulomas producing the enzyme 1α-hydroxylase, which converts 25-hydroxy vitamin D to 1,25-dihydroxy vitamin D. With sarcoidosis, hypercalcemia may be secondary to increased intestinal absorption induced by excessive amounts of 1,25-dihydroxy vitamin D. In patients with this disorder, 1,25-dihydroxy vitamin D production can be diminished by using corticosteroids, such as prednisone, as the initial therapy.

Calcitonin is an antiresorptive agent that is not effective in hypercalcemia that is due to granulomatous disease. Similarly, pamidronate works via osteoclast inactivation and, therefore, is not first-line therapy when overproduction of 1,25-dihydroxy vitamin D is the cause of hypercalcemia. Plicamycin is another antiresorptive agent whose use is limited by its toxicity, particularly in patients with renal, liver, or bone marrow disease.

Bibliography

Berliner AR, Haas M, Choi MJ. Sarcoidosis: the nephrologist's perspective. Am J Kidney Dis. 2006;48(5):856-870. [PMID: 17060009]

Item 75   Answer: D

Educational Objective: Evaluate secondary amenorrhea.

This patient should undergo transvaginal pelvic ultrasonography. If results of the initial laboratory assessment are normal, the cornerstone of the evaluation for secondary amenorrhea rests on the results of a progestin withdrawal challenge (medroxyprogesterone acetate, 10 mg orally for 10 days). Menstrual flow on progestin withdrawal indicates relatively normal estrogen production and a patent outflow tract, which limits diagnostic evaluation to chronic anovulation. Absence of flow indicates estrogen absence and/or an anatomic defect. In patients with no flow, pelvic anatomy is assessed with ultrasonography and/or MRI. The absence of menses for several months after dilation and curettage in this patient suggests severe endometrial damage or formation of scar tissue (Asherman syndrome). Therefore, an ultrasound is appropriate to assess the pelvic anatomy.

A hysteroscope is a fiberoptic device inserted into the uterus via the vagina and cervix that enables direct visualization of the endometrial cavity. It is typically not the first diagnostic test to assess for the presence of anatomic disorders that may be associated with amenorrhea because of its cost and invasiveness.

Approximately 50% of primary amenorrhea is caused by chromosomal disorders that result in gonadal dysgenesis and depletion of ovarian follicles. Turner syndrome, the most common disorder in this category, is classically associated with a 45,XO genotype and is characterized by a lack of secondary sexual characteristics, growth retardation, a webbed neck, and frequent skeletal abnormalities. Because this patient has secondary, not primary, amenorrhea, a karyotype is not needed.

The patient previously had normal menses and fertility and has no stigmata of hyperandrogenism. Therefore, 21-hydroxylase deficiency is unlikely, and measurement of the serum 17-hydroxyprogesterone level is unlikely to provide useful information.

KEY POINT

- **In secondary amenorrhea, absence of menstrual flow after a progestin withdrawal challenge with medroxyprogesterone acetate indicates estrogen absence and/or an anatomic defect; when such absence occurs after dilation and curettage, the possibility of Asherman syndrome must be considered.**

Bibliography
Yu D, Wong YM, Cheong Y, Xia E, Li TC. Asherman syndrome—one century later. Fertil Steril. 2008;89(4):759-779. [PMID: 18406834]

Item 76   Answer: A
Educational Objective: Manage amiodarone-induced thyroid function changes.

Amiodarone has been associated with several abnormalities in thyroid function, including amiodarone-induced thyrotoxicosis (hyperthyroidism [type 1] and thyroiditis [type 2]), hypothyroidism, and inhibition of thyroxine (T_4) to triiodothyronine (T_3) conversion. Because of the drug's high iodine content and fat solubility, its effects on the thyroid gland have been reported to persist from months to up to 1 year. The results of this patient's thyroid function studies are consistent with decreased T_4 to T_3 conversion with a concomitant increase in the serum thyroid-stimulating hormone level, which can occur with use of amiodarone. The decision to discontinue amiodarone can be complex. Amiodarone is usually not discontinued unless it fails to control the underlying arrhythmia. In patients with hypothyroidism who must continue amiodarone, thyroid replacement therapy is indicated. In patients with previously normal thyroid gland function who discontinue amiodarone, hypothyroidism often resolves.

Amiodarone-induced thyrotoxicosis can be a management challenge. Theoretically, antithyroidal drugs are preferred in type 1 (hyperthyroidism) and prednisone therapy in type 2 (thyroiditis). In practice, however, a combination of both may be needed in patients with either type.

Whereas propranolol is known to affect T_4 to T_3 conversion, other β-blockers, such as metoprolol, are not. Discontinuing metoprolol in this patient is unlikely to restore normal thyroid function.

Omeprazole and other proton pump inhibitors can affect hormone absorption in patients on thyroid hormone replacement therapy. Given that this patient is not receiving levothyroxine, the use of omeprazole does not explain her findings.

Sertraline appears to enhance thyroid hormone metabolism but does not cause the abnormal results on thyroid function tests seen in this patient.

KEY POINT

- **Amiodarone has been associated with thyrotoxicosis, hypothyroidism, and inhibition of thyroxine (T_4) to triiodothyronine (T_3) conversion.**

Bibliography
Gheri RG, Pucci P, Falsetti C, et al. Clinical, biochemical and therapeutic aspects of amiodarone-induced hypothyroidism (AIH) in geriatric patients with cardiac arrhythmias. Arch Gerontol Geriatr. 2004;38(1):27-36. [PMID: 14599701]

Item 77   Answer: B
Educational Objective: Diagnose hypoparathyroidism after thyroidectomy.

The most likely explanation for this patient's hypocalcemia is hypoparathyroidism. She has hypocalcemia because of inadvertent removal of or damage to the parathyroid glands during thyroidectomy, which has led to hypoparathyroidism. Absence of parathyroid hormone (PTH) action causes a lack of stimulation of osteoclasts with lack of mobilization of calcium from bone, increased urine calcium loss, and resultant hypocalcemia. Additionally, 1α-hydroxylase is downregulated, with a resultant decreased production of 1,25-dihydroxy vitamin D. This decreased production impairs the absorption of calcium and phosphorus in the gut.

Anxiety-induced hyperventilation can induce a decrease in the ionized calcium level. As the partial pressure of carbon dioxide falls, there is a dissociation of hydrogen ions from albumin to compensate for the respiratory alkalosis. This dissociation leads to increased binding of calcium ions to albumin, which causes the ionized calcium level to decrease. This decrease can be sufficient to induce clinical features of hypocalcemia. However, the total calcium level does not decrease, as it has in this patient.

Tissue resistance to the action of PTH occurs in the rare congenital condition of pseudohypoparathyroidism. Despite increased PTH levels (not decreased, as in this patient), patients with this condition have hypocalcemia and hyperphosphatemia. Phenotypically, patients with pseudohypoparathyroidism have a short round face, short neck, and short fourth metacarpal bone.

Pseudo-pseudohypoparathyroidism refers to the condition in which patients have the phenotypic appearance of pseudohypoparathyroidism but normal calcium and phosphorus levels because of normal PTH secretion, function, and action.

KEY POINT

- **Hypocalcemia following neck surgery is likely due to hypoparathyroidism.**

Bibliography

Shoback D. Clinical practice. Hypoparathyroidism. N Engl J Med. 2008;359(4):391-403. [PMID: 18650515]

Item 78   Answer: D

Educational Objective: Identify secondary causes of diabetes mellitus.

This patient's findings are most likely caused by ectopic secretion of adrenocorticotropic hormone (ACTH). He had rapid onset of diabetes mellitus associated with features of excess glucocorticoid and mineralocorticoid activity (metabolic alkalosis, unprovoked hypokalemia, and hypertension). Cortisol binds to the glucocorticoid receptors to exert its effects in various tissues. However, at high concentrations, such as in this patient, cortisol also binds to the mineralocorticoid receptors in the kidney; hence the observed increase in mineralocorticoid activity can occur. Examination findings include features consistent with excessive ACTH secretion: hyperpigmented mucous membranes, proximal myopathy, and elevated levels of cortisol and ACTH. Notably, the patient had a rapid onset of disease that is more typical of a malignant process than an ACTH-secreting pituitary tumor (Cushing disease). A chest radiograph to detect a small cell lung cancer is a reasonable next diagnostic step for this patient who is a cigarette smoker and has findings of excess cortisol and ACTH.

Both adrenal adenoma and carcinoma are unlikely diagnoses. These disorders will suppress, not elevate, the ACTH level because of the autonomous production of cortisol.

KEY POINT

- **A secondary cause should be strongly considered in patients with rapid onset of diabetes mellitus in the absence of risk factors.**

Bibliography

Arnaldi G, Angeli A, Atkinson AB, et al. Diagnosis and complications of Cushing's syndrome: a consensus statement. J Clin Endocrinol Metab. 2003;88(12):5593-5602. [PMID: 14671138]

Item 79   Answer: C

Educational Objective: Evaluate hyponatremia caused by desmopressin treatment in a patient with diabetes insipidus.

This patient's hyponatremia is most likely the result of excessive water ingestion. Patients with central diabetes insipidus cannot concentrate their urine and respond to subcutaneous desmopressin administration by decreased urine output and increased urine osmolality. Desmopressin can cause hyponatremia if a person continues to drink without any fluid restriction, particularly if their fluid intake is excessive, although progressive nausea usually limits the intake. For patients with chronic central diabetes insipidus, allowing breakthrough polyuria to occur by temporarily reducing or stopping desmopressin can prevent hyponatremia and enable recognition of the patients in whom the disease remits. Patients who develop diabetes insipidus after trauma or neurosurgery have been noted to recover normal urinary concentrating ability and normal urine output as late as 10 years after the initial insult.

Cerebral salt wasting, a syndrome characterized by hypovolemia and hyponatremia, usually occurs within 10 days of a neurosurgical procedure or disease, particularly subarachnoid hemorrhage. Cerebral salt wasting is an unlikely diagnosis in this patient in the absence of hypotension or other signs of hypovolemia.

In patients receiving desmopressin who develop severe hyponatremia and a low urine output, cortisol deficiency should be part of the differential diagnosis. Cortisol deficiency is unlikely in this patient because she is on an adequate dosage of replacement cortisol.

The syndrome of inappropriate antidiuretic hormone secretion seems an unlikely cause of hyponatremia in a patient who has a recent diagnosis of diabetes insipidus and responded to an appropriate dosage of desmopressin.

KEY POINT

- **Continued drinking without fluid restriction while taking a fixed dose of desmopressin can cause hyponatremia.**

Bibliography

Loh JA, Verbalis JG. Disorders of water and salt metabolism associated with pituitary disease. Endocrinol Metab Clin North Am. 2008;37(1):213-234, x. [PMID: 18226738]

Item 80   Answer: D

Educational Objective: Evaluate hyperthyroidism as a cause of loss of glycemic control in a patient with diabetes mellitus.

Measurement of this patient's thyroid-stimulating hormone (TSH) level is most likely to diagnose the cause of her deteriorating glycemic control. The deterioration in glycemic control in patients with previously stable diabetes mellitus should always raise the suspicion of an underlying illness that may increase insulin resistance or diminish insulin production. This patient's symptoms of diaphoresis and weight loss and her deteriorating glycemic control suggest thyrotoxicosis; in the postpartum setting, women with type 1 diabetes have an increased risk of postpartum thyroiditis. An excess of thyroid hormone increases hepatic glucose production and can contribute to new deterioration in glycemic control in diabetes. Therefore, her TSH level should be checked.

The levels of antitransglutaminase antibodies are elevated in patients with celiac disease, which does occur with increased frequency in patients with type 1 diabetes. Diarrhea is a clinically significant finding in approximately 50% of patients. There are no suggestive gastrointestinal symptoms of this condition other than weight loss, which is seen in this patient. However, weight loss by itself is insufficient to suggest the disease, and celiac disease cannot explain her other symptoms.

Hemoglobin A_{1c} values and postprandial glucose levels are measurements of glycemic control but do not provide any useful information about the nature of this patient's recently deteriorated glycemic control.

Cushing syndrome can be diagnosed with a urine free cortisol level. Cushing syndrome is caused by excessive amounts of endogenous or exogenous glucocorticoids causing central adiposity and is marked by weight gain, supraclavicular fat pads, round or "moon" facies, and a "buffalo hump." Other findings include violaceous striae and incidental bruising, hirsutism, amenorrhea, and abnormal libido. Antagonism of insulin action causes hyperglycemia. However, there is no evidence suggestive of Cushing syndrome in this patient, so obtaining a urine free cortisol level is not the best option.

> **KEY POINT**
>
> - **Hyperthyroidism can contribute to poor glycemic control in patients with diabetes mellitus.**

Bibliography

Vondra K, Vrbikova J, Dvorakova K. Thyroid gland diseases in adult patients with diabetes mellitus. Minerva Endocrinol. 2005;30(4):217-236. [PMID: 16319810]

Item 81   Answer: B

Educational Objective: Manage a multinodular goiter.

The most appropriate management for this patient is fine-needle aspiration biopsy of the dominant nodule. Several studies have shown that multinodular goiters harbor the same risk of thyroid cancer as solitary thyroid nodules. Most experts perform fine-needle aspiration biopsy on individual nodules greater than 1.0 to 1.5 cm in diameter or on nodules that have concerning ultrasound characteristics, such as microcalcifications or prominent central intranodular blood flow. In this patient, only the right midpole nodule meets these criteria; the other three nodules do not require fine-needle aspiration biopsy.

This patient who is currently euthyroid has a dominant thyroid nodule that is associated with a significantly increased risk of cancer. Repeating the ultrasound in 6 months could delay the diagnosis of cancer. Additionally, the routine use of levothyroxine for nodule shrinkage is not recommended because the drug is generally ineffective in reducing nodule size, cannot be used to determine whether a nodule is benign or malignant, and exposes patients to the undesirable side effects of thyroid hormone replacement, such as tachycardia and osteoporosis.

Because the thyroid-stimulating hormone (TSH) and free thyroxine (T_4) levels are normal, there is little clinical utility in obtaining a thyroid scan. If the TSH level had been suppressed, a thyroid scan and radioactive iodine uptake would have been warranted to look for a toxic nodule or toxic multinodular goiter.

> **KEY POINT**
>
> - **The risk of cancer is the same in solitary thyroid nodules and multinodular goiters; a fine-needle aspiration biopsy is recommended for nonfunctioning nodules greater than 1.0 to 1.5 cm in diameter or for nodules that have concerning ultrasound characteristics.**

Bibliography

Hegedüs L. Clinical practice. The thyroid nodule. N Engl J Med. 2004;351(17):1764-1771. [PMID: 15496625]

Item 82   Answer: D

Educational Objective: Diagnose genetic hypogonadism.

This young man has primary testicular failure as indicated by the small testes, low testosterone level, and elevated gonadotropin levels. In a young man with primary testicular failure and no history of uncorrected cryptorchidism, therapy with cancer chemotherapeutic agents, irradiation, surgical orchiectomy, or previous infectious orchitis, a genetic etiology of the infertility is likely. Klinefelter syndrome, complete or mosaic, is one of the most common causes of primary testicular failure and is the most likely diagnosis. Obtaining the patient's karyotype is therefore indicated. Not all patients with Klinefelter syndrome have the classic eunuchoid proportions and gynecomastia on presentation; some have normal puberty only to be infertile, with a low testosterone level, as adults.

The total testosterone level is unequivocally low. Therefore, measurement of other serum hormone levels, such as estradiol or free testosterone, is not necessary.

Because his follicle-stimulating and luteinizing hormone levels are high and his serum prolactin level is normal, he most likely has primary hypogonadism. Therefore, pituitary imaging to detect a pituitary tumor and testicular biopsy to determine another cause of his infertility are unnecessary.

> **KEY POINT**
> - **Klinefelter syndrome, complete or mosaic, is one of the most common causes of primary testicular failure; can present in adulthood without the stigmata of eunuchoid proportions and gynecomastia; and can be confirmed by a karyotype.**

Bibliography

Lanfranco F, Kamischke A, Zitzmann M, Nieschlag E. Klinefelter's syndrome. Lancet. 2004;364(9430):273-283. [PMID: 15262106]

Item 83   Answer: C

Educational Objective: Treat a patient whose type 2 diabetes mellitus is inadequately controlled on dual oral therapy.

In addition to her current therapy, this patient should also take pioglitazone to improve her glycemic control. According to the American Diabetes Association, most patients with diabetes mellitus should have a hemoglobin A_{1c} value of less than 7%. This patient is substantially above that target despite dual therapy with metformin and a sulfonylurea. Several options are available, including increasing lifestyle modifications, adding a third oral agent (such as a thiazolidinedione, an α-glucosidase inhibitor, or a dipeptidyl peptidase-IV inhibitor), or adding an injectable agent, such as exenatide or insulin. This patient has expressed the desire to avoid injections, at least for the time being. As a result, her options are more limited. Of the choices provided, the only one that has been shown to reduce hemoglobin A_{1c} values by approximately 1% is pioglitazone. This treatment has been endorsed by the recent American Diabetes Association/European Association for the Study of Diabetes Consensus Statement on the management of type 2 diabetes.

The glucose-lowering power of acarbose ranges between a 0.5% and 0.8% reduction in hemoglobin A_{1c}

values and is thus inferior to that of pioglitazone. Furthermore, acarbose may have substantial gastrointestinal side effects, including bloating, abdominal cramps, diarrhea, and flatulence.

Increasing the dosage of a sulfonylurea, such as glimepiride, above half the maximum recommended dosage provides little additional therapeutic benefit. Similarly, patients taking metformin, 2000 mg/d, are unlikely to get much additional benefit from increasing the dosage to 2550 mg/d (the maximum recommended dosage).

> **KEY POINT**
> - **A recent American Diabetes Association/European Association for the Study of Diabetes Consensus Statement on the management of type 2 diabetes mellitus endorses the addition of pioglitazone to the regimen of a patient with suboptimal glycemic control on dual oral therapy.**

Bibliography

Nathan DM, Buse JB, Davidson MB, et al. Management of hyperglycemia in type 2 diabetes: a consensus algorithm for the initiation and adjustment of therapy: update regarding thiazolidinediones: a consensus statement from the American Diabetes Association and the European Association for the Study of Diabetes [erratum in Diabetes Care. 2008;31(3):522]. Diabetes Care. 2008;31(1):173-175. [PMID: 18165348]

Item 84   Answer: D

Educational Objective: Treat corticosteroid-induced osteoporosis.

This patient with corticosteroid-induced osteoporosis should be treated with risedronate. Bone loss induced by exogenous corticosteroids is the most common form of secondary osteoporosis. The extent is determined by the dose and duration of therapy. Both risedronate and alendronate have been shown to increase bone mineral density (BMD) in patients treated with corticosteroids. In addition, both agents decrease the risk of new vertebral fractures by up to 70%. A dual energy x-ray absorptiometry scan to assess BMD should be performed at the initiation of corticosteroid therapy. An oral bisphosphonate, such as risedronate or alendronate, which are specifically approved as therapy of corticosteroid-induced osteoporosis by the U.S. Food and Drug Administration (FDA), should be started in patients in whom the BMD is already low. Recently, an annual intravenous infusion of zoledronate was also approved by the FDA as therapy of corticosteroid-induced osteoporosis. All patients also should receive appropriate calcium and vitamin D therapy.

Calcitonin decreases bone resorption by attenuating osteoclast activity. Its use may be beneficial in decreasing pain associated with acute or subacute fracture, but because of the availability of other medications that have better efficacy in fracture reduction, calcitonin is not considered a first-line treatment for osteoporosis and is not FDA approved for the treatment of corticosteroid-induced osteoporosis.

The prevention and treatment of corticosteroid-induced osteoporosis includes oral calcium supplementation (1500 mg/d) and oral vitamin D (800 U/d). The patient is on sufficient dosages of both vitamin D and calcium.

Raloxifene is a selective estrogen receptor modulator with suppressive effects on osteoclast and bone resorption and is associated with an increase in bone mass and decreased vertebral fractures. It is not recommended for use in premenopausal women or in women taking estrogen replacement therapy. Adverse effects include an increased risk of thromboembolism, fatal stroke, and increased vasomotor symptoms. It is not FDA approved for the treatment of corticosteroid-induced osteoporosis and would also be inappropriate for this patient because of its adverse effect profile.

KEY POINT

- Oral bisphosphonates are the therapy of choice for corticosteroid-induced osteoporosis; all patients with corticosteroid-induced osteoporosis should also receive adequate calcium and vitamin D supplementation.

Bibliography

Reid DM, Devogelaer JP, Saag K, et al. Zoledronic acid and risedronate in the prevention and treatment of glucocorticoid-induced osteoporosis (HORIZON): a multicentre, double-blind, double-dummy, randomised controlled trial. Lancet. 2009;373(9671):1253-1263. [PMID: 19362675]

Item 85   Answer: B

Educational Objective: Evaluate suspected acromegaly.

The best initial step in diagnosis is measurement of the insulin-like growth factor 1 (IGF-1) level. Acromegaly is usually caused by excess growth hormone (GH) secretion by a tumor of the GH-secreting cells of the pituitary gland. If this tumor occurs in childhood before the closure of the epiphyses, pituitary gigantism results. Patients with acromegaly develop organomegaly and tissue hypertrophy. High GH levels stimulate the liver and other tissues to increase synthesis of IGF-1, also known as somatomedin C, which exerts its actions on multiple tissues in the body and results in organomegaly and soft-tissue and bony hypertrophy. Diagnostic laboratory abnormalities include elevated GH and IGF-1 levels. This patient should have her IGF-1 level measured because a single IGF-1 level reflects integrated GH secretion, and an elevated level is highly reliable in indicating GH hypersecretion and a diagnosis of acromegaly.

GH is secreted episodically with high spike and low trough levels, which makes a single GH measurement (or even several measurements) potentially misleading. For GH measurements to be used to diagnose acromegaly, GH secretion must first be shown to be autonomous with a glucose tolerance test, which can show that GH levels are not suppressible by hyperglycemia, as they normally would be.

An MRI of the pituitary gland should only be performed after the biochemical diagnosis has been established.

Somatostatin receptors are present on GH-secreting adenomas but often not in sufficient amounts to make a tumor visible on an octreotide scan. Such testing is not part of the routine evaluation of patients with acromegaly.

KEY POINT

- Acromegaly can be diagnosed by demonstrating an elevated insulin-like growth factor 1 level in a patient in whom there is clinical suspicion of the disorder.

Bibliography

Ben-Shlomo A, Melmed S. Acromegaly. Endocrinol Metab Clin North Am. 2008;37(1):101-122. [PMID: 18226732]

Item 86   Answer: B

Educational Objective: Treat selected patients with diabetes mellitus not controlled by pioglitazone and metformin.

Exenatide should be added to the patient's regimen. She has not achieved a hemoglobin A_{1c} target of less than 7.0% despite therapy with metformin and the thiazolidinedione pioglitazone. She has experienced hypoglycemia with sulfonylurea therapy and remains reluctant to retry this medication. For similar reasons, she also refuses insulin therapy. Exenatide, an injectable glucagon-like peptide-1 (GLP-1) mimetic, is the best option for this patient because, on average, it lowers the hemoglobin A_{1c} value by approximately 1%, which would bring her value nearer the target range. GLP-1 is an incretin hormone with several actions, including the stimulation of glucose-dependent insulin secretion, the inhibition of glucagon secretion and hepatic glucose production, the delay of gastric emptying, and the suppression of appetite through central pathways that have yet to be elucidated. Exenatide also is not associated with hypoglycemia when paired with other drugs that do not increase the risk of hypoglycemia, such as metformin and thiazolidinediones. The additional major benefit of exenatide in patients with type 2 diabetes mellitus is weight loss. Exenatide is approved by the U.S. Food and Drug Administration for use in combination with metformin, sulfonylureas, and thiazolidinediones.

Acarbose is an α-glucosidase inhibitor that retards small intestinal carbohydrate absorption. Adding this drug to diabetes regimens is associated with modest hemoglobin A_{1c} reductions of approximately 0.5%. Adding acarbose to this patient's diabetes regimen is thus unlikely to allow her to achieve the target hemoglobin A_{1c} value of less than 7%.

Because many of the drugs used to treat diabetes have similar effects on reducing hemoglobin A_{1c} levels, substituting drugs is never as effective as adding drugs. Therefore, changing metformin to the rapid-acting nonsulfonylurea insulin secretagogue nateglinide is unlikely to further reduce her hemoglobin A_{1c} value. For similar reasons, substituting the thiazolidinedione rosiglitazone for the thiazolidinedione pioglitazone or switching from pioglitazone to the dipeptidyl peptidase-IV inhibitor sitagliptin is unlikely to reduce her hemoglobin A_{1c} value.

KEY POINT

- Injectable therapy with the glucagon-like peptide-1 agonist exenatide reduces hemoglobin A_{1c} values and can be used in combination with oral agents to achieve glycemic targets in patients with type 2 diabetes mellitus; the major benefits are weight loss and the lack of hypoglycemia.

Bibliography

Amori RE, Lau J, Pittas AG. Efficacy and safety of incretin therapy in type 2 diabetes: systematic review and meta-analysis. JAMA. 2007;298(2):194-206. [PMID: 17622601]

Item 87   Answer: C

Educational Objective: Manage an incidentally found adrenal mass.

This patient should be retested in 12 months. He has an incidentally discovered 2.5-cm adrenal mass but no clinical or biochemical features suggesting excess hormonal secretion. Neither the size nor the imaging characteristics of this adrenal mass raise concerns for a possible malignancy. The risk of primary or metastatic cancer approaches only 2% for tumors less than 4 cm in size. Additionally, the attenuation value of the mass is very low.

This patient is not hypertensive and has no clinical or biochemical evidence, such as excess catecholamine secretion, of a pheochromocytoma. Because a pheochromocytoma is unlikely, a metaiodobenzylguanidine (MIBG) scan, which can confirm the presence of such a tumor, is unwarranted.

Positron emission tomography (PET) is usually reserved for patients with a known malignancy to help with staging or to detect metastatic disease. PET scans can detect tumors of the adrenal gland, but there is a high (in excess of 15%) false-positive rate that makes this technique unhelpful in the evaluation of an incidentally discovered adrenal mass.

There are no indications for surgical intervention at this point in this asymptomatic patient with a nonfunctioning 2.5-cm adrenal mass with unremarkable imaging characteristics.

KEY POINT

- Small, incidentally discovered nonfunctioning adrenal adenomas with no evidence of malignancy should be managed with close observation and follow-up testing.

Bibliography

Young WF Jr. Clinical practice. The incidentally discovered adrenal mass. N Engl J Med 2007;356(6):601-610. [PMID: 17287480]

Item 88   Answer: A

Educational Objective: Treat male osteoporosis.

This patient with T-scores of -3.0 in the lumbosacral spine and -3.2 in the left hip has osteoporosis and should be treated with alendronate. Osteoporosis is a silent skeletal disorder characterized by compromised bone strength and an increased predisposition to fractures. The following risk factors are associated with osteoporosis in men:

- Prolonged exposure to certain medications, such as corticosteroids, anticonvulsants, some cancer drugs, and aluminum-containing antacids
- Chronic disease affecting the kidneys, lungs, stomach, and intestines
- Hypogonadism
- Smoking, excessive alcohol use, low calcium intake, and inadequate physical exercise
- Older age (bone loss with increasing age)
- Heredity and race (with white men seeming to be at greatest risk)

The diagnosis and treatment of any underlying medical condition affecting bone health are essential to preserve bone health. Medications that cause bone loss should be identified, evaluated, and stopped, if possible. Unhealthy habits, such as smoking, excessive alcohol intake, and inactivity, should be changed and vitamin D and calcium supplementation begun. A regular regimen of weight-bearing exercises in which bone and muscles work against gravity should be encouraged. Weight lifting or using resistance machines can also be recommended because they appear to help preserve bone density. The U.S. Food and Drug Administration (FDA) has approved three antiresorptive medications (the bisphosphonates alendronate, risedronate, and zoledronate) and the anabolic agent teriparatide as treatment of male osteoporosis. Bisphosphonates are not recommended for use in patients with an estimated glomerular filtration rate less than 30 mL/min/1.73 m².

Calcitonin is currently FDA-approved for the treatment of osteoporosis in women (but not men) who are at least 5 years postmenopausal. It has been shown in clinical trials to decrease bone loss and decrease risk of vertebral fractures; however, it has not been shown to reduce nonvertebral or hip fractures. Alendronate would be a more effective agent in this patient.

When osteoporosis is due to hypogonadism, testosterone replacement therapy should be considered unless there are contraindications. However, this patient's testosterone level is already normal.

Teriparatide is a recombinant human parathyroid hormone and a potent anabolic bone agent. Teriparatide is

FDA-approved for treatment of postmenopausal osteoporosis in women at high risk of fracture and for treatment of hypogonadal or primary osteoporosis in men with high risk of fracture. Teriparatide is more expensive then bisphosphonates and requires subcutaneous injection. Treatment with teriparatide is limited to a maximum of 2 years (concerns related to risk of osteosarcoma) and is contraindicated in patients with a history of bone malignancy, Paget disease of bone, hypercalcemia, or history of skeletal irradiation. Given its cost, subcutaneous route of administration, long-term safety concerns, and the availability of other agents, teriparatide is generally not used as a first-line drug for treatment of osteoporosis.

KEY POINT

- The bisphosphonates alendronate, risedronate, and zoledronate and the anabolic agent teriparatide are approved by the U.S. Food and Drug Administration to treat male osteoporosis.

Bibliography

Ebeling PR. Clinical practice. Osteoporosis in men. N Engl J Med. 2008;358(14):1474-1482. [PMID: 18385499]

Item 89   Answer: D

Educational Objective: Manage diabetic ketoacidosis.

This patient should be started on an insulin drip. Discontinuation of insulin pump therapy resulted in inadequate insulin coverage; as a result, the patient developed diabetic ketoacidosis, as evidenced by the plasma glucose level of 262 mg/dL (14.5 mmol/L), positive urine ketones, and an anion gap. It is imperative to recognize that patients with insulin-deficient diabetes mellitus can develop ketoacidosis with only moderate glucose elevations. This patient should now be started on an insulin drip in a monitored setting. Intravenous insulin infusion is usually the preferred method of insulin delivery in an emergency because dehydration may be severe (which decreases subcutaneous absorption) and rapid titration of insulin may be required. Her plasma glucose level should be measured every 1 to 2 hours and adjustments made to the insulin infusion, as required, to gradually normalize her glucose level and reverse the ketoacidosis. After the metabolic abnormalities have been corrected and the patient is ready to be transferred to subcutaneous administration of insulin (usually when the patient starts eating), intravenous and subcutaneous insulin administration need to be overlapped to avoid rebound ketoacidosis. Short-acting or rapid-acting insulins should be given for 1 to 2 hours or intermediate or long-acting insulins for 2 to 3 hours before terminating the insulin infusion to ensure adequate overlap.

Insulin glargine and neutral protamine Hagedorn (NPH) insulin are long-acting preparations that do not provide the flexibility needed to aggressively treat diabetic ketoacidosis.

The use of sliding scale insulin will not allow for adequate insulin coverage, and the ketoacidosis can be expected to progress.

KEY POINT

- Ketoacidosis can develop in insulin-deficient patients with only moderate plasma glucose elevations; an insulin drip is the most effective treatment of diabetic ketoacidosis.

Bibliography

Kitabchi AE, Nyenwe EA. Hyperglycemic crises in diabetes mellitus: diabetic ketoacidosis and hyperglycemic hyperosmolar state. Endocrinol Metab Clin North Am. 2006;35(4):725-751. [PMID: 17127143]

Item 90   Answer: D

Educational Objective: Treat low testosterone levels in a patient with a prolactinoma.

This patient should have testosterone replacement therapy. Hyperprolactinemia suppresses gonadotropin-releasing hormone production directly, and correction of the hyperprolactinemia can often restore normal testosterone production. With massive prolactinomas, however, irreversible damage to the gonadal axis may occur. This patient has had tumor shrinkage and normalization of his prolactin level; however, his follicle-stimulating hormone and luteinizing hormone levels are undetectable, his testosterone level is very low, and his symptoms persist. Therefore, the most appropriate treatment to improve this patient's symptoms of fatigue and poor libido is testosterone replacement therapy.

The cabergoline should be continued during testosterone therapy to control tumor growth. Continuing or increasing the present dosage may lower his prolactin level even further but is unlikely to increase his testosterone level.

Given the effect of his symptoms on the patient's quality of life, retesting him in 1 year is not a viable option.

KEY POINT

- In men with massive prolactinomas, irreversible damage to the gonadal axis may occur that necessitates testosterone replacement therapy, despite normalization of the prolactin level.

Bibliography

Mascarell S, Sarne DH. Clinical presentation and response to therapy in patients with massive prolactin hypersecretion. Pituitary. 2007;10(1):95-101. [PMID: 17308959]

Item 91   Answer: B

Educational Objective: Manage a prolactinoma.

This patient with hyperprolactinemia should begin taking oral contraceptives. Because she is not desirous of pregnancy, there is no critical need to restore ovulation. However, she has been amenorrheic for 3 years, which implies hypoestrogenemia and an increased risk for osteoporosis. Oral contraceptives will supply needed estrogen and, at the same time, provide contraception. Studies have now shown that oral contraceptive use is safe in women with microadenomas, and there is minimal risk of tumor enlargement.

The dopamine agonist bromocriptine has been shown to restore ovulatory cycles in greater than 80% of women. Although this agent will address this patient's amenorrhea, she will still require contraception to avoid pregnancy. A dopamine agonist would be indicated if pregnancy were desired.

Stereotactic radiation therapy can lower prolactin levels to the normal range, but it may take several years to do so. This treatment also has the potential adverse effect of hypopituitarism. In patients with prolactinomas, radiation therapy is performed as a treatment of last resort if neither medical therapy nor surgery is effective because of its rather poor risk-to-benefit ratio.

Transsphenoidal surgery has a lower efficacy than dopamine agonists in treating prolactinomas and carries a considerably increased risk of morbidity. Therefore, such surgery is usually performed only if there is no response to a dopamine agonist.

If this patient is provided reassurance with no active treatment, she will remain estrogen deficient and will consequently develop progressive bone loss. However, the chance of tumor enlargement without active treatment is only approximately 7%.

> **KEY POINT**
>
> - **Estrogen replacement may be sufficient treatment in hypoestrogenemic women with prolactinomas who are not interested in fertility.**

Bibliography

Gillam MP, Molitch ME, Lombardi G, Colao A. Advances in the treatment of prolactinomas. Endocr Rev. 2006;27(5):485-534. [PMID: 16705142]

Item 92   Answer: B

Educational Objective: Manage postpartum thyroiditis.

Postpartum thyroiditis, which occurs in approximately 5% of women in the United States who have been pregnant within a few months of delivery, is a variant of painless thyroiditis. At presentation, patients may have transient thyrotoxicosis, transient hypothyroidism, or thyrotoxicosis that is followed by hypothyroidism and then by recovery. This patient most likely has postpartum thyroiditis that is now in the hypothyroid phase after a period of transient thyrotoxicosis. The hypothyroidism can be confirmed by remeasuring her thyroid-stimulating hormone (TSH) and free thyroxine (T_4) levels. Postpartum thyroiditis and Graves disease can occur and are more common in patients who tested positive for thyroid antibodies at baseline and in those with a history of previous postpartum thyroiditis. Graves disease can improve substantially during pregnancy only to rebound significantly after delivery. In this patient, the absence of a goiter and eye disease point away from Graves disease, as does the recent development of symptoms associated with hypothyroidism.

Methimazole therapy is inappropriate for this patient because she most likely has hypothyroidism, not hyperthyroidism. If transient hypothyroidism is confirmed by a high TSH level and low free T_4 level, thyroid hormone replacement, not methimazole, can be considered for bothersome symptoms.

With postpartum thyroiditis, results of thyroid scans and radioactive iodine uptake tests will be low during the thyrotoxic phase and then become elevated during the hypothyroid phase as the thyroid gland recovers and becomes very avid for iodine as stores are repleted. Before such testing can be advised, however, the results of current thyroid function tests are required to assess the patient's thyroid hormone status and determine if scan results suggest Graves disease or, what is more likely, recovering thyroiditis.

Ultrasounds of the thyroid gland can be used to distinguish the high vascular flow of Graves disease from the low-flow pattern of autoimmune thyroiditis. A more direct test of this patient's thyroid function, however, is measurement of the TSH and free T_4 levels, which can quantify thyroid function and provide a baseline with which to compare future thyroid function test results.

> **KEY POINT**
>
> - **Postpartum thyroiditis can cause postpartum thyrotoxicosis, hypothyroidism, or a period of both.**

Bibliography

Stagnaro-Green A. Postpartum thyroiditis. Best Pract Res Clin Endocrinol Metab. 2004;18(2):303-316. [PMID: 15157842]

Item 93   Answer: D

Educational Objective: Treat fasting hyperglycemia in type 1 diabetes mellitus.

This patient should take his evening dose of neutral protamine Hagedorn (NPH) insulin at bedtime rather than at supper to counter his morning hyperglycemia, which may be a manifestation of the "dawn phenomenon." The dawn phenomenon is defined as an increase in blood glucose levels during the early morning hours (4 AM-8 AM) and is thought to be related to increased levels of growth hormone and other insulin counterregulatory hormones at this time. The dawn phenomenon is seen more often in teenage patients with type 1 diabetes than in adult patients with type 2 diabetes. Although variable, bedtime NPH insulin peaks about the right time (4-10 hours after use) to cover dawn hormone surges and will likely be more effective than the same dose given at supper time. Continuous subcutaneous insulin infusion is another option to precisely match the insulin needs of the dawn phenomenon.

Increasing the dosages of suppertime insulins or adding bedtime regular insulin when the patient's bedtime blood glucose measurement is nearly normal could cause nocturnal hypoglycemia and would not be the best way to manage his morning hyperglycemia.

KEY POINT

- Elevated fasting glucose levels often occur because of the dawn phenomenon, which is primarily due to growth hormone–induced hyperglycemia.

Bibliography

Fanelli CG, Pampanelli S, Porcellati F, Rossetti P, Brunetti P, Bolli GB. Administration of neutral protamine Hagedorn insulin at bedtime versus with dinner in type 1 diabetes mellitus to avoid nocturnal hypoglycemia and improve control. A randomized, controlled trial. Ann Intern Med. 2002;136(7):504-514. [PMID: 11926785]

Item 94   Answer: C

Educational Objective: Treat postmenopausal osteoporosis.

This patient should stop taking alendronate and instead receive intravenous zoledronate. Bisphosphonates are first-line drugs for treating postmenopausal women with osteoporosis. Alendronate and risedronate reduce the risk of both vertebral and nonvertebral fractures. Some patients with osteoporosis may be intolerant of oral bisphosphonates because of aggravation of underlying gastroesophageal reflux disease. For these patients, once yearly intravenous infusion of zoledronate is a potent and effective alternative. An injectable bisphosphonate, such as zoledronate, should also be considered when oral bisphosphonates are unsuccessful, contraindicated (as in esophageal stricture or achalasia), or likely to be poorly absorbed (as in uncontrolled celiac disease and inflammatory bowel disease) and when a patient is unable to remain upright for 30 to 60 minutes after dosing.

Approval by the U.S. Food and Drug Administration of intravenous zoledronate was based on the results of a study that documented a 7.6% absolute reduction in new vertebral fractures over 3 years compared with placebo (number needed to treat [NNT] = 13). Zoledronate also resulted in a 1.1% absolute reduction in the risk of hip fractures over a median duration of 3 years (NNT = 90).

Calcitonin is not a first-line drug for postmenopausal osteoporosis treatment. Its efficacy against fractures is not strong, and its effects on bone mineral density are less than those of other agents.

Whereas oral ibandronate is associated with a reduction in vertebral fracture rates, neither oral nor intravenous ibandronate is associated with a reduction in hip fracture rate. Therefore, ibandronate would not be the best choice in this patient with reduced bone density in the hip.

Although raloxifene, a selective estrogen receptor modulator, can prevent bone loss and reduces the risk of vertebral fractures, its effectiveness in reducing other fractures is uncertain. Extraskeletal risks (including risk of thromboembolism and fatal stroke) and benefits must be considered before starting postmenopausal women on raloxifene therapy. For this patient, the safer alternative of intravenous zoledronate is available and is recommended as first-line therapy.

KEY POINT

- Once yearly intravenous infusion of zoledronate is a potent therapy for treating postmenopausal osteoporosis.

Bibliography

Black DM, Delmas PD, Eastell R, et al; HORIZON Pivotal Fracture Trial. Once-yearly zoledronic acid for treatment of postmenopausal osteoporosis. N Engl J Med. 2007;356(18):1809-1822. [PMID: 17476007]

Item 95   Answer: B

Educational Objective: Manage pituitary tumor apoplexy.

This patient should urgently receive hydrocortisone for what appears to be pituitary tumor apoplexy. An underlying nonfunctioning adenoma was diagnosed 2 years ago. Given this patient's relatively low blood pressure and rapid pulse, adrenocorticotropic hormone deficiency is a distinct possibility. Therefore, she should be given a stress dose of hydrocortisone in the range of 50 mg every 8 hours. In acute hypopituitarism, such as occurs with pituitary apoplexy, it is necessary to administer parenteral stress doses of corticosteroids as soon as the diagnosis is suspected.

Bromocriptine can rapidly shrink a prolactinoma and thus can be useful for this purpose. The likelihood of its shrinking a nonfunctioning adenoma, however, is quite low and does not address the immediate, life-threatening issue of adrenal insufficiency in this patient.

An MRI can detect hemorrhage into pituitary tumors. However, this study should be performed only after patients have received hydrocortisone.

Although this patient may well benefit from transsphenoidal surgical decompression, such surgery is appropriate only after hydrocortisone therapy and a confirmation of the diagnosis with an MRI.

KEY POINT

- In acute hypopituitarism, such as occurs with pituitary apoplexy, it is important to give parenteral stress doses of corticosteroids as soon as the diagnosis is suspected.

Bibliography

Nielsen EH, Lindholm J, Bjerre P, et al. Frequent occurrence of pituitary apoplexy in patients with non-functioning pituitary adenoma. Clin Endocrinol (Oxf). 2006;64(3):319-322. [PMID: 16487443]

Item 96   Answer: C
Educational Objective: Evaluate hypogonadism.

This patient should have an MRI of the pituitary gland. He has acquired hypogonadotropic hypogonadism, as evidenced by his low testosterone level and low follicle-stimulating hormone (FSH) and luteinizing hormone (LH) levels. Although normal ranges are somewhat assay-dependent, testosterone levels less than 200 ng/dL (6.9 nmol/L) are considered deficient, and values consistently greater than 350 ng/dL (12.1 nmol/L) are considered normal. In a young man with hypogonadotropic hypogonadism, pituitary tumors must be excluded as a cause. Very low FSH and LH levels (<0.5 mU/mL [0.5 U/L]) strongly suggest a pituitary tumor, particularly if they are associated with a high prolactin level. Low levels of gonadotropins with a normal prolactin level are consistent with infiltration from hemochromatosis, exogenous androgen or estrogen administration, critical illness, or suppression by narcotics or corticosteroids (or a combination of these). Although this patient's prolactin level is only mildly elevated, he also has low levels of insulin-like growth factor 1, thyroid-stimulating hormone, and free thyroxine (T_4). These multiple pituitary deficits require imaging to rule out a pituitary tumor.

Until a pituitary tumor is confirmed or excluded as the cause of his symptoms, treating his mild prolactinemia with cabergoline, or his mild hypothyroidism with levothyroxine, or his testosterone deficit with testosterone replacement therapy is premature.

Testicular ultrasonography is used to evaluate a testicular mass, not to determine the cause of impaired testosterone production.

KEY POINT
- In patients with hypogonadism, very low levels of follicle-stimulating hormone and luteinizing hormone strongly suggest a pituitary tumor, particularly if associated with an elevated prolactin level.

Bibliography

Kazi M, Geraci SA, Koch CA. Considerations for the diagnosis and treatment of testosterone deficiency in elderly men. Am J Med. 2007;120(10):835-840. [PMID: 17904450]

Item 97   Answer: C
Educational Objective: Treat hyperaldosteronism.

Spironolactone therapy should be initiated in this patient. He has biochemical findings suggestive of primary hyperaldosteronism. The initial clue to the diagnosis is the unprovoked hypokalemia and urine potassium renal losses. The results of laboratory studies show an elevated serum aldosterone level and suppressed plasma renin activity, which are suggestive of hyperaldosteronism. The diagnosis is usually confirmed by using a salt load to find out if aldosterone secretion is nonsuppressible and therefore autonomous. After primary hyperaldosteronism is biochemically confirmed, the cause should be defined. CT of the adrenal glands is an excellent way to localize an adrenal adenoma. This patient's CT scan does not show an aldosterone-secreting adrenal adenoma but rather suggests bilateral adrenal hyperplasia. The treatment of choice in such instances is an aldosterone receptor–blocking agent, such as the nonselective agent spironolactone or the more selective agent eplerenone. Besides blocking aldosterone receptors, spironolactone usually lowers blood pressure and keeps it down. The combination of spironolactone with a thiazide diuretic may provide even better control and allow for smaller doses of spironolactone. If additional antihypertensive therapy is needed, calcium-channel blockers or angiotensin-converting enzyme inhibitors may be used.

Bilateral adrenalectomy is unnecessary and inappropriate in this patient with bilateral adrenal enlargement. Such treatment would make him dependent on permanent glucocorticoid and perhaps mineralocorticoid replacement therapy.

Beginning lisinopril therapy is unlikely to control the patient's hypertension or address his primary hyperaldosteronism as well as an aldosterone blocker will.

Triamterene is a commonly used potassium-sparing diuretic that does not block the effects of aldosterone on the kidney. Using it will not be sufficient in this patient with hyperaldosteronism.

KEY POINT
- Primary hyperaldosteronism caused by bilateral adrenal hyperplasia is best treated medically with a nonselective (spironolactone) or more selective (eplerenone) aldosterone-blocking agent.

Bibliography

Young WF Jr. Adrenal causes of hypertension: pheochromocytoma and primary aldosteronism. Rev Endocr Metab Disord. 2007;8(4):309-320. [PMID: 17914676]

Item 98   Answer: D
Educational Objective: Evaluate suspected benign familial hypocalciuric hypercalcemia.

The most appropriate next diagnostic test for this patient is determination of the urine calcium to creatinine clearance ratio. In this asymptomatic patient with mild hypercalcemia and an inappropriately normal parathyroid hormone (PTH) level, which implicates a PTH-dependent cause, the differential diagnosis includes primary hyperparathyroidism and benign familial hypocalciuric hypercalcemia. Benign familial hypocalciuric hypercalcemia is a rare autosomal dominant disorder characterized by lifelong mild asymptomatic hypercalcemia. This disorder, which is caused by an inactivating mutation of the calcium-sensing receptor, must be distinguished from primary hyperparathyroidism to determine the need for parathyroid surgery. Parathyroidectomy is neither necessary nor effective in patients with benign familial hypocalciuric hypercalcemia because the condition is not associated with any sequelae of primary hyperparathyroidism. First-degree relatives of patients with this condition often have hypercalcemia, and 50% of them will carry the genetic trait for the disorder.

The syndrome is diagnosed by a urine calcium to creatinine clearance ratio of less than 0.01, measured in a fasting morning spot urine collection. The formula for determining the calcium to creatinine clearance ratio is (urine calcium × serum creatinine)/(serum calcium × urine creatinine).

Measuring vitamin D metabolites would be helpful only if the PTH level were suppressed, which would suggest a non–PTH-mediated cause of hypercalcemia. This patient's PTH level is in the normal range. The 25-hydroxy vitamin D level is elevated in states of vitamin D intoxication, and the 1,25-dihydroxy vitamin D level is increased in sarcoidosis, granulomatous disease, and lymphoma.

Similarly, obtaining a PTH-related protein (PTHrP) level is unnecessary in this patient. The PTHrP level is elevated in states of humoral hypercalcemia of malignancy. The elevated serum calcium level resulting from the effect of PTHrP on bone suppresses PTH production from the parathyroid gland; the PTH level would be undetectable. Finally, most patients with humoral hypercalcemia of malignancy have an obvious malignancy, and measurement of PTHrP is usually not necessary to establish the diagnosis.

KEY POINT

- Benign familial hypocalciuric hypercalcemia is a rare autosomal dominant disorder that is diagnosed by a urine calcium to creatinine clearance ratio of less than 0.01.

Bibliography

Raue F, Haag C, Schulze E, Frank-Raue K. The role of the extracellular calcium-sensing receptor in health and disease. Exp Clin Endocrinol Diabetes. 2006;114(8):397-405. [PMID: 17039419]

Item 99   Answer: C

Educational Objective: **Diagnose exogenous use of thyroid hormone medication.**

The best next step is to measure the patient's serum thyroglobulin level. Given her access to thyroid hormone products at work and her prominent weight loss concerns, she is most likely surreptitiously taking thyroid hormone. Usually, differentiating surreptitious thyroid ingestion and thyroiditis from Graves disease is straightforward. In all three, the thyroid-stimulating hormone level will be low, and the free thyroxine (T_4) and free triiodothyronine (T_3) levels will be elevated (although not when pure T_3 is the hormone taken exogenously). Although a low radioactive iodine uptake is typical of both thyroiditis and exogenous thyroid hormone use, Graves disease is associated with a

high radioactive iodine uptake. Thus, this patient does not have Graves disease.

Given that thyroiditis is an inflammatory state, the erythrocyte sedimentation rate (ESR) level should be elevated and the serum thyroglobulin (TG) level high because of the excess thyroid release by damaged thyroid follicles in patients with this condition. TG levels are similarly elevated in disorders such as Graves disease and toxic multinodular goiter. In contrast, the use of exogenous thyroid hormone is associated with a low or normal ESR, as this patient has. Finally, the use of exogenous thyroid hormone suppresses thyroid activity and lowers TG levels. Therefore, confirmation of a low TG level in this patient combined with the already documented normal-range ESR would effectively rule out thyroiditis and make exogenous thyroid hormone exposure most likely.

Prednisone is an appropriate treatment in patients with thyroiditis and methimazole in those with Graves disease, but neither has a role in treating patients with thyrotoxicosis from exogenous use of thyroid hormone.

KEY POINT

- A low radioactive iodine uptake in a patient with symptoms of thyrotoxicosis suggests thyroiditis or exogenous thyroid hormone exposure; the erythrocyte sedimentation rate and thyroglobulin level are low in patients taking exogenous thyroid hormone and elevated in those with thyroiditis.

Bibliography

Intenzo CM, dePapp AE, Jabbour S, Miller JL, Kim SM, Capuzzi DM. Scintigraphic manifestations of thyrotoxicosis. Radiographics. 2003;23(4):857-869. [PMID: 12853661]

Item 100   Answer: C

Educational Objective: **Treat diabetic nephropathy.**

Substituting furosemide for the hydrochlorothiazide is the most appropriate next step in treatment. In a patient with progressive diabetic nephropathy, adequate blood pressure control is primary. A blood pressure less than 130/80 mm Hg is desirable; for patients excreting 0.5 to 1.0 g of protein per day, even lower levels are desirable. This patient needs additional antihypertensive treatment. With a serum creatinine level of 2.1 mg/dL (185.6 μmol/L), his estimated glomerular filtration rate (GFR) is 38 mL/min/ 1.73 m². At this low GFR, hydrochlorothiazide is relatively ineffective, and a loop diuretic, such as furosemide, is likely to be more effective in eliminating salt and water, reducing blood pressure, and increasing potassium excretion.

Dihydropyridine calcium channel blockers, such as nifedipine and amlodipine, do not have significant effect on protein excretion despite effective blood pressure reduction, can lead to additional fluid retention, and would not address the patient's hyperkalemia.

A β-blocker, such as metoprolol, will lower his blood pressure but has limited effect on protein excretion. β-Blockers can cause hyperglycemia and raise the serum potassium level as much as 0.5 meq/L (0.5 mmol/L). Because this patient already has hyperkalemia, the addition of a drug that may further increase potassium is not indicated.

Drugs that act to block the renin-angiotensin-aldosterone system, such as angiotensin-conveting enzyme (ACE) inhibitors and angiotensin receptor blockers (ARBs), may have additional renoprotective benefits besides the lowering of blood pressure. ARBs, such as irbesartan, have been shown to decrease the progression of nephropathy in patients with type 2 diabetes mellitus. However, such a benefit has not been shown in patients with type 1 diabetes mellitus, so nothing is likely to be achieved by switching from an ACE inhibitor to an ARB in this patient.

KEY POINT

- Thiazide diuretics are less effective than loop diuretics in patients with significantly impaired glomerular filtration rates.

Bibliography

Gross JL, de Azevedo MJ, Silveiro SP, Canani LH, Caramori ML, Zelmanovitz T. Diabetic nephropathy: diagnosis, prevention, and treatment. Diabetes Care. 2005;28(1):164-176. [PMID: 15616252]

Item 101   Answer: C

Educational Objective: Evaluate suspected pheochromocytoma with no adrenal masses on imaging studies.

The most appropriate next test for this patient is a metaiodobenzylguanidine (MIBG) scan. She has the classic symptoms of pheochromocytoma—palpitations, sweating, headaches, and hypertension. Additionally, biochemical testing revealed increased plasma levels of catecholamines and urinary excretion of their byproducts (metanephrine, normetanephrine, and vanillylmandelic acid). Most pheochromocytomas are located in the adrenal medulla, and some are extra-adrenal in origin. CT has sensitivities of 93% to 100% in detecting adrenal pheochromocytoma, and approximately 90% in detecting extra-adrenal catecholamine-secreting paragangliomas. MRI is as sensitive as CT in detecting adrenal pheochromocytomas and superior to CT in detecting extra-adrenal catecholamine-secreting paragangliomas. With the CT scan of the adrenal glands showing no masses, the next best localizing study would be an MIBG scan. MIBG scintigraphy is highly specific (99%) but less sensitive (80%) than CT techniques. MIBG scintigraphy is generally reserved for patients with equivocal CT results, extra-adrenal catecholamine-secreting tumors, or suspected malignancy.

An adrenalectomy is appropriate only when a tumor is confirmed. An adrenalectomy would not be indicated if the source of the catecholamines were confirmed to be extra-adrenal.

Adrenal vein sampling is a technically difficult and hazardous procedure, especially in a patient with a pheochromocytoma. The availability of the highly specific and sensitive MIBG scan should take precedence over this more hazardous procedure.

An MRI scan from the base of the skull to the pelvis might be indicated if an adrenal source of catecholamine production were excluded. MRI of the skull base to the pelvis would then be useful to detect extra-adrenal catecholamine-secreting paragangliomas

KEY POINT

- Scintigraphic localization of a pheochromocytoma with a metaiodobenzylguanidine (MIBG) scan is appropriate when a CT scan or an MRI is negative or equivocal for a pheochromocytoma.

Bibliography

Lenders JW, Eisenhofer G, Mannelli M, Pacak K. Phaeochromocytoma. Lancet. 2005;366(9486):665-675. [PMID: 16112304]

Item 102   Answer: E

Educational Objective: Diagnose glycemic status, distinguishing between diabetes and prediabetes.

This patient's current glycemic status is noncategorizable on the basis of the information provided.

The diagnosis of diabetes mellitus can be established by a fasting plasma glucose level of at least 126 mg/dL (7.0 mmol/L), a random plasma glucose level of at least 200 mg/dL (11.1 mmol/L), or a 2-hour oral glucose tolerance test (OGTT) result of at least 200 mg/dL (11.1 mmol/L). A recent expert committee statement recommended that the hemoglobin A_{1c} test be used to diagnose diabetes, but major professional organizations have not yet endorsed this recommendation. Impaired fasting glucose, impaired glucose tolerance, or both mark the transition from normal glucose tolerance to type 2 diabetes mellitus. Impaired fasting glucose is diagnosed when the fasting plasma glucose level is in the range of 100 to 125 mg/dL (5.6 to 6.9 mmol/L), and impaired glucose tolerance—an analogous prediabetic state—is diagnosed when the plasma glucose level at the 2-hour mark of an OGTT is 140 to 199 mg/dL (7.8 to 11.0 mmol/L).

This patient, whose random plasma glucose level is 158 mg/dL (8.8 mmol/L), has not met any of the established criteria for diabetes or prediabetes. He requires either measurement of his fasting plasma glucose level or an OGTT to determine his status.

For a diagnosis of the metabolic syndrome to be made, information about the patient's blood pressure, lipid levels, fasting plasma glucose level, and waist circumference is necessary. Insufficient data have been provided for this diagnosis.

- Type 2 diabetes mellitus is diagnosed when the fasting plasma glucose level is 126 mg/dL (7.0 mmol/L) or greater, the random plasma glucose level is 200 mg/dL (11.1 mmol/L) or greater, or the plasma glucose level is 200 mg/dL (11.1 mmol/L) or greater after a 2-hour oral glucose tolerance test (OGTT); impaired fasting glucose denotes a fasting plasma glucose level of 100 to 125 mg/dL (5.6 to 6.9 mmol/L), and impaired glucose tolerance denotes a plasma glucose level of 140 to 199 mg/dL (7.8 to 11.0 mmol/L) at the 2-hour mark of an OGTT.

Bibliography

American Diabetes Association. Diagnosis and classification of diabetes mellitus. Diabetes Care. 2008;31 Suppl 1:S55-S60. [PMID: 18165338]

Item 103   Answer: B

Educational Objective: Initially evaluate secondary amenorrhea.

This patient's serum follicle-stimulating hormone (FSH) and prolactin levels should be measured. Secondary amenorrhea is defined by the absence of menses for 3 or more consecutive months in a woman who has menstruated previously. Menstrual failure can be complete amenorrhea or varying degrees of oligomenorrhea, the latter being much more common. Pregnancy should be excluded in all patients prior to other evaluations. Polycystic ovary syndrome is the most common cause of secondary amenorrhea, and hypogonadotropic hypogonadism is most commonly caused by hyperprolactinemia. In cancer survivors, ovarian failure can be traced to chemotherapy or radiation treatments. Turner syndrome mosaicism and autoimmune disorders should be considered in other patients.

Laboratory evaluation is first directed toward ovarian failure, hyperprolactinemia, and thyroid disease. Therefore, FSH, prolactin, thyroid-stimulating hormone, and free thyroxine (T_4) levels are generally measured. An FSH greater than 20 mU/mL (20 U/L) suggests ovarian failure. If the woman is younger than 30 years or has primary amenorrhea, obtaining a karyotype is often recommended, even if the stigmata of Turner syndrome are not present.

If serum FSH and prolactin levels are normal on laboratory studies, the next step in the evaluation is a progestin withdrawal challenge. If the progestin challenge does not result in withdrawal bleeding, then assessment of the pelvic anatomy with ultrasonography, hysterosalpingography, or MRI would be appropriate. A high serum prolactin level requires additional pituitary evaluation, including MRI. Obtaining an MRI before this patient's serum prolactin level has been determined, however, is premature.

This patient has no symptoms of hyperandrogenemia. Therefore, measurement of her total serum testosterone level is of little value.

- After pregnancy is excluded, the initial evaluation of secondary amenorrhea includes measurement of follicle-stimulating hormone, thyroid-stimulating hormone, and prolactin levels.

Bibliography

Practice Committee of the American Society for Reproductive Medicine. Current evaluation of amenorrhea. Fertil Steril. 2006;86(5 Suppl 1):S148-S155. [PMID: 17055812]

Item 104   Answer: C

Educational Objective: Manage levothyroxine dosing in a patient with thyroid cancer.

No changes should be made to this patient's medication regimen. Patients who undergo a total thyroidectomy for benign disease require thyroid hormone replacement therapy. A typical goal is to maintain a thyroid-stimulating hormone (TSH) level of 1 to 3 µU/mL (1 to 3 mU/L). For patients who had thyroid cancer, especially those with higher-risk thyroid cancer, additional thyroid hormone is required to suppress the TSH level. TSH suppression has shown benefit is reducing thyroid cancer recurrence. Typically, patients with low-risk stage I and II disease have a target TSH level in the low-normal to just-below-normal range (0.3 to 0.6 µU/mL [0.3 to 0.6 mU/L]). However, the TSH levels of most patients with higher-stage thyroid cancer should be even lower (or even unmeasurable). Because some patients cannot tolerate this purposely induced state of subclinical thyrotoxicosis, the TSH goal can be adjusted to more of a replacement level as symptoms require. This patient had stage II cancer and no evidence of disease at present. Therefore, his TSH level of 0.3 µU/mL (0.3 mU/L) is in an acceptable range, and no adjustments to his medical regimen are necessary at this time. However, his TSH level should be regularly checked.

Measuring the patient's triiodothyronine (T_3) level is unlikely to provide any useful information because the TSH level and a patient's current symptoms are the primary targets of levothyroxine dosing in patients with thyroid cancer who require TSH suppression.

- Thyroid-stimulating hormone suppression by levothyroxine is the standard of care in patients who have thyroid cancer, with the degree of suppression determined by the severity of disease.

Bibliography

Jonklaas J, Sarlis NJ, Litofsky D, et al. Outcomes of patients with differentiated thyroid carcinoma following initial therapy. Thyroid. 2006;16(12):1229-1242. [PMID: 17199433]

Item 105   Answer: A

Educational Objective: Evaluate suspected adrenal insufficiency.

This patient has clinical and biochemical features of primary adrenal insufficiency, and the diagnosis can be confirmed with a cosyntropin stimulation test. Patients with chronic adrenal failure frequently report anorexia, weight loss, fatigue, and vague abdominal discomfort. Physical examination and laboratory studies help differentiate primary from central causes of adrenal insufficiency. Uninhibited adrenocorticotropic hormone (ACTH)–stimulating nonfunctional adrenal glands cause the patient with primary adrenal failure to be darkly pigmented. In normal persons, the cortisol level is highest in the early morning serum, ranging from 5 to 25 µg/dL (138 to 690 nmol/L). The finding of a morning cortisol level that is less than 3 µg/dL (83 nmol/L) is diagnostic of adrenal insufficiency, and a value between 3 µg/dL and 10 µg/dL (83 and 276 nmol/L) is highly suggestive of the diagnosis. This patient's clinical picture and elevated ACTH level support the diagnosis of primary adrenal insufficiency. Whereas a high morning salivary cortisol level excludes adrenal insufficiency, a low value increases its probability. The diagnosis of adrenal insufficiency depends on showing that the adrenal glands cannot produce cortisol when stimulated by ACTH. Synthetic ACTH (cosyntropin) can be administered to determine whether the adrenal cortex is capable of raising serum cortisol levels to greater than 18 µg/dL (497 nmol/L).

An insulin-induced hypoglycemia test is used as the gold standard to investigate the integrity of the hypothalamic-pituitary-adrenal axis. The hypoglycemia stimulates ACTH secretion from the pituitary gland, which in turn stimulates the adrenal glands to secrete cortisol. Given its serious potential adverse effects, the insulin-induced hypoglycemia test should be performed only by experienced endocrinologists and should not be pursued as a routine diagnostic test in this patient.

Obtaining an early morning salivary cortisol level will not provide any additional information over that already gleaned from the morning serum cortisol level and so is unnecessary in this patient.

Measurement of the 24-hour urine free cortisol level is useful only when investigating the possibility of excessive glucocorticoid secretion and would not be helpful in diagnosing adrenal insufficiency because of the wide range of normal values.

KEY POINT

- **The diagnosis of primary adrenal insufficiency requires showing that the adrenal glands cannot produce cortisol when stimulated by adrenocorticotropic hormone.**

Bibliography
Oelkers W. Adrenal insufficiency. N Engl J Med. 1996;335(16):1206-1212. [PMID: 8815944]

Item 106   Answer: D

Educational Objective: Treat type 2 diabetes mellitus with oral antihyperglycemic monotherapy.

This patient has type 2 diabetes mellitus. Various oral and injectable agents are available for the initial management of type 2 diabetes, most of which reduce hyperglycemia to a similar degree. Because of its low cost, effectiveness, good tolerability, relative safety, favorable effects on body weight, and absence of hypoglycemia as a side effect, metformin remains the best first-line agent available. In the American Diabetes Association and the European Association for the Study of Diabetes consensus statement for the pharmacologic treatment of type 2 diabetes, initial therapy with diet, exercise, and metformin was advised, barring any contraindications, such as renal insufficiency (serum creatinine level >1.4 mg/dL [123.8 µmol/L] for women and >1.5 mg/dL [132.6 µmol/L] for men). For this patient, ongoing attempts at lifestyle change are unlikely to reduce her blood glucose level further. Therefore, initiation of metformin therapy is most likely to improve her glycemic control.

Exenatide, an injectable agent, is only approved for use in combination regimens with oral agents and is inappropriate in most circumstances as monotherapy.

Glimepiride could be used but is associated with weight gain and the risk of hypoglycemia. Overall, it remains a less attractive choice than metformin in most patients, including this one.

Pioglitazone is also available for monotherapy, but its side effects of weight gain, edema, increased peripheral bone fracture rates in women, and high cost make it less attractive than metformin as a first-line therapy.

KEY POINT

- **Metformin is recommended as the initial pharmacologic therapy for most patients with type 2 diabetes mellitus.**

Bibliography
Nathan DM, Buse JB, Davidson MB, et al. Medical management of hyperglycemia in type 2 diabetes: a consensus algorithm for the initiation and adjustment of therapy: a consensus statement of the American Diabetes Association and the European Association for the Study of Diabetes. Diabetes Care. 2009;32(1):193-203. [PMID: 18945920]

Item 107   Answer: B

Educational Objective: Manage thyroid storm.

This patient should receive propranolol, propylthiouracil, and hydrocortisone. She has pneumonia complicated by thyroid storm, a life-threatening condition. Common precipitants of thyroid storm include iatrogenic causes, such as therapy with radioactive iodine, abrupt cessation of antithyroidal drugs, acute nonthyroidal illnesses, and thyroid or nonthyroidal surgery in a patient with unrecognized or inadequately treated thyrotoxicosis. A point scale has been derived to facilitate the early diagnosis of thyroid storm. Patients with greater than 45 points are likely to have thyroid storm. This patient has a score of 55 points (temperature of 39.4 °C [102.9 °F], 15 points; pulse rate of 138/min, 20 points; gastrointestinal-hepatic dysfunction, 10 points; and a precipitant cause [pneumonia], 10 points). Thyroid storm is a clinical diagnosis; there is no cutoff range of free thyroxine (T_4) or free triiodothyronine (T_3) levels that supports the diagnosis. Patients in thyroid storm require hospital admission to an intensive care unit. Appropriate therapy includes a combination of β-blockers, antithyroidal medications, saturated sodium potassium iodide plus hydrocortisone therapy, cooling of body temperature, and treatment of any underlying precipitant. Propranolol and propylthiouracil have the added benefit over atenolol and methimazole of reducing T_4 to T_3 conversion. Usually, high dosages of propranolol (240-480 mg/d) and propylthiouracil (>450 mg/d) are required to take advantage of that benefit and to adequately treat thyroid storm.

Radioactive iodine ablation can acutely exacerbate the thyrotoxic state by releasing preformed thyroid hormone from injured thyrocytes and takes many weeks (or even months) to bring about hypothyroidism. Therefore, this therapy is not appropriate for patients in thyroid storm.

Thyroid storm is a life-threatening condition, and therapy should not be delayed to perform a thyroid scan or radioactive iodine uptake test, which would only confirm the previously established diagnosis of Graves disease.

KEY POINT

- **Thyroid storm, a life-threatening condition that is diagnosed clinically, should be treated immediately with propranolol, propylthiouracil, and saturated sodium potassium iodide plus hydrocortisone; treatment of any identified precipitating cause is also essential.**

Bibliography

Nayak B, Burman K. Thyrotoxicosis and thyroid storm. Endocrinol Metab Clin North Am. 2006;35(4):663-686. [PMID: 17127140]

Item 108   Answer: A

Educational Objective: Evaluate a patient with head trauma for hypopituitarism.

This patient should have a morning (8 AM) measurement of his serum cortisol level. Studies have shown a frequency of hypopituitarism in up to 35% to 50% of patients after a motor vehicle accident or subarachnoid hemorrhage.

The most important hormonal axis to test is the hypothalamic-pituitary-adrenal axis, and an 8 AM serum cortisol measurement is the best first test to determine deficiency of this axis. An intact hypothalamic-pituitary-adrenal axis is necessary for normal health and well being, and the ability of the axis to respond appropriately to stress is critical for survival. If the basal cortisol level is equivocal (that is, between 6 and 18 μg/dL [166 and 497 nmol/L]), then

testing with metyrapone or low-dose (1 μg) cosyntropin stimulation may prove valuable. Assessment of the other pituitary axes should eventually be carried out in this patient, but the results of these tests are not as potentially lifesaving as (and thus are less critical than) the results of an early morning measurement of the serum cortisol level.

Growth hormone would be the last hormone assessed once all other deficits have been tested for and corrected. If there are three or more pituitary hormonal axes found to be deficient, a low insulin-like growth factor I level would establish a diagnosis of growth hormone deficiency.

The diagnosis of secondary hypogonadism is established if a patient's testosterone concentration and sperm count are low and serum luteinizing hormone and follicle stimulating hormone levels are inappropriately normal or low.

Because the damage is at the hypothalamic-pituitary level, measurement of the serum thyroid-stimulating hormone level is not appropriate. A serum free thyroxine (T_4) level will indicate thyroid hormone status more accurately.

KEY POINT

- **Hypopituitarism is common after head trauma, and the hypothalamic-pituitary-adrenal axis is the most critical hormonal axis to test when evaluating a patient for this condition.**

Bibliography

Schneider HJ, Kreitschmann-Andermahr I, Ghigo E, Stalla GK, Agha A. Hypothalamopituitary dysfunction following traumatic brain injury and aneurysmal subarachnoid hemorrhage: a systematic review. JAMA. 2007;298(12):1429-1438. [PMID: 17895459]

Item 109   Answer: A

Educational Objective: Manage the effect of lithium treatment on thyroid function.

This patient should receive treatment with levothyroxine. Lithium use has been associated with both hypothyroidism and hyperthyroidism, although the former appears more common. He also has a strong family history of autoimmune thyroid disease and tests positive for anti–thyroid peroxidase (TPO) antibodies. Patients with anti-TPO antibodies have a generally increased risk of developing hypothyroidism, especially those on lithium therapy. Because he appears to have underlying hypothyroidism caused by Hashimoto disease, treatment with levothyroxine is the appropriate next step.

There is no indication to consider any other therapy besides levothyroxine. Patients treated with liothyronine (triiodothyronine [T_3]-containing preparations) have wide fluctuations in serum T_3 levels because of liothyronine's rapid gastrointestinal absorption and its relatively short half-life.

Measurement of serum anti–thyroid peroxidase or anti–thyroglobulin antibodies identifies chronic lymphocytic thyroiditis (Hashimoto disease) as the cause of hypothyroidism. However, approximately 5% of patients with Hashimoto disease are seronegative for antithyroid antibodies. In mild thyroid failure, the presence of antithyroid antibodies strongly predicts progression to overt hypothyroidism. However, the best predictor of progression is the magnitude of the elevation in thyroid-stimulating hormone (TSH) level. Because this patient's TSH level is elevated and free thyroxine (T_4) level is low, the serum antibody tests offer no additional information that will assist in management.

Because the patient's bipolar disorder has been well controlled on his present regimen, the lithium should not be discontinued.

No data suggest that increasing iodine intake reverses the progression of hypothyroidism secondary to Hashimoto disease or lithium therapy. Therefore, supplementing the patient's intake of iodine will not be helpful and may even worsen the hypothyroidism.

KEY POINT

- **Patients who develop hypothyroidism while on lithium therapy may require levothyroxine therapy.**

Bibliography

Lazarus JH. The effects of lithium therapy on thyroid and thyrotropin-releasing hormone. Thyroid. 1998;8(10):909-913. [PMID: 9827658]

Item 110   Answer: D

Educational Objective: Treat male osteoporosis secondary to hypogonadism.

This patient had a clinically nonfunctioning pituitary adenoma with secondary hypogonadism and osteoporosis. He should be treated with testosterone replacement therapy. Hypogonadism is a prevalent secondary cause of male osteoporosis. Hypogonadism increases the skeletal sensitivity to parathyroid hormone and decreases intestinal calcium absorption. Because testosterone is aromatized to estradiol, it can be regarded as a prohormone for estradiol in the bone. Low bone mass in men with hypogonadism can be improved with androgen replacement, and bisphosphonates are effective in men regardless of their gonadal status. Anabolic therapy with teriparatide can likewise increase bone mineral density. Supplementation with calcium and vitamin D is also advisable.

Bromocriptine is useful for therapy of prolactinomas but has little utility for treatment of clinically nonfunctioning pituitary adenomas and will not treat this patient's osteoporosis.

Calcitonin can increase bone mass and is associated with a reduction in vertebral but not nonvertebral fracture rate. It is not as effective as bisphosphonate therapy and will not treat this patient's extraskeletal hypogonadal symptoms. Furthermore, calcitonin is not approved by the

U.S. Food and Drug Administration as therapy of male osteoporosis.

Subclinical thyrotoxicosis can accelerate osteoclastic resorption of bone. Because this patient's free thyroxine (T_4) level falls in the normal range, there is no need to decrease the levothyroxine dosage.

KEY POINT

- **Hypogonadism is a prevalent secondary cause of male osteoporosis.**

Bibliography

Adler RA. Epidemiology and pathophysiology of osteoporosis in men. Curr Osteoporos Rep. 2006;4(3):110-115. [PMID: 16908000]

Item 111   Answer: B

Educational Objective: Manage subclinical Cushing syndrome.

This patient should undergo a left adrenalectomy. Subclinical Cushing syndrome, defined as mild hypercortisolism with either no or minor manifestations of Cushing syndrome, is the most frequent finding associated with an adrenal incidentaloma. In this patient, the only clinically significant symptoms on presentation were weight gain and hypertension, and the screening tests performed for this incidentally discovered adrenal mass showed features consistent with non-adrenocorticotropic hormone (ACTH)–dependent Cushing syndrome, which indicates an adrenal origin. Although her hypercortisolism is mild, it is associated with poor suppressibility with dexamethasone, which is consistent with Cushing syndrome. Therefore, the incidentally discovered adrenal mass is functional and should be surgically removed.

With CT evidence of a dominant tumor on one of the adrenal glands and a small-sized adrenal gland on the other side, there is no need for an adrenal vein catheterization or MRI. Adrenal vein catheterization can be helpful in patients with ACTH-independent hypercortisolism and bilateral adrenal nodules.

Repeating the biochemical tests in 6 months is unnecessary because the diagnosis is already firmly established. Despite the fact that the patient has minimal symptoms, removal of the functioning adenoma now will result in less patient morbidity compared with waiting 6 months.

KEY POINT

- **Surgical adrenalectomy is the treatment of choice for functional adrenal tumors, regardless of size.**

Bibliography

Findling JW, Raff H. Cushing's syndrome: important issues in diagnosis and management. J Clin Endocrinol Metab. 2006;91(10): 3746-3753. [PMID: 16868050]

Item 112   Answer: D
Educational Objective: Treat hypopituitarism.

This patient should be treated with hydrocortisone. She has clear evidence of panhypopituitarism on her baseline testing, and no further stimulation tests are necessary. Postpartum hemorrhage can cause pituitary infarction and subsequent hypopituitarism, also known as Sheehan syndrome. Sheehan syndrome commonly presents with amenorrhea, a postpartum inability to lactate, and fatigue due to central hypothyroidism or secondary adrenal insufficiency.

Hydrocortisone must always be administered first because it is potentially life-saving. If thyroid hormone is begun before hydrocortisone, it would metabolize cortisol more rapidly, and the patient could have a hypoadrenal crisis.

Although estrogen and progesterone should be given to prevent osteoporosis and improve clinical well-being, they certainly should not be the first hormones replaced. In theory, the estrogen could increase cortisol-binding globulin, which would bind cortisol and decrease free cortisol levels; a worsening of adrenal insufficiency could potentially result if cortisol production is limited.

Hyponatremia can result from both hypothyroidism and hypoadrenalism with an inability to clear free water. Correction of the hypoadrenalism and hypothyroidism should be attempted first to see if the hyponatremia resolves before water restriction is tried. This patient's degree of hyponatremia is minimal and does not demand immediate treatment.

Growth hormone (GH) is by far the most "optional" hormone to be replaced and would only be started after other hormones are replaced. Improved muscle mass, bone density, and quality of life have been shown in several studies of adult GH deficiency treated with replacement therapy. Patients must be carefully selected in order to identify those patients most likely to benefit. GH is given parenterally and is very expensive ($10,000 to $20,000 per year). This hormone should be used in conjunction with an experienced endocrinologist.

This patient's free thyroxine level is low, so administration of levothyroxine is certainly appropriate, but this hormone should be started only after hydrocortisone is given.

KEY POINT
- **In patients with panhypopituitarism, cortisol should be replaced before other hormones.**

Bibliography
Toogood AA, Stewart PM. Hypopituitarism: clinical features, diagnosis, and management. Endocrinol Metab Clin North Am. 2008;37(1):235-261. [PMID: 18226739]

Item 113   Answer: C
Educational Objective: Diagnose the cause of hypogonadism in a patient with Cushing syndrome.

This patient has hypogonadism most likely caused by his prednisone therapy. Suppression of gonadal function is a common feature of endogenous and exogenous Cushing syndrome. The patient has been treated with prednisone. As a result, he developed clinical features of Cushing syndrome. At the same time, chronic prednisone therapy has resulted in suppression of the hypothalamic-pituitary-adrenal axis, as evidenced by his decreased serum adrenocorticotropic hormone, serum cortisol, and plasma dehydroepiandrosterone sulfate levels. Excess corticosteroids suppress the gonadal axis by inhibiting the release of gonadotropin-releasing hormone and subsequently the secretion of follicle-stimulating hormone (FSH) and luteinizing hormone (LH). This process results clinically in symptomatic hypogonadism (loss of libido and erectile dysfunction).

The low serum gonadotropin (FSH and LH) levels argue against primary gonadal dysfunction, which would be expected with Klinefelter syndrome and primary testicular failure. The testicular examination finding of soft, normal-sized testes also is inconsistent with Klinefelter syndrome, in which patients typically have small, firm testes.

The absence of other pituitary hormone deficits in this patient makes a pituitary microadenoma unlikely. The presence of a normal serum prolactin level argues against a prolactin-secreting pituitary microadenoma, and it is unlikely that a pituitary microadenoma not secreting prolactin would cause hypogonadism.

KEY POINT
- **Suppression of gonadal function is a common feature of endogenous and exogenous Cushing syndrome.**

Bibliography
Newell-Price J, Bertagna X, Grossman AB, Nieman LK. Cushing's syndrome. Lancet. 2006; 367(9522):1605-1617. [PMID: 16698415]

Item 114   Answer: D
Educational Objective: Evaluate suspected hypogonadism.

This patient's free testosterone level should be measured. His presenting symptoms are suggestive of hypogonadism. His initial screening testosterone level measurement is indeterminate, and a more reliable method of measuring testosterone, such as measurement of the free testosterone level, measurement of the bioavailable testosterone level, or measurement by mass spectrometry in a reference laboratory, is needed. Measurement of total testosterone, preferably from two blood samples collected in the early morning, is the initial diagnostic test for suspected hypogonadism. Although normal ranges are somewhat assay-dependent, values consistently less than 200 ng/dL (6.9 nmol/L) are considered low, and values consistently greater than 350 ng/dL (12.1 nmol/L) are considered normal. In patients with values that are between 200 and 350 ng/dL (6.9 and 12.1 nmol/L) or that are inconsistent with the clinical situation, the free and/or bioavailable testosterone should be measured. Free testosterone can be measured by either equilibrium dialysis or calculation, but direct assay kits are unreliable and should be avoided. Bioavailable (free plus weakly bound) testosterone is measured by ammonium sulfate precipitation and immunoassay or by calculation. If the result of this test is abnormal, then additional diagnostic studies are warranted.

Treatment of the patient with either sildenafil or testosterone replacement is not indicated until the diagnosis of hypogonadism is confirmed. In patients with hypogonadism, therapy with sildenafil or other phosphodiesterase type 5 inhibitors will not correct the symptom of fatigue.

Measurement of the patient's serum estradiol level will not help determine if his free and total testosterone levels are normal and thus not help exclude hypogonadism as a diagnosis.

KEY POINT

- In patients with indeterminate testosterone values (between 200 and 350 ng/dL [6.9 and 12.1 nmol/L]) or with values that are inconsistent with the clinical situation, the free and/or bioavailable testosterone level should be measured.

Bibliography

Rosner W, Auchus RJ, Azziz R, Sluss PM, Raff H. Position statement: Utility, limitations, and pitfalls in measuring testosterone: an Endocrine Society position statement. J Clin Endocrinol Metab. 2007;92(2):405-413. [PMID: 17090633]

Item 115   Answer: B

Educational Objective: Treat hypothyroidism in a patient on multiple medications.

Given this patient's recent symptoms, newly elevated thyroid-stimulating hormone (TSH) level, and low-normal free thyroxine level, she most likely has inadequately treated hypothyroidism. The goal TSH level for patients receiving thyroid hormone replacement is typically in the range of 1 to 3 µU/mL (1 to 3 mU/L). The best course is thus to increase the levothyroxine dosage by 25 µg (to 100 µg) and retest thyroid function in 6 weeks to ensure that the TSH is back in the target range.

Although iron taken with levothyroxine can affect the absorption of the levothyroxine, a multivitamin with iron taken many hours after levothyroxine dosing should not. Therefore, discontinuing the multivitamin is unlikely to have a beneficial effect on the TSH level.

Estrogen does not affect levothyroxine absorption but does increase thyroid-binding globulin (TBG) levels, which increases the amount of bound thyroid hormone. Patients with intact thyroid function can accommodate an increase in TBG levels and maintain normal free thyroxine (T_4) levels. However, free T_4 levels can be expected to decrease in patients dependent on exogenous levothyroxine. The timing of the oral contraceptive pill dosing will not alter this effect. When oral contraceptive pills are discontinued in such patients, results of thyroid function tests should be monitored for a potential need to decrease the thyroid dosage.

The role of desiccated thyroid hormone or a triiodothyronine (T_3) preparation in a patient with hypothyroidism is very controversial, and there is no reason to consider such therapy in this patient. In addition, combined T_4-T_3 products and desiccated thyroid contain a higher amount of T_3 to T_4 (1:4) than is present in normal thyroid secretions. T_3 in these preparations is rapidly absorbed into the circulation and may result in supraphysiologic serum T_3 levels for several hours after administration. This action can be particularly hazardous to patients with underlying coronary artery disease.

KEY POINT

- The initiation or discontinuation of estrogen-containing compounds in a patient with hypothyroidism can increase or decrease, respectively, levothyroxine dosing requirements.

Bibliography

Arafah BM. Increased need for thyroxine in women with hypothyroidism during estrogen therapy. N Engl J Med. 2001; 344(23):1743-1749. [PMID: 11396440]

Item 116   Answer: D

Educational Objective: Manage hypoglycemia unawareness in an insulin-treated patient.

This patient's dosage of insulin should be decreased. Hypoglycemia is a major rate-limiting step in achieving tight glycemic control in patients with diabetes mellitus, in particular those treated with insulin. Repeated episodes of hypoglycemia are associated with a condition known as "hypoglycemia unawareness," especially in type 1 diabetes. In this condition, the body no longer responds to mild hypoglycemia with typical symptoms (diaphoresis, tachycardia, anxiety, and tremor). Instead, neuroglycopenic symptoms, such as confusion, personality changes, and loss of consciousness, become the first manifestation of hypoglycemia. Hypoglycemia unawareness clearly relates to the frequency and severity of hypoglycemic events. In this manner, hypoglycemia begets further hypoglycemia.

Hypoglycemia unawareness can be diminished in this patient by decreasing the dosages of insulin glargine and insulin lispro by approximately 20% until his blood glucose level increases and hypoglycemia is avoided. This step allows the brain to adapt to the new ambient glycemia so that the normal adrenergic responses to hypoglycemia can be reestablished. Once this occurs, an intensification of the insulin therapy can be retried, but if problems redevelop, a permanently increased blood glucose target will be necessary.

Metformin is not approved for use in patients with type 1 diabetes mellitus. Furthermore, the addition of metformin to this patient's insulin regimen without reducing the dosage of insulin will not prevent hypoglycemia or improve hypoglycemic unawareness.

Unless the insulin dosage is concurrently decreased, simply changing the type of basal insulin from insulin glargine to insulin detemir is unlikely to increase blood glucose levels and prevent hypoglycemia.

Substituting regular insulin for the rapid-acting insulin analogue insulin lispro may actually exacerbate the incidence of hypoglycemia by delayed action on the blood glucose level. The duration of action of regular insulin is significantly longer than that of insulin lispro, with substantial insulin activity present 4 to 6 hours after injection.

KEY POINT

- **Hypoglycemia unawareness can be diminished by decreasing the dosage of insulin and scrupulously avoiding hypoglycemia.**

Bibliography

Edelman SV, Morello CM. Hypoglycemia unawareness and type 1 diabetes. South Med J. 2004;97(11):1143-1144. [PMID: 15586620]

Index